War and Moral Dissonance

This collection of essays, inspired by the author's experience teaching ethics to Marine and Navy chaplains during the Iraq War, examines the moral and philosophical dilemmas posed by war. The first chapter deals directly with Dr. Peter A. French's teaching experience and the specific challenges posed by teaching applied and theoretical ethics to men and women wrestling with the immediate and personal moral conflicts occasioned by the dissonance of their duties as military officers with their religious convictions. The following chapters grew out of philosophical discussions with these chaplains regarding specific ethical issues surrounding the Iraq War, including the nature of moral evil, forgiveness, mercy, retributive punishment, honor, torture, responsibility, and just war theory. This book represents a unique viewpoint on the philosophical problems of war, illuminating the devastating toll combat experiences take on both an individual's sense of identity and a society's professed moral code.

Dr. Peter A. French is the Lincoln Chair in Ethics, Professor of Philosophy, and the Director of the Lincoln Center for Applied Ethics at Arizona State University. He is the author of twenty books, including *Ethics and College Sports* (2004), *The Virtues of Vengeance* (2001), and *Cowboy Metaphysics: Ethics and Death in Westerns* (1997). He is a senior and founding editor of *Midwest Studies in Philosophy*, and his articles have appeared in numerous philosophical and legal journals.

D1202364

War and Moral Dissonance

PETER A. FRENCH

Arizona State University

CAMBRIDGE UNIVERSITY PRESS

Cambridge, New York, Melbourne, Madrid, Cape Town, Singapore,
São Paulo, Delhi, Dubai, Tokyo, Mexico City

Cambridge University Press
32 Avenue of the Americas, New York, NY 10013-2473, USA

www.cambridge.org
Information on this title: www.cambridge.org/9780521169035

First published 2011

Printed in the United States of America

A catalog record for this publication is available from the British Library.

Library of Congress Cataloging in Publication data

French, Peter A.
War and moral dissonance / Peter A. French.
p. cm.
Includes bibliographical references and index.
ISBN 978-1-107-00048-3 – ISBN 978-0-521-16903-5 (pbk.)
1. Iraq War, 2003 – Moral and ethical aspects.   2. War – Moral and ethical aspects.
3. Iraq War, 2003 – Psychological aspects.   4. Iraq War, 2003 – Chaplains – United
States.   5. United States. Marine Corps – Chaplains.   6. United States. Navy –
Chaplains.   7. Military chaplains – Professional ethics – United States.   8. French,
Peter A.   9. Military ethics – Study and teaching – United States.   10. United States –
Moral conditions.   I. Title.
DS79.767.M67F74   2010
172'.42 – dc22   2010023740

ISBN 978-1-107-00048-3 Hardback
ISBN 978-0-521-16903-5 Paperback

Contents

Preface

The wars in Iraq and Afghanistan have taken a physical and psychological toll on a group in the United States military that has received very little attention in the media: chaplains. Navy chaplains serving with Marine, Coast Guard, and Naval units have responsibilities for ethical education in those units and are tasked as moral advisers to command, as well as provide religious services and counseling. I begin this book with a memoir of my experiences for more than two years (2004–2006) as an instructor in intensive weeklong sessions held at bases and camps around the world teaching Navy chaplains about ethics and the virtues so that they can better fulfill their assignments in theater and during other deployments. Although I have been a university philosophy professor for more than forty years, I had never taken on such an assignment, though I did teach at Homestead Air Force Base for the Air Force during the Vietnam War. I have tried to describe what it was like for those of us on the teaching team to design and teach a suitable ethics curriculum for chaplains who are suffering through identity-challenging personal conflicts while trying to perform their multiple roles in the combat zones. The religious beliefs the chaplains espouse often clash with the realities they confront in a war that many worry cannot be morally justified, and for some chaplains, the curriculum we designed added intellectual ammunition to their concerns about the moral legitimacy of the enterprise in which they had staked their professional careers.

My experiences with the chaplains, most having just recently returned from Iraq or Afghanistan, sometimes bordered on the surrealistic and often jumped that border. Many of the chaplains were tormented by psychological demons that had inhabited them during their combat-zone deployments. Some chaplains had vivid flashback experiences during the teaching sessions. Too many of them seemed to be untreated post-traumatic stress disorder (PTSD) sufferers. All wrestled with the moral schizophrenia that they wear on their uniforms: they are officers in the war machine and they are ordained representatives of religious faiths that typically preach beliefs antithetical to the "virtues" of the military. Many of the chaplains confided some of their horrific stories to me of personally witnessed human destruction and, in their clerical roles, of listening to confessions and confused cries for psychological and theological help from Marines who had committed or had witnessed patently immoral acts during their tours of duty.

I have not felt comfortable telling the story of my Iraq War experience until recently, but for many reasons, some purely philosophical, some emotional, some pedagogical, and some because of a nagging sense of duty, I have decided to tell it. I suspect that as philosophers ensconced in our academic offices and university classrooms we seldom imagine what it might be like to try to teach Aristotle, Kant, and Mill, as well as concepts like moral conflict and honor and the nature of evil, to students who cannot drive grotesque demons out of their heads while having committed themselves both to religious ideals and military duty. It is a story of responsibility accepted and shirked on individual, collective, and corporate levels.

I have not used the names of any of the chaplains with whom I had discussions about the philosophical and religious issues that were haunting their waking and sleeping hours. Although all of the chaplains knew that what they told any of us on the teaching team would not be held in the confidence of the confessional, many poured out stories that they personally felt the need to unburden and, I believe, some wanted those stories to reach a wider audience not because they hoped they would be agents of change but because the impact of political decisions that purport to represent the will of the American public should not be kept secret from that public. Though they may have felt that most of us "can't handle the truth," they also seemed to feel that we should not be shielded from it by an antiseptic mask of political rhetoric. Some, however, simply could not help themselves. They had seen too much to be circumspect. I have not told all of their stories.

Many of the chaplains during our intense teaching sessions raised important philosophical questions on topics related to the experiences they were undergoing. Some of them spoke privately with me during breaks about topics they wanted to further explore and some raised issues that kept me awake in my base quarters jotting down notes about what I wished I had said in response to their probing. A number pointedly asked me to write on specific topics at which I had only hinted as to what my position might shape up to be. This book is the result of my responding to the philosophical provocations the experience produced.

I hope my memoir will help philosophers and students understand not only the relevancy challenges of what we teach but also the reality of the Hell in which what we teach runs smack-dab into the physical and mental carnage of human enterprises.

After the memoir, the remaining chapters of the book are attempts to deal with the topics with which the chaplains and I were most engaged, either in formal sessions or in personal discussions. The second chapter examines conceptions of human nature and the nature of moral evil. It should come as no surprise that the chaplains were concerned about both topics and that many wanted to believe that human beings are inherently good, despite the evidence before their eyes and in their nightmares. I find it easy to give an abstract definition of moral evil that is likely to be acceptable to most people regardless of their philosophical or theological commitments. However, it is much harder to concretely identify cases of wickedness that rise to the level of sheer evil. I played around with that idea for many years, mentioning it on a number of occasions to some of the chaplains, and I used some of my thoughts on the matter in a chart I devised for one of the formal sessions. In the 1980s, I wrote what might be called a "treatment" for a video presentation on evil. A paper that Richard Taylor published in which he tried to sort out the various ways we might catalogue evildoers inspired it. I borrowed Taylor's motif of a sudden vacancy in Hell when Satan is pardoned by God, occasioning the formation of a search committee, analogous to those with which academics are well acquainted, to nominate the successor. I decided to expand the original conception into a report of the dialogue among the demons on the search committee who are trying to identify different types of evildoers, aided by the views of certain classical philosophers, in order to evaluate the credentials of some nominees to sit on the Throne of Hell. I have included the resulting piece as an appendix to Chapter 2.

Chapter 3 focuses on the loss of innocence and its role in moral responsibility. Although only a few chaplains raised this matter directly with me, because I had written on the subject in *Responsibility Matters*, I used the topic as a way into a discussion of moral conflict and tragedy when I developed one of the sessions for the second year of the training. It should come as no surprise that experiences of war, particularly in urban combat zones, provoke loss of innocence in young Marines, who, despite their training and macho swagger, discover they haven't really confronted their own capacity to do and be done evil. What I wrote in the earlier book on the subject has also been recently discussed in the philosophical literature and gave me good reasons to reevaluate some of my views on the matter and respond to expansions on it developed by Michael McKenna.

In Chapter 4, I discuss forgiveness, mercy, and retributive punishment as ways of responding to moral evil. The chapter recalls distinctions drawn in the second chapter and uses the true story of Simon Wiesenthal's confrontation while in a Nazi concentration camp with a dying SS soldier who begged Wiesenthal to forgive him for atrocities he had committed against Jews during the Holocaust. The case was the one on which I focused a session for the chaplains that provoked considerable conflict because for many, their faith group commitments to doctrines of forgiveness and mercy are extremely difficult to honor in wartime situations.

One of the chaplains in a private conversation in Naples, Italy, asked me whether ethics was always just applying the formulae of certain standard theories to specific cases and, more or less, reading off the results. Perhaps part of the reason for his thinking that might be the crux of applied ethics was that in the first year of the sessions, we had spent considerable time trying to teach deontological, utilitarian, and divine-command ethical theories to the chaplains. The impression that was left with some of them, and may very well be what a number of Ethics 101 students in college get, was that applied ethics is rather like a buffet dinner with the entrees set out in trays from which one can choose to fill one's plate. What the chaplain wanted to know was whether a person could invent his or her own normative rules and principles and act on them and still be acting ethically. As I understood the question, or so I put it to the chaplain, the issue was whether there is such a thing as moral originality, and if there is, how would what is original in a person's normative principles be assessed within the field of ethics. The chaplain nodded and said he had in mind Jesus Christ. Of course he did. Chapter 5 is my attempt to deal with the identification and assessment of purported original moral principles and rules.

Chapter 6 derives from the session I created for the second year of the training course. It is on a concept that is taken to be essential to the military: honor. Honor's twin, shame, plays a structurally important role in military units, particularly in those with strong traditions of cohesion and group identity such as the Marine Corps.

I take up a very difficult topic in Chapter 7. The interrogation of detainees following the September 11, 2001, terrorist attacks by al-Qaeda in the United States became a central element in the Bush administration's prosecution of its global war on terror. The techniques that were approved for use by interrogators verged on and then crossed the line into what is identified in American and international law as torture. During the 2004 sessions with the Navy chaplains, the evidence of extensive mistreatment of detainees in the old Abu Ghraib prison in Iraq were revealed to the public in a number of graphic photographs and media stories. The chaplains expressed shame when I asked them how seeing the pictures made them feel, but some also admitted that they knew of similar treatments of prisoners and detainees by Marines. I wrote the chapter to explore some of the ways the American government tried to justify what it called "enhanced interrogation techniques" and to make a case, based on an understanding of the concept of will found in Harry Frankfurt's work, for interrogational torture as inherently immoral.

A rather bizarre case of extraordinarily severe injuries suffered by a Marine in Iraq combined with an extreme case of PTSD provoked my attempt in Chapter 8 to make a plausible case, denied by Hubert Dreyfus and others, that a person could live a worthwhile life confined to a metaverse like that provided by *Second Life*. In Chapter 9, I sort out various uses of "ought" and "must" as they are used in institutional settings. That sets the stage for "Inference Gaps in Moral Assessment" (Chapter 10), in which I argue that moral judgments about organizations and individuals cannot be inferred directly from moral judgments about the institutions of which they are concrete instantiations and in which they function professionally. My thinking about the topic arose through considering the situation in which military chaplains typically find themselves, namely, working for an organization whose primary reason for existence is to do the very sorts of things proscribed by the doctrines of the faith groups to which they belong.

Chapter 11, "Blaming Whole Populations: The American People and the Iraq War," is based on one of the earliest papers I published on the topic of collective responsibility. On revisiting the earlier paper, I radically altered it to reflect on certain episodes in the Iraq War that were recounted to me by some of the chaplains. The issue, however, that prompted the earlier paper regarding the Vietnam War is still prominent: Does it make sense to ascribe collective moral responsibility to the American people for the barbaric behavior of those who are fighting in a foreign country in the name of the American government and nation?

Chapter 12 has a very strange history. It was provoked by a discussion I had with a group of the chaplains about whether someone who was relentlessly infused since early childhood with an intolerant perspective, a particular cultural point of view, should be held morally responsible for acting on the hatreds and prejudices that are so much a part of who they understand themselves to be, individually and collectively, and their place in the world. The chaplains had in mind insurgents and terrorists who were raised in madrasahs to hate Americans, American culture, modernity, Israel, Judaism, and Christianity. Early versions of the chapter were read in Florida and in Utah, and I was prepared to give it as the Veroni Memorial Lecture at Kent State University in 2008. I argue that collective memories (or what also may be called heritage stories) are a potential source of a type of moral impairment that I call being "morally challenged." The third section of the chapter provides an account of how collective memories have the capacity to cause what Harry Frankfurt called "volitional necessity" leading to moral challenges for some people, especially in situations in which the groups of which they are members are acting concertedly. The primary point is that though collective memories may engender volitional necessity in people and render them morally challenged in certain circumstances with regard to doing the right thing, they do not convert them into moral incompetents with respect to whom the assessment of moral responsibility is inappropriate. In that section, I offer examples of how I believe some people may have become morally challenged when their leaders used their heritage stories or collective memories to incite them to the performance of untoward actions. As one of a number of examples, I mention the speeches of Slobodan Milosevic that recalled the 1389 battle on the Field of Blackbirds as a way of motivating Serbs against Kosovo Muslims. I say nothing about the morality of the Serbian people. However, after a poster announcing my forthcoming lecture was distributed on the Kent State University campus and on its website in which my discussion of the Serbian/Kosovo example was cited, there arose from the Serbian community in Ohio and then internationally an outcry of complaints and accusations regarding what some believed were my views about Serbs and Serbian culture. This escalated into an outrageously false and, I believe, libelous article on a Serbian-American website in which my views were mischaracterized as the claim that "Serbian people are rapists and killers because they are delusional about their history during the time they lived under the Islamic Law in Kosovo." I make no such claim. The Serbian-American website went on to say that I must be in the pay of the Saudi royal family, CNN, or the Kosovar Albanians. This was, of course, nonsense. Unfortunately, the audience interest in the lecture that was incited by all of that publicity was poisonous. I received a number of harassing emails from Serbs in this country and elsewhere, accusing me of racism, of being a closet Islamist, of collaboration with those who would destroy Western civilization, and much more incendiary rubbish. My life was threatened and I was told to expect a very unpleasant experience at Kent State should I dare to give the lecture. The utter irrationality and vituperative rhetoric of the attacks from the supporters of Serbia made it clear that there was little likelihood that the planned lecture would be a worthwhile philosophical experience. A Serbian priest in Cleveland, Ohio, telephoned to warn me not to give the lecture, that he knew of some people, presumably from his congregation, planning to seriously injure or perhaps kill me. I was begged to confess my ignorance of Serbian history and culture and profusely apologize for my offenses on the Serbian-American website. I was persuaded by my family and friends to cancel my appearance at Kent State even though the campus police said they would guarantee my safety and a group of Albanians from Detroit wrote me volunteering to come to Kent and, in no uncertain terms, to protect me from the Serbs. They vowed it would be the battle of the Field of Blackbirds all over again! Reading the chapter should persuade any reasonable person that the Serbs had nothing over which to get so heated.

Chapter 13 is a direct result of my using the suicide note of Colonel Ted Westhusing to focus a discussion of the duties of chaplains confronting the fragility of human beings whose deeply held convictions and commitments have been shattered by the realities of their experiences. Colonel Westhusing expressed in that note his utter disdain for the way corporations and private contractors had commandeered what he believed to be the justifiable mission of the troops in Iraq to their own monetary advantage and were also performing shoddily to the detriment of soldiers and Marines who were trying to do their jobs and get home more or less in one piece. Outstanding work on issues of corporate responsibility by Deborah Tollefsen, Denis Arnold, and Carlos Gomez-Jara Diez drew me back to my earlier work on corporate responsibility and significantly contributed to my reexamining the structure of corporate responsibility and punishment, with special attention paid to the performance of KBR, Inc., on the bases in Iraq.

The final chapter takes up the application of just war theory to the parade of missions that the Bush administration trotted out as reasons for invading Iraq and occupying the country. I am particularly interested in the purported justifications of preemptive and preventive war and also conclude with a commentary on the mission of establishing democracy as a legitimate *casus belli* when it is unclear what sort of democracy is intended and whether the culture being gifted with whatever form of democracy is in the package is a reasonable recipient.

Acknowledgments

There are, as always, many people to thank for their insights and work on the topics I have explored. I am especially grateful to Michael McKenna, Deborah Tollefsen, Ish Haji, Denis Arnold, Carlos Gomez-Jara Diez, Philip Pettit, Jeffrie Murphy, Margaret Walker, John Kekes, and Harry Frankfurt. A number of my philosophy graduate students unknowingly contributed by serving as sounding posts for some of the arguments and ideas with which I was wrestling, both during the years of the chaplain experience and as I worked on this book. The other members of the teaching team provided me with astute observations on content and introduced me to elements of military life of which I was too little aware. Thank you to Rick Rubel, Chris Eberle, Larry Lengbeyer, John Hittinger, George Lucas, and especially my daughter, Shannon French.

This book is dedicated to the men and women of the Navy Chaplain Corps with whom I spent many long hours as described in the memoir that is Chapter 1. Many have served multiple deployments in Iraq and Afghanistan, in support facilities, and on ships. All, I hope, return safely and will receive the care and honors that they have earned.

An earlier version of Chapter 6 was published in *Public Affairs Quarterly* in 2002 under the title "Honor, Shame, and Identity."

A version of Chapter 8 was written for a conference on philosophy and recreation held at the University of North Florida in November 2008.

Chapter 9 is a reworking of a paper that appeared in the *Journal of Philosophy* in October 1977 as "Institutional and Moral Obligations or Merels and Morals."

An early version of Chapter 10 was read at the Centre for Educational Research and Innovation (CERI) in Paris as part of a conference and was published in French as "Les ruptures du raisonnement déductif dans les évaluations morales: Capitalisme, entreprises et individus."

Chapter 11 is a revisitation and radical reworking of a paper first published in 1974 by Oxford University Press in a collection edited by

Held, Morganbesser, and Nagel called *Philosophy, Morality, and International Affairs.*

Parts of Chapters 3 and 13 are from my response to papers written by Michael McKenna and Deborah Tollefson honoring my work in an issue of the *American Philosophical Association, Newsletter on Philosophy and Law,* edited by Steven Scalet and Christopher Griffin (Spring 2008).

The latter part of Chapter 14 owes much to "The Meanings of Democracy: A Western Perspective," which was given at the World Congress of Philosophy in Boston and published in *Proceedings of the Twentieth World Congress of Philosophy*, Volume XI, "Social and Political Philosophy" (2001).

1

The Two-Collar Conflict

A Philosopher's Memoir of the Iraq War

Only sinners lose their souls, it's said, through evil that they do. Not Robert
Shannon. Incapable of anything but good, he lost his soul through savagery that
he witnessed, horrors that he saw. When you lose – or have ripped from you –
the spirit that directs you, you have two options. Fight for your soul and win it
back, and you'll evermore be a noble human being. Fail, and you die from loss
of truth.

Frank Delaney, Shannon, 2009, chapter 1

It was late September 2005. I was delayed at the gate of Naval Air Station Oceana in Virginia Beach, Virginia, while my orders were checked
and a pass and parking permit were issued. Oceana is the home base of
the Pukin' Dogs. A sign announcing that fact is posted beside an F-14
jet fighter just inside the gate. The Pukin' Dogs, or Strike Fighter
Squadron 143, is an operational fleet squadron that now flies supersonic
F/A18 E's. The squadron's distinguished history is honored at Oceana.
It includes service during the Korean and Vietnam wars, the Persian Gulf
War, and over Bosnia. During their 2004 cruise aboard the carrier *George
Washington*, the Pukin' Dogs were involved in forty sorties over Iraq,
including bombing runs over Fallujah during Operation Phantom Fury,
when the Marines attempted to retake the city after the failed Operation Vigilant Resolve, which had been prompted by the widely publicized
murders and burnings of Blackwater mercenaries in the city in spring
2004.

 I was at Oceana on that balmy early fall day for the validation of the
second year of a professional development training course (PDTC) on
ethics for Navy chaplains. I was a member of a small team of professors hired by a company that won the contract to teach ethics to the
chaplains serving in the Navy, Marine Corps, and Coast Guard. Our team

worked for about half a year to create a weeklong course, a sequel to the PDTC on ethics we taught in 2004 for the sea service chaplains, intended to acquaint them with various virtue concepts and character development issues and to help them deal with moral conflicts and the ethical education of the troops during their deployments in the combat zones in Iraq and Afghanistan, as well as at other postings.

Among the revelations in a Pentagon Mental Health Advisory Team report (MHAT-IV) on the ethics of the troops in Iraq was that only 38 percent of the Marines serving in Iraq believe that noncombatants (Iraqi civilians) are to be treated with dignity and respect. Chaplains serving with Marine units have responsibilities for ethical education in those units and are tasked as moral advisers to command. In 2004 and 2006, the PDTCs for the chaplains were dedicated to the teaching of ethics so that the chaplains might better fulfill their assignments. After our PDTC was "validated," we would teach the PDTC on Navy and Marine bases at locations around the world, from Okinawa to Naples, Italy, from Hawaii to Norfolk, Virginia, from Camp Pendleton to Camp Lejeune.

Somewhere in the Department of Defense or the Chaplain Corps offices, the teaching team's 2004 stint earned sufficiently high enough grades to win a second contract for the contractor that hired us, a company owned by American Indians (which, I supposed, Sitting Bull and Geronimo might have found humorous). That piece of irony was soon to be passé, however, because the company was sold twice in the course of the next year and we ended up working for General Dynamics. (There probably is something profoundly ironic in that, too.) At least the company wasn't sold to Halliburton!

The validation process involved the team teaching the weeklong course to a select group of about forty chaplains who flew into Oceana to serve as the "beta group." The senior ranking members of the Corps evaluated our performance and especially the content of the various segments of the course. Those on our teaching team who were in the Navy (two retired captains) and those who were on the civilian faculty at the Naval Academy – that is, all team members except for me – referred to the segments each of us created for the course as our "briefs." When I was first told I had to present my four briefs for validation, I assumed that meant that I would give the written material in the form of Power Point slides to some mid-level officer, perhaps a lieutenant commander, who would stamp it with some code to which only a select few in the Corps and in the bowels of the Pentagon would be privy. I was not involved with the validation process in the first year and had to be informed that I was to teach the sessions I had created in real time with the Admirals observing. That was but one of my many misconceptions or misunderstandings about the Navy way of doing and talking about things.

It was obvious to me from the beginning of my relationship with the project in 2004 that the chaplains were comfortable with the retired Navy captains on the team and to a somewhat lesser degree with those who are civilian professors at the Naval Academy. Because I had no personal connection to the Navy, I would have to earn credibility with them. That meant that I needed to learn the vocabulary of the Navy and the Marine Corps "on the run" and prove to the chaplains that in addition to knowing ethics and being able to teach it, I had a functional command of their scriptures, even though I have no religious affiliation, and could hold my own when they raised examples for discussion in the peculiar language that is Navyspeak.

In early October 2003, I was on a telephone conference call with my daughter, Dr. Shannon French, then a philosophy professor at the Naval Academy, and a retired Navy captain with whom she worked at the Academy. They informed me that they were members of a team that had constructed a syllabus for weeklong PDTCs on ethics for the chaplains. I do not know with certainty what at that time led the senior officers of the Navy Chaplain Corps to decide that the chaplains needed ethics training. A senior chaplain told me that the Pentagon had raised questions about why the chaplains were not playing a more central role in providing moral advice to command. It is, however, noteworthy that in summer 2003, the Associated Press ran a troubling story about how the Navy had punished more than forty chaplains in the previous decade "for offenses ranging from sexual abuse and adultery to fraud, a misconduct rate much higher than for other officers.... Most of the punished chaplains, 28 of the 42, were accused of sexual misconduct or harassment.... Examples: A Roman Catholic chaplain went to prison for molesting the young sons of sailors and Marines. A Seventh-day Adventist chaplain was court-martialed for an indecent assault during a counseling session. Three chaplains – a Baptist, a Catholic, and a United Pentecostal Church International minister – were punished for downloading porn onto Navy computers.... The regular officers had a discipline rate of two per 1,000, while the rate for chaplains was 45 per 1,000."

Shannon had taken on the leadership duties for the team. At their course's validation in September 2003, the senior officers of the Chaplain Corps decided that one of the original members of the team was

ineffectual. He resigned from the team when informed of that evaluation, leaving the team in a bind because the validated curriculum had
to be taught by two team members at eleven locations between January
and May 2004. I was asked to take over the former member's obligations
by teaching at San Diego, Norfolk, and Hawaii. In the early 1970s, I had
written a book on the My Lai Massacre, I had taught at Homestead Air
Force Base during the Vietnam War, and I had been a college philosophy
professor, mostly writing and teaching in ethics, for nearly forty years, so
it was assumed that I could step in without great difficulty. I agreed to
take on the assignment although I had not yet seen the syllabus I would
be teaching.

The syllabus for the first (2004) ethics PDTC was, by and large, a basic
ethics course, mostly a smorgasbord of moral theories interspersed and
usually illustrated with military stories and military examples of moral
conflict. My daughter informed me that much of the course was derived
from the required ethics course that was taught at the Naval Academy
to cadets in their second year. Although I did not recognize a pervasive
problem with the curriculum when I first examined it, during the actual
teaching it became clear that because of its primary origin, much of
the discussion of the issues focused on command decisions and not on
the sorts of experiences that typically confront chaplains. In retrospect,
I think that may have been more of a plus than a minus because after
the *pro forma* reaction of the chaplains to some of the cases – "That's a
command issue, not my problem" – we were able to elicit very candid
responses to relevant questions such as "OK, but what might the situation
or the command decision provoke that does fall within your scope of
duty when the captain or the colonel orders X rather than Y?" or "If
the commanding officer had asked for your advice when doing X was
under consideration, how would you have responded?" As events in Iraq
deteriorated, their responses to our attempts to engage them in such
ethical dialogues became more candid and shrouded in doubt and inner
turmoil.

The two team members assigned to a particular base or Marine camp
divided up the teaching assignments or briefs during the week. There
were a few team-taught segments but, by and large, it was a single team
member holding forth for a session and then sitting in the back of the
room, frequently with an admiral and almost always with a captain or
commander, observing the next session. Team members generally taught
the sessions they had created, but that left many sessions each week that
had to be taught by a team member who did not develop it. Insofar as

I had nothing to do with the creation of the Power Point slides (a Navy requirement) for each session, nor had I ever taught the material in the way it was formatted, it was decided that, wherever possible, I should teach the briefs that presented some of the more standard ethical positions such as Kantianism and utilitarianism. Sticking just to the major historical theories, however, would not suffice to my pulling my weight during the week, so I also was assigned to teach briefs on moral motivation, cultural and moral relativism, divine command theory, conflicts of duty, just war theory, truth telling, and moral numbing. Each of the sessions lasted for approximately an hour, but some were longer and one or two were only forty-five minutes or so.

After each session, the chaplains got a fifteen-minute break during which most would tank up on coffee and doughnuts in the morning and soft drinks and various geedunk – unhealthy snacks – in the afternoon. After a few of the PDTCs, someone in the higher command of the Corps insisted that more healthful food also be provided, and a plate of raw veggies appeared. After the first day, some of the chaplains would also use the breaks to approach me and the other instructor with questions. Their questions, however, frequently were not about the material we had just covered. They typically related incidents they had experienced, or "had heard that another chaplain had experienced," in country. They wanted to know if they had done the right thing when they (or the mythical chaplain of their stories) had responded to the situation in the manner they did. In the first PDTC that I taught, the stories were more or less standard wartime occurrences regarding whether a report on an incident should have been sent up the chain to higher command or whether a counseling session with the chaplain was sufficient. Later in my "tour of duty," the stories became more and more horrific, and the chaplains telling them became less concerned about disguising their involvement and their deep moral concern that something very bad was happening to them and to their moral, if not religious, status. Into the second year, 2006, their concerns became more desperate and personal and revealed significant psychological and moral damage to what one chaplain referred to as his "immoral immortal soul."

My first assignment in January 2004 was at the Anti-Submarine Warfare Training Center at Point Loma, San Diego, with a class of almost 100 chaplains. That was after the first wave of success the U.S. troops experienced following the invasion of Iraq. The slog of occupation was setting in. It was, however, before virtually everything in Iraq failed to follow the blueprints the architects of the war in the Bush administration had drawn and the ill-informed pundits in the media had enthusiastically supported. Luckily, or maybe by design, I was teamed with my daughter, who not only had years of experience in teaching much of the specific material in the PDTC but also had a good grasp of the jargon of the sea services. She took on the first few sessions, starting promptly at 7:30 AM every day, while I observed and tried to gather as much information about how to get a handle on the material for this group of "students" as I could, realizing that I would have to teach many of the sessions she was covering when she was not with me in Norfolk and at Pearl Harbor.

The week began with our being introduced to the chaplains by the captain in charge, the OSTM (on-sight training manager), as the SMEs (pronounced "smeees"), only the beginning of what seemed like an endless parade of acronyms. What the hell is a SME? The name drew to my mind creatures from an old Al Capp cartoon, little white globular alien things with stumpy legs and no arms and small black eyes. Perhaps to many of the chaplains that was exactly how we were perceived: the more or less lovable and selfless shmoos. The chaplains, hopefully affectionately but maybe facetiously, often used such expressions as "Here come the SMEs" and "Watch out for the SMEs." I remembered that it was the fate of the shmoos (or shmoon – the preferred plural) in the *Lil Abner* cartoon strip to destroy human society because humans stopped working and took full advantage of the unlimited supply of shmoon, whose raison d'etre was to sacrifice themselves for the comfort and happiness of humans. The shmoon had to be exterminated to save the human race from its own predilection to lie about idly and avail itself of the benefits bestowed on it by such creatures. I worried that we SMEs could well be the Chaplain Corps' shmoon, and that led me to wonder what the acronym really stood for. I tried out a number of possibilities while my daughter taught the introductory session, but nothing seemed to fit the bill. Then I dug out the orders we received from the Chief of Chaplains that get us through the tight security at the bases and it jumped out at me: we were referred to as "subject matter experts" – SMEs! Of course!

Almost immediately at Point Loma it became evident that there was a very wide range of academic backgrounds and intellectual interest represented by the chaplains gathered in the room. Some of their responses, when they did respond to my daughter's questions and invitations to engage in the discussion, suggested less than excited and certainly not enthusiastic intellectual curiosity. On the other hand, some were highly stimulated to explore the issues and to identify ways they might incorporate the material being taught when they returned to their units. Why was there such a divergence of intellectual rigor and analytic capacity in the group? At an early break, I inquired of the OSTM, who was keeping everything running shipshape on a tight schedule, about how someone gets to be in the Navy Chaplain Corps.

He informed me that the Pentagon has a committee, the Armed Forces Chaplains Board, that determines which religions are legitimate and thus rate having chaplains in the military. A look at their decision on Wicca suggests that they tend to accept judicial and IRS decisions as guiding their inclusion of a religion on the list. There are more than 100 recognized religions, the most recent, at least at that time, being Wicca. But not every religion has a chaplain in the service. Wicca does not, but in a recent legal case, a Wicca family won the right to have their son's gravestone in a military cemetery decorated with the five-pointed star in a circle that is the symbol of the Wicca religion. The majority of chaplains represent the traditional religions and denominations: Roman Catholic, Baptist, Methodist, Lutheran, and the like. There are a few Jewish chaplains, one of whom was an admiral, and I met one Muslim. Some less well-known religions are also represented in the Corps, including the Native American Church.

A would-be chaplain must meet certain requirements before being admitted to chaplain training. He or she must have a baccalaureate degree of not less than 120 semester hours from a college or university listed in the *Directory of Postsecondary Institutions* and have successfully completed three years of resident graduate study in theology from a school listed in the *Directory of Postsecondary Institutions*, the *Association of Theological Schools Bulletin*, the *Transnational Association of Christian Colleges and Schools Directory*, or a graduate school whose credits are accepted by a school listed in one of those directories. The aspiring chaplain must also be ordained by and have the ecclesiastical endorsement of one of the recognized churches. Given those educational criteria, there is little wonder that the intellectual interest level and the academic backgrounds of the chaplains in the room ranged from those who had undergone rigorous studies at Catholic seminaries and Jewish yeshivas to those with degrees from Bible Colleges and fundamentalist conservative Christian seminaries with very narrow curricula. In my early years as a college philosophy professor, I taught large undergraduate courses in which the academic abilities of the students varied dramatically, but I could not recall teaching such a radically diverse group in terms of academic preparation as those chaplains, even though, unlike the college freshmen, they all shared the same career or calling (as many of them would say).

Recognizing the source of my concern, the OSTM was quite blunt with me. "You're wondering about the diversity in the room? Not like your graduate philosophy seminars, is it?" I agreed with a nod. "Well, that's not all. We get a certain kind of clergy in the Corps. They're rather different from most of the parish priests and ministers you might have met." I recall chuckling as I looked out on a room in which maybe a third of the chaplains were dressed in Marine desert camouflage uniforms and boots and the rest were in stiffly pressed khaki uniforms with mirror-polished black or brown shoes. He went on, "Most of them would be disasters in a church where they had to carry out the regular parish duties of a minister, managing the church's activities and business dealings. Their faith groups are more than willing to send them to us. Some are former combatants who did their tours in the Navy, the Marines or the Army, got religion, went to seminaries, got an ecclesiastical endorsement, and joined us. Each of them has a story as to how he or she ended up in the Corps. It's not a bad life, most of the time, with assignments at bases all over the world. We have the highest retention rate in the services. Of course it's not so good during a war." Of course, we were in the middle of two wars!

Meeting the entry criteria, the would-be chaplain undergoes ten weeks of basic training at Newport, Rhode Island. Four courses comprise the training. The first six weeks is Naval Chaplains Basic Course (NCBC), followed by one week on Naval leadership (DOC), a one-week Amphibious Expeditionary course (AMEX field exercise), and finally a two-week course on Tools, Empowerment, and Ministry Skills (TEAMS). Those first six weeks are to get the chaplain recruits in physical shape, the other four acquaint them with the sea services and protocol, and offer ministerial training with special relevancy to the sorts of duties they will undertake in the Navy, the Marine Corps, or the Coast Guard. Upon completion of the training course, they graduate as lieutenants junior grade. Chaplains can rise in the ranks to admiral. I met four admirals in the Chaplain Corps while working this assignment.

Each morning's PDTC session began with a nonsectarian prayer offered by one of the chaplains, and each afternoon session closed with another prayer. The Navy requires that all prayers offered up by chaplains at public functions be nonsectarian. Chaplains are not required to give public prayers, but if they do, they must conform to the Navy's policy. After observing the ritual on the first day and the second morning, I pulled the OSTM aside during a break and rather bluntly asked, "To whom was the chaplain praying this morning?" For a moment, he stared blankly at me, then he responded, "God." "Some general god, or the god of his religion?" "Oh, I see what you're asking," he responded. "You don't think a prayer can be nonsectarian." "I don't claim to know much about theology, but it is worth thinking about," I said. He acknowledged that to be true and that he didn't really approve of the practice, but it was Naval regulations. I carried the issue a step further by suggesting that the exercise might be blasphemous to some and a violation of one of the Ten Commandments to others. He responded that some chaplains had made such a complaint about the practice, but it was always good to offer thanks to and ask for guidance from God. "So," I followed up, "you all really believe in the same god? Allah, Yahweh, Brahma, Vishnu, all the same? And what about the nontheistic Buddhists?" He smiled. "No, they are not the same." He was anxious to get away from this discussion and see to the refilling of the coffee urn, but I pushed him one step further. "You're a Lutheran. When you give the prayer, are you praying to the Christian god, even though you don't mention that or end with something like 'in the name of Christ we pray'?" He admitted that was what he thought he did. "So your prayer isn't really nonsectarian." He hesitantly nodded, then dashed off to tend to his organizational duties. I wondered if I would get a call from the company that employed us telling me that my services were no longer required, that I had carried my philosophical curiosity too far. But that call never came.

At the next break, that OSTM approached me again. "Your question about the prayer," he started. "I suppose it is not really a prayer at all unless each of those praying is in his or her mind addressing it to the god of his or her faith group. I think that is what each of us is doing in the room." "But isn't that a problem for you then? It isn't really a nonsectarian prayer, and, well, if you don't believe that the other guy's god really exists, can he be praying? He is certainly not praying to your god, the one and only true god, as you understand it." "Yes, it is one of the problems with the pluralistic environment of the Chaplain Corps. Our Code of Ethics maintains that we work collegially with chaplains of religious bodies other than our own and respect the beliefs and traditions of our colleagues." I acknowledged that I had read their Code of Ethics and that I wondered how the line in it that says that chaplains serve God and country is meant to be understood. He smiled, "Pluralistically, I suppose." A number of chaplains were, like the OSTM, intellectually and spiritually aware of the thin line they walked between being the pastoral representatives of their faith groups and being commissioned officers in the Navy.

This became much more obvious to me during teaching sessions at every subsequent PDTC during the two years in which I was involved in the project. On the right collar of the chaplain's uniform is the insignia of military rank. On the left collar is the insignia of the chaplain's faith – a cross, a tablet, a crescent, or a Dharmacakra. At virtually every PDTC, at least one chaplain would point to his two collars during the discussion of an ethical issue related to some military situation that had struck very near to home. That action was the universal symbol in the Corps that expressed the schizophrenic nature of their jobs. Sometimes it would be referred to just by the words, "two collars." During a session at Pearl Harbor, one of the chaplains expressed it as "I preach love and forgiveness and mercy and respect for other people while I work for an organization that sees itself as having only two jobs: to kill people and destroy property. How do you like that, Dr. French?"

There is an ongoing internal conflict in the Chaplain Corps between those from fundamentalist evangelical Christian churches and those representing the liturgical Protestant and Catholic churches. It raised its head during my second PDTC, at the Little Creek Amphibious Base in Norfolk, Virginia, in late March 2004. During the session on Kantianism, I was asked point blank by an older chaplain to explain how the history of promotions in the Corps could be ethical. Weren't they being treated as means and not as ends? I must have looked befuddled. I was clueless. He smiled slyly and said something to the effect that "they must not have told you about that." I looked to my colleague to see if he had any idea about what the chaplain was referring to. He shook his head. I tried to move past the question, or rather around it, giving it what they would say was a wide berth. However, another chaplain from the sullen group in the back row, one who had been silent up to that point and who seemed bored with the whole PDTC, piped up by seconding the question and saying it was something that definitely required ethical examination. Why was I shirking it? "After all, what's the point of this PDTC?" I said I would look into it, but the topic of that session was deontic ethics. The mumbling from the back row became more of a rumble. The senior chaplain who was serving as the OSTM for this PDTC cut in and told the chaplains to stay on topic. Dutifully they complied.

I sought out the questioner during the next break and asked him to fill me in. He kept a wary eye out for the OSTM while telling me that he and a significant number of his fellow evangelical chaplains, serving and retired, were party to a class action suit to move more of their number up in the ranks and into command positions in the Corps. He told me that the Corps leadership refused to acknowledge that the evangelicals are the only group that is growing in number in the Corps as well as in the ranks, especially in the Marine Corps. The number of Catholics and traditional Protestants has declined, but the leadership continues to come from those groups. "They work on a quota, don't let them tell you they don't. One third Catholic, one third liturgical Protestants, and the other third is us and all the rest of the hundred or so faith groups in the Corps," he asserted with fervor. One of his buddies joined the discussion, spewing out that they had to work in an environment polluted with bias against their faith groups. "They pass us over for promotion and give us bad ratings only because of the religions we represent. But most of the sailors and Marines are believers in our churches. The Catholics and the Lutherans are the first-class folks in this operation. They make up the selection board. They'll promote a Jew or a Muslim before one of us and of course they promote their own."

When I got the chance that evening, I googled the lawsuit and learned that a class action suit was in the courts in which a number of Navy chaplains alleged discrimination because of religious quotas that favored the liturgical Protestants and the Catholics in promotion and job ratings. Also, it alleges that evangelical Protestant chaplains have had their sermons censored, and that they have had to officiate at liturgical services while the liturgical chaplains have not had to conduct nonliturgical services. On one point, the nonliturgical Protestants were correct. The Navy figures show that Catholics and liturgical Protestants are about 32 percent of those serving in the Navy, whereas the evangelicals can claim at least 50 percent of the Marines and sailors. Eighteen percent of the Marines and sailors are Jewish, Muslim, or claim no religious affiliation. Also, the Navy board that handles promotions in the Corps consists of chaplains, unlike the arrangements in the Army and the Air Force where the selection boards are made up of personnel from branches other than the chaplaincy. The suit was pending in the courts throughout the years of our PDTCs, and occasionally comments about it from both sides popped up in the sessions. On more than one occasion, I overheard the Chief of Chaplains referred to as "that Papist," and snide remarks were made about an admiral who was Jewish. Once in a while, someone would blurt out something about those chaplains who care more about their liturgy than the Bible. Those sorts of expressions of a clear division in the ranks of the Corps occurred more frequently in the first year and virtually disappeared in 2006. They were replaced with much more pressing concerns for the mental health and well-being of the chaplains and a general apprehension that those in command were not focused on the need to care for those caregivers being emotionally devastated during and after deployments in Iraq. I cannot recall hearing anyone associating the perceived lack of care for the caregivers to the purported discrimination that was the fulcrum of the lawsuit.

One of the sessions in my first PDTC, the one at Point Loma in January 2004, was on truth telling. The Power Point slides seemed straightforward. One of the slides contained a story premised on the fact that the commodore and his staff would be conducting a command inspection of a ship on Monday. A division officer (DivO) of that ship was responsible for equipment maintenance. On the Friday before the inspection, his CPO (chief petty officer) told the DivO that he had overscheduled maintenance for the week, so he marked off four jobs that were not actually completed in order to look "all-clear" for the inspection. He promised the DivO the jobs would be completed the next week when he had his whole crew back. The next slide asked questions of the chaplains as if they were the DivO. They pretty much in unison pointed out that they are never in such a position; the questions are not relevant to their assignments. I refocused the questions by asking them what they should say to the DivO when he comes to them for advice about the position he is in. One of them facetiously said, "I'd tell him to resign." Another quipped that at least he doesn't have to worry about keelhauling or "kissing the gunner's daughter." I asked them to get serious and two or three said, "So, it's gundecking." "Happens all the time," another noted. I was in the dark again. The Navyspeak term "gundecking" threw me. Hoping they wouldn't realize I was winging it, I pressed on by asking them what would they advise in such cases and reminding them they are the moral advisers on shipboard. This elicited a full-scale account of such inspections and how the DivO must put the CPO on report, inform the commodore of the failure to complete the maintenance, and commit himself to seeing that it is done as soon as possible. Nonetheless, he is the DivO and it is his responsibility. He won't escape unscathed. I was told that too many ships sail out of harbor with incomplete maintenance on important equipment, putting crews and missions at risk. They agreed that if the chaplain knows about gundecking, he must take action.

"Action," as I came to learn at all the PDTCs, for most of the chaplains means send it up the command and then forget about it. It is then somebody else's problem. I had to point out to them on many occasions that they are required to follow it up the command and see that action is taken. It is not enough just to report it. Chaplains must follow through on their reports. Many of them were shocked to learn that two chaplains were court-martialed because they had not followed through on their reports about the My Lai Massacre. In neither of those cases, however, were the trials held.

I asked the chaplains how many of them had been made aware of cover-ups of maintenance on ships on which they were stationed. More than half raised their hands. When I followed up by asking how many reported their knowledge to the appropriate superiors, only three volunteered that they did. One said that he was told it was none of his business. "So gundecking happens frequently?" I asked. Many nodded. "Gundecking" was now part of my vocabulary even if I wasn't terribly clear as to its precise definition. Later, I verified my understanding with a lieutenant commander. It is a centuries-old naval term that refers to falsifying reports on equipment for inspections – for example, reporting that there are forty guns ready for action when there are only thirty-five. He told me that someone had explained the term to him as coming from the fact that the deck just below the top deck on British warships was called the gundeck even though there were no guns on it. It was a deception. Once I learned the term, I used it with the confidence of someone who had "come in through the hawsepipe" in other PDTCs when I taught the truth-telling session.

At Pearl Harbor in May 2004, the chaplains expounded on an astounding variety of examples of how widespread gundecking is both on ship and among the Marines in country. It became obvious to me that what lies behind the practice in many cases is an almost playful cover-up of the woeful level of force preparedness and supplies. One chaplain detailed how two Marine companies would pass equipment back and forth to each other when inspections were announced so that both would appear to be fully supplied and could account for all the equipment they were supposed to have but didn't. References to the ill-equipped troops in Iraq were often made in the media in those days, but the public, and probably the Pentagon, really didn't, perhaps couldn't, know just how ill-equipped or improperly maintained the troops were because of gundecking. The discussion of gundecking in the PDTCs revealed that chaplains know a great deal about the daily shady activities of those in their units at all ranks. But they do little with this knowledge and even sometimes abet the activities, believing themselves impotent to make any significant difference.

Though I was often perplexed and dissatisfied with the gundecking discussions, and were this to have occurred in one of my own philosophy seminars, I would have pushed the discussion much further, the minutes-to-go signs held up by the OSTM urged me to move on. I raised another question about truth telling, one in which the chaplains did not see themselves as directly engaged but one about which they had opinions that reflected their two-collar conflict. I asked them whom it is permissible to lie to in war. They all agreed that you could lie to the enemy, but matters got a bit sticky for them when it came to your own people, the Congress, the troops, and allies. I reminded them of an earlier discussion we had about Kant's moral theory and told them of Kant's exchange about lying with Benjamin Constant, in which Kant argued that it is never morally permissible to lie. They had earlier expressed a decided preference for Kantianism over the utilitarian's reliance on consequences when deciding the right thing to do in a particular circumstance. Some had expressed contempt for utilitarian ethics. However, when it came to this question, most were utilitarian through and through. What mattered were the consequences. You could lie if in doing so you were protecting your service, your ship, your unit, and, of course, your country; and you could lie to your country's citizens and their elected officials and legislators because more often than not "They can't handle the truth!" Fortunately for me, the allotted time for the session expired before I could dig more deeply into the contradictions being voiced and agreed to among the chaplains. It was, however, obvious that many found justifying lying on consequentialist grounds uncomfortable. One said that if he only had the pin on his left collar to worry about, he would probably condemn all lying. But then there was that other insignia.

At the end of the first day of the PDTC at Point Loma in January 2004, it fell to me to teach the section on divine command ethics. I offered them four possible ways to understand the relationship between a divine command and an action being good or right: (1) God orders it if and only if it is good or the right thing to do; (2) If God orders it, then it is good or the right thing to do; (3) It is good or the right thing to do if and only if God orders it; and (4) If it is good or the right thing to do, then God orders it. I asked them which captured their understanding of divine command ethics. Most discarded both (1) and (4) on the grounds that they implied that something could be good independently of God's ordering it. Most thought that in both of those cases, God would first have to evaluate the action against a preexisting criterion of goodness or rightness and then order it. In that case, God would be like a high-ranking Marine officer with a copy of the Uniform Code of Military Justice (UCMJ) and the rules of engagement. They opted for either (2) or (3) because what makes an action good is that God orders it. I asked them to consider whether any action could be good or the right thing to do if God had not ordered it. Some thought that there might be some things that were good to do even if God hadn't actually ordered them, but a substantial number "stuck to their guns." An action is good or the right thing to do only if God ordered it. Some things might be permissible because God hadn't forbidden them, but they were not good unless God commanded them.

I wondered if doing some things might be bad even if God had not expressly forbidden doing them. No takers on that question! Having never taught this sort of thing before, I was not sure where next to take the discussion, but the idea popped into my head to try the story of Abraham and Isaac with a Kierkegaardian twist. I asked them if they knew the story of Abraham and Isaac; they all nodded. Some pulled out their handy Bibles and opened to Genesis. I began to tell the story my way, more than a bit like a stand-up comic.

"OK, here's how I remember the story. While he is sleeping, Abraham hears a voice he takes to be God. (I'm not sure what it is to take a voice to be God speaking, but that happens quite a bit in the Old Testament. Remember Moses and the burning bush and Samuel arguing with God about creating Saul as King. I guess when you hear it, you just know it's not your neighbor or your CO or your mother-in-law. It's God!) God orders Abraham to take his son Isaac on a hike to Mount Moriah to offer him there as a human sacrifice to God. If it had been me, I would wonder if my neighbor was piping his disguised voice into my bedroom telling me what to do because he was sick and tired of my boy playing acid rock music so loud. But Abraham apparently had no doubts that it was God commanding him. By the way, God commands. God doesn't suggest or advise or recommend. Keep in mind, as I am sure you do, that Isaac was the very long-awaited and much-cherished son of Abraham and his wife Sarah, so this was a big deal – no ordinary human sacrifice, but still Abraham gathers up the kid and off they go. I suppose he had to tell Isaac something other than 'We're off to sacrifice you to God. Sorry, kid. That sometimes happens when God calls.' Maybe he lied to him, told him they were going hunting, having a male bonding experience, father-and-son quality time. In any event, God ordered it, so it must have been the right thing for Abraham to do. But was it really right, ethically right? Abraham gets to the point of plunging a knife into Isaac before an angel comes along and tells him he doesn't have to do it. If I did the same thing to my son, the courts would lock me up, even if I didn't actually kill him.

Take a minute and think about what Abraham has done to his familial relationships. Sarah won't be too happy when she learns about this and Abraham has to know it. What of the kid? What of Isaac? What is Isaac going to do the next time his father invites him to go out with him? 'I don't think so, Dad. There's a game on.' Will everyone agree that because God commanded it, it was the right thing ethically for Abraham to do?"

Some of the chaplains, angry at my version of the story, refused to comment, so I reminded them (or, in some cases, informed them) that Kierkegaard had considered the story carefully and had reached the conclusion that what Abraham did could not be justified ethically. He had done something immoral. He had come within an angel's wing of killing his son, of committing murder, yet Abraham is held in very high regard by three great religions, each represented in the Corps. He is not, on Kierkegaard's account, to be honored as a paragon of moral behavior. He is, in Kierkegaard's terms, the "knight of faith." He transcended ethics and embraced faith by acting on God's command despite what he had to know would be the ethical repercussions of his actions. And we should not forget that Abraham could not believe that he would not have to sacrifice Isaac. God had commanded that he do it. God didn't tell Abraham this was only a test and nothing will happen to the boy.

"So you don't think that divine commands are necessarily ethical?" one chaplain asked. I thought about that for a minute, then said that I was not ready to admit that everything God commanded in the Bible was ethical, and I worry that some of the things God does in the Scriptures couldn't be considered outstanding examples of virtuous behavior. A hand was raised and I called on what turned out to be one of the most perceptive and intellectually astute chaplains in the room. He asked if I had a problem, as he did, with the book of Job. The question and his reason for raising it were square on target. Unfortunately for me, they provoked me to continue my less-than-respectful recitation of stories from the Holy Book.

I told them that in my view, what God does in the book of Job is well outside what we understand to be ethical behavior. In my less-than-well-chosen words, "God and Satan are having a discussion in which Satan challenges God to let him prove that even the most pious, righteous, and just human will break down and curse God if he has to endure a certain level of suffering. God bets Satan that Job will endure anything and not curse God and then gives Satan permission to do his worst to Job, short of killing him. That Job in no way deserves anything that happens to him is a given. This is a cosmic game. No way around it, Job is an innocent victim of torture. Satan takes from Job his herds, his property, his family, his seven sons, and leaves Job covered with sore boils sitting on a dung heap. Job may be pissed off, but what he really wants is an explanation that will make sense of his condition. Why the torture, why the suffering? He has done nothing wrong. A group of neighbors comes by, and they discuss with Job why he is in such a state. They heap insult on his injury. Their solution is to tell Job that he must have sinned in some really major way and that he is now paying the price for his transgression. Both we and Job know that is not true. He hasn't sinned and he doesn't deserve what has befallen him. Finally, in desperation, Job calls out to God to come to him and justify why he is in such dire straits. I am not sure if Job's doing that actually lost the game for God, that isn't recounted, but what God does is, in my humble estimation, one of the nastiest things imaginable. Here is poor misused and maligned Job, full of open sores, emotionally distraught, sitting on a heap of dung and ashes, and how does God appear to him? In a whirlwind! That had to stir things up in a most unpleasant way for Job! Talk about torture! And what does God say to Job? Not, 'Sorry, you see Satan and I were having a little game.' No, He tells Job to gird up his loins like a man and don't presume to understand the ways of God and the universe. Then He goes on for about seventy verses bragging about His power, about besting the Leviathan and the Behemoth. Job doesn't need to be convinced that God is powerful. Job only wants to know what happened in the universe to cause a perfectly righteous and pious person to be so tortured. He gets no answer to that. None! Is that ethical? And there is another puzzling part of Job: God is revealed as tempted by Satan to enter into this unethical business. What's that all about?"

Toward the end of my rant on Job, I got the distinct feeling that I was really going far too far for this crowd and that it would be well beyond the pale were I to go further by raising Jung's idea that Job reveals a morally immature God who needs to learn morality from Job and will ultimately answer Job by becoming not a whirlwind but a man. In any event, the OSTM was standing up waving his "1 minute remaining" card, and the chaplain who had provoked the rant had his hand in the air. Most of the rest sat with blank faces. My daughter, however, had a "cat that ate the canary" grin on her face.

The usual end-of-the-day nonsectarian prayer followed that session. The chaplain assigned to offering it made some remarks about the glory of the scriptures (I assume that he had to mean any scriptures). I took that to signal that he did not particularly care for my takes on those Bible stories. The "amens" at the conclusion of his prayer sounded conspicuously louder than they had at the morning prayer.

The OSTM met with my daughter and me after the chaplains left the room. He told me that he could not find anything about Job or Abraham and Isaac in the validated Power Point slides. Some deviation was probably OK, but we needed to be careful because frequently in the past, chaplains got upset when material was covered that was not in the workbooks they were given. I took that as a gentle rebuke, not because the material I had called on was not in the PDTC workbook but because he had heard from some of the chaplains that my use of the Bible was offensive, even if I had not really screwed up the stories. And I had said "pissed."

The next day, one of the chaplains cornered me during a break and wanted to explain to me that God had, after all, restored Job to everything that was taken from him. I resisted the urge to tell him that the denouement of the book historically was a later addition, but I could not stop myself from asking him if he thought that made what was done to Job morally all right. "Ethically, can you torture an innocent person and after you've finished, in effect, pay him off for what you did to him? That OK?" The chaplain said that would not be ethical. "Is it OK if God does it?" He shook his head, not as a way of saying "No" but as a way of expressing his decision not to pursue this any further.

During a break that day, one of the physically more impressive chaplains, well over six feet tall and looking more like a linebacker than a clergyman, one who had recently returned from a deployment in Iraq, asked if I would chat with him in the courtyard outside of the building where the PDTC was being held. There he said that he was really impressed with my command of the Bible. I said he was probably one of the few. He said I'd be wrong about that. I admitted that I had read through it a few times. After exchanging pleasantries about our homes, he asked me if I had been saved. I told him that I was not a member of any organized faith group and I had no intention of joining one. He very politely told me that I really need to become affiliated with a church and that he would be more than willing to "counsel" with me on the matter. He represented one of the more liberal Protestant denominations, and they would surely welcome me. I thanked him for his concern, but told him that because there was far too much that I could not accept in the theologies of virtually all of the faith groups represented in the PDTC, I would remain on the outside for the foreseeable future. It was not that I had not given the tenets of those religions considerable thought,

I assured him. In fact, that was exactly why he would not be successful in any conversion exercise on me. He acknowledged that was probably true but said that he liked me and was concerned about the future of my immortal soul. I thanked him for his concern but said that if I had a soul, its fate would be my responsibility. He then told me that the rule in the Chaplain Corps is that a chaplain cannot attempt to convert a sailor or Marine who is already affiliated with another faith group, but the unaffiliated are fair game. I asked if he had much success in the conversion business in Iraq. He smiled and said there was no time. Things there are not going as well as the media over here portrays them. "It is getting ugly," he said. "If this goes on much longer, I fear we are all going to Hell." That was in January 2004.

My second PDTC was at the Amphibious Base at Little Creek, Virginia, in late March and early April 2004. Much had already changed on the ground in Iraq, and the demeanor of the chaplains at Little Creek seemed quite different from those only two months before at Point Loma. They were more sullen and introspective, or so it seemed to me. At first, I attributed the general attitude of the group of seventy or so to their being primarily Easterners (after all, I am from Arizona), Atlantic Fleet types, and the weather on the Virginia coast that week was gloomy and damp. But I was wrong. Many in the group had seen war up close in either Iraq or Afghanistan, and they were beginning to exhibit mental and spiritual fatigue.

On the second day of the PDTC, the news was all about Fallujah. Blackwater mercenaries had been taken by a mob, dragged through the streets, hung, and burned. The media pictures were brutal and assaulted the American public's sensibilities. The first and natural reaction was to get revenge, and the result was the ill-fated Operation Vigilant Resolve, with a high cost to the troops. Perhaps more important, the public, and even the media, began to view the Iraq conflict not as a glorious crusade to free an enslaved people but as the price a great nation pays for invading a sovereign, weaker nation in which its indigenous population will fight for its own land even at great cost and take whatever time it takes to rid itself of the unwanted invaders. We may have been vigilantly resolved, but they were fighting for their own land on their own land.

Some of the chaplains expressed their frustration with the Iraqi people who didn't seem to appreciate what we were doing for them. A few bluntly said that we ought to just blow up the whole country, kill them all, and get the oil. During a discussion of just war theory, one of the chaplains asked if this stuff was being taught to the midshipmen at the Naval Academy. I said that it was. He forced a laugh and I asked him why. "Because there's no point in it, is there? It has no impact on us or the midshipmen when they become officers. What does it matter if a war is just or unjust? We have nothing to do with the decision to fight. We fight it wherever they tell us to because we're ordered to. Filling officers' heads with this crap about when a war is unjust can only weaken their resolve to do their duty. How can they be good officers if they're worried that they might be fighting an unjust war?" "But you chaplains need to know what the young officers learn at the Academy about what makes a war just or unjust because some day on deployment one of them might tell you that he or she is convinced that this one is unjust. What do you say to that officer then?" "You tell the coward to resign his commission." "You don't try to tell him that regardless of whether or not the war is just, he has some power to insure that the war is not conducted in an unjust fashion?" He shrugged. I then suggested that knowing about just war theory would help in dealing with the relatives of Marines killed in a war if you could assure them that they died in a just war. Forced laughter. The same chaplain explained that when he had to meet with the wife or the mother and father of a Marine killed in the Iraq War, he assured them that their husband or son had died in the line of duty protecting America. "Protecting them from what?" I asked. "From mushroom clouds over their town, you know, from WMDs [weapons of mass destruction]." "But," I retorted, "there are no WMDs." "How do you know?" came the reply, followed by, "The Commander in Chief says there are. He's the boss, God bless him. I tell them they should be proud that their husband or son died in the service of George W. Bush." "Are they usually consoled?" I asked. "Yeah, usually, but I never get into this just war stuff. If President Bush sends us to Iraq or Afghanistan, that's all we need to know." He got up and promptly left the room, ostensibly to make a needed trip to the bathroom. I was unsure as to whether I should comment with him no longer present, or go on with the Power Point slides on just war theory, or what. A few other chaplains helped me out by remarking as to how difficult it is to make those dreaded calls at the homes of the relatives of dead Marines. It is a relief when no one asks if their husband or wife or son or daughter died for a good cause. "You pray that all you have to say is that they died doing their duty." After the session, some expressed worry that the whole enterprise in Iraq was a charade, that there was probably something important that the United States government was pursuing there, but it wasn't WMDs and it wasn't democracy for that country. There was a flicker in their expressions of doubt about the mission, admittedly from the minority of the chaplains at Little Creek. That flicker would become a bonfire in the coming years.

During a break after my teaching the session on "Moral Numbing," in which we discussed the potential moral dangers of remote-control warfare, a younger chaplain who had been serving with the Marines in Afghanistan pulled me aside. One of the cases we had examined involved a chaplain on a ship in the Persian Gulf at the beginning of the war, the "Shock and Awe" stage. He had witnessed the teams of sailors who launched the missiles destined for Baghdad leaving a pizza party, carrying out their missile-firing duties, and nonchalantly returning to the pizza. He decided that something was wildly wrong with that. Their pushing of buttons to send the deadly missiles off the ship had no moral consequences for them. Their acts were robotic. They were morally numb to what they were doing. He spoke with their commander and they decided that the sailors should watch the television broadcasts on CNN and Al-Jazeera of the destruction being caused in Baghdad. He had intuited that it is morally important in an age of virtual warfare that sailors not disassociate themselves from the fuller extent of what their acts of button pushing produce. They were not just pushing buttons or even just launching missiles. They were destroying neighborhoods, probably killing people. He told me that sailors said the pizzas didn't taste quite as good after they had seen the results of the missile launchings.

I told this story to a businessman with whom I was having lunch, and he said that what that chaplain and commander did was cruel, inexcusable. In his view, we want robotic sailors, soldiers, and Marines. All they are required to do is push those buttons. We don't want them worrying about the moral status of their actions. They should separate what they do in wartime from the rest of their lives, that is, compartmentalize that part of their lives. Be robots, if that is what it takes. "We are paying them to do the dirty work, but we shouldn't make them confront it on a personal level." I pointed out that if we take that approach, we have diminished their moral status. We are just using them as we might use a tool to do a job we want done. That was exactly what he thought should be the case. "After the war, let them get back to being moral citizens of the country without all of the ethical baggage. They'll be much happier." None of the chaplains expressed similar views when the session on moral numbing was taught, but as the war continued and the mental condition of the troops and the chaplains deteriorated, I sometimes wondered if the businessman didn't have a point, albeit a point that could find very little ethical support. The moral and psychological weight of the war was being borne by those in combat and the caregivers on which the combatants depended, while those who concocted the war, engineered it, manufactured it, marketed it, seemed to bear none of that burden. Nor, as I discovered in my second tour of PDTCs in 2006, did they provide adequate care for those on whom they had allowed the burden to fall.

The young chaplain that had cornered me during the break had a certain look in his eye that I later learned to identify as the "thousand-yard stare." "Doc, you serve in war?" I told him that during Vietnam I had taught on Homestead Air Force base but had never been in combat. "A Fobbit, huh? Never killed anybody, huh?" "Never." "Ever see a good friend of yours get the brains blown out of his skull?" "No." I asked what a Fobbit is. He chuckled. "Some of us are, most aren't. A Fobbit is what we call somebody that stays behind the wire. You know, never goes out on patrol, never faces fire. Most of the guys, military and especially contractors, stationed in Iraq and Afghanistan are Fobbits." I asked where the term comes from and he told me that the bases are FOBs, forward operating bases. "They stay in the shire, like Hobbits, you know, Fobbits." I nodded. There seemed to be considerable disdain for Fobbits among those who venture outside the wire, outside the shire. He went on to tell me that while he was serving with a unit fighting the Taliban, a Marine with whom he had becomes good friends, whom he had "brought to Christ," was shot and killed a few yards away from him. He went on to say that it made him so furious that he picked up the fallen Marine's rifle and was about to start firing in the direction of the Taliban unit when his RP (Religious Program specialist who is trained to protect chaplains in combat areas) stopped him. The RP said, "Chaps, I got your back. Put the rifle down. You got other things to do here." After a minute or two, he dropped the rifle. "Doc, I really wanted to kill some of them sons of bitches and I would have, if that RP hadn't been there. I'm sure of it." I said that I understood the frustration that he must have felt being in the midst of a firefight and watching Marines die. He touched his collars, lingering longer on the cross. Then he shook his head. I thought I heard him say as he walked away to get a soda, "Maybe next time." With the help of his RP, he had won a battle against the personal demons that tempt many of the chaplains in combat zones, but did he doubt he would have the moral courage to repeat that success on his next deployment? Did he really want more to be a Marine than a chaplain?

There were a number of chaplains that I met who seemed to me to be frustrated would-be Marines. They are in a very difficult bind, and it is not made easier by stories that seem to be in the culture of the Corps about chaplains taking up weapons in desperate situations. I sat down in the back of the room as my colleague began teaching a session. I opened the workbook and leafed through the Power Point slides, wondering if the PDTC syllabus actually addressed the real ethical problems the chaplains were facing.

At another break, a chaplain asked if we were going to talk about harassment issues. I couldn't recall any specific places in the syllabus where the topic was raised, but I remembered that at Point Loma, when my daughter and I asked the chaplains what issues they typically had to address, a number mentioned sexual harassment. The chaplain asked if he could tell me a story that I might use in future PDTCs. He said that as a young lieutenant, he was walking down a passageway on ship with his senior chaplain and met an LN3 (Legalman Third Class). He introduced the LN3 to the senior chaplain and told him, in a jocular tone, that she had missed a few of his chapel services. The senior chaplain, also in a playful voice, told her that she had been "a bad girl," but then he grabbed her by the arm, pulled her toward him, and slapped her on her butt. The LN3 ran off. The young chaplain was stunned and wondered what he ought to do. Perhaps he should go to this senior chaplain and tell him that what he had done was wrong. Perhaps he should tell the story to the XO (the executive officer). But before he decided what he should do, the LN3, with tears in her eyes, came into his office. She said that he had witnessed what had happened and she wanted to know what he intended to do about it. He asked her what she wanted him to do, and she told him that she was going to press charges and that she was counting on him to stand by her. She'd had enough of "this sort of thing." The chaplain admitted to me that he was afraid he had just blown his career in the Navy when he agreed to support her account of what had happened. She brought charges and the senior chaplain was sent to Admiral's mast where he was reassigned to a small command. His reassignment, however, did not occur for six months, during which the chaplain had to serve under him. The chaplain himself was then reassigned to the oldest ship in the Navy, homeported in La Maddalena, Sardinia. He was passed over for promotion for some years before finally being promoted, though he never received a poor fitness report.

My third assignment was at Pearl Harbor in Hawaii in May 2004. It was a smaller group of chaplains, mostly from Pacific bases. We met in the conference room in the BOQ (Bachelor Officers Quarters). That is not the proper name for such buildings any longer, but everyone called it the BOQ. It was a rather stolid group at first. My SME colleague and I cruised through the first day or so of sessions like old pros. I had, despite the rebuke to not include things that were not on the validated Power Point slides, used the standard game-theory matrix for Prisoner's Dilemma to provoke discussion on moral motivation, and the OSTM didn't object. There was a pall over the room and it was no secret why that was the case.

Pictures from Abu Ghraib prison had been all over the TV that morning and throughout the week. When it came my turn to teach the session on *jus in bello*, justice in war, I could not resist opening with the question, "How does Abu Ghraib make you feel?" Not a word in response. Dead silence, downcast eyes! I resisted the philosophy teacher's impulse to fill the void. Painful dead silence! Minutes past; a lieutenant commander raised his hand. "Ashamed."

"Does he speak for the rest of you?" There was nodding around the table. "Why are you ashamed? Marines didn't do the torturing of those prisoners. There wasn't a Navy chaplain at Abu Ghraib." The floodgates were breached and most of the chaplains contributed to a discussion of how it feels to see Americans in the military doing such heinous things. Has the war come to this? One chaplain volunteered that Marines he knew of had done equally despicable things to Iraqi civilians. Some rode the tired old horse of "a few bad apples." A number expressed their pro-and-con emotional reactions and the reactions they witnessed in their units when scuttlebutt about what was going on at Abu Ghraib and other detention centers made the rounds. A few tried to justify what the soldiers had done by using the Bush administration mantra that we didn't know the whole story, perhaps these were really bad guys. That was shouted down with "Nothing justifies it" and "Don't be pathetic," but there was definitely a sense in the room that something would justify the torture and mistreatment of prisoners at Abu Ghraib, if only we were privy to some classified information. It was clear that even the staunchest supporters of the war and the Bush administration were grasping at straws. They seemed to realize as they did so that something very bad had occurred and that rather than being an aberration, it may be a symptom of what sort of war they were in. The war, it seemed, was not one that could satisfy all of the conditions of a just war that they had been discussing in the PDTC.

I refocused on the question of what ought a chaplain do were one stationed at that prison and aware of the goings on. The standard answer was that a chaplain ought to report what he or she had learned up the chain. "That's all?" I asked. Some maintained that he or she ought to try to put a stop to it, but others wondered how a chaplain could accomplish that in the circumstances. The general view was that the soldiers serving as prison guards at Abu Ghraib were acting under orders. A chaplain might be seen as trying to contravene orders. One lieutenant noted that any orders that called for such torture and inhumane treatment of prisoners would be immoral and illegal. He was asked whether he had yet been deployed to Iraq. He said that he had not. That seemed to rob him of his credibility but, of course, what he said was correct.

I injected into the discussion a theme that we had used from the first PDTC. "Are you chaplains not supposed to be Nathan?" I asked them. They were caught off-guard by that question and took a few minutes to recall the reference. "You are the moral advisors to command. You are supposed to stand before authority and unflinchingly speak the unvarnished truth. Remember Nathan to David, 'You are the man.'" I doubted there were many Nathans in the room or at any of the PDTCs. They were probably more like the chaplain who composed the weather poem on Patton's orders. In fact, in the second series of PDTCs, when I asked how many had been told to offer up Patton-like prayers by commanders, most of the hands in the room were raised, and stories of being asked to give prayers to slaughter as many of the enemy as possible or make the missiles fly true to their targets were recited. (I assumed that these would have been nonsectarian prayers.) When asked if they complied, generally the response was that they had not written or given a prayer in exactly the way they had been asked to do so. They had modified it to make it more palatable to their theology.

In the second year's PDTC, we had the chaplains listen to Mark Twain's "War Prayer." Some were uncomfortable at hearing Twain's vividly grotesque interpretation of how God might hear what appears to be a preacher's simple prayer for victory over the enemy army in the Civil War. Others said that they would no longer be able to pray for victory. They would restrict themselves to praying for the safe return of the Marines in their units from engagements with the enemy.

One day at lunch in Hawaii, the admiral, Chief of Chaplains, gave a brief talk in which he said that at least there was no chaplain at Abu Ghraib. The admiral was wrong. There was an Army chaplain at Abu Ghraib. Some of the chaplains later told me that they knew that chaplain personally. During our preparations for the second PDTC, I was informed that attempts to interview that chaplain had proven unsuccessful. So rather than try to concoct a session about a chaplain dealing with torture and war and warriors turned into sadists, I developed a session on moral courage for the second PDTC focused on Specialist Joseph Darby, who had slipped an anonymous note about the torturing at Abu Ghraib under the door of investigators. When it was revealed that Darby had "broken" the case, he was ostracized by the people in his hometown and called a rat for turning on his fellow soldiers. The chaplains, to my surprise, were reluctant to praise Darby. They would not call him courageous, despite what he suffered, because he had not gone properly up the chain of command. In a few instances, I sensed the same disapproval of Darby that permeated his unit and made his life back home a living hell. That led me to wonder if another chaplain than the one who actually served at Abu Ghraib would have made any difference. There was reluctance in the chaplains to interfere, even though their literature tells them that they need to be cognizant that "by my presence" is sometimes a powerful deterrent for the troops not to engage in unethical behavior. One of them told me in private that those who have not been over there have no idea what it is like to deal with the type of recruits that now are in the services. I asked him what he meant and he said that especially in the Army, the ranks are filled with every kind of gang member you can imagine. "There's Bloods, Crips, Gangster Disciples, Hells Angels, MS-13s, Mexican Mafia, Aryan Brotherhood, you name it. Not so many in the Marine Corps, but what do you expect in prisons run by those guys. And in the villages. . . . God help the women, especially the young girls. They think a chaplain's gonna make a difference? Sure."

A Pentagon study, described in a *Time* report in May 2009, identified 165 cases of sexual assault among troops serving in Afghanistan and Iraq in 2008. That was an increase of 26% from 2007. Worldwide, there were 2,923 cases of sexual assault reported among U.S. service members.

After Abu Ghraib, the PDTCs were never the same. At every PDTC, some of the chaplains, in some cases, a majority in the room, were openly struggling to retain their sense of personal and professional identity. Perhaps because I was the oldest member of the team or because I had no direct affiliation with the Navy or the Pentagon, the chaplains seemed unable to constrain themselves from telling me their worst stories and asking me to tell them what they should have done, and if what they did was the right thing. They wanted my approval. Often, I did not approve, but I lied and told them that what they did was the right thing in the circumstances. How ethical is that? At the end of each day of a PDTC in the second year, I would return to my room on the base feeling that I had been entrapped in the immorality of the war in which truth had been the first victim. But what I felt was nothing compared to what the chaplains were feeling by the fall of 2005 and the spring of 2006.

The first two days of validation at Oceana in September 2005 went well. The third day was a different story. I already taught my four briefs. They needed some fine-tuning before we could take them "on the road" to the bases in the winter and spring of 2006. Two were a bit long, and one was too complicated. I worked on them while sitting in the back of the meeting room in the BOQ where the validation was being conducted. About forty chaplains were stuffed into the room. Most were Christians, but there were a few Jews and a Muslim in the group. Two admirals and other senior officers were scattered around the room.

After the first two days of each PDTC, I had to find some way of effectively teaching material developed by another team member even if, as was true of some sessions, I neither knew much about the subject nor agreed with its inclusion in the course. In working with a team, compromises had to be made on subject matter as well as on the thrust of sessions. In our team preparation sessions, I discovered that I was not especially good at compromising, particularly when dreading the fact that I would have to stand up in front of a group of up to 100 chaplains and try to get this stuff across to them. Given her background at the Naval Academy, my daughter seemed to handle these sorts of matters far better than me. She created session topics on character, the chaplain's pre-war role, the chaplain's role in combat, and ethical issues in the transition from combat. I organized sessions around the topics of moral courage, honor and integrity, moral conflict, and virtuous responses to moral evil. The other team members created the remainder of the sessions. At a team development meeting, a series of exchanges occurred when I objected to the use of material from the Boy Scouts in a section on character development because of the offense it could give to gay chaplains. A retired Navy captain told me that there are no gay chaplains. I corrected him that there are gay chaplains and that during the previous year's PDTCs, some had revealed to me that they were gay. That captain, who was the team leader for the second series of PDTCs, ended that discussion abruptly by telling me, almost ordering as a captain is wont to do, never to tell anyone on the team or in the Chaplain Corps that I know of any specific gay chaplains because those chaplains would have to be "booted out" of the Navy. It was don't ask, and for God's sake, don't tell! "Don't go there," I was emphatically told by everyone else on the team when they sensed I was ready to tack into a full-blown discussion of the morality of that policy. References to the Boy Scouts eventually were struck from the Power Point slides.

During the time since the previous ethics PDTCs had ended, the Marines in Iraq experienced nearly a year and a half of increasingly bloody conflict. The loss of American lives escalated with no end in sight. When we met the chaplains serving as the beta group at the Oceana validation of the new PDTC, I noticed a distinct change in their demeanor from those of the PDTCs of 2004. They greeted each other with nods and waves, but the lightheartedness I had witnessed in them at Point Loma in January 2004 was conspicuously absent. A person's bodily movements often reveal his or her inner self to others, even if unintended. Many of the chaplains showed up at Oceana with heavy hearts. During the first two days, we had little inkling of just how heavy, but soon there would be no doubt.

During a session on the third day, one of our SME colleagues asked what seemed like a reasonable question: "How many of you keep a log or a notebook or a diary of your experiences during deployment?" Most of the hands went up. He then asked if they read them and a chorus of "No's" and "No ways" echoed around the room. His puzzlement at this was answered with poignant stories that poured forth as if the sluice gates at a wastewater treatment plant had burst, first from one side of the room, then the other. One husky chaplain dressed in a Marine desert camouflage uniform stood and recounted that when he came home from a deployment, his wife and mother-in-law asked him to read some of his diary to them so they could better understand what he had been through in Iraq. After reading less than a page, he could not continue. He could not control his tears and the nauseous feeling rising in his gut. He left the room with his wife and mother-in-law calling after him to return. As he told the story, tears began to well in his eyes again. He brushed them away. "I couldn't do it. I just couldn't do it," he muttered. A chaplain near him put an arm around his shoulder. He brushed that off and walked quickly out of the room. Two chaplains followed him.

Another chaplain who had been deployed in a medical unit said that she knew her journal was filled with horrible stories that would make anyone sick, but there was no way she was ever going to read it or let anyone else read it. My colleague tried to tell them that it was important for the Corps to keep these sorts of records if only to help future chaplains. Someone laughed sardonically and another mumbled that if they did, it would be difficult to get recruits. Those around him muttered agreement.

I turned to the OSTM for the validation and asked if the chaplains were required to keep journals or diaries. He said it was not a requirement but that it is strongly recommended, especially in the combat zones so they can write down their experiences and in so doing both provide a record for the Corps and help expunge them from their own minds. It is referred to as "Lessons learned." "That's not working very well, is it?" I asked. He acknowledged that many of them had to deal with emotionally difficult situations because the war had become so confusing and chaotic. I suspected that the traumas they were observing and counseling were creeping into their psyches like the Blob from the 1950s horror movie, rolling over them, and absorbing them along with those Marines for whom they were there to provide care, solace, and theological escape.

At my first PDTC of 2006 in San Diego in February, at the chapel not far from Marine Corps Air Station Miramar (MCAS Miramar), my daughter again joined me. On the first day, one of the chaplains pulled me aside. He had just returned from Iraq and wanted to ask me a question. There was tiredness in his voice, as if it was a strain to talk. "Doc, I was north of Baghdad with my unit. They had been fighting for the better part of two days, clearing out a suspected nest of insurgents. It wasn't as bad as some engagements, mostly door-to-door, not many incidents. I don't think any of the guys got a scratch. This E-3," he paused when he noticed that I didn't understand the reference. "This lance coolie, lance corporal," he clarified, and I nodded, "came up to me shaking with tears running down his face. He told me that he had rescued two young Iraqi kids who had been walking towards the fire zone and brought them back behind the lines. The Gunny told him to get rid of the kids, find their folks, and get back to work. He set off with the kids, not understanding anything they were saying. Behind a wall he found their father crouched down, hiding. The children rushed to him and he gathered them in his arms. The lance corporal headed back to his unit," the chaplain continued, "but after he got only a few yards he heard shots behind the wall. He rushed back and found the two children shot dead in the head lying in pools of blood. Their father stood over them with a pistol in his hand. He shouted at the lance corporal something in Arabic that sounded like a curse and he put the gun to his head and killed himself." I stared at the chaplain and I think I asked him what else happened. In any event, he continued. "The E-3 came to see me that night and told me the story. He said he couldn't get the images of those children out of his mind. He believed he had done something wrong by taking them to their father, that he had somehow condemned them to death. I told him it wasn't his fault and that you can never tell what's going on in these people. He was just following the Gunny's orders. I saw him a couple of days later. He looked terrible. He couldn't sleep. I told him that he had to forget it. It's war. Stuff happens. I said I would read the Bible with him. He said he wanted to be alone and he wandered off. They found his body a couple of days later floating in the river." I think I muttered "Christ!" The chaplain looked me in the eyes for a moment, and then he lowered his head. "Doc, I did the right thing?" "Yeah," I said. "I don't know what else you could do. You can't help everybody." "Yeah, sure," he muttered and left me standing at the back of the chapel, wondering what I was supposed to say. I certainly wasn't going to quote something from Kant to him.

On November 19, 2005, the Haditha Massacre occurred. Marines killed twenty-four civilians, including women and children, many in their homes. The general in charge of the Marines in Al Anbar learned that some civilians had been killed in Haditha that day but regarded the deaths as an unfortunate consequence of war in that region of Iraq. At the preliminary hearing for the captain who was charged with dereliction of duty for failing to investigate the massacre, the general claimed that the targeting of civilian women and children at Haditha was something he learned only on February 12, 2006, when a *Time* reporter questioned the Marine report on the incident. A chaplain in the PDTC in San Diego described the Haditha case to me in some detail in January 2006. He told the story to me, I believe, as a way of unburdening himself. He said that he heard from some of those in his unit that their Humvee hit a roadside bomb and that a lance corporal was killed that morning. The squad leader, a staff sergeant, shot five Iraqis – a taxi driver and four teenagers – who were standing by a white car with their hands interlocked behind their heads or, the chaplain tried to recall, maybe their hands were bound. The staff sergeant fired eight or so rounds into them, point blank, the chaplain said. The staff sergeant and a lieutenant then led a squad to three houses. They fragged the houses and rained gunfire on them. Elderly folks, women, and children were inside. Eight were dead in one house, seven in another, and four in a third. The mother of a three-year old was shot trying to shield her daughter, but the daughter was already dead. "One of the sergeants went into the houses and . . . ," the chaplain paused but did not look at me. Then he continued in a soft voice, "he pissed, urinated, on the corpses." "Why?" I wondered. "He was angry because his lance corporal was the one killed by the roadside bomb. I saw the pictures one of them took of the bodies with his cell phone camera. It was murder, wasn't it?" All I could think to say was, "Did you report it?" He shook his head. "They know about it, believe me. You don't try to cover up something, if you don't know it was bad." He was right about that. When the general was interrogated by military investigators, he is reported to have said, "It was just here is something that happened, and it was on to the next thing." It was not so easy for that chaplain to move on to the next thing.

Five months after the San Diego PDTC, Representative John Murtha, a retired Marine colonel, said on CNN, "There was no firefight, there was no IED that killed these innocent people. Our troops overreacted because of the pressure on them, and they killed innocent civilians in cold blood."

Some of the chaplains expressed fear that their Marines had abandoned ethics altogether when dealing with the Iraqi people. I wondered if they included themselves in that assessment. They used Biblical references such as "Garden of Gethsemane experiences" to describe the turmoil they were undergoing both personally and vicariously when they had to listen to the stories and concerns of the Marines in their units. The image of Gethsemane reminded me of the account in Luke's Gospel in which Jesus is described as "being in an agony . . . and his sweat became like great drops of blood falling down to the ground." Was that how they felt? Also the Garden of Gethsemane was where Judas betrayed Jesus. Did they also feel betrayed?

On the morning of the fourth day of that PDTC in San Diego, I began the session on humanitarian intervention that focused on the genocide in Rwanda by asking the chaplains if they knew what the mission is in Iraq. I expected they might say it was humanitarian. Dead silence. Then one timidly offered, "There is no mission in Iraq. We are just there." An animated discussion ensued in which some argued that maybe the mission has become humanitarian now, but others insisted that it was always about oil and the sooner we admit that to ourselves, the easier it will be to get over it. Later, an admiral told me not to ask that question again. Consequently, I could not restrain myself from asking it at the other two PDTCs I taught that spring. The answer that there is no mission in Iraq became the standard response, until a chaplain pulled me aside during a break at the PDTC in Naples, Italy, in May 2006 to express his opinion that the only mission in Iraq is to kill and maim Americans and Iraqis in order to bolster inept administrations in Washington and Baghdad and make tons of money for the contractors. "We should have been in New Orleans and on the Gulf Coast where we could have done some good. That's our country," he said.

At the end of the PDTC in San Diego, Shannon had to endure criticisms from an admiral about what he regarded as her lack of respect for a certain docking operation and the seriousness of lines crossing when a ship is pulling alongside an auxiliary ship to take on fuel and supplies. The irrelevance of this chastisement compared to the serious psychological issues that the PDTCs exposed and that drew no comment at all from him remains a mystery. We assumed that he was putting the SMEs in their place, showing off how much he, a chaplain, albeit an admiral, knew of delicate maneuvers of ships at sea, and that he was also diverting our attention from the dirty linen that the chaplains were hanging out for us to see.

My daughter also joined me for the PDTC at the Kitsap Atomic Submarine Base in the state of Washington in March 2006. Except for an unseasonable snowstorm, this PDTC was more or less uneventful. We encountered a Marine chaplain who disrupted many of the sessions by intoning in a booming homiletic voice that every Arab in the Middle East should be killed. The other chaplains tried to quiet his interruptions with little success. The OSTM for the PDTC told us that they would be deciding on his fitness for deployment. Perhaps his most disturbing characteristic was the way he positively relished recounting the goriest details of episodes he had experienced on his most recent deployment with the Marines in Iraq. He seemed to have embraced the insignia on his right collar, but Shannon and I wondered if his blustering about the blood and guts strewn about hovels was not a defense mechanism shielding a psychologically distraught person who had seen too much and who had tried to care for too many.

At various points in some of the sessions, we used clips from films or television shows to focus the chaplains' attention on the crux of a topic or, admittedly, to break up the monotony of a teacher droning on about virtue or morality in war. The topic of a session on the third day was the chaplain's role in combat.

At validation in Oceana, the lights in the room were dimmed, and on the screen a clip played from *The Longest Day*. The clip was about a chaplain, traveling with the troops at night in Normandy, who loses his communion set during a river crossing. Bullets are zinging around and bombs exploding, but the chaplain insists on diving into the river to find the set.

"Turn that goddamn thing off!" a chaplain shouted from somewhere on the left side of the room. "Turn it off. Now!" A number of chaplains near him rushed over to see what was the matter. He had covered his ears

shooting her was within the rules of engagement and justifiable. Two days later the sergeant told his platoon commander that he could no longer fight and refused to go on another mission. The chaplain reminded the sergeant that refusing to fight was a court-martial offense, but that did not faze him. His platoon ostracized him and he was called a coward. After a number of meetings with the chaplain and transfer to another platoon, about three months later, the sergeant was sent home. While on leave in his hometown, he heard a firecracker on the Fourth of July and dropped to the ground outside a store thinking he was being shot at. The sergeant started drinking profusely and picked fights in bars, where he often ended up bleeding and had to be pulled off of customers. He could not control his temper or his drinking, and he could not sleep. He returned to the Marines at Camp Pendleton and was diagnosed with post-traumatic stress disorder (PTSD). He tried to reenlist to become a Marine recruiter, but his reenlistment was denied on the grounds that he had failed to obey orders in combat, was a coward, and refused to return to Iraq to prove that he was fit for combat duty. He was given an honorable discharge. "No joy!" The chaplain's voice dropped. Some of the others in the room also muttered, "No joy." I asked one of the SMEs, a retired Navy captain, what that meant. "What it sounds like," he replied. "An unsuccessful mission." I began to wonder if PTSD could be caught by those ministering to the troops even if they were not themselves witnesses to the carnage and did not experience the daily chaotic threats to their lives and limbs and brains that characterized the way the war had evolved for the fighting troops. There certainly was enough "No joy" to go around. The unwarranted death of the Iraqi woman in the black burqa in Ash Shatra was only the first act in a tragedy for so many involved in the war, for so many there in the room at Oceana, involved in a drama that would have no cathartic denouement.

I looked up at the screen while the chaplain was speaking. The Power Point slide read: "A mother and a father may be willing to give their beloved son or daughter's life for their country, but I doubt they would be willing to sacrifice their child's soul." It was a quote from Shannon's book on *The Code of the Warrior*.

Thankfully, time expired for the day's validation sessions. The chaplains filed solemnly out of the room past us. One of them tipped his head rather sheepishly to me. Another said in a muffled voice, "That was great. We need that sort of thing." We SMEs nodded back, incredulous.

At each of the PDTCs, stories provided to the team by the chaplains were incorporated into the syllabus and used to provoke discussion of the ethical roles to be played by a chaplain when deployed in a combat zone. During my final PDTC at Naval Support Activity (NSA) Capodichino in Naples, Italy, in May 2006, I was discussing the case of a chaplain in Afghanistan assigned to a Marine battalion. The Commanding Officer (CO) of the battalion had a habit of publicly humiliating those under him. On a particularly difficult "hump," one of the Marines collapsed from exhaustion. The chaplain stopped and gave the stricken Marine some water from his canteen. The CO yelled at the chaplain, "Chaplain, you get the fuck out of there. You're weakening my Marines. Don't show kindness to my warriors." Some of the Marines in the battalion told the chaplain that degrading them was one thing, but demeaning the chaplain was clearly offensive and improper. The chaplains in the PDTC were supposed to tackle the question of whether the chaplain in the story had an obligation to report the treatment he received at the hands of the CO to higher authority.

They struggled with the question on a number of grounds. The majority felt that reporting it up the line would do no good because the higher ranking officers would side with the CO of the battalion. "They always do." Some said that word of such disloyalty by a chaplain would filter around the Marine Corps and negatively affect the chaplain's next assignment. He would likely get a bad fitness report and his promotion chances would be ruined. Also, because action would not likely be taken against the CO, if the CO learned of the chaplain's report going over his head, he probably would become more abusive. As it had on many previous occasions, the two-collar conflict again surfaced. "When they don't like what we are doing, they remind us that we are Navy officers first and foremost." That, of course, is not biographically true. They all had been ordained clergy in their faith groups before putting on the uniform. So it must be, from the Navy's point of view, an issue of priorities. The right collar outranks the left. I often got the impression that many chaplains would not see it that way, if push ever came to shove.

High-ranking chaplains interjected in various discussions, especially those dealing with moral courage and moral conflict (two of my briefs), that chaplains must never forget that they are ranking Navy officers and that they have a duty to provide leadership while also carrying out their obligation to serve as the moral compasses for the units to which they are assigned. "Most of you, and the Corps in general, have shirked that duty, have not taken your role as Navy officers seriously," said the captain who had just taken command of Navy Region Europe in a make-no-mistake-about-it officious tone. After his harangue, the others behaved more like chastised children than military officers, and the room was filled with the sounds of silence. At the next break, the captain told me that the chaplains regularly need to be reminded that they are not in the Navy just to hold religious services, listen to confessions, and comfort the injured and widows. He felt that too often chaplains let opportunities to make an ethical difference in command decisions and daily operations slip by. He attributed some of their inaction to protecting their careers, but he said that is a general problem throughout the military, all the way up to the top.

Following up on the captain's admonition, I asked the chaplains why they would do what they recommended, which was, in effect, to do nothing. A chaplain has to do the best he can in a circumstance like that, they said, almost in unison, and it is counterproductive to cause the CO to become angrier with you or with the Marines you may be helping. The Marine Corps is not going to replace a commanding officer who is getting results because a chaplain complains about his leadership style and the language he uses to motivate the battalion and his underlings. One of the chaplains who had been silent up to that point spoke up. "That's just how it is. I know that officer and I know that chaplain. When you're dealing with that kind of guy, you want to keep confrontations to a minimum. You got to go along to get along. You've got to swallow it sometimes."

After the session, that chaplain told me that he was the chaplain in the story and that there was much more to it. The CO broke the morale of the junior officers and seemed to relish every opportunity to abuse and humiliate the chaplain. His favorite phrase that typically accompanied his chastising the chaplain for weakening his Marines was "I know Jesus Christ and he would be ashamed of you." The chaplain, without the slightest show of humor, went on to say how he found that odd because the CO was a nonpracticing Muslim. I held back the urge to ask how one is identified as a nonpracticing Muslim. Is a nonpracticing Baptist still a Baptist? A lapsed Catholic still a Catholic? I suspected that what he might have meant was that the CO was of Arabic descent, and that he assumed that meant he was a Muslim or was once a Muslim. Of course, there are many Christian Arabs and, I suppose, atheist Arabs, as there are some Irish Buddhists and Irish atheists.

At Naples, I partnered with an outstanding young philosopher from the Naval Academy. That PDTC received the highest ratings from the attending chaplains of any of the PDTCs in 2006. I think one reason for its success was that a local chaplain served as the OSTM because the usual representative from the Corps offices or the Navy Chaplains School was unable to attend. The Naples OSTM allowed us to control the length of the sessions to suit the way the discussions of the topics were going. We did not cut off fruitful interchanges just because the time set in the syllabus had expired.

The chaplains in attendance were mostly veterans of Iraq and Afghanistan, and many seemed to be suffering emotionally from their experiences, as anyone aware of what they had undergone would expect. The Chief of Chaplains of Navy Region Europe pointed out to me that the chaplains were clearly having a difficult time mentally, as he himself was, having just returned from Afghanistan, and that he noticed that many had put on some weight. He felt certain this was due to consumption of more beer and alcohol than they had done in the past. He had attended the validation at Oceana and knew the content of those sessions in the PDTC that had provoked distressing emotional reactions from some of the chaplains. I expected that he might ask us to tone down those sessions for this group, but instead he asked us to especially stress those topics, to work on the postwar issues and not to shy away from exposing the emotional underbelly of service in Iraq and Afghanistan. "In the end," he said, "they need that more than ethical theories. They need to get it out and think about how it is affecting their lives. If they don't, all the other stuff won't really make much difference." I got the impression he was speaking for himself as well as for the chaplains he commanded.

My SME colleague and I took his request to heart, with the result that the better part of a day bristled with engaged discussion that was not really academic philosophy or ethics but that brought out pervasive issues related to the role of caregivers in combat that should attract the attention of those writing academically about just war and humanitarian intervention. That discussion focused primarily on deprivations and depravations endured in Iraq. One of the chaplains, however, had enough. He protested that he was sick and tired of hearing about the stress and agony of those in Fallujah or Baghdad. He was the chaplain at a hospital in England ministering to the injured from the war and, he believed, he had undergone as much as any of them, including the breakup of his marriage.

During the discussion of humanitarian intervention, the case of Captain Luc Lemaire of the United Nations forces in Rwanda was especially provocative in the Naples PDTC. (In some accounts, Lemaire is referred to as a lieutenant.) In 1994, Lemaire commanded ninety soldiers, who were protecting 2,000 Tutsis in the Don Bosco school compound in

Kigali. Large numbers of armed Hutus gathered outside the compound threatening to enter and kill all of the Tutsis. Lemaire received a call from headquarters ordering him to remove his troops from the compound to assist in the transportation of Europeans and their pets to the Kigali airport. The Tutsis begged Lemaire to turn their guns on them if he was going to follow those orders. They preferred to be shot by the UN force than hacked to death by the machete-wielding Hutus. Lemaire followed his orders, and the 2,000 Tutsis were hacked to death. We highlighted the gruesome tale with clips from the movie *Hotel Rwanda*, in which a somewhat similar scene is depicted regarding a UN commander, though without the gruesome outcome in the school compound.

The chaplains were shocked by the story. I do not believe that they had not heard of the genocide in Rwanda, but they had not understood it in such vivid terms, nor were they aware of the command decision by the UN headquarters to protect Europeans seeking to get to the airport rather than Tutsis under immanent threat of death. The question I asked to open the discussion was, "Suppose that you were a chaplain assigned to Lemaire's unit and he asked you what he should do when ordered to leave the Tutsis in the compound to their fate?" The first reaction from some of the chaplains was that they would tell him that he should follow his orders. That provoked others to virtually shout that a chaplain should insist that Lemaire and his troops not leave the compound. Lemaire should call back to headquarters and try to explain the seriousness of the situation at the compound. Let the Europeans wait. I interjected that Lemaire had apparently done so, perhaps on two occasions, and that headquarters repeated his orders to leave the compound. One of the chaplains said that were he the chaplain with the unit, he would stay with the Tutsis. "And be hacked to death by the Hutus?" someone asked. "Yes," responded the chaplain. "That is where a chaplain belongs, not supporting a clearly misguided and immoral order." "But most of you throughout the week have been telling me that following orders was your first priority. And when we discussed an episode of the *M*A*S*H* series, almost all of you said that Hawkeye was in the wrong for doing the humanitarian thing rather than just informing command of the situation and then following command orders," I said.

Most of the chaplains agreed that the Rwandan situation, however, was different. Some maintained that if his chaplain could not convince Lemaire to stay and protect the Tutsis, to disobey his orders, that chaplain should take a stand and urge the troops to do so. Maybe by doing so he would shame them into taking the ethical action in the circumstances even if it meant refusing to follow orders. "That's mutiny," someone called out. "On what grounds should he do that?" I asked. "Are you now utilitarians counting how many will be benefited?" No, they weren't, they said. They were trying to stop a massacre. If you have a good chance of preventing such an evil outcome, you must try. If you are unsuccessful in getting Lemaire and/or his troops to stand their ground in the compound, then all you can do is join the victims. "What good would that do?" one of the chaplains asked. Another responded that it would put the chaps (they are typically referred to by the troops as "chaps") on the side of the angels. I resisted the urge to say it would do so literally. Instead, I asked them if they were willing to say that a chaplain in this case should both urge a commander to disobey orders from his superiors and, in any case, disobey orders himself. Most said that was exactly what was required. "Why? Throughout the week you have insisted that you must never counsel disobedience of superior orders." One chaplain spoke up, "Because I should have done it more than once." Another said, "It's easier in this case, because you've told us the outcome. On the ground there's so many unknowns. You don't know that the Hutus will really hack all of the Tutsis to death." "Come on," someone else said. "They were doing it all over Rwanda. Of course they were going to do it. Are you going to hide behind such a remote possibility?" "You might as well say that God might interfere and prevent the massacre," another interjected. "Worse than that," someone else said. "You could tell yourself that if they were massacred it was God's will. That takes our responsibility utterly out of the equation."

An African American chaplain asked whether the United States had any forces in the country. Rather than ask him why he wanted to know, I just responded that after the incident in Somalia, the Clinton administration refused to do anything about the genocide in Rwanda. He shrugged. I might have continued the discussion, but I could sense that it was becoming very uncomfortable for a number of the chaplains, especially after the chaplain had said that he should have behaved more courageously in Iraq, presumably to try to prevent bad things from happening in the unit to which he was assigned.

Before I could cut off discussion, a chaplain who had been silent up to that point began in almost a whisper. "It was race. Protect the Europeans because they're white. Let the Africans kill each other. Who cares? Let the Sunnis and the Shia fight it out in Iraq. None of us would be so noble as to stay in that compound when the troops left. Most of us would be first on the bus. Don't kid yourselves. Right collar takes precedence. Orders are orders." "You can't do much dead," added another chaplain. Another fired out, "It's moral courage and we don't have it, like the captain said." "Don't be so tough on us. A chaplain can only do so much. 'By my presence' only goes so far," retorted another. The chaplain was referring to a mantra that is used in the Corps to remind the chaplains that much of their ministry will be carried on just by their being present in situations. Marines and sailors will be reluctant to behave badly when the chaps is around. But there is another side of that coin: if Marines and sailors are behaving badly and the chaplain is around and doing nothing to express his negative reaction to their behavior, they will take his presence to be a tacit approval of what they are doing and so regard it as having a moral seal of approval. An African American chaplain brought the discussion of the Rwandan genocide to a close. "If you aren't standing with those Tutsis when the UN troops pull away from the compound, God help you. Who the hell do you think stands up for humanitarian behavior in the military, if not us?"

One of the chaplains during the break asked me if there were any repercussions for Lemaire or his superiors following the massacre. I said that I hadn't been able to find enough online about Lemaire to answer about him, but that the commanding general of the UN forces in Rwanda, Romeo Dallaire, was medically released from the Canadian Forces after being diagnosed with PTSD. There was a general "hmmm" from the chaplains who had gathered around us, an acknowledgment that they empathized. I told them that he suffered from clinical depression, attempted suicide on a number of occasions, and in 2000 was found on a park bench in Ottawa, Canada, in a near coma brought on by a combination of intoxication and anti-depressants. After recovery, he has become a humanitarian advocate and served in the Canadian senate.

At the end of the third day of the PDTC in Naples, I was teaching that infamous session on the ethics of care that still began with the homecoming scene from *The Best Years of Our Lives*. I was surprised that this group of chaplains saw so much more rejection, fear, and humiliation in the encounter between the paraplegic sailor, his family, and fiancée than other PDTC groups had drawn from the scene. I wasn't at all certain that what they were recounting was up there on the screen. Some of it, I suspected, was being played on the screens in their minds.

After urging discussion of caring for traumatically damaged psyches upon return from combat, the Power Point slides focused on the problem of warriors bottling up their emotions for fear of displaying a weakness of character. The issue to be discussed was supposed to revolve around the way the ethics of care could provide chaplains with better tools for dealing with Marines in combat zones than some of the other types of formal moral theories that had previously been discussed in the PDTC. Another slide noted that nurturing the virtues of care ethics could help Marines retain their humanity in combat.

I did something during that session that had not been done in other PDTCs. I pulled out the report on the suicide of Colonel Ted Westhusing. Colonel Westhusing was a philosophy and English literature professor at West Point. His Ph.D. dissertation in philosophy was on honor. He was a devout Catholic with a wife and three children. He volunteered to go to Iraq, fervently convinced that it was a just war. On June 5, 2005, he was found dead in his trailer at Camp Dublin. It was a suicide, one of twenty-two suicides in Iraq by American troops that year.

There were 102 suicides in the Army in 2006. One hundred forty soldiers committed suicide in 2008, and in the first three months of 2009, there were fifty suicides. One hundred eighty-seven Marines attempted suicide in 2008. Forty-one were successful. It is the second leading cause of death in the Marine Corps. More Marines kill themselves after returning from deployments in Iraq or Afghanistan, but the numbers in country are also rising. The Marine Corps has not drawn any connections between deployments and suicide attempts. The Corps is willing to link the rise in suicides to an increase in the pace of rotations to the war zones of Iraq and Afghanistan but not to deployments there. The Marine Corps commandant was reported as saying that the suicides are not because of service in Iraq but because of the "ops tempo" in general.

Colonel Westhusing left no doubt. He worked under the command of General David Petraeus on training Iraqi forces. Interviews in Colonel Westhusing's file following his suicide indicated that his greatest strength of character was his sense of integrity, which was also the most likely reason for his death. He felt that he had to go to Iraq to shore up his credibility as a professor at West Point. He had argued with other philosophy professors at the Academy that the American mission satisfied the conditions of a just war, both in cause and execution. He was certain that serving there would confirm both conditions for him.

While carrying out his duties, Colonel Westhusing found himself regularly in conflicts with contractors, primarily over fraudulent expenses and the participation of mercenaries in the killing of Iraqi civilians. His suicide note included the claim that his superiors, such as General Petraeus, tolerated corruption and human rights violations.

Colonel Westhusing became convinced that the values of the military that he prized, such as duty and, especially, honor, were replaced in Iraq by the values of unfettered capitalism. Profit supplanted honor. According to the report that I read to the chaplains, his suicide note read in part, "I am sullied – no more. I didn't volunteer to support corrupt, money-grubbing contractors, nor work for commanders only interested in themselves. I came to serve honorably and feel dishonored. I trust no Iraqi. I cannot live this way. All my love to my family, my wife and my precious children. I love you and trust you only. Death before being dishonored any more. Trust is essential – I don't know who to trust anymore. Why serve when you cannot accomplish the mission, when you no longer believe in the cause, when your every effort and breath to succeed meets with lies, lack of support, and selfishness? No more. Reevaluate yourselves, cdrs [commanders]. You are not what you think you are and I know it."

I then quoted from Army psychologist Lt. Col. Lisa Breitenbach's report on Colonel Westhusing. She opined that the colonel had placed too much pressure on himself and that he was too rigid in his thinking, that he had difficulty understanding how monetary values could take priority over moral ones in war. She said that was a major flaw in his character. She wrote, "Despite his intelligence, his ability to grasp the idea that profit is an important goal for people working in the private sector was surprisingly limited. He could not shift his mind-set from the military notion of completing a mission irrespective of cost, nor could he change his belief that doing the right thing because it was the right thing to do should be the sole motivator for businesses."

When I finished reading, the room was dead silent. One of the chaplains sighed deeply. I turned to him. He bobbed his head up and down, then said without affect, "So his character flaw was that he had a moral character." Another followed suit by asking if that was the real lesson of this PDTC. I quickly backtracked by telling them that I wasn't sharing the Westhusing story for that reason. My point was to solicit from them how they would handle someone who came to them with deep ethical concerns similar to those that apparently motivated Colonel Westhusing to commit suicide. That provoked a meager amount of comment. Most who tossed in a word said they had already been confronted by a number of disaffected and depressed cases like Westhusing's. The discussion, however, turned sharply back to the reasons the colonel shot himself and not how to handle with care comparable cases.

They wanted to talk about corruption they had witnessed, the creep of the mission, the loss of the mission, the difficulty in explaining to the Marines why the contractors from Blackwater were being paid salaries many times greater than the U.S. troops to do similar things. Some expressed their self-doubts about their beliefs about the justice of the war and recounted debates about the ethical bases for the war they had with other chaplains and members of their families and friends stateside (they refer to America as CONUS, which, after struggling with the acronym for a while, I learned from the OSTM means "continental United States"). "It is not just seeing the carnage, Doc," one of them told me. "War's war. It's like that guy said in that note. It's what you held in here," he pointed to his head, "that you don't want to let go and that you can't get to fit with what you experience in theater. You want it to be noble, honorable, 'cause that's what you told everyone and yourself that it has to be. Then it ain't."

Someone else noted sarcastically that hardly anybody back in CONUS cares about Iraq anymore, anyhow. "They've moved on and we're slogged in. FUBAR." I knew what that meant.

We never got to most of the Power Point slides for that session, but no one complained. When the session was over, one of the chaplains pulled me aside and gave reality to the quote from Shannon's book. "Doc, the mother of one of my Marines contacted me when I returned from my last deployment and asked, 'Chaps, I knew that my boy could lose a limb or even his life when he joined up, but why did they have to take his soul?' Doc, what the hell was I supposed to tell her?" I think I asked what he did tell her and he shrugged. I remember looking at him and slowly shaking my head, indicating that I would only say something trivial if I offered anything at all. Both of us left the room feeling utterly inadequate.

Throughout the week at Naples, discussions often slipped into concerns expressed by the chaplains that adequate attention was not being paid to their mental health by the Corps. A number of times, and especially during the prolonged discussion of *jus post bellum* and the ethics of care, I urged the chaplains to convey their concerns in that regard to the admiral, the Chief of Chaplains, who attended the final afternoon of the PDTC when the chaplains gave presentations to him regarding ways to improve the chaplain's role in character education and ethical development in various levels of the sea services. These "Presentations to the Flag Officer" were to be based on the week's training sessions and were given by three groups, selected by rank. The lower ranking chaplains were to focus on creating a character-development program suitable for a ship. Supervisory chaplains were to prepare a brief that advised the First Marine Division Commanding General concerning what elements should be included in a character-development program that would be implemented throughout the division. The group chaplains were to design a brief for the Commander Naval Education and Training Command on the institutionalization of character development in the sea services.

On the morning of the day the admiral arrived in Naples, the chaplain chosen to open the session prayed that he and his fellow chaplains would "speak truth to power." His prayer was not answered. None of the chaplains said a word to the admiral about the need for the care that many of them required. After the admiral left, the captain told them that he understood their needs and that he intended to visit all of them in his command and discuss how the Corps can help them handle the difficulties they are enduring. He encouraged them, no matter what rank, to share with him the emotional and mental ghosts that were haunting their lives.

At the close of validation in Oceana on that late September 2005 afternoon, the team met with the admirals and some of the senior officers of the Chaplain Corps for evaluations and debriefing. The officers did not look happy. I turned to the retired Navy captain who coordinated and task-mastered our efforts to create the PDTC. He was referred to as the POC in the e-mails the team got from the contractor. Another acronym that was a mystery to me! When I finally got a chance to ask Shannon what it stood for, she off-handedly said, "Point of Contact," as if it was so obvious.

"Can they just fire us?" I asked our POC.

"I guess," he said hesitantly.

I decided that they probably wouldn't fire all of us. Maybe one or two of us will be canned, as in the previous year when they insisted on the removal of the original member I had replaced. I had nothing to do with the last two day's sessions, so I was convinced that I was safe. I was counting on the money and the trip to Italy. What about my daughter? The sessions that really set things off were her creations.

All of the chaplains having left the room, we sat down at a round table. The Chief of Chaplains looked stern, but first deferred to the other officers for their comments. They told us, in no uncertain terms, that the session on transitioning from battlefield situations must be cut from the course. We SMEs sat silently. Our POC jotted a note. I looked into the faces of the other SMEs and realized that they were not going to speak. I piped up.

"Admiral, your chaplains need help. They can't even watch a clip from *The Best Years of Our Lives*." The admiral, whom we knew as a kind and thoughtful man, an intellectual with a first-class academic background, looked away and in the direction of a captain and a master chief. "My staff has told me that we are addressing their needs," he said. Some of the team members and I shook our heads. "Not too well, from what we saw today," I said.

The admiral nodded, "We haven't taken care of our own."

Emboldened I pushed gently. "We shouldn't cut that session, but we can modify it to lessen the impact on those with PTSD." A captain harrumphed, and then snapped in an officious tone, "This is supposed to be a course in ethics. Leave the psychology to the Navy shrinks. You're the wrong people to raise these issues."

Shannon responded with assurance that the session is about ethics, about what a chaplain ought to do in the chaplain's role when dealing with Marines suffering from postdeployment problems in their lives, such as PTSD. The captain retorted that the chaplains ought to just send those Marines to the shrinks. "Shrink referral is one of their tasks." One of us reminded them that the chaplains are also suffering, sometimes maybe even worse than the young Marines in their units.

"Chaplains are Naval officers," came the terse reply from the admiral. I am sure that at least the civilians on the SME team wondered how that was relevant. "So was that Marine sergeant," I thought, but didn't say. Oh well, he was noncommissioned. Maybe that was supposed to make some important difference when it comes to being able or not to deal with trauma.

I pressed on, though not really knowing where to go with this and hearing the voice of our POC in the back of my mind reminding us umpteen times during our deliberations while creating the PDTC that we are contractors. We work for them. The customer is always right. Of course, the customer is often wrong. We said that at a number of team meetings. We are, by their own identification of us, subject matter experts. Shannon and I insisted in those meetings that we have a fiduciary relationship to the chaplains. They may know the proper form of liturgy in baptizing a baby, and the protocol on shipboard, but we are the experts when it comes to the teaching of ethics and the concepts of virtue. They acknowledged that in the title they gave us. We are the "pros from Dover," in the words of Hawkeye and Trapper John in the movie *M*A*S*H*. If they knew the stuff we were hired to teach them, there would be no need of the PDTCs, and the Pentagon reports would not conclude that there is a crisis in ethics among the Marines in Iraq.

I, more or less humbly, reminded the admiral, "They are also human beings and they are obviously hurting and need to discuss these issues. Kant probably had no idea about a soldier's heart or shell shock or post-traumatic stress disorder, but the foundation of his ethics is that all human beings deserve respect and should always be treated as ends in themselves and not merely means. We can hardly teach ethics to chaplains in the midst of this pathetic war and not deal with their own moral and psychological dilemmas. They just are not separable."

One of the team members voiced agreement. The retired Navy captains seemed stunned at what they probably regarded as talking back to the admiral and throwing in a philosophical reference to boot. The admiral had an excellent Catholic education in philosophy and theology. A thin smile crossed his lips and he replied. "Modify that session. Cut out the clip from *Frontline*. The chaplains know each other. Word gets around. They will know that chaplain and what happened to that sergeant." He motioned toward the meeting room. "We don't need that sort of situation to arise at Pendleton or Lejeune."

Another admiral was more adamant. "That guy is now out there with the Veterans Against the War. They use him in some of their ads. He speaks at their rallies. We can't have that at the bases, especially the Marine camps. It demeans the service."

The members of the team, except for Shannon and me, responded with a crisp "Yes sir." The segment regarding the sergeant was forever expunged from the PDTC syllabus, and Shannon's brilliant session on returning warriors was scrubbed, to be replaced by a toned down one on the Ethics of Care that, during my last PDTC in Naples, I maneuvered, by using the case of Colonel Westhusing, into provoking a serious and disturbing discussion of honor, integrity, mission, and suicide. The admirals and the others in charge of the Navy Chaplain Corps were not there, and there is no hint of even the possibility of such a discussion in the Power Point slides they validated.

For a moment, the room in the BOQ at Oceana was quiet. I don't think we were sure that the validation of our PDTC was over or whether another shoe would drop and more changes in content, if not changes in personnel, would be ordered.

A deafening roar of jet engines broke the silence, filling the room. We looked up with trepidation, as if the ceiling were going to fall down on us.

The Pukin' Dogs were flying over the building.

As long as I live, I shall know for a certainty that I shall never again encounter anything as awful. If I ever again see anything so terrible, I will know that I have died without salvation and that I am in Hell. And that is the name – Hell – we gave to Belleau Wood.

Frank Delaney, *Shannon*, 2009, chapter 22*

---

*The Battle of Belleau Wood was fought during June 1–26, 1918. On June 6 alone, the Marines suffered 1,087 casualties, including 31 officers. One thousand eight hundred eleven United States forces were killed and 9,777 injured during the full extent of the nearly month-long battle. The fictional Captain Robert Shannon, a chaplain who served with the United States Marines at Belleau Wood in Delaney's novel, writes what I have quoted as he is trying to recover from severe shellshock (PTSD).

2

Our Better Angels Have Broken Wings

Human Nature and the Nature of Evil

The mystic chords of memory stretching from every battlefield and patriot grave to every living heart and hearthstone, all over this broad land, will yet swell the chorus of the organ when again touched, as surely they will be by the better angels of our nature.

Abraham Lincoln, *First Inaugural Address*

I. Human Nature

"I have seen so much hell on my two deployments in Iraq that I'm finding it hard to believe that humans were made in the image of God, that we are essentially good. Satan can go on an extended vacation. We are more than wicked enough," a chaplain who served with Marine units in Iraq told me at NSA Capodichino.

Many theologians and some moralists have defended conceptions of the basic or inherent goodness of humans. British moral sense theorists, notably Francis Hutcheson, contended that humans are naturally benevolent and are endowed with moral emotions or second-order affections and moral reactive attitudes that give rise to virtues and principles or standards of the morally good and bad. Hutcheson wrote:

> The Author of nature . . . has made virtue a lovely form, to excite our pursuit of it, and has given us strong affections to be the springs of each virtuous action. . . . The Author of nature . . . has given us a MORAL SENSE, to direct our actions. And to give us still nobler pleasures: so that while we are only intending the good of others, we undesignedly promote our own greatest private good. . . . There is no such degree of wickedness in human nature, as in cold blood, to desire the misery of others, when it is conceived no way useful to our interests. . . . We have practical dispositions to virtue implanted

49

in our nature.... There is a universal determination to benevolence in mankind.... Human nature is formed for universal love.[1]

For Hutcheson, human nature is attracted to virtue, but the "natural good" – or pleasure experienced and sought by humans – and the morally good are distinct. Stephen Darwall comments: "Moral good... is realized only by the motives of a moral agent and is something we recognize in disinterestedly approving these motives when we contemplate them. Moral good is irreducible to natural good. Nevertheless, Hutcheson is keen to argue, moral goodness is a natural property."[2] Moral goodness, for Hutcheson, is a quality of our actions (various forms of benevolence) that causes us, because we are so constructed by the "Author of nature," to experience approbation when we contemplate those actions.

A word about Hutcheson's comment about wickedness is also in order. I take Hutcheson to be holding the dictum, typically ascribed to Socrates, that humans do not willingly do evil for its own sake. He is not, of course, claiming that humans do not do wicked deeds to each other when they believe doing such things will further their own natural goods or when it is useful to their interests.

Hutcheson's account of natural human goodness is reminiscent of the conception of human nature found in the works of the Chinese philosopher Meng-tzu, or Mencius. "There is no man who is not good.... As far as what is genuinely in him is concerned, a man is capable of becoming good," said Mencius.

> That is what I mean by good. As for his becoming bad, that is not the fault of his native endowment. The heart of compassion is possessed by all men alike, likewise the heart of shame, the heart of respect, and the heart of right and wrong.... Benevolence, dutifulness, observance of the rites, and wisdom are not welded on to me from the outside; they are in me originally.[3]

Charles Darwin, who argued that morality is a natural outgrowth of human nature and that natural selection would favor the strengthening of our inherent moral sense, takes a not-dissimilar position on inherent human goodness.[4] He was influenced in his thinking on this by his reading of another moral sense theorist, David Hume.

[1] Francis Hutcheson, *An Inquiry Concerning the Original of Our Ideas of Virtue or Moral Good*, (1725, 1738).

[2] Stephen Darwall, *The British Moralists and the Internal "Ought" 1640–1740* (Cambridge, 1995), 211.

[3] Mencius, *The Book of Mencius*, translated by D. C. Lau (London, 1970). Reprinted in *Theories of Human Nature*, edited by Donald Abel (New York, 1992), 79–81.

[4] Charles Darwin, *The Descent of Man* (London, 1888).

These conceptions of human nature as inherently good have a very long pedigree. Well back in that lineage are the predominant theological interpretations of the early chapters of the book of Genesis. Humans are made in the image of or after the likeness of God and so are, presumably, naturally good, for "God saw everything that he had made, and behold, it was very good" (Genesis 1:31). The doing of evil or wicked deeds by humans is a corruption of inherent human nature and must be attributed to forces or sources external to the core of human nature, an echoing of Mencius, although undoubtedly without knowledge of his work. In Genesis, the corruption is attributed to a woman's proclivity to give in to temptation or, arguably, to her curiosity, a desire for wisdom (knowledge of good and evil). No account is provided regarding the content of what must have been Eve's persuasive argument to Adam also to partake of the forbidden fruit. It just says that she gave some of the fruit to him and he ate it. Perhaps Adam saw that although God had backed the command against eating or even touching the fruit with the threat of imminent demise, Eve had not dropped dead on the spot under the tree.

The description of Adam and Eve's Fall has the appearance of an account of the behavior of curious young children confronted with a prohibition against touching or eating something that is alluring, if only because it is forbidden, when they think the adults are not watching. Irenaeus argued that "the Fall" was an act of immaturity. He wrote: "God made man lord of the earth... but he was small, being but a child. He had to grow and reach full maturity... man was a child; and his mind was not yet fully mature; and thus he was easily led astray."[5]

In any event, human nature, as we are led to believe on many, indeed standard, Christian theological interpretations of "the Fall," remains good inherently, as created, though irrevocably polluted. Imagine a lake high up in the Rocky Mountains that was originally crystal-clear pure spring water. Now, however, slag deposits from molybdenum mining irreversibly pollute it. Does it make sense to say that the lake is essentially pure, though never again a source of potable water? Perhaps.

I find the story of Adam and Eve utterly baffling for many reasons, some of which I have written about at length elsewhere.[6] I find it puzzling that God left out knowledge of good and evil from the minds of his created humans who were supposed to be in God's image. My suspicion, also, is

---

[5] St. Irenaeus, *Adversus Haereses*, translated by W. W. Harvey (1857).

[6] Peter A. French, "Losing Innocence for the Sake of Responsibility," *Responsibility Matters* (Lawrence, 1992), chapter 3.

that the fruit of that tree provides only rudimentary knowledge, lacking the subtlety of mature moral reasoning but giving the devourer a taste for more, and that God, who planted or caused the tree to be planted, may have had only that much knowledge of good and evil at the time of the creation of the garden. Much in the Bible suggests to me that God is not morally mature and, perhaps, that God is learning morality or evolving morally as events involving his creations unfold. God's moral learning experiences might be analogous to how humans might develop moral sensitivities by watching particularly good films or dramas enacted on a stage. The radical disanalogous factor, however, is that God gets to decisively interact in the historical moment with the human actors in a way that we in the movie theater do not. We are merely audience; God is also a cast member. In fact, God gets to play the lead in the drama that is the Bible. Such an historical god, a god with a biography, I suppose, is not consistent with the conception of God as infinite or maybe eternal, although it could be consistent with an immortal god. The *Catholic Encyclopedia* says, "When we say that God is infinite, we mean that He is unlimited in every kind of perfection or that every conceivable perfection belongs to Him in the highest conceivable way."[7] Worrying about the historicity of infinite, immortal, and/or eternal gods, however, is probably farther down a sidetrack than I ought to venture here. That ground quickly becomes distinctly swampy.

The "in the image" business mentioned by the chaplain in Naples surely is not to be taken literally as a physical replica. I have seen enough of us humans, including in the mirror, not to be tempted to think we are godlike in physique. I have always assumed that the image of God that is essentially in humans, as per the creationist's story, must have something to do with potential moral characteristics, mental abilities, reason, and the like. Perhaps Adam and Eve were really created as, Irenaeus argued, children, not the mature adults that various artists have depicted. "In the image of God" might then mean only having certain capacities, capacities God has or has actualized, that might develop under certain conditions in humans. With that said, it seems odd that ingestion of a particular fruit would endow one with knowledge other than the taste, texture, and so forth of that kind of fruit. But eating a forbidden fruit, one forbidden by a powerful authority, albeit one that may not yet have matured morally either, when followed by punishment or at least a tongue lashing, could

[7] Available online at http://www.newadvent.org/cathen/06612a.htm.

well induce knowledge of one's capacity to do bad things – a first step, perhaps, toward gaining knowledge of good and evil.

What happens to Adam and Eve after devouring the forbidden fruit is curious. Their eyes were opened "and they knew they were naked." So they make aprons of fig leaves for themselves. Of course, they were not blind before the Fall, so the eye-opening bit is figurative and the aprons, supposedly to cover their genitalia, are a mark of shame. But, why do that if they are ashamed that they ate the fruit of the tree of knowledge of good and evil, countermanding the orders of God? Perhaps they should have covered their mouths or cut off their hands. Sex seems to have had nothing to do with their defiant act. I imagine that they may have explored their bodies and had sex some time, perhaps many times, before the incident with the forbidden fruit. After all, God had not prohibited sex in the garden. Genesis 1:28 has God saying to Adam and Eve, "Be fruitful and multiply, and fill the earth and subdue it."

Although this is very cloudy, it may be that the writers of Genesis wanted to link evil and shame with sex. Additionally along those lines, God adds severe pain to childbearing as part of the punishment of the woman. In that, God shows something less than moral consistency. He orders sex, at least for procreation, but "greatly" multiplies the pain of birth. A rational woman might well decide to take the sex whenever she can as long as pregnancy can be prevented. The punishment on the woman for the sin of disobedience is imposed only when she bears children. So it is not sex that is punished, but procreation, something that has itself been ordered by God. God also pronounces to the woman that "your desire shall be for your husband, and he shall rule over you." I assume the idea is that the husband will want sex for reasons of procreation and so the punishment will be exacted. There is also a hint that God is installing a sex drive in the woman, presumably also in the man, and that, combined with the man's desire to have a brood and a lineage, will ensure that sex is primarily, if not exclusively, carried on for reasons of procreation. Whatever this part of the story is supposed to explain, it displays a lack of moral maturity on God's part and leaves the punishment of women for this great original sin to some degree of chance and open to the mitigation of painkilling drugs.

But, as the story goes on, after all of the chastising and condemning, God is less concerned that humans now have knowledge of good and evil than that they may use their new gained wisdom to reason that being ordered not to do something makes sense only if the recipient of those orders possesses the ability to do what is prohibited. The serpent is merely the fall guy in the story. The serpent does not tempt the woman or beguile her; God does by issuing the prohibition. The serpent only tells the inquisitive woman the truth: "You will be like God, knowing good and evil."

There is a second forbidden tree in the Garden of Eden, the Tree of Life; consuming its fruit would make humans immortal, and God will have none of that. So humans are cast out of the Garden and into a world that should not be all that miserable, for, after all, it was also created by God and deemed by its creator as good.

There are, as some philosophers have made their reputations pointing out, many senses of "good," and perhaps when God pronounced all of the creation as good, what was meant was that each part was good for whatever purpose it was to serve, an instrumental good, as it were. Everywhere outside of Eden was to be a place for the continual punishment of humans for their sin, if only with the pangs of regret at what was lost, so if the rest of the world is good, it might be good only for that purpose and not intrinsically good. Hence the expression, "No place is paradise!"

The Lincoln quote suggests that although there are better angels in our nature, perhaps, worse angels or downright devils are hanging out in there as well. But are they there essentially?

Further passages in Genesis express or suggest the corruption or pollution conception of human nature: we are inherently morally good, in the image of God as per the earlier passages in Genesis, but corrupted and not just corruptible. A passage that is puzzling in some aspects but clear enough in its point is Genesis 6:1–6:

> When men began to multiply on the face of the ground, and daughters were born to them, the sons of God saw that the daughters of men were fair; and they took to wife such of them as they chose.... The Nephilim were on the earth in those days, and also afterward, when the sons of God came in to the daughters of men, and they bore children to them. These were the mighty men that were of old, the men of renown. The LORD saw that the wickedness of man was great in the earth, and that every imagination of the thoughts of his heart was only evil continually. And the LORD was sorry that he had made man on the earth, and it grieved him to his heart.

One interpretation of this passage tells us that angels, "the sons of God," were sent to Earth to teach morality and that when seeing women, "daughters of men," they became enamored of them and had intercourse with them. This resulted in the birth of the Nephilim. The Nephilim were giants responsible for ancient monumental architecture but also corruptors of humans. Humans, on this account, are victims not of their own morally defective natures but of the corruptors. This passage, despite its reference to every thought in the hearts of men being "evil continually," on all of the interpretations I have found, does not contradict the idea that humans are by nature good. But these corrupted humans reached a stage of immorality that even God regards as irredeemable. The subsequent passage begins the story of the great flood. "So the LORD said, 'I will blot out man whom I have created from the face of the ground, man and beast and creeping things and birds of the air, for I am sorry that I have made them.'" This, some might discern, is rather morally immature of God, a bit of a tantrum, for though there may be adequate reasons to capitally punish the humans, what moral reason could there be to do away with all the animals and birds? Of course, theologians will point out that the fuller story is that God decides that one human, Noah, is righteous, uncorrupted, and that the various created species will be saved, if not all of the existing instantiations of those species.

Mencius expresses the idea that humans are corruptible, although not inherently corrupt, in a reported disputation with Kao Tzu. Kao Tzu identifies human nature with water, which if given an outlet in any direction will flow in that direction. He maintains, "Human nature does not show any preference for either good or bad." Mencius, however, replies that although water does not show a preference for either east or west, it always flows downwards. Human nature, he maintains, is good in the same sense as water is disposed to flow downwards. However, water can be diverted and dammed so that it does not flow downwards. Just so, Mencius says, humans can become bad by turning against or being diverted from their "native endowment."[8]

Saint Augustine famously argued that the natural drives of human nature are invariably good, but that all humans have an inescapable tendency to do evil, and he attributes the latter to the Fall of humans recounted in Genesis 3, discussed previously. That tendency is original sin. There is, however, a conceptual tangle that is hard to unknot in the Augustinian account. The cause (I suppose it is proximate because there is said to be a direct causal chain involved and its causal power does not seem diminished with the passing of generations) of our being born sinful, indeed conceived and born in sin, is Adam's and Eve's transgression with the fruit of the tree; of knowledge of good and evil. But Adam and Eve sinned in innocence; they were not conceived in sin, which, on the Augustinian account, must have been a unique sin, whereas all of the

[8] Mencius, 80–81.

rest of the members of the human race since that fateful day are morally tarnished before they are even born, victims of Adam and Eve, beset with an unnatural but not divestible blemish on their moral character. So, the first sin is of a distinctly different character than all those that have been subsequent to it. Adam and Eve did not munch on that fruit because they had an unnatural disposition to defy the orders of God, a tendency to do evil. If they had such a disposition, they would also have been a victim of original sin. But where then was its source? It was surely not in their created nature, for that was good as so pronounced on by God and stressed by Augustine. My strong suspicion with regard to all of this is that God was too hasty when surveying his creation after the sixth day. Alternatively, as the misogynists no doubt will suggest, the removal of one of Adam's ribs to make a woman altered that good creation and allowed the introduction into him of the unnatural tendency to do evil, including to disobey direct commands of God. But that altering wasn't Adam's handiwork. It was God's.

The Chinese philosopher Xunzi famously maintained that there is a fundamental moral fault in human nature; we are innately evil. No better angels, only fallen ones! For Xunzi, we must radically alter our natural tendencies or we will fall into endless conflict with each other as we try to satisfy our innate desires for self-aggrandizement. Important for Xunzi, humans are not irredeemably cast into a Hobbesian state of nature. Although human nature is bad or antithetical to morality or, at minimum, blind to morality, human nature is corrigible. Humans are inherently evil, but perfectible. When controlled and properly directed by rules, regulations, and rituals, they can become good and, as Xunzi maintains, have a natural desire for the good, precisely because they lack it. You cannot have a desire for something you already have inherently or essentially.

> Following human nature and indulging human emotions will inevitably lead to contention and strife, causing one to rebel against one's proper duty, reduce principle to chaos, and revert to violence. Therefore one must be transformed by the example of a teacher and guided by the way of ritual and rightness before one will attain modesty and yielding, accord with refinement and ritual, and return to order. From this perspective it is apparent that human nature is evil and that its goodness is the result of conscious activity.[9]

---

[9] *Sources of Chinese Tradition*, edited by Wm. Theodore de Bary and Irene Bloom (New York, 1999), 2nd edition, 1, 180.

For Xunzi, the idea seems to be that if we have to learn and work at something, it cannot be natural to us. "The nature is what is given by Heaven: one cannot learn it; one cannot acquire it by effort. . . . What cannot be learned or acquired by effort but is within us is called the nature. What can be learned and, through effort, brought to completion is called conscious activity."[10] The moral task of humans is one of transformation, and that is accomplished in rites and rituals, training, and modeling. In effect, renovating oneself is an educational and even a political task, and one not far removed from the conversion that Thomas Hobbes envisions from humans in a state of nature to humans in a civil state.

Hobbes's view is not that we are naturally wicked, although that idea is not infrequently attributed to him, probably because his descriptions of human behavior when it is unconstrained by social coercion sound like accounts of beings that are naturally wicked. Hobbes, however, does not permit the use of moral language to describe humans when they are in the state of nature. For Hobbes, humans in the state of nature are premoral. In that state, "the notions of Right and Wrong, Justice and Injustice have no place."[11] Humans act in the manner Hobbes describes in the state of nature because they are self-interested and rational, but, unlike Xunzi, that is not synonymous with evil. Hobbes does not morally condemn humans in the state of nature. If anything, he writes about them with a certain compassion and pity. They are the victims of their own rationally self-interested natures and in need of salvation through the sword of the state enforcing covenants and converting the values of self-interest to reflect cooperative needs. Maoists transformed Hobbesian self-interested rationality into their concept of basic evil very much in keeping with Xunzi's conception. Maoists, Baogang He writes, "believed that self-interest is the source of evil and that moral destruction lies deep in the individual self as a sort of 'original weakness.'"[12]

Laurence Thomas rejects the innate evil conception of humans, while admitting that humans have been responsible for so much evil that it is not surprising that we might think it is a defining characteristic of the species. He offers what he calls the "fragility-goodness conception"[13] of human nature, an account that owes much, Thomas acknowledges, to

---

[10] Ibid.

[11] Thomas Hobbes, *Leviathan* (1651), chapter XIII.

[12] Baogang He, "Designing Democratic Institutions and the Problem of Evil: A Liberal Chinese Perspective," *The Just Society*, edited by Ellen Frankel Paul, Fred D. Miller, Jr., and Jeffrey Paul (Cambridge, 1995), 302.

[13] Laurence Thomas, *Vessels of Evil* (Philadelphia, 1993), 15.

Martha Nussbaum's analysis of Greek tragedy and philosophy in her book *The Fragility of Goodness*.[14] Thomas claims that "human beings are not generally disposed to perform great self-sacrifices on behalf of strangers, nor are humans generally disposed to harm others. On the contrary, they are naturally moved by the weal and woe of others, and they want to eliminate suffering. The problem, however, is that human beings are especially fragile."[15] By that, Thomas means that our natural propensities, more or less the ones cited by Hutcheson, are very easily thwarted. We do not take delight in causing harm to others, and generally the sight of humans suffering repulses us. In much the manner of Peter Strawson's account of our reactive attitudes, Thomas maintains that we are generally indignant when witnessing the inflicting of undeserved harm on another human being, and we are generally revolted by the idea of personal participation in such harm causing. Put simply, we are not naturally disposed to do evil acts on each other. But we, in fact, do perform such acts on others, and that can be explained only by the assumption that in such cases and for any number of reasons or blocks our basic sensibilities are "deadened" and we "break."

Human nature is such that we are vulnerable to act in ways that block our own better instincts, in ways that are not touched by, but banish those better angels of our nature. We are prone for various reasons, most of which are buried in the complex and conflicted character of humans *qua* humans, sometimes to revel in the undeserved suffering of others. We do evil or are in complicity with evil although we are not innately evil, a view that is not far removed from Mencius's conception.

What inclines us to this vulnerability to evil, and what form does it take? I suspect that Thomas would cite such standard motivations as self-interest, fear, cowardice, and the like. To the question of why we are prone, as we are often, to resist what the Thomas account regards as our essential propensities and to act contrary to them, he seems to say only that we are just that way, we are fragile and that is what fragile entities sometimes do. Fragility entails the disposition to break under certain conditions.

Thomas's fragility-goodness model may seem to be marginally superior to the innate evil model of someone like Xunzi, at least on the grounds that it facilely accounts for displays of benevolence, altruism, and other

---

[14] Martha Nussbaum, *The Fragility of Goodness* (Cambridge, 1986).
[15] Thomas, 15.

non-self-directed moral virtues, whereas Xunzi accounts for the occurrence of such virtues in human behavior as the outcome of training and the inculcation of habits. Repression of the desire to do evil, typically in the form of social norms, ritual practice, or legal restrictions, coupled with the fear of punishment or some sort of unwanted social reaction, is required, Xunzi might argue, to make an explanation of human goodness plausible. Undeniably, human beings sometimes do demonstrate genuine concern for others and their plights. Some even cross the road and provide succor to the suffering on the other side. On the fragility-goodness model, we should expect such behavior from each other at least occasionally without undergoing training, but not on the innately evil model in the absence of the inculcation of good habits.

The fragility-goodness account of our nature suggests that we are inclined to be weak of will and frequently and often too easily distracted from doing those things that positively respond to the urging choruses of our better angels. However, it would be a mistake to classify all human evildoing as a product of our vulnerability to give in to the attractions or temptations of wickedness, sometimes cleverly disguised, despite our desires to do otherwise. Although, as J. L. Austin opined,[16] we sometimes succumb to temptation with finesse, not all episodes of moral weakness are the result of weakness of will.

The fragility-goodness model of the human condition seems to underlie what might be called the Christian conception of tragedy. W. H. Auden, in a brilliant essay on "The Christian Tragic Hero,"[17] identified the difference between classical Greek tragedy and the conception of tragedy that governs the plots of Shakespeare's plays and, Auden's example, Melville's *Moby Dick*. Unlike the Greek tragedy of necessity, the Christian tragedy is the tragedy of possibility or, rather, of possibilities squandered, possibilities for salvation. The tragedy is that the hero seals his or her own fate by failing to take advantage of opportunities that would have produced a different outcome than the destruction that he (or she) will merit and meet. The hero is a basically good person who suffers from the sin of pride, knowing he (or she) is not nearly godlike, but acting as if he (or she) is. Although Ahab's fate in *Moby Dick* is predicted, it is not necessary. Until his actions seal it, matters might have

---

[16] J. L. Austin, "A Plea for Excuses," in *Philosophical Papers* (Oxford, 1961, 1970, 1979), 198, fn 1.

[17] W. H. Auden, "The Christian Tragic Hero," *New York Times Book Review* (16 December, 1945), 1, 21.

gone differently, for example, at a number of points he might have broken off the hunt for the white whale. Oedipus has no such opportunities
to escape his fate. He is born to it.

I, contrariwise, wonder if a fragility-evil model of human nature that
depicts us as innately both evil and fragile might have as much explana-
tory power as the fragility-goodness model. Our vulnerability to the temptation to occasionally do a good deed could explain why we fail on such
occasions to act as villainously as the evil angels of our nature would
have us.

It may be worth noting that Lincoln's phrase is actually less optimistic
than it sounds and than he probably intended. His choice of words is "the
better angels of our nature." "Better" not "best" nor even "good." Better
than what? Presumably, better than those angels of our nature that are
not very good, perhaps evil angels of our nature, the genetic remnants
of our Nephilim ancestry. The implication seems to be that in human
nature there reside angels (or dispositions) of various degrees along a
moral scale.

Rather than adopt a model of human nature that has it primarily
as good or evil or one or the other but fragile, it is closer to what is
observable in human behavior to hold the view that humans are capable
of behaving in ways that aptly can be described as good and in ways that
we should unabashedly call evil. In neither case does doing so reflect
an innate nature. The conception I am suggesting is akin to the view
Mencius assigns to Kao Tzu. That is not to say that we have no essential
moral nature but rather to say that at best, we should be more modest
in this regard, holding what might be called a capabilities conception of
the moral nature of humans that says very little about the predictability
of our behavior. Perhaps the less said the better. The task of morality
and ethics is hard enough without having to be conceived as taking on
cosmic forces of evil emanating from within each of us, and it would
have little to do were we uncorrupted, naturally good beings. Perhaps
the only real virtue in an inherently good but corrupted model of human
nature is that it may provide the moralist with some meager hope that the
ethical enterprise, to some degree, may succeed. However, to call up again
the imagery of the polluted mountain lake, as I look out across the lake
now contaminated beyond reclamation, what value is the knowledge
that it is innately pure spring water? Water, anywhere I suppose, may
be pure or contaminated to various degrees until it is polluted to such a
degree that it cannot be purified and potable. It might even be said that
it is the nature of water to be susceptible to being contaminated, and

that pure water these days is hard to find. Water just is H_2O in various stages of pollution. Humans are just humans in various stages of moral degradation. Lincoln appeals to our better angels and some humans no doubt respond positively. My more pessimistic view is that those angels more often than not in most people have broken wings and cannot take flight to move us beyond what our often convoluted and confused sense of rational self-interest motivates.

I agree with Yan Jiaqi that evil is universal in that sense that all of us have the potential to do evil deeds,[18] and with Immanuel Kant, in *Religion Within the Limits of Reason Alone*, when he talks of the "natural propensity in man to evil."[19] Kant sees the propensity to evil as arising in three different ways or in three different degrees. These are the weakness of the human heart, the impurity of the human heart, and the corruption of the human heart. But Kant also talks of the "seed of goodness implanted in our species,"[20] and that sounds rather like Thomas's fragility-goodness model. Recognizing the potential, even an inclination, in oneself to do evil is, as I have elsewhere maintained, crucial to moral maturity.[21] Importantly, however, it is not a consciousness of some universal innate moral nature in humans, even one that we often fail, for a variety of reasons, to actualize. It is the awareness, at once both frightening and fascinating, repulsive and seductive, appalling and alluring, horrible and provocative, of one's own capacities to injure, to hurt, to harm, to offend, to victimize. No human nature model is necessary to account for that, and none is wanted.

II. The Nature of Evil

Moral evil – as distinct from what is usually called natural evil, such things as tornadoes and hurricanes, a distinction drawn by Kant[22] – is human behavior that jeopardizes a person's or a group's aspirations to have a good life or lives by willfully inflicting undeserved harm on him or her or them. There are those who believe that there are no natural evils. For example, the Bethlehem Baptist Church, Elder Affirmation of Faith,

---

[18] See Yan Jiaqi, *Wode sixiang zichuan* (*My intellectual autobiography*), translated by D. S. K. Hong and Denis Mair (Honolulu, 1992).

[19] Immanuel Kant, *Religion Within the Limits of Reason Alone*, translated by Greene and Hudson (New York, 1960), 24.

[20] Ibid., 50.

[21] See note 6.

[22] See, for example, p. 15.

revised in November 2003, reads: "We believe God has subjected the creation to futility, and the entire human family is made justly liable to untold miseries of sickness, decay, calamity, and loss. Thus all the adversity and suffering in the world is an echo and a witness of the exceedingly great evil of moral depravity in the heart of mankind." Apparently, for the Bethlehem Baptists, tornadoes tearing through towns and trailer parks, hurricanes inundating major cities, cancers striking down children and adults are divinely ordered punishments to which those enduring them are justly subjected. They are not mere natural disasters that the inhabitants of the earth must endure in the normal course of events. They are caused by God's retribution for the "moral depravity" of the human race. Carrying out the logic of the Affirmation, I suppose that such natural disasters and calamities are not to be classed as evils at all. Just punishments are not evils because they are deserved harms. For the Bethlehem Baptists, all evil is what Kant and others call "moral evil."

Moral evil (hereafter just evil) can involve such things as intentionally causing in people undeserved physical and emotional pain and suffering, feelings of helplessness and separation from what they most care about and for, violating their trust, and the like. Importantly, evil is not only inflicting physical injury; in some of its dastardlier instantiations, it may be entirely psychological. Nel Noddings captures some of what I mean by evil when she writes that "the most basic form of evil is pain. Physical pain, when it does not promise a better end state (right here on earth), is an evil we should avoid and relieve. Separation is evil because of the deep psychic pain it causes. . . . Helplessness too is associated with psychic pain."[23] Crucially, evil leaves victims who did not deserve the pain, suffering, or deaths they endured at the hands of their victimizers, evildoers. Evil, regardless of the complexity of the analyses of its perpetrator's mental states, is primarily about victims. Victimization is the identifying characteristic of evil. Evil can be banal, monumental, or casual, but it cannot be victimless. It can be the result of major or minor imperfections or corruptions of character, sheer motivational wickedness, negligence, or failures, large and small, at various stages of the machinery of human action. But it always involves victims. Those victims are other humans, directly or indirectly. A few years ago, an arsonist set one of the largest forest fires in Arizona history. Not only did it destroy trees and brush and critters that live in the woods of the Rim Country of Arizona, it also destroyed homes and businesses. However, had it only destroyed the

---

[23] Nel Noddings, *Women and Evil* (Berkeley, 1989), 118.

forests, humans would still have been victims, losing something precious in their lifetime, as reforestation will take many decades. Victimization of other humans is at the hardened heart of evil.

Many religious people also will class as evil what they regard as violations of divine injunctions. In my view, God cannot be a victim of human actions, so I regard violations of those injunctions that relate solely to rules regarding religious observances as blasphemies or sacrilege or impieties, but not as moral evildoing. Interestingly, in the Ten Commandments, only three of the Commandments describe blasphemous actions. The others involve victimizing or disrespecting humans and so catalogue some moral evils.[24]

Lewis Carroll's poem "The Walrus and the Carpenter" in *Through the Looking Glass* offers a cogent, if comic, example of the import to the concept of evil of victims over the mental gyrations of evildoers.[25] The Walrus and the Carpenter convince a number of oysters to take a walk with them on the beach. They rest on a rock and proceed to eat the oysters despite the pitiful protests of the meal. The Walrus starts to cry and expresses compassion for the plight of the oysters. "I weep for you," the Walrus said, "I deeply sympathize." Then, with tears pouring down his cheeks and holding a handkerchief before his eyes, he gobbles up the largest oysters of the bunch. The Carpenter shows no sympathy or pity for the meal and continues to eat. Soon, all of the oysters are devoured. Alice and Tweedledum and Tweedledee discuss the poem. Alice, as Jonathan

---

[24] Disobedience is not evil, even disobedience of God. Eve and Adam by eating the fruit of the Tree of Knowledge of Good and Evil were not evil and that was not an evil act. Children when they deliberately disobey their parents in similar matters are not evil. To be evil, a person must inflict pain and suffering where and when it is not deserved. To be evil is to victimize, and when it is preferential, it is profoundly wicked. It could be argued, as Augustine might, that Adam and Eve by their act of disobedience victimized the human race, especially women who must endure pain when giving birth, something that, presumably, they would not have to suffer had Eve not taken a bite of the forbidden fruit. But God pronounced that sentence on women, not Eve alone. God told Adam and Eve they would die were they to eat of the forbidden fruit, not that all pregnant women would give birth in pain and agony. However, it might be argued that Eve is still the victimizer because she angered God and in that anger God caused women to suffer the pains of labor. God, however, is then reduced to an out-of-control reactor who was set off by Eve. The Biblical God is hardly that. God makes decisions, God acts volitionally, God is not just a player, God is the player. So God, we must assume, could have understood what Eve did as childish disobedience and responded as a parent might with a scolding and deprivation of something desirable for a period of time. But condemning all women forever and undeservedly to suffer at childbirth.... Well, that's another story!

[25] Peter Heath, *The Philosopher's Alice* (New York, 1974).

Bennett might suggest,[26] offers that the Walrus is the better of the two
diners because "he was a little sorry for the poor oysters." She is reminded
that, nonetheless, he ate more of the oysters than the Carpenter did and
that he probably held the handkerchief in front of his face to shield
his gluttony from the Carpenter. Alice then shifts her support to the
Carpenter because he didn't eat as many as the Walrus. But, it is pointed
out by one of the Tweedles that he ate as many as he could snatch.
Alice, convinced, declares that they are both evil. What really matters
morally is the empty oyster shells. Victims are what are important in the
determination of whether or not evil has been done. This is also the
case when undeserved harm is an unintended but unavoidable result of
a person or group intentionally doing something else, what John Kekes
calls "unchosen evil."[27] In Chapter 9, I discuss such a case as an exemplar
of moral tragedy.

The mental states, the conscience or lack thereof, the quality of will
attributed to the evildoer might play a central role in justifications of
responsibility ascriptions, blameworthiness, and the appropriateness of
punishment, but not in the determination of whether or not an act or a
person is evil. For example, there is a moral difference between killing
someone and experiencing the same or very similar mental states as one
would were one actually to kill a real human when "killing" a virtual
entity (an avatar) in a cyberspace design platform. Perhaps such behavior in a virtual environment indicates a bad or a dangerous character, a
dangerous quality of will, someone to guard against in any environment,
but surely there is a distinction with a difference between suspecting a
person of having bad character traits and identifying him or her as an
evildoer. Intuitively, let alone legally, there is a yawning chasm between
people who actually kill and those who contemplate doing it, between
those who kill real humans and those who kill virtual entities that look
like humans, even if there were no significant difference in their mental states. Suppose we borrow from the literature on "moral luck" and
concoct a thought experiment in which two equally negligent drivers are
driving down a residential street talking on their cell phones or texting
on their Blackberries. One of them is lucky not to hit and kill a pedestrian
who is crossing the street, whereas the other is unlucky and kills a little girl
whom he would have seen had he been paying attention. In some of the
"moral luck" literature, the intuition that comparing the two incidents

---

[26] Jonathan Bennett, "The Conscience of Huckleberry Finn," *Philosophy* 49 (1974).
[27] John Kekes, *Facing Evil* (Princeton, 1990), chapter 4.

is supposed to produce is that the two drivers are both morally blameworthy. The fact that Driver 2's negligent driving resulted in a death is
a matter of bad luck. Although I postpone the discussion of justifying
blame and punishment until Chapter 4, it should be obvious that both
drivers cannot be blameworthy for the same things. Both, of course, warrant blame for negligent driving, but surely both are not to blame for the
death of the little girl. Only the second driver can be held responsible for
that. What Driver 1 did not do – kill a pedestrian – is not something for
which he can be held responsible, although we might very well say while
chastising him, "See what you could have done, like Driver 2, you could
have killed a child." Judith Jarvis Thomson[28] disagrees. She maintains
that we have a principle of responsibility that reads as follows: "Whatever
we do, our doing of it is no more to our discredit than are those purely
mental acts by which we do it."[29] This principle points Thomson to the
conclusion that whatever degree of moral blame might be appropriate
for the second driver would also be appropriate for the first. Whatever
moral indignation would be justifiable in the one case would be equally
justifiable in the other. That idea – or, as Margaret Walker puts it, the
"troubling assumption" – is "that actually causing the harm one risks merits no more blame than merely risking the harm without causing it."[30]
On my account, Driver 2 did something evil, whereas Driver 1 did not.
That's a big difference.

There are philosophers who think that the raison d'etre of ethics is
to make people good, and there are those who believe that the most
important thing any ethics could do is to stress the need to minimize the
causing of undeserved harm. Those are not, to be sure, incompatible.
Obviously, if we succeeded in making everyone good, we would eradicate
the undeserved harm, the evil, which is caused by intentional and negligent human actions. That, however, is a pipe dream. We live in a world
in which a great deal of undeserved harm and injury are suffered, and
despite the expenditure of vast quantities of ink on treatises focused on
goodness and making people good and on doing the right thing, evil has
hardly been alleviated. Frankly, humans are moral cannibals.

We prey on each other and search for moral justifications or excuses for
our doing so. Humans not only murder, mutilate, rape, and perform all

[28] Judith Jarvis Thomson, "Morality and Bad Luck," *Metaphilosophy* 20 (1989), 203–221,
   reprinted in *Moral Luck*, edited by Daniel Statman (Albany, 1993), 195–216.
[29] Statman, 199.
[30] Margaret Walker, "Moral Luck and the Virtues of Impure Agency," in *Moral Luck*, 237.

manner of physical injuries on each other, they also, often cleverly, steal funds, dreams, hopes, plans, and the like from each other, leaving behind, if they are still alive, distraught, demoralized, despondent, sorrowful, defeated, grief-stricken, inconsolable victims. We have perfected the art of victimizing in virtually every area of human endeavor. It is humans who create Ponzi schemes to bilk other humans of their savings; who elect to take their countries into unnecessary wars and justify those wars with elaborate lies and public relations schemes; who bankrupt once-viable firms with risky investments, after which they desert the firms with astronomical bonuses or golden parachutes in their pockets. It is a mistake to think that the paradigmatic cases of evil are physically brutal. Many involve no physical contact with the victim at all. Humans devour each other's spirits – sometimes with subtlety, often tactlessly – more frequently than they physically mutilate or kill. When we speak of the "Law of the Jungle," we mean something much more akin to "dog eat dog" or "the strong shall devour the weak" than Rudyard Kipling's famous poem about the moral rules of the Wolf Pack.

III. The Laws of the Jungles

> Now this is the Law of the Jungle – as old and as true as the sky;
> And the Wolf that shall keep it may prosper, but the Wolf that
>   shall break it must die.
> As the creeper that girdles the tree-trunk the Law runneth
>   forward and back –
> For the strength of the Pack is the Wolf, and the strength of the
>   Wolf is the Pack.

As J. L. Mackie pointed out, Kipling's poem "states the basic principles of social co-operation. Its provisions are a judicious mixture of individualism and collectivism."[31] The theme of the poem is that unrestrained competition between members in a collective, a group, is destructive of both those individual members and the groups to which they belong. But what is the alternative? The poem cites a number of rules for wolf behavior that allow for individual wolves to realize the "profits" from their own expertise and daring, while not damaging the potential for the pack as a whole to achieve a commodious lifestyle. The well-being of the pack and the individual's well-being are interlocked, and that requires constraints

---

[31] J. L. Mackie, "The Law of the Jungle: Moral Alternatives and Principles of Evolution," *Philosophy* 53 (October 1978), 206.

on individual self-aggrandizement. The implicit guarantee in following Kipling's Law of the Jungle is that both selfishness and altruism have a protected place in the pack, although altruism is backed by sanctions, in fact, by capital punishment.

One of the more persistent problems of ethics has been the one framed by the question, "Why be moral?" That problem often is posed as a conflict between what is straightforwardly maximal for an individual person to do in specific circumstances and what is recommended by the principles or rules of ethics and so is communally optimal in those circumstances. The anticipated outcome corresponds to what Kipling insists the Law of the Jungle achieves for the pack: maintaining optimal social conditions for the collective and the individual over the long run by enforcing cooperative strategies and encouraging the rejection of individual selfishness as the exclusive strategy.

Simple game theory in the form of Prisoner's Dilemma or Richard Dawkins's example of a species of birds parasitized by dangerous ticks[32] may be used to illustrate the way the individual/collective welfare situation may be formulated. The problem for Dawkins's birds is that no bird by itself can remove the ticks from its head, and a tick in the head is deadly. If none of the birds will groom another, the species will eventually perish. There are three types of birds among Dawkins's bird species when it comes to grooming other birds by removing ticks from their heads. Some are Suckers, some are Cheats, and some are Grudgers. Suckers will groom any bird that needs grooming. Cheats will accept grooming from any other bird, but will not groom anyone, and a Grudger will groom a bird that has groomed it and any stranger, but if the stranger does not reciprocate, a Grudger will not groom it again. A species needs to achieve what Dawkins calls an "evolutionarily stable strategy," an ESS, to avoid extinction. Were all the birds Suckers, the species would achieve ESS. It would be a community of saints and it would not need a law for its jungle. Add in the Cheats to the collective and as they multiply, the Suckers soon will die off because Suckers will groom other birds, including Cheats, but the increasing number of Cheats will never groom them. A collective of nothing but Cheats, however, is not stable, so it also will become extinct because no one gets groomed. Add in the Grudgers, and when the Grudgers achieve a critical mass in the population, the Cheats, having destroyed the Suckers (which is a good thing because the Suckers endanger the Grudgers because they are, in effect, giving away grooming

---

[32] Richard Dawkins, *The Selfish Gene* (Oxford, 1976).

for free, so the Cheats can still prosper), will die off and the Grudger way of life will be an ESS. The Law of that Bird Jungle will take the form "Be done by as you did," which will morph into "Groom only birds that groom you." A stable reciprocal altruism will recommend itself to all of the birds in the collective.

Because I am more at home talking about Prisoner's Dilemma-type situations than grooming birds with ticks in their heads, I shift to that ground and offer a simple example. Suppose that X has a neighbor (N) with whom X engages over time in an Iterated Prisoner's Dilemma-type situation. X and N have two choices in those engagements: (1) to cooperate, and (2) to not cooperate. The moves and associated payoffs for X and N are as follows: if they cooperate, they can achieve a Pareto optimal outcome in which both gain something. If they both choose not to cooperate, both lose an equal amount, but each will lose less than will be suffered by either should that person cooperate when the other does not. If one cooperates and the other does not, the noncooperator will gain much more than from the joint cooperative action and the cooperator will lose more than if both do not cooperate. Which Law of the Jungle, Kipling's or the one more commonly identified as such – namely, adopting a strategy of straightforward maximization – should guide X's actions? The cooperative policy, Kipling's Law, seems not to be sufficiently self-recommending to override the motivation of selfishness. Some further persuasion to do the cooperative thing would be needed and that cannot be rational persuasion. After all, if a player could be rationally persuaded to always be cooperative, the "Why be moral?" problem, understood as the "Why cooperate for the collective good?" problem, would evaporate.

Richard Posner, I think correctly, analyzed the 2008 economic crash in the United States as resulting from people quite rationally acting on profit-maximization motives, ignoring what they believed to be a small probability of the failure of the capitalist economy if everyone were to follow suit. Short-term focused rationality does not need to take up the possibility of everyone in the game adopting the same policy. Its concern is immediate gratification. Those in power positions in some of the largest financial institutions in the world were individually rational but collectively irrational.[33] The rationality of behaving as they did is inherent in a capitalist economic system that had been redesigned by deregulation and easy money (low interest rates). It would be highly improbable that those who represent the "big financial players" in such a system could be

---

[33] Richard A. Posner, *A Failure of Capitalism* (Cambridge, MA, 2009).

persuaded that they or their organizations should act irrationally by not, for example, maximizing profit by investing in the sub-prime mortgage and derivatives markets.

Nonrational persuasions tend to be coercive, just as Kipling's Law of the Jungle makes it plain that a wolf that does not abide by it "must die." Acting ethically, it seems fair to say, essentially involves accepting constraints on the straightforward maximizing of one's own interests in social interactions when such maximizing will not produce Pareto optimal outcomes; that is, when cooperation and mutual benefit will not otherwise occur. X's acting cooperatively, however, can be rationally justified only if producing a Pareto optimal outcome between N and X is a part of a course of action that maximizes X's utility or is incidental to such maximization.

The standard argument, following the work of Robert Axelrod,[34] has been that if the same players iterate Prisoner's Dilemma, a strategy that apparently is not straightforwardly maximizing will recommend itself to rational players. That strategy is Tit For Tat (TFT). In other words, Dawkins's rational Cheats will adopt the Grudger strategy. A Tit For Tatter in Iterated Prisoner's Dilemma cooperates on the first move and then plays whatever the other player has played on his or her previous move. So, if the Tit For Tatter's opponent does not cooperate in response to a cooperative move, on the next move the Tit For Tatter will not cooperate and will continue not cooperating until the other player responds with a cooperative move. This is a version of reciprocal altruism. In terms preferred by Mackie, "reciprocal altruism is shown in gratitude for benefits and further benefits in response to gratitude."[35] Gratitude is the reactive attitude on the flip side of the coin from resentment. Grudgers among Dawkins's birds are reciprocal altruists. But are they and X and N acting ethically? Granted that reciprocal altruism within a group produces a stable cooperative group or is an ESS for the group, is it also an ethical principle?

Peter Danielson once praised TFT (which I am calling a version of reciprocal altruism) as a basic ethical principle,[36] and I agreed with him.[37] It certainly has the appearance of "an impartial, mutually beneficial principle." But all is not as it appears. The TFT strategy seems to

[34] Robert Axelrod, *The Evolution of Cooperation* (New York, 1984).

[35] J. L. Mackie, "Genes and Egoism," *Philosophy* 56 (October, 1981), 554.

[36] Peter Danielson, "The Moral Significance of Tit For Tat," *Dialogue* 25 (1986), 449–470.

[37] Peter A. French, *Responsibility Matters* (Lawrence, KS, 1992), chapter 2.

require a player to make moves that, were they evaluated in isolation, would be judged irrational because they are not maximizing. However, they are integral elements of a complex action that will maximize for the player and consequently for an opponent. So TFT in Iterated Prisoner's Dilemma games actually is straightforwardly maximizing because using that strategy, as tournament results purportedly demonstrate, actualizes the best situation for the player among the situations that the player has available to him or her. That might be taken as a reason to doubt that it is an ethical principle, assuming that a version of egoism should not be mistaken for ethics.

It might be thought that TFT is a basic ethical principle that happens to be the straightforward maximizer's preferred strategy in Iterated Prisoner's Dilemmas. TFT and, for that matter, the attitude of the Grudger, simply fails to qualify as an ethical principle. Neither the Tit For Tatter nor the Grudger in their respective situations requires constraint on the attempt to maximize. By adopting TFT (or Grudger), one will stand a better chance of realizing one's best outcome in iterated episodes. (The tick problem does not disappear after all the Grudgers have been groomed. Ticks are persistent!) That does not make TFT (or Grudger) an ethical principle, although it is a principle to which a number of people, especially those in business, are appealing when they insist that "good ethics is good business." Danielson concedes, "TFT is not a moral principle because in Iterated Prisoner's Dilemma it is straightforwardly in the agent's interests."[38] To achieve the ethically preferred outcome, players do not have to impose on themselves consideration of the interests of others. If they just act rationally selfish, the cooperative outcome will materialize. So-called ethical egoism, though not ethical, is not self-defeating.

Although there are many more types of interaction situations about which Game Theory and Rational Choice Theory have much to say, including single-play Prisoner's Dilemmas and Chicken, discussing them, though edifying, adds little more to the basic problem: there seem to be no rational reasons to be moral, if being moral is defined in terms of steadfastly constraining selfishness in favor of adopting cooperative policies for the sake of the cooperative outcomes to be realized. Straightforward maximizers do better than cooperators, but if they are to survive to enjoy their profits, they eventually, like Dawkins's Grudgers, adopt reciprocal altruistic principles, and cooperative outcomes are sustainable if only for selfish reasons.

[38] Peter Danielson, *Artificial Morality* (London, 1992), 46.

Grudge and TFT encourage self-love and self-referential altruistic principles. There is nothing wrong with either self-love or self-referential altruism, but those interests are far narrower than what is generally understood as the scope of the ethical. Self-referential altruism may extend out as far as the collectives to which one belongs, including, I suppose, one's country where it subsumes patriotism; but, in most cases, it does not encompass the human race. Where self-reference wears thin, rationality no longer provides justification for cooperative behavior.

In *The Scope of Morality* I wrote:

> None of us individually may have a good prudential reason in specific cases to be moral . . . that is better than the good reasons we have to be purely self-interested. . . . Although one may have a self-interested reason to do what there is a moral reason to do, from the point of view of rationality one cannot have only a moral reason to do what there is a moral reason to do that is better than the prudential reason one has to do something else in that instance. . . . An unbridgeable gulf remains between what is reasonable for the individual to do and what morality often demands . . . the greater personal risks are run in acting morally.[39]

I am still convinced that the gulf is unbridgeable and that acting ethically by constraining one's straightforward maximization (constraining self-love and self-referential altruism) cannot be rationally justified. Tit For Tatters or Grudgers cannot be faulted from the point of view of rationality for not adopting a personally risky, even if morally admirable, cooperative policy that reaches beyond family, friends, associates, and those for whom they are grateful for one reason or another.

Kipling's Law of the Jungle includes a powerful coercive element, namely, the threat of death for the lawbreaker. Why is that? Could it be that gratitude is not a dependable moral emotion, whether in wolves or humans? Or is it that wolf nature, like human nature, is not inherently good, although it is rational? Self-referential altruism has its limits, something unambiguously observable in the behavior of those in criminal organizations like the Mafia. The supposed better angels of human nature, suffering from damaged wings, have a minimal flight range. The threat of extreme punishment in Kipling's Law of the Jungle alters the payoffs for failing to reciprocate from a manageable risk to something to be given serious weight when deciding which strategies to adopt. Where the coercive power behind law is absent, as in ethics (and in deregulated financial markets, as noted by Posner), rationality is no helpmate to ethics, nor, for that matter, is human nature, and evil is often the result.

---

[39] Peter A. French, *The Scope of Morality* (Minneapolis, 1979), 151–153.

Appendix
An Evil Fantasy
The Minutes of the Search Committee from Hell[40]

God, in an act of divine mercy if not wisdom, pardoned Lucifer, fitted him out in a new set of wings and a harp, and let him return to heaven to rejoin the angelic orchestra. A vacancy thereby existed in the deepest circle of Hell: the chief executive officer, the lord of the underworld. Only someone thoroughly wicked, incorruptibly evil, would be suitable for the position. A search committee of demons was organized to identify a worthy successor to Lucifer, to find someone who surpasses all others in moral depravity.

First meeting

Members present: Beelzebub (the committee chair), Asmodai (the lustful), Berith (the murdering blasphemer), Astaroth (the vain one), Mephistopheles (the soul-catcher), Screwtape (the demonic counselor), and Lilith (the seducing succubus).

Beelzebub called the meeting to order and reminded the members that God's actions in pardoning Lucifer gave them a unique opportunity to define the future vision and mission of Hell. He assured the committee that he is committed to seeing that evil not be trivialized or reduced to the mere absence of goodness. The committee's job, he explained, is to select the absolute paragon of evil with the audacity of wickedness, one who will revitalize the demonic activities throughout the universe, and it must do a better job than the previous committee, which had picked someone God could forgive.

Mephistopheles worried that God may have so vast a capacity for forgiveness that the committee ought not to be concerned about the possibility that even the best choice for the job might be pardoned one day and join the angelic hosts. All the committee can do is find the candidate that will make that harder for God to do, said Screwtape, and cited a precedent in scripture that made it clear that God's prerogatives were limitless, but that, historically, God can get really angry and when acting out of anger condemns souls to eternal damnation. The committee must find someone so repulsive to the divine sensibilities that it will take eons for God to overcome his anger and forgive him or her. Mephistopheles

---

[40] Suggested by Richard Taylor, "The Governance of the Kingdom of Darkness," *Southern Journal of Philosophy* (1971), 113–118.

wondered if Screwtape was reading from the Old or New Testament. Beelzebub chuckled; the others sat in glum silence.

Lilith opined that Hell needed a change. It was high time a woman got the job. She noted that the Christian theologian Tertullian claimed that woman is the "devil's gateway."

Astaroth wondered if this was her idea of affirmative action.

After a brief tussle and an exchange of verbal unpleasantries, the chair restored order and Lilith and Asmodai reminded the committee that the Bible contains many references to women as inherently evil and unclean, and the early Christians would not let a menstruating woman in a church. Berith noted that hundreds of thousands, possibly millions, of women had been witches and were killed during the witch hunts of the fifteenth through the eighteenth centuries in Europe and America. Beelzebub smiled broadly and acknowledged credit for his part in spurring on the witch hunts. Lilith noted that many of those tortured and burned were self-confessed. They told of flying to forest clearings for orgies with demons. Berith suggested that one of them might be a good candidate for the vacancy. Asmodai scoffed that those women were frauds and that Berith well knew it. None had ever made it to the true depths of Hell. Some were in purgatory and a few were now in heaven. He explained that those so-called, self-proclaimed witches had been persuaded by Lucifer to anoint themselves with unguents made from henbane, nightshade, mandrake, and belladonna. If humans rub such a concoction on certain sensitive parts of their bodies, they feel like they are flying. They were hallucinating on atropine. It absorbs through the skin, and causes a lengthy sleep and dreams of wild rides, frenzied dancing, and sex. Beelzebub snickered that it made selling the burning entertainments so much easier when the women were confessing and telling such lurid stories on themselves. Mephistopheles made it clear that he would not support putting a mere druggy on the Throne of Hell. Asmodai retorted that erotic hallucinogenic orgies sounded heavenly to him. He was told to get serious by the rest of the committee. The chair had to be roused from a nostalgic reverie for those good old days.

Lilith made another pitch for a female lord of the underworld by reminding the committee that the Greeks, and not just the Christians, saw women as the source of evil in the world. She quoted from Hesiod: "For the price of the fire, Zeus made an evil thing for mankind. For the renowned smith of the strong arms took earth, and molded it, through

Zeus's plans, into the likeness of a modest young girl . . . when, to replace good he had made this beautiful evil thing, he led her out where the rest of the gods and mortals were . . . wonder seized both immortals and mortals as they gazed on this sheer deception, more than mortals can deal with. For from her originates the breed of women, and they live with mortal men, and are a great sorrow to them . . . so Zeus of the high thunder established women, for mortal men an evil thing."

Beelzebub shut down the general discussion of the topic and decreed that this time around, the search committee would pay special heed to female candidates. He then specified what he believed they had to look for in the credentials of the candidates. He reminded the committee that evil involves inflicting physical and psychic pain, injuring people, making them feel helpless, separating them from what they hold most dear. Lucifer was a master at causing physical and emotional pain for its own sake. That is the sort of thing that should be of paramount concern in the committee as they rank-order the candidates. The committee members nodded agreement.

The chair opened a laptop and clicked on a file. Inside that file were other files labeled with the name of a nominee. Inside each nominee file were documents providing the nominee's resume, supporting data, and letters of recommendation. Despite having cast the sole negative vote against her appointment, Lilith was selected to serve as "God's advocate." She was tasked to see if she could uncover convincing reasons why the nominees were not the embodiment of sheer wickedness, the instantiation of evil to the nth degree. Lilith asked the committee to first narrow the field before she took on the job. Astaroth surfed through the files and moved that the only two females who were nominated should be on the short list to satisfy Lilith's concern that women were not given their due in Hell. Seconded by Berith and passed unanimously. Beelzebub, who had read the documents in the files before the meeting, moved that they consider on the short list four more nominees. He read off the names he preferred and, without objection, the committee agreed to start with the six. They were Lucretia MacIntyre, Charles Manson, Ernst Kaltenbrunner, Bubba Horne, Winston Churchill, and Griselda Blanco.

Lilith moved to adjourn the meeting so that she could prepare her cases and consult with the Cads and the Lys. That would require a journey to Limbo, so she moved that the next meeting of the committee be in a week. Without objection, the meeting was adjourned and the next meeting scheduled in a week.

Second meeting

All committee members present.

Beelzebub called the meeting to order. Lilith was asked to report on her meeting with the Cads and the Lys. Berith wanted to know who these people are and why Lilith went to see them. Lilith explained that over the millennia, two distinct groups of philosophers formed in Hell. One called itself "the academy," "Cads" for short. The other, "the lyceum," popularly known as the "Lys." Their philosophical debates provide one of the few entertainments in Hell, but demons have to go up to Limbo to hear them and that apparently is too much of a bother for most of the senior demons. There is a rumor, unconfirmed, that HBN (Hell Broadcasting Network) will soon be telecasting the debates if they can persuade David Hume to moderate.

Limbo, Lilith reminded the committee members, is a neither-here-nor-there sort of place with only reflective lighting from the real fires deeper down in Hell. Nonetheless, it was not difficult to locate Socrates, the grand old man who is held in the highest of esteem by the Cads. She reported that Socrates asserted in categorical terms that the committee's task is fated to failure. No one, not even a demon of the highest order, can do evil for its own sake, he claimed. No one does wrong willingly. If evildoers really knew what they were doing, they could not choose to do it. Depraved behavior can be the result only of deprivations, bad social conditions, mental diseases, and unavoidable ignorance. Beelzebub snickered that sometime they have got to bring this Socrates fellow down into the deeper circles to meet some of the evildoers residing there. Once he got into a dialogue with most of them, he would have to radically revise his dictum.

Aristotle, leader of the Lys, offered her more hope of finding a truly evil candidate, Lilith reported. He argued that there are two sources of human evildoing: weakness and wickedness. He warned that the committee should distinguish between two cases, one in which an evildoer actually has good moral principles but fails to act on them, and one in which the evildoer acts on bad moral principles. Failure to act on good moral principles occurs because the candidate was weak of will or because the candidate just didn't give those principles proper weight in the circumstances.

Lilith took out a sheet of paper on which she had drawn a chart based on her understanding of what she had heard in Limbo. The chart was passed around to the committee members and then laid out on the table. For the sake of the committee's minutes, it is herein reproduced.

The Person Did Something Morally Wrong Because of . . .

Weakness of Will	Amorality
Although he/she knew what was morally right, he/she could not resist his/her desire to do what was morally wrong.	Although he/she knows what is morally right, he/she gives moral considerations no weight when acting.
Perverse Wickedness	Preferential Wickedness
He/she has false moral beliefs on which he/she acted.	He/she chose to do what is morally wrong because it is morally wrong.

Astaroth studied the chart before noting that if he read it correctly, the committee has to find a candidate who chooses to do morally wrong deeds just because they are morally wrong and not for any other reason no matter how satisfyingly wicked the things that the candidate has done may appear on the surface. Screwtape pondered over that and asked if they had to exclude someone who was deeply committed to and acted on a set of beliefs that he or she believed to be morally correct, even though the beliefs were really morally bad or false. Berith looked puzzled. Screwtape explained that someone might be committed to certain beliefs that the person wrongly thinks are morally justifiable. But they are not. Just the opposite is the case. The person acts on those beliefs and causes some spectacularly awful things to happen to people. As long as the person still holds and acts on those beliefs, albeit believing them to be morally good principles and the like, is that not evil enough for the purposes of the search committee? Mephistopheles noted that virtually every political leader with whom he had recently traded an election for their immoral souls would fit that description. They all think the perverted beliefs they hold are positively brimming over with moral goodness.

Lilith interrupted to tell them that all of the ancient Greek philosophers with whom she discussed the issue insisted that the search committee could never find someone who actually fell into the most evil category with any regularity. They were in some agreement that the most evil one can get is perverse wickedness, and that if you really believed that what you were doing was morally wrong, you could not do it, or at least you could not prefer it because you believed it was morally wrong. She reported that she also met with a small group of former Christian theologians, who were sharply divided between those whose philosophical roots were with the Greeks and those who claimed scriptural or revelatory sources for their doctrines. The latter maintained that preferential wickedness is not only possible, it is prevalent among humans and that they had spent the bulk of their ministries trying to combat and condemn it. To a person, those in that group had not the foggiest idea why they were in Hell and expected a reprieve any moment.

Asmodai drew the committee's attention to weakness of will. He maintained that in his experience, knowing the morally right thing to do but not being able to bring oneself to do it is rampant among humans, and what a blessing that it is. Beelzebub worried that although many folks in Hell were there because of chronic weakness of will, it would hardly seem right for the Prince of Darkness to be someone who knows and wants to do what is right but just cannot control himself or herself at the crucial moment, and only then does the wicked thing he or she knows should not be done. The head of Hell would not be much worse than the chubby kid who, even though she knows she should not eat the chocolate cake and does not really want to eat the cake because she really wants to fit into the bikini she bought, cannot stop herself from devouring it. Our leader, if that were the case, the committee chair concluded, would be pathetic, even pitiable. The committee agreed that would never do. Mephistopheles singed the air of the room with invective against Milton, Goethe, and Marlowe for portraying Satan and himself as tragic creatures who despite wanting always to do evil, cannot help but contribute to the good. Lilith scolded him that although he may have that right with Milton and Goethe, Marlowe, her favorite playwright in Hell, should not be painted with the same brush. Although he did not relent, Mephistopheles brushed the argument aside and the general discussion continued.

Screwtape asked Lilith if she had met Freud when she was doing her research. She had not. Screwtape admitted that he had done some reading up in preparation for the meeting and found that Freud and some others identified evil with acts of aggression, with the urge to destroy, to wreck, to kill, and claimed that aggression is an innate human drive. Evil is giving in to your natural urges. Berith laughed and then expressed the view that truly wicked persons are very much in control. He said he has always been, laughing laconically. They are not merely giving in to some urge in a ravenous fashion. They can be quite deliberate and in rational control of themselves. Lilith nodded agreement also, noting that not all aggression is morally wrong. Aggression plays many positive roles. Developmental psychologists claim it is an important element in play and crucial to socialization. They say that children need direct physical clashes with others to develop sympathy. Astaroth shuddered.

Asmodai added that love might become more dangerous than naked aggression. Lilith hissed at him that he would never know that firsthand. He nodded and rattled off other motivations – such as greed, avarice, sloth, and fear – that have the potential of being more powerful malevolent motives than aggression. There was general agreement around the table.

Beelzebub called for order and insisted it was time to consider the six candidates they had placed on the short list. The first file he asked them to open on their laptops was that of Charles Manson.

Manson's was a self-nomination and was not accompanied with many letters of recommendation. Screwtape noted that Manson had tried passing himself off as Jesus Christ. He quipped that when that did not work, the Prince of Darkness probably seemed to Manson to be a natural next step in his career.

Astaroth read from the file that Manson organized the August 1969 Tate/LaBianca murders in Los Angeles. He sent members of his "family," a motley collection of runaway teenagers he controlled with LSD, to brutally slaughter six people more or less selected at random. The murders were gruesome. His plan, if it could be called that, was to start a race war with the killing of affluent whites in such a way that, he believed, blacks would be blamed. He believed the blacks would prevail in the war but would not be able to govern, and so he would be called by the victors from his hiding place in Death Valley to rule the world. He said he got the whole idea from the Beatles song "Helter Skelter."[41]

Astaroth expressed the opinion that this guy was more crazy than evil. Lilith, playing her part as God's advocate, spoke up. She noted that Manson really had no moral principles. He did wicked things, but he did not see inflicting pain on others as evil. He is indifferent to morality.

Beelzebub nodded agreement, but Asmodai wanted clarification as to whether Lilith was saying that Manson does not know the difference between right and wrong.

Lilith expressed the view that Manson is probably a psychopath who never thinks about the interests and welfare of others. When he hurts them, it is almost incidental. The terrible things he does probably are not really acts of conscious wrongdoing. At best he is amoral, she opined. Screwtape noted that whether at best or at worst the next Lord of the

[41] See David Cooper, *The Manson Murders: A Philosophical Inquiry* (Cambridge, 1973).

Underworld must be a conscious wrongdoer and so someone who knows at every level of knowing that what he or she is doing is immoral and still prefers to do it, not someone who gets his ideas from listening to old records from the 1960s. The committee agreed that there will always be a place in Hell for Manson, but not an executive position.

Almost simultaneously, they each moved Manson's file to the trash.

Berith opened Griselda Blanco's file and perused it. After a few minutes, he cleared his throat and read aloud from one of the documents in the file stating that Blanco was one of the most vicious drug dealers in history. She was known to the United States' DEA as "the godmother" and to her enemies in the drug trade as "the black widow." She used her lovers and members of her family as hit men and cocaine couriers, then when they got in her way, she killed them herself or had them killed. She announced to her gang of cutthroats that if anyone crossed her, he would die. To punctuate her resolve to use murder to govern her subordinates, she told them, "If my mother does something to me, I'll kill my mother, too."

Astaroth noted that Blanco moved at least 200 kilos of cocaine a month into the U.S. market, averaging $96 million per year in income. In 1976, she delivered $40 million worth of cocaine to her Boston, New York, and Miami pushers hidden throughout the Columbian tall ship "Gloria" while it participated in the "parade of tall ships" celebrating the bicentennial of American independence. The search committee members laughed.

Lilith chimed in that Blanco also ordered the infamous Dadeland massacre in a shopping mall in Miami in July of 1969. Beelzebub wondered aloud if Griselda Blanco would not only withstand the scrutiny of God's advocate but also satisfy her desire to see a woman as the CEO of Hell.

Lilith shook her head. She admitted that Griselda has an impressive list of credentials and that, unlike Manson, she was not acting out a fantasy. But she is like Manson in one important respect: she just does not care that she is doing wicked things. She knows that what she does is morally wrong, and that fact does not faze her. She is amoral or morally indifferent. Where the cocaine business is involved, she just does not care if she inflicts pain and suffering, although she knows it is wrong to do it. We know she knows the difference between right and wrong because she taught her children sound moral principles. She has going for her that she is a conscious wrongdoer. But, Lilith proposed, Blanco does not do evil for its own sake. She does it for the money and, maybe, for the power. If she could have made that kind of money doing something good, she would have been a paragon of virtue. The committee decided that it could not depend on Griselda Blanco to continue her wicked ways, dumped her file in the trash, and moved on to the next candidate.

That was Winston Churchill. His candidacy was based primarily on his wartime decisions to continue the terror bombing of German cities instead of concentrating on strategic targets. Without convincing military reasons and against his own publicly professed moral principles, he ordered the firebombing of Dresden. More than 100,000 civilians were massacred. Churchill jubilantly announced that the fire bombings were making the ordinary people of Germany "gulp . . . a dose of the miseries they have showered upon mankind."

Screwtape noted that Churchill has Manson and Blanco beat in sheer numbers of dead victims. And he has administrative experience that will be a plus running Hell.

Lilith interrupted the committee's general grunts of approval by insisting that the quality, not the quantity, of the evil should matter in the choice of the next Lord of the Underworld. She explained that Churchill is not as wicked as the body count makes him look. He was morally negligent, but he was not doing evil for its own sake. He failed to exercise self-control. He probably decided not to think from the moral point of view about what he was ordering. Many political leaders suffer from the same sort of moral weakness of will. Besides which, she pointed out, you could lay his body count next to that of Hitler, Stalin, Pol Pot, or Attila and it would not be so impressive. This is not about counting dead bodies; it is about moral depravity for its own sake, not patriotic gore. Churchill probably realized that if he concluded that the bombing of the German cities was morally wrong, he would not have been able to order it. But he did not want to lose the opportunity to terrorize the Germans. He let his emotions block him from avoiding moral wrongdoing.

Screwtape noted that a document in the file says that Churchill admitted to feeling badly about the Dresden bombings later in his life. That must disqualify him. There is no place for remorse on the Throne of Hell.

Lilith drew the committee's attention to the file of Lucretia MacIntyre. She recounted that Lucretia contracted AIDS but continued to have sexual experiences with as many men as she could lure to her bed. Most of them got the disease. She just could not resist her sexual desires. After her affairs, she felt regret. She was not like the Texas hooker who used to write in lipstick on the mirrors of her clients' hotel rooms, "Welcome to the wonderful world of AIDS." She was fully aware that she was doing wrong. But like Churchill, she failed to make her behavior conform to her own moral principles.

Asmodai expressed the opinion that there is no reason for the committee to believe that Lucretia will not eventually gain control of herself and resist future temptations to do evil things. She is, plain and simply, weak of will. The committee unanimously discarded her candidacy, although Lilith expressed unhappiness that they had eliminated the female candidates.

After securing the committee's permission to champion a candidate, the chair, Beelzebub, put forth the case for Ernst Kaltenbrunner. He noted that Kaltenbrunner was one of the first twenty-two men charged with crimes against peace, war crimes, and crimes against humanity in Nuremberg in 1946. He was tireless in exterminating Jews, supervising the death camps at peak efficiency. Berith noted that Kaltenbrunner even looks like a killer, a large man, with a thick neck, piercing eyes, a scar from the left of his mouth to his nose, and bad teeth. Beelzebub continued by noting from the file that Kaltenbrunner insisted he was acting in the best interests of his country, and admitted that he knew he was ordering the killing of millions.

Asmodai expressed the opinion that Kaltenbrunner is a perfect candidate, but Lilith, playing her part as God's advocate to the hilt, cut off the general praise for Kaltenbrunner. She admitted that Kaltenbrunner did not mess up in the execution of his actions. His resolve was always firm, his planning never slipshod. But she drew from the file his plea before the Nuremberg Tribunal in which he claimed that he had not appreciated what he was doing. He firmly believed that he did what he morally ought to have done.

Screwtape expressed doubts about her point. He wondered how it could be possible for someone to believe that it is morally right to cause and morally wrong to stop such suffering, if that is in one's power. "How could anyone who knows what 'morally wrong' means think what Kaltenbrunner did was right? How could he think it was his moral duty?"

Beelzebub suggested that Kaltenbrunner was a German patriot. Screwtape, however, responded that he could understand doing what Kaltenbrunner did believing it was one's patriotic duty but not one's moral duty.

Lilith referred the committee to her graph. Kaltenbrunner's actions, she said, were perversely wicked and driven by his perverse belief that the Jews must be destroyed to save civilization. She noted that he said that if he were a Jew, he should be exterminated. He went to his execution proclaiming that his contributions to the Final Solution were his moral duty.

Astaroth admitted that he liked perversion as much as the next devil, but that he realized that there could be no guarantee that Kaltenbrunner would not turn around tomorrow and adopt sound moral beliefs. He is dedicated to doing his moral duty, as he sees it. Lilith agreed and noted that the problem with Kaltenbrunner, and any perverse wrongdoer, is that the committee cannot depend on him to continue to hold perverse moral principles. Asmodai added that the committee risked becoming a laughingstock in Hell if it selected a Prince of Darkness who turned into a point of light.

The final candidate from the original short list was Bubba Horne. Berith pointed out that as a teenager, Bubba made a practice of beating up other teenagers, usually those smaller than himself, and mugging older people from whom he also stole whatever money he could find on them. He would zoom by on his bicycle and upset women carrying packages of groceries from the market. As their fruits and vegetables lay strewn about in the parking lot, he would pull up and snatch a banana or an apple and eat it in front of the dazed shopper. After a while, however, he found unfulfilling this sort of harassing of people that were no real threat to him.

Astaroth interrupted to point out that Horne had said that in his personal statement in the job application. Berith snarled annoyance at having been interrupted, then continued to summarize Horne's resume. He noted that Horne went through a sort of enlightenment experience in which he decided to change his tactics. He took up the study of ethics, attended ethics classes at a number of local universities, studied from the acknowledged ethical experts, and devoured books on different ethical theories. "He says in his application that what he realized was that he could use moral principles against ordinarily good people. He could expose their private failings and reveal to them and to the public their moral shortcomings, no matter how minor. He could hoist them on the moral petards they claimed to hold as basic principles of behavior." Berith agreed and noted that Horne really worked hard at perfecting the art of doing it without mercy. He got considerable joy out of watching people who cared about their moral and their social standing wriggle on the hook of the very ethical principles by which they professed to live.

Mephistopheles was impressed with Horne and called him a moral assassin. Asmodai agreed and brought up Horne's list of work experiences from the file. He had moved from job to job to expand his opportunities to inflict psychic moral suffering. He had been a salesman and then spent nearly a decade as a preacher in one of the mega-evangelical churches. His flock hung on his every word and regarded him as a virtual prophet of biblical proportions. He decided to end that gig in a way that would devastate the faith of many of his parishioners by announcing from the pulpit that he was a practicing homosexual and that he found his sexual lifestyle, although it was condemned by the teachings he had frequently proclaimed from that same pulpit, more overflowing with what is sacred in the eyes of God than a life lived by abiding by the tenets he had preached. Of course, he was not a homosexual. He left his wife and children to live with a woman from his former congregation whom he had seduced after choir practice. Just as he had hoped, many of the parishioners of his church condemned themselves for having been so deceived and deserted religion altogether. Some followed what they thought was his lead and took up profligate lifestyles that led to their ruin and the ruin of their families.

Horne soon deserted his mistress, moved to Washington, DC, and began a new career as a political reporter. He had a field day in that job, ruining a number of political careers.

Screwtape noted that Horne went on to become an ethics teacher at a small liberal arts college. Horne knew he was twisting the purpose of ethics by using its rules and principles to hurt people, but he masterfully demolished the self-worth of his targets, ruined their reputations, and brought their spirits crashing down. He slyly tempted his victims, just ordinary people, into indiscretions, and then self-righteously exposed them to public humiliation and degradation. And he usually managed to appear ethically pure and personally distressed at the extent of the immorality he was uncovering.

Berith could find nothing in Horne's file that negatively affected his candidacy. He noted that Horne believes that what he does is morally wrong, but he does it for its own sake. And he does it with relish. He uses ethics to hurt people, and he is damned good at it.

Lilith pointed out that Horne could succeed only with people who care about being or appearing ethical. He could not do a thing with Manson or Blanco or Kaltenbrunner or any of those on the search committee. She wondered if he would have much of an effect on MacIntyre or even Churchill.

Beelzebub pointed out that there was no record that Bubba Horne had ever killed anyone. All of the other candidates had killed, and some had done so in nearly uncountable numbers. Screwtape wondered why killing people should matter that much. It was never certified as to how many humans, if any, Lucifer had actually killed.

Asmodai spoke about how Bubba Horne has the attitude that killing people is too much of a bother and shortens the duration of the pain he joyfully, devilishly, administers. He makes his victims suffer because of their own professed moral convictions and their inability to live according to them. "Think of the burdens of shame and guilt he must be loading on the backs of otherwise pretty good folks. It is positively diabolical!"

Lilith objected that all Bubba Horne did was practice ethics without kindness. Screwtape wondered if unkind ethics was really ethics at all. Mephistopheles asked where in Kant or the utilitarians does it say you have to be kind when making moral judgments or when exposing another's moral shortcomings to him or her. Kindness in those cases is supererogatory, if it has any moral status at all. It is not required.

Beelzebub wondered aloud how it would look if the Prince of Darkness were really a defender of ethical principles.

Berith called for a vote. Beelzebub requested that the committee postpone for a day the taking of the vote because the turn of events had caught him offguard and he did not feel he had taken sufficient time to study the Horne file. Berith's motion failed for the lack of a second. It was agreed that the committee would postpone voting on the short-list candidates until the next day. Lilith asked for an additional day because she was not happy with the short-listed candidates and would like the time to examine the other files to determine whether a worthy candidate, preferably a woman, had been overlooked. Her motion also failed for lack of a second. The committee adjourned.

The search committee did not meet the next day or ever again. Lucifer was tossed out of heaven for behavior unbefitting an angel, and flung back into the depths of Hell where he settled back comfortably on the throne. A memorandum was posted thanking the search committee members for their service, which was no longer required. The members of the search committee were not displeased by this outcome and returned to their regular jobs.

3

Responsibility for Innocence Lost

In "The Loss of Innocence and the Things that Remain,"[1] Michael McKenna takes up what he calls my "controversial thesis that we morally competent adults have an obligation to usher innocents from their moral condition, and this involves opening children up to the possibility of evil." McKenna addresses questions I originally neglected in a chapter of my *Responsibility Matters* on "losing innocence for the sake of responsibility."[2] These questions are crucial to a serious consideration of the crux of my thesis that adults have a moral responsibility to facilitate the loss of innocence in children.[3] I used that chapter in developing the first draft of the second year's PDTCs session on moral conflict issues. The topic, it turned out, troubled a number of the chaplains who had observed firsthand how innocence lost is all too often replaced with anger and brutality rather than any hoped-for moral wisdom. Some chaplains spoke with me about their worry that confronting one's loss of innocence was most likely to be postponed by Marines with whom they were deployed in favor of losing some other part of themselves in a bottle or by taking out the rage their experiences in Iraq had aggravated when they returned to CONUS and confronted their own children and spouses.

In order to avoid confusion, the type of innocence McKenna and I are talking about is a moral status, not a particular state with respect to

---

[1] Michael McKenna, "The Loss of Innocence and the Things that Remain," *American Philosophical Association, Newsletter on Philosophy and Law*, edited by Steven Scalet and Christopher Griffin, Spring 2008, 7, 2, 5–9.

[2] In *Responsibility Matters* (Lawrence, KS, 1991).

[3] I should note that although McKenna gives me considerable credit for exploring the issue of loss of innocence, I learned a great deal, as I noted in that chapter, from the earlier work on the subject by Herbert Morris. See Herbert Morris, "Loss of Innocence" in his *On Guilt and Innocence* (Berkeley, 1976), 139–161.

an untoward event. The innocent, in the sense in which McKenna and I are interested, might be described as in a state, vis-à-vis the ascription of justifiable moral responsibility, comparable to that of Adam and Eve before the Fall. Innocence, in this sense, is the purity of moral virginity. It is not the purity of always acting as morality prescribes.

The innocent are not subject to moral standards. They are not held accountable to moral norms, principles, and rules. The story in Genesis associates this type of innocence with a lack of a certain sort of knowledge, namely, ignorance of right and wrong. When Adam and Eve lose their innocence, their eyes "are opened" and they notice that they are naked, but nakedness per se must have little to do with the matter because they were not wearing clothing from the first. As I noted in chapter 3 of *Responsibility Matters*, we may assume that they frolicked around the garden naked and played games, possibly even "house," before that fateful day in which they added a certain fruit to their diet. Before the Fall, surely they saw they were naked but they did not *see that* they were naked. After all, they weren't blind. If they had been blind, they would have much less to remember, and so regret, about their loss of paradise.

We see a lot of things without *seeing that* we see them. In *seeing that* x there is usually seeing x, though not always, but in seeing x there is not a *seeing that* x to be unpacked. "Seeing" seems closer to "laying eyes on" than to "knowing that" or "noticing." Suppose I were to say that I saw Denzel Washington in a movie last week. Someone might have told me after the movie was over that I had just seen Denzel Washington give an exceptional performance. Try as I might I cannot recall what he looked like or what part he played. Yet, I would not be lying were I to tell my friends that I saw Denzel Washington in a movie last week. Seeing does not require being able to identify correctly what is seen. Suppose I were to say that I saw Washington play the part of the college president in the movie. That is something I could not have seen. What I saw was Washington playing the debate coach. I could not have watched the movie and failed to see Washington playing the debate coach. But I did not see that Washington played the debate coach.

I may see someone kidnap a child without seeing that he is kidnapping a child. Someone might say of me, "He saw the kidnapping take place," but surely that does not entail that I saw that a kidnapping was taking place. Still, I might be an excellent witness for the state when the kidnapper is apprehended. On examination in the witness stand, I might admit that I saw a man usher a child into an automobile. I may testify that I saw the child struggle with the man. I saw the kidnapping;

I now know that it was a kidnapping, but I did not *then* see that it was a kidnapping. Even if I never were to find it out, I still saw the kidnapping. At the risk of overburdening this example, it is worth mentioning that the kidnapper might have seen me and that he could truthfully say of me, "He saw the kidnapping," even though I would not say, "I saw the kidnapping." The motif of the criminal attempting to eliminate a witness who does not know he or she is a witness nor of what he or she is a witness is not an uncommon plot in the movies or in suspense fiction. The criminal's concern is, however, well grounded because one can see something even though one does not see that it is the certain kind of something that it is.

One cannot be taught to see, neither does one learn to see. One sees or one does not see. A child may be outfitted with new glasses to improve his seeing, but he cannot learn seeing as he can walking, writing, or subtraction. "Seeing that," however, reports a cognitive accomplishment. To see that *x* is *y*, one must at least know some rudimentary things about *x*'s and *y*'s. N. R. Hanson had something of this sort in mind when he wrote, "'Seeing that' threads knowledge into our seeing."[4] In every "I see that . . ." and in every "I saw that . . ." an "I know that . . ." can be unpacked. When saying one "sees that *x*," one is also claiming to "know that *x*." This is especially clear in the past-tense usage. When I say, "I saw that *x* is *y*," I am both giving others my authority for saying that *x* is *y* and reporting on the way I came to be in the position to make my claim to know. Consequently, others hearing my utterance of "I saw that *x* is *y*" are entitled to say they know that *x* is *y*. They are not entitled to say that they saw that *x* was *y*, although they might say that because of my utterance, they had come to see that *x* is *y*. "I saw that *x* is *y*" and "I see that *x* is *y*" offer the speaker's guarantee (his transmissible authority) as well as his support for his guarantee that *x* is *y*.[5]

Actually, the passage in Genesis speaks of Adam and Eve knowing that, not seeing that, they were naked. Coming to know, like seeing that, depends on the acquisition of concepts and a vocabulary, which provide a way to describe things and events, a way to understand them, and, often, a way to feel about them – in short, a conceptual enrichment. "Naked" does not simply mean "without clothes." Knowing one is naked, for example, may involve such feelings as shame, guilt, remorse, and regret.

[4] N. R. Hanson, *Patterns of Discovery* (Cambridge, 1958), 22.
[5] Obviously, this account echoes views about saying "I know *x*" that were defended by J. L. Austin in "Other Minds," *Philosophical Papers* (Oxford, 1961).

I maintained in *Responsibility Matters* that loss of innocence must include learning to redescribe actions and events in ways that were not previously possible for a person; further, it crucially involves acquiring a certain kind of conceptual understanding. The conceptual shift from innocence to moral maturity involves the loss of the ability to seriously use childhood illusions to describe actions – one's own and those of others – and events. Central to the loss of innocence is gaining knowledge of one's capacity to do and be done evil. That knowledge must be learned by what Bertrand Russell called acquaintance and not solely by description.[6] McKenna nicely summarizes my position when he writes, "to lose her innocence, one must have some experience in which she, so to speak, faces the moral reality of the world herself, and in doing so, comes to have a deeper conceptual understanding of the moral topography of the world and her place in it."[7]

My claim that innocence must be lost by learning of evil not only by description but also by acquaintance suggests to some that I am treading a very fine line between ushering a child into moral responsibility and child abuse. After all, knowing evil by acquaintance can be a very unpleasant, extremely hurtful, and sometimes identity-shattering experience. Still, my point is that it is not enough to expose children to literature, fictional or nonfictional, or take them to "coming-of-age" films. Although most people probably will learn more about evil by description than by acquaintance – and that, of course, is a good thing – members of the moral community must grasp their own potential to be the subject and object of evil by personal confrontation. Otherwise, it will be only an "academic" matter for them (using that term in its pejorative sense).

After rejecting a number of alternative accounts of what Eve may have learned from eating the fruit of the tree of knowledge of good and evil, I decided, like Morris, that all Eve really needed to taste in that first bite of the forbidden fruit was an immediate acquaintance with her capacity to do and be done evil. All the rest required for moral maturity could occur incrementally and much of it through knowledge by description. The fruit was not especially loaded with information. It was just a fruit, some say a quince, others an apple. Ingesting it was not swallowing a chip of thousands of YBs of rights and wrongs. It was the bite, not the bytes, that mattered.

---

[6] Bertrand Russell, *Problems of Philosophy* (Oxford 1912), chapter 5.
[7] McKenna, 6.

As McKenna rightly notes, on my account, the loss of innocence is a cultural artifact. It does not occur naturally. "For a person to grow into the state of a morally responsible agent, she must, so to speak, come to acquire a relationship to her moral world that is created by social conditions and expectations that are not of her making, nor of nature's."[8] Consequently, mature members of a moral community have a moral obligation to aid in bringing about the loss of innocence for their children. There are what might be identified as Hobbesian reasons for this requirement placed on the mature members: If a community does not consist of competent moral agents, contracts and promises cannot be relied on as stable social arrangements and the community will crumble. McKenna writes:

> More generally, we want our children to grow up to be morally virtuous, and hopefully, even morally heroic. They cannot do that and remain mere innocents. Hence, the obligation is upon us. But if it is, and certainly French is correct that it is, then the disturbing implication stares us in the face. If the loss of innocence requires direct acquaintance with evil, then our obligation to our children is, at least, to create the conditions in which they face it.[9]

McKenna, however, makes an important point challenging my claim that loss of innocence is always accompanied by the sort of gain required for full membership in the moral community. He points out that a child who has been sexually molested may well lose his or her innocence while not gaining the knowledge that he or she can also do evil. I agree that being a victim, even understanding that you are a victim, does not necessarily lead one to the realization that you are also capable of being a victimizer. And this must be especially true in cases of greatly disproportionate power situations. It is also unlikely that sexually abused children gain from those horrific experiences an understanding of intimacy in mature moral terms. However, some may experience the reactive attitude of resentment, and that may be an incremental step toward their gaining knowledge of evil in the requisite sense for moral maturity. It is difficult for me not to imagine that a sexually molested child would not experience resentment, and some may, sadly, experience shame. Those reactive attitudes, as Strawson famously maintained, rest on a set of expectations of respect, goodwill, and the protection of personal dignity that have "common roots in our human nature."[10]

---

[8] Ibid.
[9] Ibid.
[10] Peter Strawson, *Freedom and Resentment and Other Essays* (London, 1974), 16.

Although that set of expectations may reside in human nature, the reactive attitudes that give rise to our moral assessments of ourselves and others typically need to be cultivated. A molested child may have certain feelings with respect to the molester but be confused as to what those feelings are or unable to sort out conflicting feelings that the episode triggered, a point Seneca made persuasively.[11] In some of the widely publicized cases involving the Roman Catholic clergy, the child may believe or be led to believe by the molester and the institutional accoutrements of the situation in which the abuse occurs that what the priest is doing to him or her is a loving or caring act, even a sacred one, and will not grasp its true moral significance for some time, often years, when the appropriate negative reactive attitudes then take hold. No matter how painful psychologically, moral maturity with respect to that part of the person's life then emerges.

I am not claiming that there might be some good in child abuse. There never is. In fact, the trauma of an abusive situation may block or greatly delay the abused child's gaining moral knowledge. In some cases, it may numb the victim or lead to regression as a way of coping with the experienced horror. In such a case, the victim cannot face the moral reality of his or her experience and so cannot be expected to gain a deeper conceptual understanding of mature moral description. The language of rape, assault, molestation, and the like finds no foothold when the dominate image in the child's mind is that it was an experience that gave pleasure to an authority figure, a stepfather, a priest, or a favorite teacher. In any event, we should not overlook the fact that typically most children experience evil and their ability to do evil without extreme trauma and incrementally.

Experiencing evil as both subject and object on the battlefield or in a "dirty" war of house-to-house incursions like the one in many of the villages of Iraq also can have a numbing or a blocking effect on moral maturity. Philosophers are not well suited by training to offer much useful advice regarding the threshold of evil at which trauma supplants knowledge acquisition. There clearly is such a threshold, and if it is crossed during some moral developmental stage, the outcome may be regression or denial of the relevance of moral characterizations of actions, as well as the temporary or permanent loss of the individual as a productive member of the moral community. It is yet to be determined whether in war situations this can be overcome by robotics, neuropsychology, and

---

[11] See Seneca, *Letters of a Stoic* (Baltimore, 1969), Letter XC.

brain-machine interfaces used to "wire" the brains of soldiers to fighting machines and to relay images and instructions directly to the brains of soldiers. That there is a threshold has been demonstrated innumerable times in military and civilian situations.

McKenna profitably explores my claim that gaining mature membership in the moral community involves losing the "illusions of innocent description." Humans could biologically mature, carry on their lives, reproduce, and die without ever invoking moral conceptual descriptions of their actions and the events in which they are involved. Were that generally the case, the human race would then be in something not unlike Hobbes's state of nature (on the negative side) or the Garden of Eden before the Fall (on the positive side). I imagine such premoral humans in somewhat the way Kierkegaard describes the life of the aesthete. He writes, "When a man lives aesthetically his mood is always eccentric because he has his center in the periphery."[12] Like a child at play, and Kierkegaard uses reference to childish behavior in his characterization of living aesthetically,[13] the interest of premoral humans in one thing or one activity or one person or group of persons soon wanes and they look for something new and different. Perhaps Eve was curious about the fruit of the forbidden tree not so much because it was forbidden but because it was different. Would it taste sweeter, more robust, tannic, spritzy, foxy? Alasdair MacIntyre provides a description of people of this sort. He writes that they are

> those who see in the social world nothing but a meeting place for individual wills, each with its own set of attitudes and preferences and who understand the world solely as an arena for the achievement of their own satisfaction, who interpret reality as a series of opportunities for their enjoyment and for whom the last enemy is boredom.[14]

I think there is much to be learned from McKenna's account of the "illusions of innocent description" as the cultural artifacts of a simplistic moral order used to begin the indoctrination of children into morality. That is an important step in the loss of innocence that I previously passed over too lightly. I was particularly concerned with the way losses of innocence often assault a person's confidence in the continuity of their self. My examples of that phenomenon were taken from two nineteenth-century British novels – *Pride and Prejudice* and *Wuthering Heights* – but

[12] Soren Kierkegaard, *Either/Or*, trans. by Walter Lowrie (Garden City, 1959), 2, 235.
[13] Ibid., 192.
[14] Alasdair MacIntyre, *After Virtue* (Notre Dame, 1981), 24.

I failed to explore the fact that fearing loss of innocence may not be because one fears loss of one's sense of self, as is the case with Catherine Earnshaw in *Wuthering Heights*. It probably more often is the internal discovery by those moving into maturity that they do not really know how to replace the comfortable illusions of childhood that have shaped their world and given it meaning with mature moral ones that lack the magic, charm, simplicity, finality, and joy that were embedded in the illusions of innocent description. "We are uncertain what to do, or how to live. We are left aware that we need a far more nuanced map of our moral surroundings, but how are we to acquire it?"[15]

It seems to me that moral philosophers have been less than successful in providing a conceptual map for navigating the mature moral world that is appropriately nuanced for the purposes McKenna mentions. Typically, the maps we draw are either too sketchy, leaving far too much to insufficiently developed moral imaginations, or too comprehensive to be of much help to those at crossroads in need of uncomplicated directions.

Importantly, McKenna moves the discussion into an issue that few philosophers, myself included, have examined. It revolves around the question suggested by what he persists in calling my "controversial thesis": How should adults parent their children? Parenting is an especially morally significant human activity. We all know that it can be done well or poorly, but on what criteria, what grounds, what benchmarks, should it be judged? Certainly, how the child "turns out" must be considered, but that often-used phrase is ambiguous and lacking in anything more than the mere suggestion of criteria. Eliminating career and financial measures and concentrating on moral maturity as a primary goal of parenting, we can ask what innocence-ending experiences are morally appropriate?

In chapter 3 of *Responsibility Matters*, I had not credited our culture with having rituals designed to facilitate a child's exposure to evil and the risks humans run in interpersonal encounters. McKenna corrects me with reminders of some of the transitional experiences children endure, or are forced to endure, in which they get "to explore the underbelly of the moral world." His examples, although not rituals in the sense I had in mind, admittedly have a certain ritualistic character to them. He writes:

> There are...such rituals as confirmation for Christians, or the bat or bar mitzvah for Jews. Even setting these sorts of examples aside, in our society we often have something similar to the rituals French has in mind: teenagers graduate and go off to college; a young person heads off to boot camp; an

---

[15] McKenna, 8.

oldest son or daughter is brought into the family business, or expected to take on parenting duties for younger siblings or nursing duties for a sickly family member. In virtually all of these cases, the transitions involved provide the opportunity for exposure to the underbelly of the moral world: a college student can cheat, squander money, have uninhibited sex and experiment with dangerous drugs, all without fear of the watchful eye of mom or dad; a soldier in boot camp is actually taught in exquisite detail the techniques for taking human life; a child brought into the family business might face for the first time the opportunity to exploit or cheat others for personal gain; and so on.[16]

More important, and McKenna recognizes this, we need to pay attention to the use by parents of the illusions of childhood that will be discarded upon moral maturity. Proper parenting requires that the illusions that are "fed" to a child must "contain the seeds of basic, true moral insights." The myths we teach to the young and on which they build their childish illusory conceptions of the moral order normally will remain moral anchors during the shattering experience of loss of innocence when the magic is replaced with the mundane. Parents need to take advantage of the illusions of childhood to find morally sound lessons, for example, that a person's moral worth and merit cannot be discerned solely from her physical appearance. Anchoring that notion in the child's repertoire will serve as a foundational concept as the child outgrows or is torn away from the magic of fairy godmothers, good witches, elves, dwarfs, wolves dressed up as grandmothers, Prince Charmings, and all the rest and must deal in mixed motives, principles of utility, and questions of integrity in morally complex and conflicted encounters with others. One way in which the parent may prepare the way for the transition is for the parent to encourage, in Feinberg's terms, "the habit of critical self-revision." What this comes to in parenting is fostering, bit by bit, story by story, a critical stance in the child toward those childish illusions of the moral order. "Why," McKenna hopes the child will question, "did Snow White have to be so beautiful or so white?" What a marvelous question. If the child does not ask it, what then? My guess is that such an omission indicates a failure of parenting because the seeds of moral conceptual maturity are, in fact, planted in the story and in many of the illusions of childhood, and not despite but because of the representation of those stories in Disney films and in the illustrations in books for children.

I recall that when my daughter was a child of ten or so she told me that she hated *Alice in Wonderland* but loved *The Wizard of Oz.* When I expressed

---

[16] Ibid.

dismay because I favored the Lewis Carroll tale for its philosophical aspects, she told me that Alice is alone in a frightening world, but Dorothy, although also in a frightening world, makes honest and loyal friends who, despite their individual deficiencies, with courage, love, and intelligence face the evils with her. Such virtues morally matter in the transition from innocence to moral maturity. It is a far cry from child abuse to bring one's children to the critical stage of engaging with their illusions, whether prepackaged or self-created, in which they raise – often to themselves – those questions that eventually shake the foundations and topple the towers of their childish conceptions of moral order and responsibility. Big bad wolves can look like loving grandmothers! All the better to eat you! The explanations parents provide for why the tales turn out as they do need to be grounded in a sound moral conceptual framework on which the child can construct his or her moral edifice. Such a well-constructed edifice will ideally serve as something of a bulwark for their sense of self during their loss of innocence on the streets of Samara, Najaf, Sadr City, or in the mountains of Afghanistan; it will make the adoption of new descriptions of the world in which they must exist more palatable and perhaps less shattering.

4

Virtuous Responses to Moral Evil

As discussed in Chapter 2, moral evil is human action that jeopardizes another person's (or group's) aspirations to live a worthwhile life (or lives) by the willful infliction of undeserved harm on that person(s). For present purposes, I am not concerned with trying to clarify what is meant by "a worthwhile life." I say more about that notion in Chapter 8. Here, it may be understood in broad terms and might even be defined idiosyncratically from person to person, person to group, and group to group. "Willful" is meant to rule out mere accidents, unforeseeable consequences, nonnegligent inadvertence, and the like. Harm is undeserved when it is not a morally justifiable hostile response to wrongdoing.

In the Appendix to Chapter 2, I offered a chart that purports to categorize different ways in which humans come to do morally wrong, indeed evil, things to each other.

The Person Did Something Morally Wrong Because of . . .

Weakness of Will	Amorality
Although he/she knew what was morally right, he/she could not resist his/her desire to do what was morally wrong.	Although he/she knows what is morally right, he/she gives moral considerations no weight when acting.
Perverse Wickedness	Preferential Wickedness
He/she has false moral beliefs on which he/she acted.	He/she chose to do what is morally wrong because it is morally wrong.

In this chapter, I am interested in how we can, individually and/or collectively, responsibly respond to moral wrongdoing, to evil. When I raised this topic with the Navy and Marine chaplains and provided them with my chart, I also had them consider an account by Simon Wiesenthal of an experience he endured in a Nazi concentration camp.[1] Wiesenthal was taken from a work detail to the bedside of a dying SS soldier. The soldier told him about having been with his unit in a town square and being ordered to herd as many as two hundred Jewish men, women, and children toward a house. A truck brought cans of petrol and some of the Jewish men were ordered to carry the cans into the house.

> Then we began to drive the Jews into the house. A sergeant with a whip in his hand helped any of the Jews who were not quick enough. There was a hail of curses and kicks. The house was not very large; it had only three stories. I would not have believed it possible to crowd them all into it. But after a few minutes there was no Jew left on the street.... Then the door was locked and a machine gun was posted opposite.[2]

The command was given to throw live grenades into the house. When the SS soldier and his comrades did so, the house burst into flames. He continued to tell Wiesenthal the story.

> We heard screams and saw the flames eat their way from floor to floor.... We had our rifles ready to shoot down anyone who tried to escape from that blazing hell.... The screams from the house were horrible. Dense smoke poured out and choked us.[3]

The Nazi grabbed Wiesenthal's hand and after Wiesenthal pulled it away, he again grabbed it and squeezed it tightly while continuing his story.

> Behind the windows of the second floor, I saw a man with a small child in his arms. His clothes were alight. By his side stood a woman, doubtless the mother of the child. With his free hand the man covered the child's eyes... then he jumped into the street. Seconds later the mother followed. Then from the other windows fell burning bodies.... We shot.... Oh God!... I don't know how many tried to jump out of the windows but that one family I shall never forget – least of all the child. It had black hair and dark eyes.[4]

The Nazi, whose name was Karl, sat up in the bed and continued, his hands prayerfully folded.

> I want to die in peace.... In the long nights while I have been waiting for death, time and time again I have longed to talk about it to a Jew and

[1] Simon Wiesenthal, *The Sunflower: On the Possibilities and Limits of Forgiveness* (New York, 1976).
[2] Ibid., 41.
[3] Ibid., 42.
[4] Ibid., 43.

beg forgiveness from him. Only I didn't know whether there were any Jews left.... I know that what I am asking is almost too much for you, but without your answer I cannot die in peace.

Wiesenthal completed the story:

Now there was an uncanny silence in the room.... Here lay a man in bed who wished to die in peace – but he could not, because the memory of his terrible crime gave him no rest. And by him sat a man also doomed to die – but who did not want to die because he yearned to see the end of all the horror that blighted the world.... I stood up and looked in his direction, at his folded hands.... At last I made up my mind and without a word I left the room.[5]

Wiesenthal and many others have questioned whether he did the right thing, the moral thing, by refusing to forgive the dying soldier.

As a starting point for trying to answer that question, suppose we ask which of the categories on my chart the SS soldier was in when he committed the crime for which he sought forgiveness? It may be easier and more morally justifiable to forgive someone who was weak of will than someone who better belongs in one of the other three categories. That, however, may be persuasively disputed. If a person is too weak of will to do what he or she knows is the right thing to do, does not that reveal a blamable character flaw, a quality of will that is seriously deficient in that it has not developed the capacity to resist temptations when it recognizes what it morally ought to do? Such a lack of moral fortitude might be excused under certain conditions, but surely not all cases in which it reveals itself, and especially those in which extreme harm to others is the result of its inability to align its will with what it knows it should do or refrain from doing. In any event, the story Karl tells hardly offers a convincing case that he was weak of will that day in that town square. He does not report that he grasped what he morally ought to have done, nor does he hint that he wanted, in some prevolitional sense, to do what he ought to do but could not because he gave in to the lure of doing otherwise. This was not a case similar to that of an obese woman, wanting and resolving to lose weight, who stares into a bakery window and knows she should not buy and eat the pastries on display, but who nonetheless buys and consumes the pastries because she cannot resist her desire for them.

Arguments with some plausibility might be made that the SS soldier was acting amorally in the square and during his service in the Nazi

[5] Ibid., 54–5.

cause, a cause he had embraced from his days in the Hitler Youth. The argument might go that despite knowing or believing that what he was doing that day was morally wrong, he chose not to give moral considerations any weight when he decided what to do and obediently followed orders because he regarded that as the best thing for him to do in the circumstances. He may have believed that there were strong prudential reasons for him to do what he was ordered to do. He might have reasoned, although there is no evidence that this ever happened, that had he refused to follow the orders to kill the Jews, he would have been shot on the spot or sent into the burning house himself to perish with the Jews in the conflagration. Such an explanation of his actions, however, fails to take into consideration a very significant detail of the story. The soldier was no ordinary German recruit or draftee, fighting for his country, following superior orders out of a habit drilled into him. He was a member of the SS, Heinrich Himmler's elite military units whose members were chosen according to Nazi racial purity doctrines and their devotion to the Nazi ideology, and who conducted the Final Solution tactics intended to exterminate Jews and others that were identified as undesirables by the Third Reich. He was a "true believer." Alan Berger, commenting on Wiesenthal's story, noted that even on his deathbed, the SS soldier "perpetuated the Nazi stereotype, Jews were not individuals with souls, feelings, aspirations, and emotions."[6] He wanted a Jew brought to his bedside and any Jew would do. It just happened to be Wiesenthal, and he wanted that Jew to serve as the janitor of his conscience, a menial task that the arbitrarily chosen Jew would not perform.

The Nazi soldier seeking forgiveness from Wiesenthal so that he can die at peace seems best to belong with the perversely wicked when he participated in the extermination of the Jews in that square. We can reasonably conclude that, as an SS soldier, he was committed to the deviant Nazi ideology that preached that it was morally permissible, indeed morally required, to kill Jews. On his deathbed, of course, he abjured that ideology and seems to have adopted one, perhaps a reversion to his youthful Catholicism, that convinced him that he did something that is morally wicked and that he needs to be forgiven for his participation in an atrocity in order to die shriven and enter heaven. It is evident from his account that Wiesenthal was appalled by the Nazi's story and his request for forgiveness. But how should he respond if I am right that the appropriate way to think of Karl with respect to the atrocity in the square is that he

---

[6] Alan L. Berger, Comment in *The Sunflower*, 119.

asks forgiveness for a perversely wicked deed? Karl also may be asking forgiveness for having lived a perversely wicked life, of which the atrocity in the square was but a vivid focal event. Could it be that only on his deathbed does he recognize his life for the moral monstrosity that it was?

It might be thought that perverse evil is less wicked than preferential evil because the perversely evil person believes himself or herself to be doing right. He or she then may be quite conscientious, which is something of a virtue or is often thought of as one, in carrying out what he or she believes to be his or her moral duty. That is often referred to in the literature as the "conscientious Nazi problem." The preferentially evil person, knowing or believing that what he or she is doing is morally wrong and preferring to do it, has no refuge in virtue. However, in the end and as discussed in Chapter 2, doing evil is causing another person to suffer undeserved harm, and the epistemic state of mind of the evildoer should not diminish that crucial fact.

Perverse evil is the only sort the ancient Greeks, committed to the Socratic dictum that no one does evil willingly, seemed to think was possible. As Mary Midgley pointed out, the dictum affirms the view that there is a "unity of all human motivation. It says that, where there are radical moral clashes, involving charges of wickedness, at least one party must be assumed to be wrong. . . . It is in fact the manifesto of extreme practical rationalism."[7] But such a view ignores or rules out a basic fact about humans: that there is an amazing variety of human motivations, in no way a unity nor in any way subsumable to practical rationality.

Kant also rejects the possibility that humans can be preferentially evil. He writes: "We are not, then, to call the depravity of human nature *wickedness*, taking the word in its strict sense as a disposition (the subjective *principle* of the maxims) to adopt evil *as evil* into our maxim as our incentives (for that is diabolical); we should rather term it the *perversity* of the heart, which then, because of what follows from it, is also called an *evil heart*."[8]

Midgley also noted that philosophers typically shrink from identifying the most egregious evildoers as preferentially wicked. However, rather than adopting the "madness" or insanity hypothesis, they resort to crediting such evildoers with having adopted some sort of idiosyncratic, although consistent and well conceived, alternative moral theory that

[7] Mary Midgley, *Wickedness* (London, 1984), 20.
[8] Immanuel Kant, *Religion Within the Limits of Reason Alone*, translated by Theodore Greene and Hoyt Hudson (New York, 1960), 32.

requires them to perform what we regard as wicked deeds.[9] Their evil is, then, perverse and the Socratic dictum is preserved.

Perverse wickedness, however, is often difficult to distinguish from preferential wickedness. Perverse wickedness, following Ronald Milo,[10] might be conceived from either a cognitivist or a noncognitivist perspective, although we would still have to allow that beliefs regarding what one is doing are involved. Cognitivists will maintain that "the agent of a perversely wicked act does something that is morally wrong because he is ignorant that acts of this sort are morally wrong and falsely believes that such acts are right."[11] Noncognitivists might maintain that a perversely wicked act "consists in doing what is morally wrong because of one's acceptance of *bad* moral principles."[12]

Either of these accounts might appear cogent. Think of a murderer who raped, tortured, and mutilated his victim before killing her. For the noncognitivist, moral principles are expressions of attitudes. So the noncognitivist will focus attention on the sort of convictions the murderer holds most deeply, what he cares about most. Those, by the noncognitivist's definition, are his moral principles. We would expect to find that for him the rape, torture, and murder of defenseless women is of little concern unless the victim is a relative, a loved one, an associate, and so forth. His wickedness is perverse because it does not offend his most deeply held attitudes.

The cognitivist's account will focus on the murderer's ignorance of moral principles. His perverse wickedness reflects a bad moral character. In fact, it is precisely because he has a bad moral character that he is ignorant of proper moral principles. Why, however, should the possession of a bad moral character render such a person ignorant of moral principles? Milo asks: "If one adopts a purely cognitivist account of the nature of moral beliefs – i.e., if one holds that to believe that a certain act is wrong is to accept as true a proposition to this effect, then how does one explain why having a bad character... prevents a person from grasping the truth of this proposition?"[13] What blocks a person with a bad moral character from granting the truth of propositions to the effect that what he or she is doing, or did, is morally wrong?

[9] Midgley, 61.
[10] Ronald Milo, "Wickedness," *American Philosophical Quarterly* (January 1983), 70.
[11] Ibid.
[12] Patrick Nowell-Smith, *Ethics* (London, 1954).
[13] Milo, 71.

Aristotelians might say that perversely wicked people are so morally sick that their intellectual capacities are impaired. They are afflicted with cognitive blindness or cognitive myopia. That imagery, however, provides no insight into how perverse wickedness produces ignorance or blocks knowledge of moral principles. If that cannot be explained, then it is conceivable that someone could have a preference for doing something while believing the proposition that the thing preferred is the morally wrong thing to do in the circumstances or under any circumstances. Some people just do what they prefer doing regardless of the fact that they believe it to be morally wrong or improper to do it. Such design platforms in cyberspace as *Second Life* seem to provide people with the opportunity to act out preferences they believe to be morally wrong because that is what they prefer. There is nothing of incontinence about it.

As Milo noted,[14] the basic problem for a cognitivist's conception of perverse wickedness resides in the beliefs they ascribe to the evildoer. They must assign to Karl beliefs to the effect that it is morally right to burn Jewish families to death. He must believe that committing such atrocities is not morally wrong. It is morally permissible or, even, morally required, or so he must believe. In effect, to make the fuller account of perverse wickedness along these lines plausible, it must be believed that there are no acts such that if one knows what it is for an act to be morally wrong, one *must* believe that acts of that kind are morally wrong. In other words, for any act, it must be possible to believe that either it is morally right or morally wrong, never only morally right or only morally wrong.

Surely, Karl knew that what he was doing was burning alive human beings. If someone knows what it is for an act to be morally wrong, could that person not know that acts of that sort are morally wrong? Karl, we may suppose, had command of a perfectly adequate moral vocabulary. So, it seems to be the case that he did not care that he acted in violation of moral principles of the sort that committing or participating in the committing of mass murder is morally wrong, or that he cares more, for whatever reasons, about performing acts that violate those principles than he does about acting in accord with them.

Aristotle departs from his defense of perverse wickedness because he cannot adopt the position that there are no kinds of acts such that if one knows what it is for an act to be morally wrong, one must believe that those acts are morally wrong. He tells us that there are some types of actions

[14] Ibid., 73.

"whose very names connote baseness, e.g., adultery, theft, and murder. These and similar . . . actions imply by their very names that they are bad. . . . It is, therefore, impossible ever to do right in performing them: to perform them is always to do wrong. In cases of this sort, let us say adultery, rightness and wrongness do not depend on committing it with the right woman at the right time and in the right manner, but the mere fact of committing such action at all is to do wrong."[15] On Aristotle's account, where murder, adultery, and theft are concerned, a person cannot be perversely wicked. Persons who do such things are preferentially, not perversely, wicked. So Karl was preferentially wicked. Further, if someone does not know what it means to believe that some action is morally wrong, that person cannot have beliefs about the rightness or wrongness of what he or she is doing in the first place, so he or she cannot properly be described as perversely wicked. The most we could say about that person is that he or she (sometimes) just prefers to do things that he or she should know are morally wrong or bad.

Noncognitivists hold that "believing an act to be morally wrong consists . . . in having a certain kind of con-attitude towards it."[16] The attitude or the disposition to choose one way rather than another is the extent of the matter. There is "nothing to be ignorant of or falsely believe."[17] One's moral principles simply are one's pro or con attitudes toward actions and events. For the noncognitivist, it may look as if preferential wickedness is not possible, at least as long as choice is determined by pro-attitudes. Only the degenerate or mentally disturbed would act counter to their pro-attitudes. Wickedness, then, should always be perverse.

Patrick Nowell-Smith writes: "If a man consistently, and over a long course of years, tries to get the better of his fellows in all transactions of daily life or if he is never moved by the consequences of his actions for other people, we might say, colloquially, that 'he has no moral principles.' But this clearly means, not that he has no moral principles or that he has good ones and continually succumbs to temptation to act against them, but that he has bad moral principles."[18] For the noncognitivist, revelation of a person's preferences is revelation of his or her moral principles. And some person's moral principles are perverse.

---

[15] Aristotle, *Nicomachean Ethics* (1107a).
[16] Milo, 72.
[17] Ibid.
[18] Nowell-Smith, 266–7.

Nowell-Smith, however, overlooks equally acceptable alternative readings of the situation that are still within the scope of noncognitivism. We could just as well describe Karl as having bad moral principles rather than as having morally bad principles.[19] In either case, he is acting on his pro-attitudes. Noncognitivists must call those pro-attitudes "his moral principles" and then judge them to be bad ones. Noncognitivists, however, need not maintain that people who are acting on their pro-attitudes must believe that they are doing what is morally right when, for example, they are doing something so despicable as participating in the commission of mass murder.

A noncognitivist, trying to explain perverse wickedness, might maintain that a person doing evil deeds because of his or her dominant pro-attitude toward the pursuit of his or her own ends must believe that failing to do so would be a moral failing. There is, however, as much reason for a noncognitivist to maintain that the evildoer believes that what he or she is doing is morally wrong, while preferring it to all other possible actions in the circumstances. Why should the noncognitivist hang the belief that what he or she is doing is morally right around the neck of the evildoer? In the end, both the cognitivist and noncognitivist have wicked people perversely preferring their own ends that conflict with standard moral prohibitions.

A number of those with whom I have shared the Wiesenthal story disputed my reading that Karl's is a case of perverse wickedness. Many of the chaplains, for example, saw him as preferentially wicked. None were willing to regard him as weak of will because it is only well after the fact, and not until he is dying and his Catholic fears of eternal damnation take center stage in his mind, that he seems to view his past actions as evil. We have no reason in the story to believe that he resisted, even for a moment, tossing a grenade into the house or firing on the Jewish family that jumped from the window. None of those with whom I discussed the story were inclined to include him among the amoral, even the temporarily amoral that day in the town square. It is, however, tempting to imagine that when joining the SS, he willfully suspended whatever sound moral beliefs he may have had, vowed not to allow them to interfere with his actions in his SS capacity, and then on his deathbed reclaimed them, applied them to the appraisal of at least one incident in his life, and found himself morally and spiritually wanting. But, it is far more likely

---

[19] A point suggested by Milo. See Milo, 73.

that when joining the SS, he thoroughly adopted its doctrines and policies as an alternative moral belief system, having already been well schooled in its ideology, and deposited whatever other moral beliefs he may have held prior to that point in the trash bin of his brain, from which they may have reemerged along with old religious beliefs, as he lay dying, and raised for him the frightful specter of the flames of Hell.

Although a number of those with whom I have discussed it have insisted that there is sufficient evidence in the story to support categorizing Karl as preferentially wicked, I am not convinced. If he was preferentially wicked, he must have known or believed that what he did in the square was morally wrong and chosen to do it for that very reason. It seems, however, that he either believed that what he was doing was right or that what he was doing was "beyond good and evil," actions without moral status or not amenable to moral appraisability. A number of chaplains who placed Karl in the ranks of the preferentially wicked regarded as supporting evidence for their characterization of him that his begging Wiesenthal for forgiveness was an additional intentional diabolical act of preferential wickedness: trying to co-opt a condemned Jew in a concentration camp into complicity with his wickedness.

Were the SS soldier's actions, or his life, properly describable as preferentially wicked, it should be harder to forgive him than were he weak of will, selectively amoral, or even perversely wicked. Nonetheless, many chaplains, especially the Catholics, maintained that when a person sincerely asks for forgiveness, it must be granted to him. Sincerity is, of course, the issue, even with such a liberal conception of forgiveness. For the Christian, that matter turns on the concept of repentance that I presently examine. I am, however, first concerned with Wiesenthal's response to Karl.

Wiesenthal must have been both bewildered and angry at the SS soldier's request, or was it an order from a captor to a captive? I am tempted to think of it in the latter terms because it carries out the Nazi ideology of superiority, but the story suggests the former: that Karl was in a supplicant mode, if not to Wiesenthal, then because of Karl's conception of what his early religious background required of him. That, however, may be too much of a stretch. If Karl were "returning to the fold," as it were, why would he not ask for a Catholic chaplain to hear his confession? It is not unimaginable that an SS Catholic chaplain, though not a Jesuit because they had been removed from the Wehrmacht in 1941, would have heard Karl's confession and granted him absolution, unless, of course, the chaplain was himself a committed Nazi – and most apparently were because of the Nazi screening process for chaplains. Karl might have had reason to believe that forgiveness for doing what a good Nazi was ordered to do would not be forthcoming from such a chaplain. In any event, Karl believed that a Catholic priest could not forgive his offense(s). Only a Jew, a representative of the victims, not his church, would do.

I imagine Wiesenthal angry at this outrageous intrusion in his unjustly burdened bare existence, trudging at manual labor, waiting the execution order that would commit him to the fate of his relatives. Aristotle devotes Section 5 of Book IV of the *Nicomachean Ethics* to a discussion of anger. He makes it clear that anger cannot be a virtue because it is a passion (NE 1105), but it can be virtuous when it reflects a certain state of character and leads to certain actions. Aristotle endorses the view that anger at the right things or people in the right time is praiseworthy and, importantly, not getting angry at the things or persons at which one should be angry reveals a serious character flaw. I want Wiesenthal to have been seething with a moral anger he could not ostensibly display.

Aristotle worries that it is difficult to determine how, with whom, at what, and for what duration one should be angry because he fears that the anger to which a person of good character is disposed can slide down a slippery slope into obsessive anger, bad temper, if not kept in check by reason. He counsels erring on the side of a deficiency, but getting angry and acting on that anger not only is not a flaw in character, it can be an indication of a good character. Those unable to raise their passions to the level of anger in situations when confronting the immoral behavior of others are moral failures.

Jeffrie Murphy maintains that anger is at the foundation of "the moral order itself."[20] It is an indicator of care, of honor, of self-respect, and respect for others. If we do not react angrily when our values are attacked, our friends are harmed, and family members are injured or insulted, who are we but, as Aristotle says, slaves without moral fiber? Moral anger, which we may define, following Aristotle, as the virtuous anger provoked in the good-tempered person by the wicked actions of others and, perhaps, oneself, demands action. It is morally incomplete without it. It is a sign of good character to have the passion in the circumstances, but a failure of character, perhaps a lack in another virtue, such as courage, not to try to take appropriate action. For Wiesenthal, that action was to leave the room without saying a word of forgiveness, the only hostile response that Wiesenthal had within his control.

[20] Jeffrie Murphy, "Two Cheers for Vindictiveness," in his *Getting Even* (Oxford, 2003).

Some of the chaplains argued that it is morally fitting that the Nazi suffer the most overwhelming pangs of guilt until death overcomes him, but that Wiesenthal would have done a more virtuous thing by forgiving him and relieving his anguish than by silently leaving the room, walking back to the work detail that may have been only postponing his own extermination at the hands of those committed to the ideology the dying SS soldier espoused. Wiesenthal's options are rather limited. It is not within his power to administer or order a physical punishment that might be commensurate with the wrong Karl has done. He can either utter the words of forgiveness or say nothing and leave, as he did. Wiesenthal, by saying nothing, chooses the punishment of condemnatory silence. Many of the Christian chaplains with whom I discussed the case maintained that Wiesenthal acted badly. He had it in his power to relieve suffering and chose not to do so. They insisted that he should have told the dying SS soldier that he forgave him as an act of mercy, even if he, perhaps rightly, believed that he had no authority in the circumstances to forgive what had been done. My inclination is to side with those who hold that Wiesenthal responded to moral evil in the most appropriate way he could in the circumstances. But, if those with me on this also believe that what he was doing by remaining silent is turning the matter of a fitting response to moral evil over to the moral universe, leaving the punishment of the SS soldier to heaven, then we part ways, as I presently argue.

What was the SS soldier asking of Wiesenthal? What is it to forgive and when is it morally justified? Forgiveness is a difficult concept to explain. As Murphy has pointed out, it is easier to say what it is not. It is not forgetting, excusing, or justifying, and although it might, at least in its verbal expression, play a significant role in showing mercy, as was suggested by some of the chaplains, it is not mercy. Joseph Butler, as pointed out by Murphy, maintained that forgiveness is "a moral virtue (a virtue of character) that is essentially a matter of the heart, the inner self, and involves a change in inner feeling more than a change in external action."[21] Butler referred to it as "forswearing resentment." To forgive is to willfully overcome the negative reactive attitudes we naturally have toward those who have wronged us, damaged us, deprived us of what we rightfully deserve. It may involve giving up the legitimate feeling of victimization and the retributive passions, the hatreds and the angers, that accompany having been victimized.

---

[21] Ibid., 13.

In 2002, I was a guest on a National Public Radio show along with a professor from California who was an advocate of forgiveness as a psychological therapy. My appearance was prompted by the publication of my book, *The Virtues of Vengeance*, and the September 11, 2001 terrorist attacks. After the host had gleaned from both of us the core elements of our respective books, the show was opened to calls from listeners. One of those calls came from a woman from the state of Washington who reported that she had been brutally raped by two men and left for dead. The men were eventually caught by the police, tried and convicted of their crimes, and are serving lengthy prison sentences. The woman told us that she did not especially care that they were now incarcerated because she had forgiven them. She wanted to know whether she had done the right thing. The forgiveness writer asked her how she felt and she said that forgiving them had lifted an emotional burden from her and that she was able to sleep better at nights. He applauded her, maintaining that she was living proof of his theory that forgiveness is the way for victims to heal their psyches after victimization, to free themselves from the heavy chains forged by debilitating anger at their experience of humiliation and loss. I was then asked for my reaction. I said that I understood that forgiveness is something that occurs within the victim, if it is going to happen at all, and that it may relieve the person doing the forgiving of painful attitudes such as anger, hatred, vindictiveness, and the like that have a tendency to consume their energies. However, I worried that in doing so, it may also diminish, if not annihilate, the victim's self-respect when he or she realizes what it entails.

The negative reactive attitudes, especially resentment, are powerful bulwarks of self-respect. Forswearing them when they are entirely appropriate, when you have been the victim of malevolent undeserved harm, cannot be a good thing. It could indicate that either you do not think you have rights not to be victimized or that you do not take those rights very seriously. Being undeservedly harmed by someone conveys to the victim that the wrongdoer regards the victim as less worthy than himself or herself.[22] Rapists, for example, express to their victims by the very act of rape that they regard them as no better than means to the satisfaction of their desires and goals, as objects to be used and discarded, and certainly not as what Kant would call "ends-in-themselves." The danger in forgiveness is that the victim may unwittingly be endorsing the

---

[22] A point made by Jean Hampton in Murphy and Hampton, *Forgiveness and Mercy* (Cambridge, 1988), chapter 2.

wrongdoer's message of such an inequality of worth. Also, I do not see how forgiveness could be morally virtuous if it is done for selfish reasons such as allowing one to sleep better at nights or to promote one's mental health. I recall that I concluded my response to that case by saying that it was reassuring to know that the state of Washington was not swayed by the caller's readiness to forgive her rapists and that it was punishing them to the full extent of its law.

Butler was wrong that forgiveness is a virtue. Or rather, if it is a virtue, it is a conditional one. Forgiveness can be a virtue, what Murphy calls "a healing virtue," only when it is consistent with the victim maintaining self-respect and when it is done for moral reasons. Murphy provides what seems to be a fairly exhaustive list of morally acceptable grounds for forgiving a wrongdoer, some of which are merely practical: the wrongdoer has suffered enough, the wrongdoer has undergone an apology ritual, for old time's sake.[23] Each of those reasons, though not always peculiarly moral, allows the separation of the wrongdoing from the wrongdoer and invites reentry of the wrongdoer into the moral community, although probably the other members, especially those who were the offended parties, will adopt a cautionary stance toward the wrongdoer. The element in forgiveness, however, that is crucial from a moral (and theological) point of view seems to be that the wrongdoer sincerely repents of the wrongdoing.

What is it to repent? Michel de Montaigne, in his essay "On Repentance," writes that he rarely repents because his conscience, although far from pure, is generally content. The suggestion is that repentance is driven by a disturbed conscience owing to the actions one has performed. One can only repent having done things that are in one's power. Montaigne notes that vice leaves remorse in the soul and, because such remorse is burdensome, repenting is the way to alleviate it. "Repentance is simply a recanting of our will and an opposition to our fancies."[24] Montaigne also points out that repentance is easy to counterfeit. "Its essence is abstruse and secret; its externals are easy and ostentatious."[25] For Montaigne, repentance is a private mental act, an interior acceptance of responsibility for what one has done badly. It, as described by Murphy, also involves "the repudiation of that evil, and the sincere resolve

---

[23] See ibid., 24.
[24] Michel de Montaigne, *Essays*, translated by J. M. Cohen (London, 1958), 237, 239.
[25] Ibid., 245.

to do one's best to extirpate it."[26] But all of that is within the mind of the wrongdoer, and it is not difficult to see why Montaigne believed it is often counterfeited. Only the wrongdoer, and presumably God, could know that the evil deed has been repudiated and that a commitment has been made to remove it. The latter, of course, is hardly possible in the case of murder, let alone mass murder. The dying SS soldier can do absolutely nothing to extirpate his crimes, and so he cannot sincerely resolve "to do one's best to extirpate" them. If repentance requires such a resolve, then Karl cannot repent. He can only regret.

Murphy argues for a social dimension in repentance. He adds a clause to the account of repentance as a purely mental act: to repent is also to "resolve to atone or make amends for the harm one has done."[27] But Murphy's additional social dimension will not help Karl. There is no way that he can atone, no way he can make amends. If Murphy is right, and I think he is, that repentance requires not only taking responsibility for the evil one has done but repudiating it, extirpating it, and resolving to atone for it by making appropriate amends, Karl cannot repent, and if he cannot repent, he should not be forgiven.

Some years ago, I published a paper on what I called the Principle of Responsive Adjustment, or PRA.[28] PRA expresses the idea that after an untoward event occurs, the person(s) who materially contributed to it is (are) expected to adopt certain courses of future action that are likely to insure the prevention of repetitions. PRA incorporates "moral expectations" of behavioral adjustments. PRA, however, is more than an expression of such expectations. It allows that in the case where the original offending behavior could not be shown to be intentional and expected adjustments in behavior and behavioral patterns are not made, and in the absence of strong evidential support for nonadjustment, the offender(s) may be held fully morally responsible for the earlier untoward event because it is, in effect, captured in the intention to repeat the offending behavior. PRA explains our practices of reevaluating persons, the actions and their characters, in the present with regard to past events in which they were a causal factor. PRA specifically addresses cases where it was not possible or not easy to identify the original offending behavior as intended by the person who materially caused it. Some critics referred

[26] Murphy, *Getting Even*, 41.
[27] Ibid.
[28] Peter A. French, "A Principle of Responsive Adjustment," *Philosophy* (October, 1984), 491–50.

to PRA as allowing "a second bite of the apple." That, of course, was not strictly speaking correct, for a second bite, on PRA, captures the first bite in the net of moral responsibility, whether or not the first bite could be shown to have been intentional. I say much more about PRA in Chapter 13. A scholar of Jewish philosophical history once asked me if PRA was the other side of the coin from Joseph Albo's theory of repentance. I had to admit that I had no idea to whom he was referring, inviting a brief course in Albo's account of repentance.

Albo was a fifteenth-century Spanish Jewish philosopher. My understanding of his conception of repentance is rudimentary at best. As I understand him, Albo maintained that persons are to be held responsible only for their intentional acts,[29] a view that many moral philosophers, including Kant, would endorse. On Albo's view, an identifying feature of an intentional or voluntary act is that the agent, in performing it, wants it to remain in his or her biography. A piece of behavior performed under duress or in some other compulsory manner, accidentally, or even negligently is not something for the doing of which the person wants to be held accountable when his or her moral responsibilities are tallied. Albo folds, some might say twists, that notion into his repentance theory. He holds that if the person sincerely repents having done something, including something he or she did intentionally, the person is attesting that the thing done really was not intentional, that he or she does not wish it to have been done, that it should not be recorded among the things he or she voluntarily did, and should not be morally counted against him or her. Sincere repentance is a retroactivity tool for altering the intentionality status of evil deeds.

There are a number of passages in the Bible in which God is reported to have hardened the heart of some villain or other. A considerable amount of discussion has taken place among Biblical scholars over the years as to what "hardening the heart" of someone is suppose to accomplish.[30] Without going deep into the details, in the famous case of Pharaoh and the Israelites in Exodus, some argue that God hardens Pharaoh's heart so that he will not be swayed by the plagues or the pleas of his people to believe he has no choice but to free the Israelites, but instead will have to make a free choice between freeing them and keeping them

---

[29] Joseph Albo, *Sefer ha-'Ikkarim* [*Book of Principles*], translated and edited by I. Husik, (Philadelphia, 1929).

[30] For examples, see David Shatz, "Freedom, Repentance, and Hardening of the Hearts: Albo vs. Maimonides," *Faith and Philosophy* (1997).

in bondage. In other words, he will not hear the emotional pleas of the heart when he makes his decision. Presumably, he will then act in accord with his character and be held fully responsible for his choice. He could then sincerely repent and, according to Albo's theory, remove the evil deed from his moral ledger. There is, however, another view of hardening of the heart, cited by David Shatz. It is that hardening the heart closes, rather than opens, the agent's options. The agent chooses to do something morally wrong and, with a hardened heart, cannot avoid doing it. Hardening the heart is the punishment of the wicked because they cannot repent and revise their biography by making it that they did not do the evil deed intentionally. They are locked in, as it were. During the early plagues, it is Pharaoh who is described as hardening his own heart, deciding that he will not free the Israelites from bondage, that he will not give in to the terror of the plagues. But then God hardens Pharaoh's heart, saying that he is "making sport of the Egyptians." The plagues of locusts and of darkness occur and Pharaoh cannot free the Israelites, his heart having been hardened by God. After the Passover, the killing of the first born of the Egyptians, Pharaoh lets Moses and Aaron lead the Israelites out of Egypt, but then God again hardens his heart and he pursues them, eventually into the Red Sea. The punishment of the hardened heart is the closing of doors on the potential of repentance to cleanse one's conscience, to wash away the sin.

The SS soldier, on an account like Albo's, could sincerely repent on his deathbed, but he also might be described as having hardened his heart in the town square and so repentance may not be available to him. Karl may well have been a person with a conscience, but he repressed it, hardened his own heart, and as death approaches for him, he wants to expunge the deed. Cynthia Ozick wrote about Wiesenthal's story:

> We condemn the intelligent man of conscience because there is a difference, because, though at heart not a savage, he allowed himself to become one, he did not resist. It was not that he lacked conscience; he smothered it. It was not that he lacked sensibility; he coarsened it. It was not that he lacked humanity; he deadened it.... The intelligent man of conscience also shovels in the babies, and it does not matter that he does it without exaltation.[31]

Consciences are artifacts and, like any artifact, they can be flawed, sometimes grotesquely. Because they are products of culture, there is no guarantee that doing the right thing as one's conscience demands is forgivable when it turns out to be a very wrong thing to have done. Suppose that

---

[31] Cynthia Ozick, "Notes Toward a Meditation on 'Forgiveness'," *The Sunflower*, 219.

Ozick is right and that Karl was a man of conscience, doing what he believed to be right in that square, deadening his humanity, not allowing sympathy for his victims to deter him from his duty. Perversely wicked, yes, but forgivable?

In 1974, Jonathan Bennett published a paper that has provoked considerable discussion and has been widely anthologized.[32] Bennett provides an analysis of Huckleberry Finn battling his conscience about whether he should return Jim, the runaway slave, to his owner. Huck's sympathies for Jim triumph over the dictates of his conscience, which insists that he would be doing wrong were he not to return the runaway. After writing a letter to Jim's owner telling her where to find Jim, Huck says that he laid the letter down and started to think of how by writing the letter he had avoided going to Hell for helping a runaway slave. Then he recalls the raft trip down the river and the good times he had with Jim and how Jim had cared for him. He picks up the letter and reports:

> I was a trembling, because I'd got to decide, forever, betwixt two things, and I knowed it. I studied a minute, sort of holding my breath, and then says to myself: "All right, then, I'll go to hell" – and tore it up. It was awful thoughts and awful words, but they was said. And I let them stay said; and never thought no more about reforming . . . as long as I was in, and in for good, I might as well go the whole hog.[33]

We applaud Huck's decision and his resolve. We might applaud Alyssa Peterson for refusing to continue to torture prisoners in Iraq and feel, in her case, sorrow for the fact that she committed suicide because she could not live with what she had done.[34] But Bennett goes on to argue, based on the same principle that led us to praise Huck, that Heinrich Himmler was a morally better person than Jonathan Edwards was. Himmler directed the SS, including Karl's unit, and orchestrated many of the atrocities of the Third Reich. He certainly can be credited, as he credits himself, with a considerable bit of the responsibility for the Holocaust. Yet, in some of his speeches, he expressed the difficulty he experienced in restraining his sympathies, as a "decent fellow" would, for the plight of those being exterminated by his orders. He was well aware of the great pain and suffering he was causing. He also believed it necessary for him

---

[32] Jonathan Bennett, "The Conscience of Huckleberry Finn," *Philosophy*, 49 (1974), 123–34.

[33] Mark Twain, *The Adventures of Huckleberry Finn* (Cambridge, 1958, first published 1884, 1885), 179–80.

[34] See Chapter 7.

to sympathize with his victims to, and only to, the extent that he could avoid becoming a "heartless ruffian." It wasn't about them. It was about him.

Jonathan Edwards, in his sermons, Bennett reminds us, showed no sympathy, no love nor pity, for the damned souls he describes as roasting in Hell. Edwards, unlike the chaplains in the PDTCs I taught during the Iraq War, believed that moral standards are independent of God's wants and are accessed by God when determining the fate of humans. God metes out justice but does not determine what is just. So when punishing the damned eternally in the most hideous ways, God is acting justly and for God not to do so would be unjust. Indeed, the saved, in whose company Edwards numbers himself, when seeing the "calamities of others" in Hell, will have their sense of enjoyment and blessedness in heaven heightened, and they will have no sorrow or sympathy for the damned, and it is right that they should do so.

Edwards, unlike Himmler, never ordered anyone killed; however, Bennett's account paints him as the more evil of the two. Why? Himmler, like Karl, was caught up in a wicked morality that dictated his duty to exterminate millions of people, and he acted on that duty despite his emotions. Yet, he had the emotions and had to stifle them, even to the point of physical illness. Bennett makes him begin to sound like a victim himself. Like both Huck and Edwards, he is infused with a wicked morality, a perverse conscience, that determines for him what his duty must be. Huck rejects duty in favor of sympathy; Himmler acts dutifully (as his morality dictates, to kill Jews) but with sympathy for his victims. Edwards lacks sympathy for the damned and also, presumably, acts dutifully in endorsing his morality. He adjusts whatever feelings of pity he might have had "so that they conform to the dictates of some authority."

And what did the SS soldier Karl do in the square? Perhaps he was like Himmler, his leader. However, as he nears death and the prospect of eternal damnation, his sympathies bud out. Or do they? Perhaps his concern, as in the square, is still only for his own well-being. How much like Himmler is he then? Or is he more like Edwards in that he never really has sympathy for his victims or for the Jew he has brought to his bedside?

Ozick brings the point into clear focus when she writes: "Forgiveness is pitiless. It forgets the victim. It negates the right of the victim to his own life. It blurs over suffering and death. It drowns the past. It cultivates sensitiveness towards the murderer at the price of insensitiveness towards the victim. . . . The face of forgiveness is mild, but how stony to the slaughtered."[35] Ozick's point is that only retributive punishment befitting the offense places pity where it belongs: for the victims. When the wrongdoer fittingly is punished, the victim is shown pity for the suffering and harm endured, and the full extent of the wrongdoing is displayed not only to the offender but to the moral community. Anything short of that is unfair to the victims. That retributive duty is not owed to the wrongdoer, contra Robert Nozick's view that punishment promotes the interest of the wrongdoer by connecting that person back to moral values after he or she had become detached from them.[36] The justification of punishment is grounded in the morally primitive notion of desert,[37] and that entails that all the rights and benefits to be derived from an act of punishment accrue to the victim who was the object of the undeserved harm inflicted by the wrongdoer. The retributive duty to punish is owed to victims, not to wrongdoers.

There are additional reasons not to respond to perverse wickedness, or any kind of wickedness, for that matter, with forgiveness. You cannot forgive a wrongdoer if you do not have standing to resent the harm, which is to say that you cannot forgive unless you are the victim of the wrong or designated by the victim to deal with the wrongdoer. Smail Balic, responding to the Wiesenthal case, commented: "Rectifying a misdeed is a matter to be settled between the perpetrator and the victim. A third party has no proper role other than mediator."[38] Abraham Heschel added: "No one can forgive the crimes committed against other people."[39] If those who were undeservedly harmed by the SS soldier are all dead, and he and his comrades saw to that, there is no one from whom he can beg forgiveness for the deed. Picking any available Jew will not do.

Robert McAfee Brown makes a further point that provokes examination of the metaphysics of dealing with moral evil in any way other than by a hostile response, retributive punishment. Brown wrote regarding the Wiesenthal case, after admitting that he could not forgive Karl: "If God forgives such deeds, does not that likewise strain to the breaking point

---

[35] Ozick, 216–217.

[36] Robert Nozick, *Philosophical Explanations* (Cambridge, 1981), 374–80.

[37] By that I mean that my claim that those who commit acts of willful wrongdoing deserve hostile responses is simply what it means to say that an act is morally wrong (or an act is one of willful wrongdoing).

[38] Smail Balic in *The Sunflower*, 111.

[39] Abraham Heschel in *The Sunflower*, 171.

any contention that the universe of God's creation is a moral universe?"[40] The universe, however, is not moral, a viewpoint suggested by a poem by Stephen Crane:

> A man said to the universe: "Sir, I exist!"
> "However," replied the universe
> "The fact has not created in me a sense of obligation."[41]

In Thornton Wilder's *The Bridge of San Luis Rey*,[42] a short novel worthy of philosophical scrutiny, a footbridge over a gorge on the road between Lima and Cuzco collapses, killing five people. A monk, after examining the biographies of the victims, concludes that by collapsing the bridge at just that time, God was both punishing the wicked and calling the good to an early heavenly reward. The underlying conception that sustains the monk in his analysis is the one referred to by Brown: that there must be a moral order to the universe that was established and is maintained by an invariably morally good God. When people die nonnatural deaths, and this should be especially evident if they die in what appear to be accidental disasters, so-called "acts of God," it must be for reasons of moral desert, and those reasons should become evident when their lives are exposed to moral appraisal. God, or the universe, handles the matter of responding to moral evil and, for that matter, moral good.

An interstate highway bridge collapsed in Minneapolis in the summer of 2007, killing a number of people. Unlike the monk in Wilder's story, we want to know what was the matter with the bridge. Did it have design flaws or maintenance issues? We have sympathy for those who died and for their family members, but we do not expend investigative efforts to uncover whether each of those who perished in the Mississippi River deserved to die at that moment either because they were morally wicked or saintly. There is a profound difference in the way the monk and most of us conceive of the universe, the role of God, and the place of humans in it. But is there a convincing argument to support the thesis that the universe or its Creator will deal in morally justifiable ways with wrongdoers?

I am not a Biblical scholar, as I often reminded the chaplains, but certain Biblical texts are perplexing with respect to the claim that there is a god in charge of the universe who is invariably morally good and

---

[40] Robert McAfee Brown in *The Sunflower*, 122.
[41] Stephen Crane, *War Is Kind*, 1899.
[42] Thornton Wilder, *The Bridge of San Luis Rey* (New York, 1927).

can be counted on to administer just deserts to wrongdoers. One oft-cited text suggesting God, at least the god described in the Bible, does not always respond in a morally defensible manner to human events is in Numbers 31: "And the LORD spake unto Moses, saying, avenge the children of Israel of the Midianites. . . . Now therefore kill every male among the little ones, and kill every woman that hath known man by lying with him. But all the women children, that have not known a man by lying with him, keep alive for yourselves."

What God ordered following a battle between the Israelites and the Midianites was the wholesale murdering of thousands of captured women and male children. This was to be done as an act of revenge against the Midianites, whose women, it is recounted in Numbers 25, "began to play the harlot" with the men of Israel and then invited the men of Israel to make sacrifices to the Midianite gods. Some of the commentators maintain that the Midianites used their women to lure Israelite men into adulterous sexual liaisons and orgies culminating in the worship of Baal, a rival god to the God of the Israelites. That behavior angered God against the Midianites and, apparently, accounts for why any Midianite woman who is not a virgin was ordered slaughtered. The text of Numbers 25, however, just says that "the people began to play the harlot with the daughters of Moab. These invited the people to the sacrifices of their gods, and the people ate, and bowed down to their gods." That sounds rather more like the fault should fall on the men of Israel, and the story goes on to recount that God orders all of the chiefs of Israel to be hung "in the sun" in order to placate the anger of God. So God's orders to avenge Israel against the Midianites in the manner described in Numbers 31 seems to have somewhat less a basis in the preceding account of the dealings between the Midianites and the Israelites than some of the commentators maintain, at least on my reading of the texts. In any event, the God of Numbers 31 is hardly a paragon of morality. There seems to be no morally good reason for the slaughter of the young boys of Midian or the enslavement of the virgin girls, for example. There may be a prudential reason to kill the young boys: they are likely to grow up to be Midianite warriors and so a future security threat. But that is hardly a moral reason. Whether or not the punishments ordered by God are capricious or draconian, they do not seem to be morally appropriate. My point in noting the example is that the Bible does not provide unambiguous support for the idea that the universe is a moral order governed over by a moral and just divine power that will mete out morally justifiable responses to moral wrongdoing, forgiving where appropriate, punishing as called for, and even showing mercy on befitting occasions.

A. S. Pringle-Pattison identified in Kant's ethics a commitment to the morally ordered universe:

> The real postulate or implied presupposition of ethical action is simply that we are not acting in a world which nullifies our efforts, but that morality expresses a fundamental aspect of reality, so that in our doings and strivings we may be said, in a large sense, to have the universe somehow behind us.... The universe is a divine moral order, not a power hostile or indifferent to the life of ethical endeavor.[43]

Kant was aware that to the ordinary observer of human affairs, there seems to be something capricious, random, at best amoral about the distribution of happiness and unhappiness, pleasure and pain, success and failure, misery and joy, profit and loss, reward and punishment in human life. Why do good people suffer and evil people prosper, if the universe is either a good place or in the control of a good god? Why is virtue not invariably rewarded and wickedness always punished? The universe itself should maintain the moral order, or the divine controller of the universe should insure it so that the apparent randomness of the distribution of desirable and undesirable states is only temporary.[44] The latter is a view found in Kant's *Second Critique*.

---

[43] A. S. Pringle-Pattison, *The Idea of God in Modern Philosophy* (Oxford, 1920), 35.

[44] There are naturalistic and nonnaturalistic accounts of karmic causality in the literature. For the classical Hindu, it is dispositional. An action with a moral quality causes an event on the ordinary event causal chain, and it also causes the actor to form a disposition. The dispositions so formed, or karmic residues, at a propitious future occasion, will cause the actor to behave in a way that will produce in the actor happiness if the originating action was virtuous or unhappiness if it was wicked. These dispositions, or *samskaras*, are tendencies to act, think, experience, interpret, and so forth in such a way as to have the morally appropriate effect on the actor. The law of karma allows that actions have an immediate causal effect on the actor: the production of the residues or dispositions. This dispositional account of karmic effects, although it may better satisfy our intuitions than an account of causation over extreme temporal distance, runs afoul of those intuitions in another important respect. Karma not only is supposed to implant dispositions in us to do things that will make us happy or unhappy in the future, it is supposed to affect the very environment in which we will live and in which the dispositions will manifest themselves. The bodies of our future lives, the environments in which we will live, our health, genetic structure, wealth, social status, and so on are supposed to be influenced by our karmic residues. How that is supposed to occur is difficult to explain within the residues theory. Sankara and those in the Nyaya system favored a mediated and supernatural causal account. They argued that there must be a god to supervise or administer karmic effects in the material world. Only a theistic administrator can guarantee the union of virtue with happiness and wickedness with unhappiness and the environmental changes necessary for them to occur.

J. B. Schneewind points out that for Kant, "morality requires each of us to make ourselves perfectly virtuous... [and] it also requires that happiness be distributed in accordance with virtue."[45] These two requirements of morality, the perfection and the distribution requirements, Kant maintains, can be met only if two metaphysical postulates are the case: the immortality of the human soul and the existence of God. To satisfy the moral perfection requirement, humans require far more than a finite lifetime.[46] But Kant was well aware that virtue does not cause happiness. A supreme power in the universe is needed to insure the appropriate distribution of happiness. "Happiness proportioned to that morality, and this on grounds as disinterested as before, and solely from impartial reason... must lead to the supposition of the existence of God, as the necessary condition of the possibility of the *summum bonum.*"[47] Acting in accord with the Categorical Imperative produces moral worthiness, and moral worthiness is the supreme achievement humans can attain. But, as Schneewind notes,[48] that is not the *summum bonum.* That requires that happiness and punishment be distributed according to moral worthiness. God, Kant argues in the *Second Critique,* insures a causal link between human virtue and happiness and between moral wickedness and suffering. Morality is "not properly the doctrine how we should make ourselves happy, but how we should become worthy of happiness."[49] The moral worthiness of humans causes God to distribute happiness in the appropriate proportion. That is, the moral qualities of actions have a causal effect on the life of the agent – albeit mediated by God – even if in a life after death. Were Kant right about the role of God and the moral order of

[45] J. B. Schneewind, "Autonomy, Obligation, and Virtue" in *The Cambridge Companion to Kant,* edited by Paul Guyer (Cambridge, 1992), 332.

[46] Immanuel Kant, *Kant's Critique of Practical Reason and Other Works on the Theory of Ethics,* translated by T. K. Abbott (London, 1873, 1909), 218. Kant writes: "The realization of the *summum bonum* in the world is the necessary object of a will determinable by the moral. But in this will the perfect accordance of the mind with the moral law is the supreme condition of the *summum bonum.* This then must be possible, as well as its object, since it is contained in the command to promote the latter. Now, the perfect accordance of the will with the moral law is *holiness,* a perfection of which no rational being of the sensible world is capable at any moment of his existence. Since, nevertheless, it is required as practically necessary, it can only be found in a *progress in infinitum* towards that perfect accordance, and on the principles of pure practical reason it is necessary to assume such a practical progress as the real object of our will. Now, this *endless* progress is only possible on the supposition of an endless duration of the existence and personality of the same rational being (which is called the immortality of the soul)."

[47] Ibid., 220–21.

[48] Schneewind, "Autonomy, Obligation, and Virtue," 333.

[49] Kant, *Critique of Practical Reason,* 227.

the universe, we would not have to concern ourselves with responding to moral wrongdoing. In his later works, however, although still convinced that the universe is a moral harmony, Kant advocates significant retributive roles for humans to play in virtuously responding to moral evil.

Very much less optimistic and far more realistic about the moral workings of the universe, John Kekes notes: "Living a reasonable and decent life is neither necessary nor sufficient for overcoming the moral indifference of nature."[50] People everywhere do wicked things, and many of them get away scot-free and end up fat, happy, and rich in the bargain. That is just a basic fact of life. Neither the universe nor a divine power external to the universe seem to be moved by the evil that humans perpetrate on each other. There is no assurance that moral evil is dealt with in a morally justifiable way, at least in an ordinary lifetime, when it matters most to the victimized and society at large. Any moral theory, Kant's in the *Second Critique* included, that rests on the postulates of a morally ordered universe, the existence of a supernatural judge and appropriator of happiness and misery, and human immortality is sheer nonsense "on stilts." The universe is the venue, nothing more. Moral order, if there is ever to be any such thing, will be a human artifact. Whatever is to be done to those who perpetrate moral wickedness is either going to be done by humans or it is not going to be done at all.

We have an option in responding to evildoers we cannot forgive, even those we believe are unforgivable: not punishing them or not punishing them to the full extent they deserve, showing them mercy. Wiesenthal could have realized that he had no authority to forgive the SS soldier, but he, nonetheless, might have told Karl that he forgave him for participating in the atrocity as an act of mercy to make it possible for the Nazi to die with a soothed conscience. Mercy is not forgiveness. Forgiveness involves overcoming certain passions: the negative reactive attitudes such as resentment and moral hatred. Mercy is acting because of certain passions such as compassion, pity, and love. Mercy is compassionate forbearance. It is a gift that the wrongdoer does not merit and it can be shown only to those who deserve to be punished for what they have done. John Tasioulas characterizes mercy as "the putative ethical value that justifies leniency in the infliction of punishment that is due in accordance with justice."[51] Not all acts of leniency are acts of mercy. The leniency

[50] Ibid., 24.
[51] John Tasioulas, "Mercy," *Proceedings of the Aristotelian Society*, New Series, 103 (2003), 101–132, 101–102.

must be for reasons typically classed as charity. Tasioulas identifies those reasons as ones that "reflect a generalized love of humanity; in particular, a concern to alleviate serious misfortunes that the human condition is prey to."[52]

Insofar as no one can deserve mercy, there can never be a moral obligation on anyone to be merciful, though some have suggested that there may be what Kant called an "imperfect duty" to be merciful. On my view, mercy is always supererogatory. The only grounds on which being merciful to a wrongdoer could be justified, particularly to one that does not warrant forgiveness, must be moral grounds. Mercy is justifiable only if there are morally relevant features, other than the demands of retributive justice, that are to be found in the wrongdoer's situation vis-à-vis the wrongdoing. Mercy can be shown only to a person. As is the case with forgiveness, it never touches the moral evaluation of the deed. It does not lower the amount of retributive punishment that the wrongdoer deserves.

Tasioulas offers four features or grounds for mercy. Each may be suggested by asking a relevant question: Does the evildoer suffer from a morally debilitating condition? Are there charitable reasons for leniency? Does the evildoer suffer from some grave misfortune that will be exacerbated by the administration of the full measure of the punishment that is deserved? Has there been sincere repentance? Enough has been said about the fourth ground, although Tasioulas expands repentance to include undergoing "profound remorse," radically reforming one's character, and "making apologetic reparation to those wronged."[53] The SS soldier in Wiesenthal's story cannot meet all of those conditions. The Grim Reaper will not give him the requisite time, and there is no way to make "apologetic reparation" to the dead.

By a "debilitating condition," Tasioulas has in mind upbringing and social and economic conditions. In Chapter 11, I discuss how certain cultural and social impacts on willful acts should be treated when they are offered as excuses for untoward behavior. Suffice it here to say that I am not persuaded that they provide a very persuasive reason for being merciful to an evildoer. There may be charitable reasons for being merciful in cases in which an understanding of a situation's wider context may provide a convincing explanation for a wrongdoer's actions, even though the failure of the wrongdoer to overcome obstacles to behaving

---

[52] Ibid., 102.
[53] Ibid., 118.

morally that were inherent for him or her in the situation reflects badly on the character of the wrongdoer.

In the third type of case, mercy might be extended to someone in the throes of a severe illness that has nothing whatever to do with the person having done something evil. Mercy then may take the suffering of the evildoer into account and mitigate deserved punishment, a classic case of lenience. The SS soldier, for example, is dying of wounds most definitely not inflicted in the square where he participated in an atrocity and for which he seeks forgiveness. It is reasonable to think that the suffering he is undergoing physically is being exacerbated by his continued feelings of guilt and remorse, which could be relieved by an insincere utterance of forgiveness by the randomly chosen Jew. Such an utterance might be understood as an act of compassion driven by humanitarian concerns.

Despite what Murphy argues about mercy being an autonomous moral virtue,[54] I agree with those who worry, including Saint Anselm, that it may never be virtuous to be merciful. If a wrongdoer deserves a certain punishment and is not forgivable, not to administer that punishment or its full extent is tempering justice. I think this is especially true if the wrongdoing is particularly grave, as most certainly is the case with the SS soldier. He willfully participated in murder and genocide, and it was not the case that he did not know what he was doing when he was helping exterminate Jews. To temper justice is to do an injustice, and that is generally understood to be a vice. Consequently, acting mercifully toward a wrongdoer may be a vice.

Moshe Bejski makes another powerful point against mercy as a virtuous response to moral evil. He argues that an act of mercy in the case of the SS soldier "would have been a kind of betrayal and repudiation of the memory of millions of innocent victims who were unjustly murdered."[55] I suppose there must be occasions when being merciful is a morally good thing to do primarily because it makes restoration and reconciliation possible. But those must be cases where the evil done is not preferential or as grotesque as that committed by Karl and his fellow SS soldiers, even if in their cases it was perverse because they had, for whatever reasons, adopted norms of behavior that were a far cry from justifiable moral principles.

There is, as mentioned throughout the chapter, another way to deal with moral wrongdoers. It is to perform a retributive duty, that is, to

---

[54] Jeffrie Murphy and Jean Hampton, *Forgiveness and Mercy* (Cambridge, 1988), 166.
[55] Moshe Bejski in *The Sunflower*, 115.

punish them. Punish them because that is what they deserve and do so to the fullest morally allowable degree. In the words of Gilbert and Sullivan from *The Mikado*: "Make the punishment fit the crime." There are all manner of arguments about exactly what punishment fits the crime in specific cases and how generally "fitness" is fairly to be determined.[56] There is no precise set of mechanical rules or a definitive set of conditions that determines whether or not a particular punishment fits the offense. Fit in the case of punishment is what H. L. A. Hart called a defeasible[57] or "open-textured" concept.[58] A concept's application is defeasible if we cannot contrive a complete list of sufficient conditions of its felicitous application because any or some member of such a set is always open to a defeating condition that would void the concept's use – that is, make it inappropriate or infelicitous in the circumstances. We can comfortably offer a list of conditions for such a concept's application only if we conjoin with that list a caveat indicating that the presence of certain features in the circumstances voids the applicability of the concept.

The defeasible conditions for fit punishment could range over descriptions of relevant factors regarding the offense, the authority of the punisher, the age of the offender, and so forth, and the inability of the offender to understand the message of punishment, that is, why he or she is being punished. If the punisher is unable to deliver the message in a way that is unambiguous to the offender, fit probably is not achieved. There are a number of different ways in which the offender may lack the ability to understand the message. These might include diminished mental capacity, mental illness, physical impairment, language incompetence, and so on. On the other hand, the fault may lie with the punisher, who may fail to deliver the message successfully in a variety of ways or for a plethora of simple or complex reasons.

There is another aspect to punishment that should be noted: the impact on the moral status of the punisher of insuring that moral wrongdoers receive the punishment they deserve. In the *Metaphysics of Morals*, Kant tells what some writers refer to as the "notorious" Island Story. Imagine a community on an island that has caught, convicted, and imprisoned murderers who are awaiting their executions. The members of the community decide to abandon the island and disperse throughout the world.

---

[56] See French, *The Virtues of Vengeance*, chapter 7, "The Tailored Fit."

[57] See H. L. A. Hart, "The Ascription of Responsibility and Rights," *Proceedings of the Aristotelian Society*, 1948–49, 171–94.

[58] H. L. A. Hart, *The Concept of Law* (Oxford, 1961), 124.

Kant writes that before the diaspora can begin, "the last murderer remaining in prison would first have to be executed."[59] What moral reason could there be for the community members to kill murderers who are unlikely to have any further impact on those members' lives? There are unlikely also to be any deterrent consequences of the islanders carrying out the death penalties. Potential murderers are not likely to desist from their felonious deeds upon learning that in a now-defunct island community convicted murderers were executed.

Kant argues that the murderers must be executed "so that each has done to him what his deeds deserve and blood guilt does not cling to the people for not having insisted upon this punishment."[60] His account is both retributive and consequentialist. It is consequentialist with respect to the members of the community. One of the two reasons to carry out the punishment is so that the community members will not carry the "blood guilt" with them as they take up residence in other communities. The "blood guilt" to which Kant refers is not the "blood guilt" of the murderers' crimes. That is handled retributively with the executions of the murderers. The "blood guilt" the islanders would bear would be due to their failure of moral duty to fit punishment to the crime according to "the strict law of retribution." The murderers on the island do not have a right to be punished. If they had such a right, they probably would not want to exercise it. The retributive duty to punish wrongdoers is what is owed to their victims. It is the victims who have the rights that cannot be ignored or abrogated. Where the offenses are monstrous, where it is immoral to forgive, and no conditions for mercy are present, we have a moral obligation to the victim(s) to punish to the fullest extent of fit. Our very conception of moral wrongdoing is the source of that obligation.

Wiesenthal's response to the plea of the SS soldier for forgiveness, his refusing to do it, may be construed as an act of punishment. It is, of course, the only form of punishment that Wiesenthal, in the circumstances, can administer. Is it fitting? Not really, though I suppose much depends on how important the SS soldier believes the forgiveness of a Jew is to how he will spend the eternal life his Catholic faith promised him. He seems to think it is essential to cleansing his guilt and, presumably, to making salvation for him possible. Whether or not there is an afterlife for him or anyone or a heaven or a hell is irrelevant. He deserves to believe that he

---

[59] Immanuel Kant, *The Metaphysics of Morals,* translated by Mary Gregor (Cambridge, 1996), 106.
[60] Ibid.

will be eternally punished in the most horrific way. Of course, Karl surely deserves much more than to die with a troubled conscience. By killing him, the war has accidentally mitigated the punishment he deserves. Perhaps he should consider himself lucky. I share Ozick's condemnation of him: "Let the SS man die unshriven. Let him go to hell."[61]

[61] Ozick, 220.

5

Assessing Attempts at Moral Originality

In the *Tractatus Logico-Philosophicus*, Wittgenstein remarks parenthetically, "Ethics and aesthetics are one and the same."[1] Within the structural framework he develops in the *Tractatus*, normative judgments cannot express propositions because there can be no value in the world of facts. Normative judgments are concerned with what "is higher" or what lies outside the accidental world of the facts. Consequently, there can be no normative facts, so normative judgments cannot be truth-apt. However, for Wittgenstein, the good or the bad exercise of the will "alters the limits of the world, not the facts, making it a different world for the happy man from the world of the unhappy man."[2] Ethics provides normative categories, such as good and bad, right and wrong, for assessing exercises of the will or the creations they produce. Aesthetics provides comparable categories for evaluating exercises of will (performances), creations, or works; but, it is generally held, it does so for altogether different reasons than ethics, hence, the provocative nature of Wittgenstein's remark.

Following Wittgenstein's lead, it would seem that ethics and aesthetics must either apply a different norm of correctness than the truth norm to assessments within their realms or adopt some version of an error theory to account for what in their assessments appear to be expressions of belief that have propositional content, a central claim identified with J. L. Mackie's account of ethics.[3] Nishi Shah correctly describes the basis of Mackie's view with respect to moral discourse:

> The objective purport of moral discourse requires that values be part of the fabric of the universe, but the universe, at least as it has been disclosed to

---

[1] Ludwig Wittgenstein, *Tractatus Logico-Philosophicus*, translated by D. F. Pears and B. F. McGuinness (London, 1961), 6.421.
[2] Ibid., 6.43.
[3] J. L. Mackie, *Ethics: Inventing Right and Wrong* (London, 1977).

us by the natural sciences, contains no such "queer" properties. Nor have the natural sciences disclosed any perceptual or other capacities that would allow us to detect the presence of such properties, even if they did exist.[4]

If we reject error theory as an account of normative discourse, the alternative norm of correctness in ethical assessment might be some version of social utility or of an agent-focused or agent-based conception of virtue.[5] In aesthetics, it might be a norm of beauty, although there may be other higher-norms in each field that define "ethically good" or "aesthetically good." "X is ethically good" commends X, Mackie's term, as satisfying certain requirements or interests as fixed by a moral norm.[6] Along the same lines, "Y is aesthetically good" commends Y as satisfying certain requirements or interests as fixed by an aesthetic norm.

Matters become cloudy when the denial of the truth-aptness of normative discourse is open to either a cognitivist or a noncognitivist interpretation. If normative assessments such as my wife's judgment "Georgia O'Keeffe's *Ram's Head, White Hollyhock and Little Hills* is beautiful" expresses her belief that the painting is beautiful, then we may ask whether her belief is correct. The norm of correctness for beliefs usually is that they are correct if and only if they are true, so the belief that the Georgia O'Keeffe painting is beautiful is true if and only if that Georgia O'Keeffe painting is beautiful. A noncognitivist would say that this norm of correctness for beliefs, as applied to my wife's assessment of the painting, is not itself a belief and so is not truth-apt. A cognitivist would say that this norm of correctness is a truth-apt belief, so the belief ascribed to my wife has the normative property of being correct if and only if its content is true. The position I recommend might be seen as somewhere between both of these views. It is to admit that normative assessments are truth-apt in that they express beliefs and in that regard they are false; however, applying the truth norm to them is unproductive if we are trying to understand normative discourse. Some other higher-norm, other than the truth-norm, should be preferred to settle correctness in judgments in normative discourse. What I am recommending may be a form of fictionalism although I don't think anything much hangs on the label. In any event, I am not here interested in pursuing that issue. In response to a Navy chaplain's provocative question, I want to investigate

---

[4] Nishi Shah, "The Limits of Normative Detachment," draft presented at the University of California, Berkeley, October 23, 2008.

[5] See Michael Slote, "Agent-Based Virtue Ethics," *Midwest Studies in Philosophy*, XX (1996), 83–101.

[6] Mackie, 54–65.

whether the aesthetically valued property "original,"[7] perhaps a requirement or interest fixed by a higher-norm that licenses the attribution of
aesthetic goodness to a work, might have a twin in the ethical assessment of actions and proposed principles of behavior. What would moral
originality be like?

I

The idea that originality may be a positive ethical evaluative category,
as it is often taken to be one in aesthetic criticism, is not evident in the
standard textbook ethical theories. From a Kantian or utilitarian point
of view, one will be credited for doing one's duty or what is right in
one's circumstances, but no additional moral credit is awarded for doing
so in a new or novel way. Also, aesthetic assessments of artworks are
generally thought of as work specific and not universalizable, whereas
moral judgments about actions or agents typically are supposed to be
universalizable and that is often regarded as an element in the norm of
correctness of ethical judgments.

   Works of art are *works*, and that, as Colin Radford claims, entails that
they are the product of a particular person's (or persons') inspiration
and skill and are made at a particular time and a certain place, and all of
those factors are essential to their production as the specific, unique exercises of will that they are.[8] A common feature of comparative aesthetic
assessments is that what is judged to be aesthetically meritorious in one
work is not necessarily meritorious when it appears in another work no
matter how much the second resembles the first. Although artworks may
be replicated, they cannot be re-produced; although copies may be made
of them, positive aesthetic judgments on the originals seldom transfer to
the copies. The originality of works of art, often cited by critics as a consideration in their aesthetic assessments, however, is not always a positive
factor because some works that may claim originality are aesthetically
atrocious and that characteristic of them usually trumps any claim they
may have to being of aesthetic merit because they are novel. Sometimes
the "shock of the new" is just plain shocking to aesthetic sensibilities and
better tossed on the junk heap.

   Two distinct concepts of originality occur in the assessment of artworks.
One, original$_1$, is just an historical claim of newness and is neither a

---

[7] See Immanuel Kant, *Critique of Judgment* (1790), translated by J. C. Meredith (Oxford, 1978), section 46.

[8] Colin Radford, "Fakes," *Mind* (January 1978), 76.

positive nor a negative aesthetic evaluative. It is not a normative claim; it is a statement of fact, and propositions expressing it are truth-apt and respond to the truth-norm. The other, parasitic on the first, original$_2$, is a positive assessment of aesthetic merit, a normative judgment of aesthetic goodness, of that aspect or aspects in which the work is novel, original$_1$. A critic, upon walking into an art gallery and seeing a recently hung show of paintings by an unknown artist, may, without sarcastic overtones, utter, "That's original." By that, the critic may mean that the paintings are unlike any the critic had previously seen, or the critic may mean that the paintings, in some respect previously unobserved by him or her in other paintings, have a positive aesthetic merit that may make them valuable as works of art. With regard to original$_2$ in art criticism, Bruce Vermazon maintains: "A minimal requirement on the original object seems to be that the respect in which the object differs from past objects must also be one respect in which the object is good."[9] Some works may be identified as original$_1$ ("Nothing like that's been done before"), but the properties of those works that set them historically apart from others may not be regarded as aesthetically valuable, may not be a respect in which the works are assessed as aesthetically good, by those experiencing them or in a position to aesthetically assess them. ("It's original, but it's terrible!") Art critics and audiences are trained or raised to a comfort zone within existing paradigms of art and may find it intellectually and emotionally difficult to commend novel pieces, to extend the criteria of aesthetic goodness much beyond the boundaries of those paradigms. Once certified as aesthetically meritorious by the art community or an appropriate subgroup within it, however, the aesthetic goodness of the historically original properties of a piece that contribute to its being aesthetically good of its art form will remain so even after the novelty of the piece has worn off. At least, it will unless there is a tectonic shift in the accepted conception of aesthetic goodness relative to that art form, unless the concept of aesthetically good comes to have a radically modified norm of correctness in aesthetic discourse. Was disco music ever good? In effect, a work's aesthetic merit resides in its experiential or presentational properties and not in its place in the history of its art form. Simply put, originality, understood as newness or novelty (original$_1$), is insufficient to convey aesthetic merit on a work because it is not a normative assessment.

---

[9] Bruce Vermazon, "The Aesthetic Value of Originality," *Midwest Studies in Philosophy*, XVI (1991), 271.

The uniqueness of humans and/or the peculiar historical contexts in which they act have not been of serious consideration in the dominant ethical theories at least since the Enlightenment. For example, arguments that antebellum American southerners who kept slaves and treated them as property should not be morally denigrated because that was the existing norm in their social world, the way of life in which they were raised, and so on, are likely to be dismissed as unacceptable exculpatory excuses from negative moral assessments of their characters and actions. More generous moralists may allow some mitigation owing to historical circumstances, but generally not to the point of altogether erasing all moral condemnation. Think, for example, of the way Thomas Jefferson's slaveholding is typically assessed. I take up this subject again in Chapter 11.

Historical references aside, it seems that whatever we as individuals may be that makes us essentially different from each other, that makes us unique individuals historically situated, has not been a determining factor in the way standard textbook ethical theories construct their accounts of the moral assessment of our actions, works, or characters. Those differences that mean so much to us as individuals are homogenized or forgotten behind veils of ignorance and in moral principles, standards, and rules that require a uniformity of treatment and impartiality. If we judge any person's actions to be good or bad, we are told that we are logically and morally bound to make the same judgment of the relevantly similar actions of any other person or of the same person on another occasion in similar circumstances. Failure to do so is to make a special case out of the subject of our assessment, and that would violate such ethical norms as fairness, justice, and equality of treatment among all members of the moral community.

In most standard moral evaluations of human actions following rules and adhering to principles tends to discourage anything in human actions that might be called "morally meritorious originality." A person might be praised for finding clever, even new (original$_1$), ways of meeting moral obligations – for example, fulfilling a promise to accompany you on your walk by riding along side of you on a yak and not only thereby doing what was promised, but giving you unexpected mirth – but not if that person defines his or her moral obligations in an idiosyncratic or novel manner. In such cases, the default position is to judge the actions negatively. Historically original decision principles or personal-behavioral imperatives are not encouraged or praised when they are introduced. Perhaps they should not be. They certainly should not be just because they are novel. In that regard, they are in the same boat as historically original works of art facing stolid aesthetic critics. The onus of justification falls on the novel.

Individuals generally are not licensed by standard ethical theories to make special cases of themselves or to declare their actions morally justified on the basis of a moral principle or rule they have invented, whether in a flash of inspiration or after weeks of contemplation on the nature of justice. Suppose a warrior in the heroic culture portrayed by Homer failed to behave according to the warrior code and acted compassionately toward a hated enemy on the battlefield. When chastised by the society of his peers, he is not likely to sway them from their disapprobation of him by maintaining that he was behaving rightly in the combat situation because he now abides by a moral principle he has invented that requires him to love his enemies and turn the other cheek.

Many of the traditional ethical theories might be thought of as requiring behavior that copies, duplicates, and replicates actions following or according with preferred principles and rules. In similar circumstances, any member of the moral community should act this way. High moral marks go to conformity. That is hardly the case in the aesthetic assessment of works.

Even if two works are indistinguishable in all experiential details, they may be judged radically differently. In such cases, originality (original$_2$) may have the casting vote on aesthetic merit. One painting may be a Turner original – *Snow Storm–Steam Boat off a Harbour's Mouth Making Signals in Shallow Water, and Going by the Lead. The Author Was in this Storm on the Night the Ariel Left Harwich* – the other, a virtually identical copy made by an art student at the Tate Gallery where the Turner is hung. The Turner gets very high marks. It is aesthetically good, very good. The student's work, no matter how competent, is a good copy, but just a copy. There is no sense in which it can be original$_2$. It is pleasing to me, and were the student to sell it to me, I would hang it in my office, but I would be unethically misleading the art student were I to tell her to just keep replicating the Turner and what she produces will be aesthetically good.

Art works are not unique when it comes to some of the factors that play a crucial role in the assessment of their aesthetic merit, a point made by T. E. Wilkerson.[10] "Good" may be an aesthetic normative when uttered by art teachers in reference to a student's choice of color, use of shapes and shading, and so forth. What may be called presentational assessments

---

[10] T. E. Wilkerson, "Uniqueness in Art and Morals," *Philosophy*, 58 (July 1983), 307.

of works generally are universalizable. If a painting is aesthetically good as an organization of shapes or in its use of colors, all accurate copies of that painting must be judged good in that sense as well. An accurate copy of the *Mona Lisa*, were such a thing possible, would be just as good presentationally as the original hanging in the Louvre. And the same, of course, can be said of the work of the Tate art student and the Turner hanging in the gallery. Wilkerson summarizes this point: "If one painting is aesthetically successful because of its use of light and color contrast, then so is any other relevantly similar painting."[11] Some things "work" aesthetically within an art form, others just do not... until they do. And there's the rub!

Art history's focus on masterpieces may be responsible for the fact that we tend to forget about presentational normatives when we think about aesthetic assessment. Think of the notorious case of van Meegeren's *Meeting at Emmaus*. The painting was done in the style of Vermeer and presented to and accepted by the art world as a Vermeer. When it was thought to be a work by Vermeer, it was appraised one way, but when it was discovered that van Meegeren had painted it in the twentieth century to pass it off as a Vermeer, its monetary and aesthetic value radically sunk. How could that happen? It is the very same painting on the very same canvas. Art critics, curators, and the general public were hoodwinked with respect to its place in the history of painting, but when the deception was discovered, why should the value of the work change? The painting qua painting did not change. If it was aesthetically good when it was believed to be an eighteenth-century Vermeer, why should it not be still aesthetically good after we learn it was painted by van Meegeren? With respect to presentational aesthetic assessment, how can it be of less merit when discovered to be a forgery?

Meeting at Emmaus's loss of aesthetic, as well as monetary, value typically will be explained in terms of what it is for a painting to be a Vermeer as opposed to being a van Meegeren. "We value Vermeer's works much more highly than van Meegeren's, however similar they may be, because Vermeer was fashioning a new style, while van Meegeren was merely reproducing a style long outdated and well within the competence of a talented modern artist."[12] Basically, Vermeer's paintings, or at least some of them, were original$_2$. Van Meegeren's painting can make no such claim, even if it satisfies presentational norms.

[11] Ibid.
[12] Ibid., 308.

Works by Duchamp and Picasso were original$_1$ when first exhibited and were not met with critical praise, although in time they were assessed to be original$_2$, and fashioned new styles, founded new paradigms, launched new movements, and conspicuously altered then-current fashion in visual art. The first person to paint a portrait of Elvis Presley on black velvet also was, no doubt, doing something original$_1$ but not something that was also good aesthetically in the aspect in which it was original. The first black-velvet painting of Elvis might bring a fair price at an antiques auction but not because of its aesthetic merit.

Most artworks, of course, may be judged as accomplishing nothing especially original$_1$ or original$_2$, although they are decent enough works in presentational terms within the style or milieu in which they were created. That might be the case with both the Tate student's copies of Turner paintings and van Meegeren's "Vermeers." Or, they may fail on all counts, presentational and as originals$_2$, and be consignable to a dumpster. Aesthetic assessments of specific works in which originality$_2$ plays the deciding role (e.g., "fashioning a new style") are not universalizable. When done by X, a particular work is good, but when replicated or imitated by Y or by X, it does not have the same aesthetic merit. James Wood, reviewing Ernest Hemingway's final novel in the *New York Times Book Review*, writes:

> The danger of a truly original style, of course, is that it has smooth copiers but does not have rough equals. That which is imitable is neutered by repetition. What cannot be imitated is what is truly original, not necessarily because it was so great but because it was, simply, first; it has a hard and unbreakable primacy.... What is great in him [Hemingway] is that, as it were, he preceded his own bad influence.[13]

Originality$_2$ as a positive factor in aesthetic assessment seems clearest to me in the visual arts, some of the performance arts, in music composition, and in creative writing. I am reluctant to talk about the role of originality in classical music performance because I know so little about the way performances, for example, of Mozart's *Symphony No. 40 in G Minor*, aesthetically should be evaluated. The composition surely gains high marks for its originality$_2$, but I wonder whether classical music performances are to be critically evaluated more on how well they replicate a certain established standard rather than on their improvisation,[14] whereas

---

[13] James Wood, "Hemingway's Final Novel," *New York Times Book Review* (July 11, 1999), 15.
[14] See Aron Edidin, "Look What They've Done to My Song," *Midwest Studies in Philosophy*, XVI (1991), 394–420.

improvisation in jazz is highly prized. In any event, as with jazz, in many forms of music performance and surely in composition, originality$_2$, including innovative variations on an existing theme, is the goal of the musician and the composer. In popular music of the 1950s, where I am more at home, Fats Domino's *Ain't That a Shame*, Little Richard's *Long Tall Sally*, and Ivory Joe Hunter's *I Almost Lost My Mind* have far greater aesthetic merit – because they are original$_2$ compositions and performances – than the same songs covered by Pat Boone (which should not even count as variations on the originals, although some might describe them as "smooth copies"), despite the popularity of the Boone releases among white audiences when they were released.

It may be virtually impossible, as Wilkerson notes, to "sustain the distinction between judgments that concentrate on the content of a work of art, on what we see [read, hear, etc.], and judgments that concentrate on the genesis, on the historical location, of the work."[15] What is highlighted in aesthetic assessments depends on the evaluator "giving proper weight to certain features at the expense of others," and that frequently requires information about the historical context in which a work was created. "We need to know which details are important, which criteria of success or failure we should use, which artistic gestures are in context striking or not, significant or not, deliberate or not."[16]

One way in which a work might satisfy the criteria of original$_2$ is, as Vermazon maintains, by transforming something recognizable or expected into something unfamiliar.[17] A writer grabs and holds the audience's attention by using familiar words in a jarring, disorderly rhythm, inflections drumming a beat that propels the plot. Think, for example, of David Milch's use of "fuck" in its multiple variations in the dialogue of the characters in the *Deadwood* series. Alternatively, recall the defamiliarization of Georgia O'Keeffe's flowers and Marcel Duchamp's *L.H.O.O.Q.*, a postcard-type reproduction of the *Mona Lisa* on which he drew a mustache and goatee. Was Duchamp just defacing a famous painting or forcing the viewer to see something iconic in a different, ironic, unfamiliar way and, indeed, given the title he used for it, in a mildly obscene way, telling those who knew the French pun, "She is hot in the ass"?

Presentational aesthetic norms acquire their content from the dominant paradigms of correctness established in a particular art form and

[15] Wilkerson, 308–309.
[16] Ibid., 309.
[17] Vermazon, 272–73.

from basic empirical facts about the medium in which they are applied, or from what may be called, after the later Wittgenstein, the grammatical propositions of that art form. "The colour octahedron is grammar; since it says that you can speak of a reddish blue but not of a reddish green, etc."[18] When a work (original$_1$) is presented, evaluators typically apply the dominant presentational evaluative norms. What is new or novel about the work may achieve what those norms require to be considered aesthetically good. It is then judged to be original$_2$. The original$_1$ work, however, may not satisfy the current norms of aesthetic goodness of its art form. It may offend them in radical ways. It may be ungrammatical. Nonetheless, critics and/or the artist may argue that when a higher-norm of correctness for aesthetic goodness is understood in a certain way, the work deserves to be assessed as aesthetically good. The work is out of the old box but resists being tossed in the dumpster of artistic failures. It demands a rethinking of the box because there is something about what is novel about it that is aesthetically considerable, that shouts out for praise, and that can't be ignored. The work still may be rejected because the existing norms are stubborn and significant changes in them require considerable persuasive argument. It surely isn't beautiful, but then perhaps beauty should not be the higher-norm. If such an argument is ultimately successful in persuading the relevant art community that the work is aesthetically good when that is understood in a way different from what had been the received position, the work will gain the status of original$_2$. It is not that tastes just inexplicably change. Tastes, by and large, trail the argumentative struggle to define aesthetic goodness, the higher-norm, in an art form. The sorts of arguments that will be most readily persuasive in this regard no doubt will have a foundation in existing presentational rules and grammar and will offer nuanced versions of those rules or expansions on the grammar of the art form. Radical norm revision will take more time to have an impact on the relevant portion of what Arthur Danto called the "artworld." Was a novel work that offended the norm of correctness in aesthetic evaluation current at its inception aesthetically good before a new norm, one that it satisfies, replaced the older norm? Was *Les Demoiselles d'Avignon* aesthetically good when Picasso first showed it in 1907?

  Les Demoiselles d'Avignon violated the existing norms of painting nudes insofar as the nude women in it are overtly on sexual display, staring

---

[18] Ludwig Wittgenstein, *Philosophical Remarks*, edited by Rush Rhees, translated by Raymond Hargreaves and Roger White (Oxford, 1975), #39.

out at the viewer, perhaps inviting the viewer into their brothel. They are deformed, and some wear or hide behind what appear to be African tribal masks. The painting is predominantly created in diagonal lines and angular planes rather than the Impressionist's color and light, giving it a violent undertone. It is cubist in its attempt to depict three dimensions without the use of perspective. *Les Demoiselles d'Avignon* was greeted with virtually unanimous negative critical responses. Georges Braque called it a "caustic and bitter use of paint." Matisse thought it was a joke. Even collectors of Picasso's earlier paintings, like Gertrude Stein, were horrified at what they regarded as the ugliness of *Les Demoiselles d'Avignon*. Today, the higher-norms governing assessments of aesthetic goodness having been changed in the relevant community, *Les Demoiselles d'Avignon* is among the most prized possessions in the Museum of Modern Art, considered a masterpiece.

II

Following the lead of the use of "original" in aesthetic assessment, may we distinguish when "morally original" describes new or novel principles of behavior that violate existing ethical norms of correctness in the circumstances (original$_1$) from when "morally original" describes novel principles that can be justified as morally good or right and so are genuine alternative ethical norms to those currently in fashion (original$_2$)? Uses of "original" in ethical assessment probably most frequently occur in moderately negative judgments by those adhering to the status quo, as in "Well, that was original!" accompanied by a certain amount of tsking.

As with aesthetic cases of originality$_2$, we should expect that principles espoused in putative moral originality$_2$ cases will incorporate many of the status quo norms of correctness in behavior while modifying, replacing, or discarding only a few, or they may introduce a wholesale change in the norms of moral correctness or ethical goodness. Wholesale shifts in moral norms will meet with the greatest resistance and require more persuasive argumentation than minor changes if they are to be accepted as new bases for the ethical assessment of conduct.

Note the exchange, intended by the author to be humorous although with serious underpinnings, among Doolittle, Higgins, and Pickering in George Bernard Shaw's *Pygmalion*:

DOOLITTLE. If you want the girl, I'm not so set on having her back home again but what I might be open to an arrangement. Regarded in the light of a young woman, she's a fine handsome girl. As a daughter she's not worth her keep; and so I tell you straight. All I ask is my rights as a father; and you're the last man alive to expect me to let her go for nothing.... Well, what's a five-pound note to you? And what's Eliza to me?

PICKERING. I think you ought to know, Doolittle, that Mr. Higgins's intentions are entirely honorable.

DOOLITTLE. Course they are, Governor. If I thought they wasn't, I'd ask fifty.

HIGGINS [revolted]. Do you mean to say, you callous rascal, that you would sell your daughter for £50?

DOOLITTLE. Not in a general way I wouldn't; but to oblige a gentleman like you I'd do a good deal, I do assure you.

PICKERING. Have you no morals, man?

DOOLITTLE [unabashed]. Can't afford them, Governor. Neither could you if you was as poor as me. Not that I mean any harm, you know. But if Liza is going to have a bit out of this, why not me too?... I ask you, what am I? I'm one of the undeserving poor: that's what I am. Think of what that means to a man. It means that he's up against middle class morality all the time. If there's anything going, and I put in for a bit of it, it's always the same story: "You're undeserving; so you can't have it."... I don't need less than a deserving man: I need more. I don't eat less hearty than him; and I drink a lot more.... Well, they charge me just the same for everything as they charge the deserving. What is middle class morality? Just an excuse for never giving me anything. Therefore, I ask you, as two gentlemen, not to play that game on me. I'm playing straight with you. I ain't pretending to be deserving. I'm undeserving; and I mean to go on being undeserving. I like it; and that's the truth. Will you take advantage of a man's nature to do him out of the price of his own daughter what he's brought up and fed and clothed by the sweat of his brow until she's growed big enough to be interesting to you two gentlemen? Is five pounds unreasonable? I put it to you; and I leave it to you.... Undeserving poverty is my line. Taking one station in society with another, it's – it's – well, it's the only one that has any ginger in it, to my taste.

HIGGINS. I suppose we must give him a fiver.

PICKERING. He'll make a bad use of it, I'm afraid.

DOOLITTLE. Not me, Governor, so help me I won't. Don't you be afraid that I'll save it and spare it and live idle on it. There won't be a penny of it left by Monday: I'll have to go to work same as if I'd never had it. It won't pauperize me, you bet. Just one good spree for myself and the missus, giving pleasure to ourselves and employment to others, and satisfaction to you to think it's not been throwed away. You couldn't spend it better.

HIGGINS [taking out his pocket book and coming between Doolittle and the piano]. This is irresistible. Let's give him ten. [He offers two notes to the dustman].

DOOLITTLE. No, Governor.... Ten pounds is a lot of money: it makes a man feel prudent like; and then goodbye to happiness. You give me what I ask you, Governor: not a penny more, and not a penny less.

PICKERING. Why don't you marry that missus of yours? I rather draw the line at encouraging that sort of immorality.

DOOLITTLE. Tell her so, Governor: tell her so. I'm willing. It's me that suffers by it. I've no hold on her. I got to be agreeable to her. I got to give her presents. I got to buy her clothes something sinful. I'm a slave to that woman, Governor, just because I'm not her lawful husband. And she knows it too. Catch her marrying me! Take my advice, Governor: marry Eliza while she's young and don't know no better. If you don't you'll be sorry for it after. If you do, she'll be sorry for it after; but better you than her, because you're a man, and she's only a woman and don't know how to be happy anyhow.

HIGGINS. Pickering: if we listen to this man another minute, we shall have no convictions left. [To Doolittle] Five pounds I think you said.[19]

Doolittle's principles are morally original$_1$ but, idiosyncratic as they may be, are they also morally original$_2$? He certainly thinks they are, and later in the play an American philanthropist endorses them by bequeathing Doolittle three thousand pounds a year on the condition that he lecture on ethics six times a year for the Moral Reform World League because Higgins had extolled Doolittle to him as the most original moralist in England. What are Doolittle's principles? (1) A father may sell his daughter for five pounds on the condition that the buyer must have honorable intentions regarding her. If the buyer does not have honorable intentions, the price is fifty pounds and then only to "oblige a gentleman." (2) A person should know himself and not dissemble, even for a personal gain. (In that regard he hardly deviates from the existing ethical norms, albeit many of those who subscribe to those norms probably honor that one in the breach more than does Doolittle.) The old-school moralist, faltering in the face of the "shock of the new morality," Colonel Pickering, having failed to be convincing with the principle that it is immoral to sell one's children, insists that Doolittle should not be paid the five pounds for his daughter because Doolittle will squander the money. Doolittle takes Pickering to be suggesting that he will save the money and disabuses Pickering and Higgins of that by insisting on another of his principles. (3) Funds earned in such an exchange should be spent in a way that distributes happiness across or benefits as wide a population as possible. Doolittle explains that in spending the five pounds on a party he will be giving pleasure to his misses and himself, employment to those who will provide the strong drink and entertainment, and a sense

[19] George Bernard Shaw, *Pygmalion* (1916), Act II.

of satisfaction to Higgins, who will realize his five pounds was spent to benefit so many. (4) Too much money defeats happiness with prudence. A reason not to accept ten pounds for his daughter is that amount would make Doolittle feel prudent, and that would block his munificence.

Are Doolittle's novel principles morally good ones? Is he a most original$_2$ moralist? His second principle is hardly revolutionary, and although he puts it to an unorthodox justificatory task, in itself it seems a morally good one. Principle 3 looks to be a version, again somewhat strained when put to work by Doolittle, of the principle of utility. Principles 1 and 4 are more clearly novel, but are they morally good principles? What makes a principle a moral good one?

Recalling Wittgenstein's *Tractatus* position or Mackie's account of ethics, it cannot be that good moral principles can be formulated as propositions that correctly state objective facts, although they may be formulated in a way that makes them appear to be truth-apt. There are no moral properties in the universe that make moral principles good or right were those properties to be instantiated in them, nor are sentences that state moral principles true (or false), there being nothing in the universe to make them so. No moral principles are revealed in the scientific study of the universe; no powers that compel motivation for us to do one thing rather than another are to be found "out there." In Mackie's terms, "morality is not to be discovered but to be made."[20] Morality is a product of our organizing and governing our circumstances and relationships (to other people, animals, inanimate objects, the earth, etc.) by rules and principles and policies, and those are located, sometimes constitutively, in our institutions and practices. We may think that our moral principles are institution transcendent, embedded in the facts of the universe, but that is a fiction, a "presupposition failure," sustained by and given false credence in the very institutions in whose rules and principles the concept of moral goodness (and badness) is given content. This does not mean that certain all-too-naturally-human proclivities and attributes are not causally responsible for the sorts of social organizations and institutions we have, more or less out of necessity, created. Mackie writes that "a moral sense, law, and justice are needed to enable men to live together in communities"[21] in the face of "limited resources and limited sympathies [that] together generate both competition leading to conflict and an

---

[20] Mackie, 123.
[21] Ibid., 108.

absence of what would be mutually beneficial cooperation."[22] The purpose of moral principles (or of morality) is to counteract in us, as much as that is possible, those limitations, to make our lives less likely to be, in Hobbes's famous terms, "solitary, poor, nasty, brutish, and short." Moral principles characteristically set constraints on harm-causing behavior, or confer moral status and establish limits on behavior relative to status, or endorse and attempt to husband the conditions conducive to the flourishing of benevolent and sympathetic sentiments toward others that may confer biological advantages on the species, if not always insuring individual aggrandizement. Novel moral principles are good if they tend to do such things and bad if they do not. It is very hard to see how Doolittle's first principle fits any of those criteria, although it might be understood, in an admittedly jaundiced way, as establishing limits on behavior relative to the status he confers on daughters. But that is a stretch, albeit not so far as might first be thought after reading the way fathers are allowed to sell their daughters in Mosaic law and other ancient legal texts.

Consider another example that might qualify as moral originality: the Sermon on the Mount. In the Sermon, Jesus gives his version of the Golden Rule (Matthew 7:12) as "So whatever you wish that men would do to you, do so to them," but that is not especially original with Jesus, and I am also not thoroughly convinced that, at least in that version, it is a good moral principle. It makes one's own proclivities the deciding factor and so pays no heed to whatever perversities persons may have or wish they had when they decide how they will treat others. What does seem original₁ is the litany, found in Matthew 5:21 to 5:48, of revisions and radical changes Jesus makes in the Mosaic laws. In each of those cases, he begins by telling his followers, "You have heard that. . . ." He then recites a version of Mosaic law, such as "You shall not kill." This is then followed by his revision, "But I say to you. . . ." In each case, he seems to make the new principle more inclusive and, frankly, more demanding:

> You have heard that it was said to the men of old, 'You shall not kill; and whoever kills shall be liable to judgment.' But I say to you that every one who is angry with his brother shall be liable to judgment; whoever insults his brother shall be liable to the council, and whoever says, 'You fool!' shall be liable to the hell of fire.[23]

In this case, Jesus is not eradicating the old principle and substituting a new one. He is augmenting the old one. Another example of the same

[22] Ibid., 111.
[23] These are translations from the Revised Standard Edition of the *Bible*.

sort: "You have heard that it was said, 'You shall not commit adultery.'
But I say to you that every one who looks at a woman lustfully has already
committed adultery with her in his heart." There are examples, however,
in which he is commending a radical new principle as a substitute for the
old:

> You have heard that it was said, "An eye for an eye and a tooth for a tooth."
> But I say to you, do not resist one who is evil. But if any one strikes you on
> the right cheek, turn to him the other also; and if any one would sue you
> and take your coat, let him have your cloak as well; and if any one forces
> you to go one mile, go with him two miles. Give to him who begs from you,
> and do not refuse him who would borrow from you. You have heard that it
> was said, "You shall love your neighbor and hate your enemy." But I say to
> you, Love your enemies and pray for those who persecute you.

His "turn the other cheek" and "love your enemies" principles are
original$_1$, and they are morally good in the aspects in which they are novel
because they do what morally good principles do: constrain the causing
of harm and promote conditions for human social flourishing. They are
original$_2$ and retain their moral goodness as principles by which to assess
human behavior after their novelty has worn off because, of course, it
has and they have.

Getting radically new principles accepted, so that they actually function as moral assessment guiding in a community, however, requires
more than pointing out that they are consistent with what morally good
principles are to look like. They must become morally normative for a
significant number of community members. In the case of the "turn the
other cheek" and "love your enemies" principles, that has not occurred,
despite the proselytizing for them in Christian churches. They remain
prospective moral norms and hold a certain place of honor owing to their
source. Some individuals and faith-based groups have adopted them at
various times through the centuries. They seem to be morally original$_2$
with the Sermon on the Mount. But among moral principles, they are
rather less than functioning norms in contemporary moral assessment
and more like museum exhibits, occasionally displayed, dusted off, and
reproposed (generally from the pulpit), applauded, and then returned
to a glass case. I am not in a position to know whether they were significant factors in the widespread adoption of Christianity in Europe, but I
suspect they were not. European history certainly does not reflect their
adoption as moral norms.

Emersonian self-reliance may be another example of moral
originality$_2$. The self-reliant person, for Emerson, has a kind of intuitive

vision of the good that is neither the "common good" nor the "greatest good for the greatest number of people." He writes: "When good is near you, when you have life in yourself. . . the good, shall be wholly strange and new. It shall exclude all other being. . . . We are then in vision."[24] For Emerson, to achieve a proximity to the good in one's actions, a person must dare to be different in the face of the pressures of social conformity, and he implies that the outcome will be human flourishing. He writes:

> I will have no covenants but proximities. I shall endeavor to nourish my parents, to support my family, to be the chaste husband of one wife, – but these relations I must fill after a new and unprecedented way. I appeal from your customs. I must be myself. . . . I will not hide my tastes and aversions. . . . If you are noble, I will love you; if you are not, I will not hurt you and myself by hypocritical attentions. . . . I do this not selfishly but humbly and truly.[25]

Self-reliance, for Emerson, requires the rejection of the traditional moral norms. He recognizes that he is prone to the charge of antinomianism or, as Nietzsche put it, to the adoption of a "*laisser aller*" position in place of morality.[26] Emerson denies that this is an implication of his ethics of self-reliance. To reject traditional morality is not to reject self-discipline, a point Philippa Foot makes in her examination of Nietzsche's position,[27] and one that is also true of Emerson's. He maintains that there are "two confessionals." He calls them the direct and the reflex ways. The reflex is the way of the non-self-reliant person who trusts the moral evaluation of his or her behavior to others, to the established moral and legal standards of the community. The self-reliant person is his or her own direct moral "task-master."

It is not that there are no moral normatives for the self-reliant. Emerson maintains that self-reliance "denies the name of duty to many offices that are called duties," and it dispenses with reliance on ethical codes. Emerson's direct confessional demands "something godlike in him who has cast off the common motives of humanity and has ventured to trust himself for a task-master." The self-reliant person becomes the moral doctrine and the law to himself or herself. There is, maybe obviously and on purpose, the echo of the Kantian moralist giving himself or herself the moral law.

[24] Ralph Waldo Emerson, "Self-Reliance" (1841) in his *Essays* (New York, 1926).
[25] Ibid., 53.
[26] Friedrich Nietzsche, *Beyond Good and Evil*, translated by Walter Kaufmann (New York, 1966), #188.
[27] Philippa Foot, *Virtues and Vices* (Oxford, 1978), 90.

Emerson's is a morality of inner strength that eschews any self-deception, not unlike one of the principles espoused by Doolittle. It requires motivational independence and self-sufficiency, demanding the curbing or moderating of typical human desires to align them with available resources, and resisting greedy impulses. For Emerson, all expressions of inner strength are morally meritorious without appeal to their consequences. Weakness of will is not tolerated.

Emerson, not unlike Nietzsche, associates the virtue of self-reliance with the language of art. He writes:

> Insist on yourself; never imitate. Your own gift you can present every moment with the cumulative force of a whole life's cultivation.... Every great man is an unique.... Shakespeare will never be made by the study of Shakespeare.... Dwell up there in the simple and the noble regions of thy life, obey thy heart and thou shalt reproduce the Foreworld again.[28]

An Emersonian principle stating a putative moral norm might be, "Expressions of inner strength or self-reliance are morally good." That principle does not entail that because it is morally good in circumstances C for X, expressing her inner strength, to do A, doing A is morally permissible for anyone, even in circumstances similar to those in which X did A. Doing A may express the inner strength of X in those circumstances, while not being an expression of the inner strength of anyone else or of X in other circumstances. There are no standard expressions of inner strength.

Is Emerson's inner-strength principle a morally good one? It is if it can be convincingly argued that it satisfies the higher-norm of morality, not if its content is true. If it does satisfy that norm, it is original$_2$, but, as with aesthetic originals, originality then is not a morally significant property of the principle. The expressions, "She is a moral original" or "His principles are morally original," when intended as positive moral assessments, contain both a factual claim – a belief that either does or does not satisfy the truth-norm – as well as a moral evaluation – a belief that is correct or not, depending not on whether what the speaker believes is true or false but on whether what the speaker believes conforms to a higher moral norm – that utilitarians will identify with the principle of utility, Kantians with duty, and others with, for example, agent-focused virtue or agent-based virtue.[29]

[28] Emerson, 60–1.
[29] See Slote or Peter A. French, *The Virtues of Vengeance* (Lawrence, 2001).

6

Public and Private Honor, Shame, and the Appraising Audience

According to the *Oxford English Dictionary*, uses of the term "honor" in English date to 1375. All pertain to credit, reputation, and a good name. Honor has to do with being worthy of high esteem, even veneration, and typically privilege, but it can also relate to nobleness of mind; for example, honor as "self-respecting integrity." I introduced the concept of honor to the chaplains with a Power Point slide containing a quote from Alexander Hamilton: "There is in every breast a sensibility to marks of honor."[1] Below the quote was a drawing of the duel between Hamilton and Aaron Burr in which Hamilton was killed and Burr's political career ruined. The irony was intentional.

Robert Ashley, the founder of the library of the Middle Temple, London, wrote a treatise, *Of Honour*, somewhere between 1596 and 1603.[2] Ashley's little book is believed to be the earliest attempt by an Englishman to provide a systematic treatise on the subject. A number of Italian writers tackled the topic before Ashley, but it would be some years later that Thomas Hooker took it up in *An Essay on Honour* (1741) in English. It would not be a stretch to characterize most of Shakespeare's *Histories*, but especially *Henry IV* (Parts I and II) and *Henry V*, as directly concerned with honor, both as a serious matter and as a source of Falstaff's humor.

Ashley was concerned about two sorts of misunderstandings about honor, one that could be attributed to Montaigne, and the other that he identified as a serious problem among his peers, and that the chaplains

---

[1] *Federalist Papers*, Number 40, Paragraph 13, 263.

[2] Although the exact date of publication is uncertain, it must be within that time frame because it is dedicated to Sir Thomas Egerton, Keeper of the Great Seal of England, and Egerton held that post during those years.

identified as a major concern in the military. The first was the treatment of honor as merely a name bestowed by people on themselves and of no real value. The second was the overly ambitious pursuit of honors, rank, and recognition. Ashley argued that each distorted a concept that when properly understood is, he believed, an essential foundation of morality. Ashley claimed that honor is the most divine of attributes because it is offered up both to God and to those who are held in the highest regard among humans. "There ys nothing amongst men more excellent then honour," he wrote. He attributed our desire for honor to nature. It is, he maintained, a primitive motivation and is necessarily joined to human felicity. Hence, honor is "to be preferred before all other especiall good thinges" such as wealth, health, friends, children, noble lineage, and so forth.[3]

Ashley's debt to Aristotle is clear throughout his treatise. For example, Ashley's placement of honor among those things good in themselves but linked to happiness echoes Aristotle's "honour, pleasure, reason, and every other virtue we choose indeed for themselves (for if nothing resulted from them we should still choose each of them), but we choose them also for the sake of happiness, judging that through them we shall be happy."[4]

Ashley, departing from Aristotle, identified in honor a special power that the other virtues lack. His insight is that honor has the power to keep those who possess it away from all vices. Honor is, in itself, desirable and those who have it gain "all delight of the mind" such that they would not ever want to part with it. To avoid losing it, one must resist the temptations of all the vices. In fact, Ashley is convinced that without honor, all of the other virtues will perish and people will go about doing "each foule and wicked deed."

Ashley's conception of the moral role of honor can be found in most honor-driven societies and organizations. What it sometimes means in those groups, however, is that deeds that would otherwise be vices are not considered to be wrong if done in the name of honor or honor preservation. In societies like the antebellum American South, for example, it also could mean that the commission of acts that would be vices if performed by others are not counted as such when done by

---

[3] All quotes are from Robert Ashley, *Of Honour,* edited by Virgil Heltzel (Huntington Library, San Marino, CA, 1947), which is a printed version of his handwritten paper book of twenty-six leaves.

[4] Translations of Aristotle are by David Ross, *The Nichomachean Ethics of Aristotle* (Oxford, 1925). The quotation is from 1097b.

"honorable men."[5] Dueling, for example, was against the law in New York when Hamilton challenged Burr, so the duelists were rowed across the Hudson to hold their encounter with pistols in New Jersey. Dueling was also illegal in New Jersey, so seconds and others who were assembled were made to turn away from the scene so they would not be able to testify that they saw pistols or the firing of pistols.

In responding to his ambitious colleagues, Ashley distinguished between honor and glory. Glory is a reflection of fame, recognition, and what Ashley called "magnificence." Honor, however, does involve recognition. It "is a certaine testemonie of vertue shining of yt self geven of some men by the iudgement of good men." There are two sorts of recognition, the sort that one gets from the multitude, which is what Ashley meant by glory, and the sort that comes from the judgment of good men. The gloss on Aristotle is evident. In reference to the appropriately proud person, Aristotle wrote, "It is hard to be truly proud; for it is impossible without nobility and goodness of character. It is chiefly with honours and dishonours, then, that the proud man is concerned; and at honours that are great and conferred by good men he will be moderately pleased, thinking he is coming by his own or even less than his own . . . but honour from casual people and on trifling grounds he will utterly despise" (NE 1124a). Ashley's treatise was, in large measure, a caution to his peers to guard against ambition and ostentation.

Ashley identified two necessary aspects of true honor. First, it is a habit of virtue in the honorable person. But second, it is found or judged to be in that person by "good men iudging aright." Ashley explained why the judgment of good men is important when he wrote:

> Because that Honour which ys said to be in any ys not only in him as yf yt depended wholy on him, but also in others, whoe must loue and commend that vertue in him which they seeme to allow of. Therefore the cause of bestowing the honour which draweth vnto yt and requireth approbacion ys in the man which is honored, but the accommodating thereof in those which allow of him for his vertues sake. And do therefore make much of him and esteeme him.[6]

Honor, for Ashley, is inseparably personal and communal. The communal aspect guarantees shame avoidance, fear of ill-repute, that most discussions of the topic take to be essential to honor. Hence, Ashley's account of honor set the paradigm that has dominated the topic: that

---

[5] See Bertram Wyatt-Brown, *Southern Honor* (New York, 1982).
[6] Ibid., 52.

though honor may have, at least in the best cases, to do with inner feelings and demonstrable virtues, it is driven by considerations of communal pressure in the form of shame avoidance. Honor, as Ashley suggested, may proceed from the display of such habitual virtues as honesty in which an agent may take pride, but it requires an audience, and, for Ashley, an audience composed of those of the highest moral standing.

Ashley warned that people are prone to value the opinions of the vulgar multitude, rather than those of the virtuous, choose the wrong audience, and have only vainglorious popularity to show rather than true honor. So, essential to the conception of public honor is a determination of the group that forms one's appropriate audience. Public honor presupposes a definition of the honorable, of one's tribunal of honor.

Social stratification seems to be tied up in a Gordian knot with public honor. The way this was typically handled in communities with honor norms was to demarcate classes. "A man is answerable for his honour only to his social equals, that is to say, to those with whom he can conceptually compete."[7] A dramatic way to see how this phenomenon worked might be to look at the history of dueling, especially because I have already raised the story of Burr and Hamilton. Pieter Spierenburg notes that male honor, as revealed in the history of violent rituals such as the duel in Europe, "has at least three layers: a person's own feeling of self-worth, this person's assessment of his worth in the eyes of others, and the actual opinion of others about him."[8] Duels were never fought across class lines. The insult of someone of a lower class was never a threat to one's honor. Challenges to honor were social-station specific. Apologists for upper-class dueling throughout Europe in the nineteenth century maintained that the practice promoted civilized behavior, taught men self-mastery and the proper forms of social interaction, and even established fraternal bonds between the participants.[9]

---

[7] J. G. Peristiany, *Honour and Shame* (Chicago, 1966), 31.

[8] Pieter Spierenburg, *Men and Violence* (Columbus, 1998), 10.

[9] "Having survived it, former enemies are like brothers" (Spierenburg, 11). Spierenburg explains, "If we take it at face value, we must assume that the prospect of having to face an opponent in arms restrained men in social intercourse; they thought twice before they said a wrong word.... The implicit assumption is that honorable men actually do not want to fight at all and do everything to avoid it" (Spierenburg, 9). A shared honor code defined the class of "gentlemen." When two gentlemen fought a duel, the courts, controlled by the gentlemanly class, were generally lenient, but should two tradesmen engage in a deadly affair of honor, most likely the courts would treat the victor as a murderer. In 1918 in France, Georges Breittmayer published a new dueling code in which he "decreed that anyone of draft age could duel and hence belonged to the same

The social stratification that supports public honor seems to be an essential element in what I have elsewhere called a spatial conception of morality.[10] In such a morality, human identities are station identities. Personal identity is exhaustively given in terms of locations and associations that form and define a social grid. Who you are is a matter of where you are within the social structure. F. H. Bradley, a fair candidate as a spatial moralist, makes the point that an individual human being, insofar as he or she is "the object of his [or her] self-consciousness," is characterized and penetrated "by the existence of others." The content of a self is a pattern of relations within a community. "I am myself by sharing with others, by including in my essence relations to them, the relations of the social state."[11] The primary moral obligation for Bradley is self-realization, and that, in large measure, amounts to finding one's position or station and acting accordingly. To find one's place, of course, requires identifying the places of others, not all others, but a significant element of that part of the social grid in which one is located. Bradley tells us that "to know what a man is you must not take him in isolation.... What he has to do depends on what his place is, what his function is, and that all comes from his station."[12] In a spatial morality, the primary moral motivation is to measure-up, not to be seen as inadequate to the tasks that define one's identity.

A Bradleyian conception of the social structure that supports an ethics of duty and stations has very obvious similarities to the stratified structure of the military, in which a spatial ethics dominates and explains why the standard answer to what should a chaplain do when confronting morally improper behavior and situations was "send it up the line. It's not in your purview." And it explains the chaplains' surprise upon learning that moral issues at every level are in their scope of duties, that they are to deal with such cases and see them through to morally appropriate conclusions. Not to do so is a dereliction of duty.

Ashley located the social force that works the magic of honor in keeping people away from vices in the fear of ill-repute, shame avoidance. Plato makes a similar claim for shame in both the *Republic* (465a) and the *Laws* (671c). A number of philosophers have provided illuminating studies

---

honor group. He only excluded men who had avoided military service or engaged in disreputable activities during the war" (Spierenburg, 11).

[10] See Peter French, *Responsibility Matters* (Lawrence, 1992), chapter 5.

[11] F. H. Bradley, *Ethical Studies* (Oxford, 1876, 1989), 173.

[12] Ibid., 173.

of the concept of shame.[13] It is generally agreed that shame relates to failures, shortcomings, feelings of inadequacy and inferiority, and the unwanted exposure of weaknesses or the fear of such revelations rather than involving transgressions of moral codes or laws. When one is ashamed, the normal response is to conceal oneself, to try to mask oneself. Shame has a distinctly visual aspect. It seems mostly to depend on the way one looks to oneself and on the way one wants to be seen by others and the way one thinks or knows one is seen by others.

Suffering shame is an identity crisis. Shame anxiety, psychologists report, is a feeling of radical isolation from one's social image. Gerhart Piers and Milton Singer claim that shame arises out of a tension between the ego and the ideal ego, and they differentiate it from guilt, which, they claim, arises out of a tension between the ego and the superego.[14] The ideal ego in a spatial morality is defined by the social conventions that set the expectations for stations, roles, and genders. John Kekes, in a similar vein, claims:

> Shame is caused by the realization that we have fallen short of some standard we regard as important. Those who are incapable of this emotion cannot be seriously committed to any standard, so they are apt to lack moral restraint. Shame is a sign that we have made a serious commitment, and it is also an impetus for honoring it, since violating the commitment painfully lowers our opinion of ourselves.[15]

Honor is typically twinned with shame and mirrors many of its characteristics. J. G. Peristiany, in a famous anthropological study of the values of Mediterranean societies, echoed Ashley's and Aristotle's accounts of honor as being necessarily both a personal and a public conception of the value of a person.[16] Honor relates, as Peristiany notes, to a person's claim to pride, both as seen by the person and by his or her peer group. The public honor game, played by people in various cultures, is the game of collecting validations of personal image from those one regards either as one's equals or one's betters and avoiding shame. The image a person

---

[13] Of note are Gabrielle Taylor's *Pride, Shame, and Guilt* (Oxford, 1985); Arnold Isenberg's "Natural Pride and Natural Shame" in *Explaining Emotions*, edited by A. Rorty (Berkeley, 1980); and John Kekes' "Shame and Moral Progress" (in *Midwest Studies in Philosophy*, XIII, 1988). I have also written some on the subject. See *Responsibility Matters*, chapter 5, and "It's a Damn Shame," in *Freedom, Equality, and Social Change*, edited by C. Peden and J. Sterba (Ithaca, 1989).

[14] Piers and Singer, *Shame and Guilt* (New York, 1971).

[15] John Kekes, *Facing Evil* (Princeton, 1990), 282.

[16] J. G. Peristiany.

attempts to validate in these games is a social ideal that is reproduced in the individual aspiring to personify it and is validated or not by its creators and sustainers. If one achieves the "right to pride," one achieves status, but status and the right to pride are elements of the social identity that is not solely, if at all, constructed, though it is internalized by the individual agent. In effect, it is a type of conformity. There should be little wonder that those in the military regard honor as a primary virtue.

Any claim to pride is "mere vanity," according to Peristiany, unless it is granted, validated, or certified by the members of the relevant social unit. Failure of validation constitutes humiliation for the individual and, most important, is the basis for shame. "Public opinion forms therefore a tribunal before which the claims to honour are brought, 'the court of reputation' as it has been called, and against its judgements there is no redress. For this reason it is said that public ridicule kills."[17] In a similar vein, John Rawls writes about shame that it "implies an especially intimate connection . . . with those upon whom we depend to confirm the sense of our own worth."[18]

Peristiany postulated a reciprocal honor/shame model to explain the social patterns of the Mediterranean region. That paradigm has had a continuing impact on anthropological studies not only of that region but others as well. The basic idea is that "honor and shame are reciprocal moral values representing primordial integration of individual to 'group.' They reflect, respectively, the conferral of public esteem upon the person and the sensitivity to public opinion upon which the former depends."[19]

There is a distinctly sexual aspect to the reciprocal honor/shame model in many societies of the Mediterranean region. Honor seems to be understood as an essentially male value, though shame, by which it is measured, is understood primarily in terms of the chastity of women. In other words, male public honor, in very large measure, is dependent on the sexual behavior of females in those societies. A man's honor is founded on and maintained by his woman's chastity. Carol Delaney, whose anthropological research was done in Turkey, explicates honor/shame reciprocity in terms of procreation issues. "Minimally, the value of males derives from the social perception of their ability to engender; it is the foundation

---

[17] Ibid., 27.
[18] John Rawls, *A Theory of Justice* (Cambridge, MA, 1971), 443.
[19] David Gilmore, *Honor and Shame and the Unity of the Mediterranean* (American Anthropological Association, 22, 1987), 3.

upon which honor is built."[20] Delaney notes that honor so understood creates high levels of anxiety in the males of the community because their honor, their social standing, balances precariously on the sexual behavior of the females. With the rural lifestyle of most of the communities as a conceptual background, the female is thought of in terms of a field that is the property of her husband, to be sown only by him. The yield of that field is the source of honor for the man, but only if it is the child of his own seed. His honor is lost if he has not been able to unambiguously insure his paternity.

Delaney notes: "Shame is an inevitable part of being female."[21] The only honor a woman can have is by remaining fully aware of her inherent shamefulness and behaving accordingly. But, she has a certain dominion over her husband's honor. She, Delaney maintains, does not possess the "seeds of honor," but her sexual behavior can render her husband dishonorable and put him "in the position of a woman and . . . therefore shamed." The ancient pollution doctrine is also invoked to explain the transference of her sexual promiscuity to her husband's shame. "Since seed carries the essential identity of a man, it leaves an indelible imprint which no amount of washing can erase. A woman who has had sexual relations with any man other than her husband becomes physically polluted, and through her, her husband's honor is stained."[22] In discussing the honor/shame culture of the antebellum American South, Wyatt-Brown refers to woman as dangerous. "They could present a husband, father, or brother with an illegitimate child and thereby cast doubt on the legitimacy of the line and desecrate the inmost temple of male self-regard. . . . In the American South, it is no wonder that men feared women."[23]

The sort of honor that is the subject of the anthropological research done on the Mediterranean and antebellum Southern cultures clearly is "public, positional, or external honor" because of its necessary dependence on an audience. According to Wyatt-Brown, there were three primary components of public honor in the antebellum South. Honor is

first the inner conviction of self-worth . . . second . . . the claim to that self-assessment before the public . . . [and] third . . . the assessment of the claim by the public, a judgment based on the behavior of the claimant. In other

[20] Carol Delaney, "Seeds of Honor, Fields of Shame," in *Honor and Shame and the Unity of the Mediterranean*, 40.

[21] Ibid., 40.

[22] Ibid., 42.

[23] Wyatt-Brown, 54.

words, honor is reputation. Honor resides in the individual as his under-standing of who he is and where he belongs in the ordered ranks of society.[24]

The literature on honor and its reciprocal, shame, is dominated by discussions of its audience or peer group dependence. If external evalu-ation by a relevant group is required, how can honor be personal? That was a question that perplexed a number of the chaplains during my dis-cussion of the concept that dominates the military's conception of ethics. To answer it, I propose to follow a well-trodden trail regarding the same question in the case of honor's reciprocal. Does shame really require an audience?

Kekes claims that shame both alerts us to our shortcomings and makes us feel deficient on account of them. An audience is supposed to be crucial in both of those aspects of shame. As a number of writers have noticed, there are two different judgments that occur in a shame situa-tion. One is the critical evaluation by such an audience and the other is the critical judgment by the agent. The latter is based on whatever standards of behavior the agent has internalized, and these standards may or may not be similar to those applied by the audience in its judg-ment of the agent's actions. Douglas Cairns summarizes the situation in the following way: "the critical judgment of oneself which is constitutive of shame is never formally identical with any critical judgment of the audience."[25] That, of course, must be the case because whatever judg-ment the audience makes, it cannot be one of shame, though it may include the judgment that the person should be ashamed of what he or she has done.

A number of different outcomes are possible when an audience assesses a person's actions, any of which can produce shame in the person so assessed. The audience might be positively or negatively impressed by or indifferent to the person's actions. The person might endorse or reject the audience's judgment, but even if the person endorses a positive audience response, the result could be that the person is ashamed. For example, the person may view the audience's approval as conditioned by their having placed him or her on a social level below what he or she believes to be appropriate to his or her self-image. The person may agree with the audience and consequently feel shame. If the audience is indifferent, the person may experience shame at having failed to impress them. In any event, the shame judgment is solely that of the person, and

---

[24] Ibid., 14.
[25] Douglas Cairns, *Aidos* (Oxford, 1993), 15.

it is made with respect to or against some standard or ego ideal that the person has internalized. So, what role does the audience really play in the matter?

Gabrielle Taylor has carefully and convincingly explicated the function of the audience in shame. She notes that "in feeling shame the actor thinks of himself as having become an object of detached observation, and at the core to feel shame is to feel distress at being seen at all."[26] What is crucial in shame is that the person achieve what Taylor calls a "higher order" critical point of view with which he or she can identify. The concept of the audience, whether real or imagined, affords the person access to that point of view. The audience per se, then, is not crucial to shame, but the person's taking up that detached observer point of view is. It is that point of view, of seeing oneself as being seen, or possibly being seen in a certain way, as exposed, that motivates the self-critical and self-directed judgment that produces shame reactions.

The role of the audience then is metaphorical. Shame crucially involves seeing, but it must be seeing oneself, not as one wants to see oneself, but as one might be seen from the perspective of what Taylor calls "a possible detached observer-description."[27] Further and essentially, to be ashamed, the person must have decided that he or she "ought not to be in the position where (he or) she could be so seen, where such a description at least appears to fit."[28]

The audience in shame is a conceptual crutch. Rawls and others have been too influenced by the shame-culture discussions of the anthropologists and so look for actual audiences. But the role of the audience is not played by the person either, a mistake made by Cairns.[29] The catalyst of shame is that the person accesses another visual perspective, one detached from his or her own, with respect to his or her actions. This is not self-awareness and self-criticism; at least not in the way those notions are usually described. A person can be self-aware without being also aware of the possible descriptions of his or her behavior that might be preferred by a detached observer, by an audience. It involves internalizing a point of view or observational perspective on the actions one performs that is other than one's attached perspective. It is to see

[26] G. Taylor, 60.
[27] Ibid., 66.
[28] Ibid., 66.
[29] Cairns, 18.

oneself as the person who *may* be seen as doing X, although one may not see oneself as doing X.

Shame not only is retrospective, it also may be, perhaps often is, a delayed reactive emotion, stalled by the agent's inability to activate its cognitive catalyst. Some time may elapse before a person is able to see himself or herself as possibly being seen to be doing X when he or she was, to his or her mind, doing Y. When the person is able to see his or her doing Y in the circumstances as capable of being seen as his or her doing X, to make the self-conscious detached comparison, he or she may feel shame to think that "someone like me, indeed I, could be seen to be doing X."

The point of view of the possible detached observer, however, is not the person's internal judgment of shame. It is not that the agent says to him or herself, "I am ashamed, degraded, because such and such an audience could perceive what I have done in such and such a way." If that were the case, if there is no such audience or if the audience could not observe the person's actions in the circumstances, and the person knows that is the case, then the person could not feel shame for what he or she did. Taylor makes the point succinctly, "It is because the agent thinks of herself in a certain relation to the audience that she now thinks herself degraded, but she does not think of this degradation as depending on an audience. Her final judgement concerns herself only: she is degraded not relatively to this audience, she is degraded absolutely."[30]

An actual audience is not essential to shame. Is that also the case with honor? I think it is. Imagine that the role of the audience in honor mirrors that of the audience in shame. Honor standards may be internalized in much the way detached-observer shame judgments are. A person may feel honor in the sense of self-respecting integrity, in the absence of an actual audience, or Ashley's "certaine testemonie of vertue shining of yt self geven of some men by the iudgement of good men." The "judgment of good men" may refer not to the actual judgment of a peer group, organization, or community but to the judgment a person can make of his or her actions as they would be made by a group of qualified detached observers. Vision is the appropriate metaphor. How could I be seen were I seen doing what I am doing? If a likely way I might be seen is under what might be called a "personal honor description," then I may feel that my actions maintain or enhance my sense of self-respecting integrity. What is

[30] G. Taylor, 68.

important is not that others, even an audience composed of exceptionally good and discerning people, do in fact so judge me. What is important is that I recognize that I can legitimately see my actions as taking such a description even though I may not, myself, describe them that way. Honor of that sort could well be called personal or private honor. It does not come with medals and public acknowledgments.

In such personal honor, as well as shame, the audience is a conceptual crutch, one that may be returned to its corner when the person has internalized the detached observer perspective on his or her actions.

Public or positional honor, as the term testifies, requires the actual approbation of others, usually those in an acknowledged peer group. If this account is correct, then the anthropologists' honor/shame reciprocal model is faulty. Public honor is not the reciprocal of shame, though it might be the reciprocal of public shaming. Of course, public shaming can be internalized by its object and become shame. That is, by suffering the public display of disapprobation and contempt, being shunned, jeered at, laughed at, cursed, or cast out, persons may well adopt the viewpoint and standards of the others and thus conform and experience the painful self-directed feeling of shame. But, they may not.

Personal honor depends on the standards of behavior one internalizes, on which detached observation point of view one adopts. That point of view could be identical to that of public honor. In that case, one sees oneself as being seen by the public or by some segment of the public, one's military unit perhaps, and, of course, one does not want to be seen as the person doing X, where one knows or believes that X is disapproved by that collective. The external elements of personal honor, in such a case, are indistinguishable from those of public honor. One has simply internalized a public honor perspective, treating the positional honors that the organization or group conveys as the major or only reason to feel honorable. That is nonaccidental compatibility of personal and public honor.

Personal and public honor may be accidentally or incidentally compatible in at least three ways. The detached observational point of view one adopts could be based in deontic values as understood or interpreted in some standard moral theory. For example, it could be Kantian in that one might adopt the detached observational point of view of the rational community and derive one's sense of personal honor from seeing one's actions as seen by the members of that community. Insofar as any single member of the rational community is as good an observer/evaluator as any other, to see one's actions as seen by the rational community could be just to see one's actions as seen by oneself when one has adopted the perspective of a rational agent. In Kantian terms, that would be to see one's actions as by one's will becoming a universal law for all people.

Another detached observational point of view that might attract a person of personal honor is one that is based in fundamental aretaic values that are external to the agent, such as the "good life" or Aristotle's *eudaimonia*. Personal honor, in that case, comes from seeing one's actions as being seen by those who know the constituents of human well-being or the good life.

Alternatively, one might adopt the detached observational point of view of seeing one's actions (or oneself) as seen by one (or by a group) whose fundamental aretaic values are based in inner strength. If one takes such a point of view, then one's honor is entirely interior to oneself. That does not, however, mean that one is one's own audience, an audience that is bound to be appreciative. It means that one sees one's actions as seen by those who see the sort of actions one is performing under certain descriptions, as doing Z, where Z either is or is not a description of behavior that evidences inner strength in the agent.[31] Personal honor may well up in the person who can see his or her actions as seen as displays of inner strength and self-reliance utterly without regard to what description may be given to one's behavior from any other detached observational point of view. That may be what honor amounts to for an Emersonian.

[31] See Michael Slote, "Agent-based Virtue Ethics," *Midwest Studies in Philosophy*, XX (1995), 83–101.

7

Torture

For the purposes of this Convention, the term "torture" means any act by which severe pain or suffering, whether physical or mental, is intentionally inflicted on a person for such purposes as obtaining from him or a third person information or a confession, punishing him for an act he or a third person has committed or is suspected of having committed, or intimidating or coercing him or a third person, or for any reason based on discrimination of any kind, when such pain or suffering is inflicted by or at the instigation of or with the consent or acquiescence of a public official or other person acting in an official capacity. It does not include pain or suffering arising only from, inherent in or incidental to lawful sanctions.

Article 1: United Nations "Convention Against Torture and Other Cruel, Inhuman or Degrading Treatment or Punishment."[1]

Torturers throughout the centuries may have found some consolation if not positive moral endorsement in what could be described as the scriptural sanction of torture. No higher a moral authority than God does a fair share of it in the Bible. And if God can engage in cruelty, then those who would imitate God may feel justified in using techniques that involve inflicting severe physical and psychological pain and suffering, especially if they are doing so in the service of what they believe to be the right or the good, and despite the United Nations Convention prohibiting such techniques. In the Middle Ages and Renaissance, monarchs and church potentates caused all manner of suffering to be visited on enemies, heretics, and women thought to be practitioners of witchcraft, assuming or citing scriptural endorsement. "Absolute control, cruelty, and torture would be signs of power and godlikeness; they would be evils in everyday life (in, for example, English common law) but good when

---

[1] December 10, 1984 – Entry into force June 26, 1987 – Signed by the United States of America on April 18, 1988, and ratified on October 21, 1994.

exercised by legitimate authority."[2] One of the many things that make the book of Job such a difficult text for moralists must be the cruelty (physical and mental) allowed by and then inflicted by God on a perfectly righteous man, all to win a bet with Satan. Little wonder that many torturers, acting in the name of the state and believing their government's officials sanction their actions, display little compunction about what they are doing to fellow human beings. Some, however, come to realize that when torturing a fellow human being, they have stepped over the threshold into evil, and it weighs heavily on their conscience despite whatever governmental directives may have been concocted to justify torture techniques or what orders they may have been given by superior officers.

Alyssa Peterson (mentioned in Chapter 4), a 27-year-old devout Mormon from Flagstaff, Arizona, for example, served with C Company, 311th Military Intelligence BN, 101st Airborne. She was an Arabic-speaking interrogator, trained at Fort Huachuca, and in September 2003 she was assigned to the prison at Tal Afar airbase in Iraq. After two nights of participating in "the cage" in "enhanced interrogation" techniques that included walling, cigarette burning, punching, and being blindfolded while naked, only to have the blindfolds removed to reveal the presence of women in the cage, Peterson refused to continue interrogations. She committed suicide on September 15, 2003, at the base. One of her fellow interrogators reported that Peterson had trouble keeping her personal feelings out of the exercise of her professional duties. Peterson believed that her participation in torture demeaned her to the point where she could not continue to live with what she had done in the name of serving her country. The torturer as victim of torture!

On August 1, 2002, Jay S. Bybee, Assistant Attorney General, wrote a U.S. Department of Justice Memorandum on the letterhead of the Office of Legal Counsel to John Rizzo, Acting General Counsel of the CIA. The White House released a redacted copy of that memorandum to the public in the spring of 2009. The memorandum was titled "Interrogation of al Qaeda Operative." Bybee wrote that it was his understanding that the operative in question, Abu Zubaydah, has information regarding terrorist networks in the United States or Saudi Arabia and plans for attacks against either U.S. targets or the interests of the United States overseas. It is clear from the memorandum that Rizzo asked the Department of Justice if the CIA interrogation teams could move the interrogation of Zubaydah into

[2] Nel Noddings, *Women and Evil* (Berkeley, 1989), 219.

an "increased pressure phase." Bybee's response went on in detail for eighteen pages and sets the basis for the use of what reasonably may be called torture as a technique of interrogation by U.S. operatives. He granted the CIA permission to engage in the new phase on Zubaydah for up to thirty days and allowed that they may use ten techniques to "dislocate his expectations regarding the treatment he believes he will receive and encourage him to disclose the crucial information."

The ten techniques Bybee specifically approved are attention grasp, walling, facial hold, facial or insult slap, cramped confinement, wall standing, stress positions, sleep deprivation, insects placed in a confinement box, and waterboarding. He granted that they could be used in an "escalating fashion, culminating with the waterboard, though not necessarily ending with this technique." Bybee provided a description of each of the techniques. He noted that some of the techniques are designed to show the person exposed to them that his or her physical space can be easily and at will invaded by the interrogator. They are intended to "induce shock, surprise, and humiliation." Some of the techniques, such as walling, are intended to produce muscle fatigue. Sleep deprivation is to be used to reduce the person's ability to think straight, and Bybee allowed up to eleven days of forced wakefulness for that purpose. The insect in his confinement box was especially designed for Zubaydah because the CIA, presumably, learned that he had a fear of insects. It was suggested that a caterpillar would do the trick. Waterboarding, according to Bybee's memorandum, has the effect of precipitating "suffocation and incipient panic, i.e., the perception of drowning." If forty seconds on the waterboard was not successful, permission was given to repeat the procedure.

Bybee cited Section 2340A(1) of the United States Code that defines torture as "an act committed by a person acting under the color of law specifically intended to inflict severe physical and mental pain or suffering (other than pain or suffering incidental to lawful sanctions) upon another person within his custody of physical control." Bybee decided that the use of the first nine techniques does not violate the Section 2340A prohibitions. Waterboarding, however, "constitutes a threat of imminent death," so it fulfills the "predicate act requirement under the statute." But, Bybee concluded that because it does not inflict prolonged severe mental pain or suffering, it does not violate the statute and insofar as the intent of the interrogators is not to inflict severe pain and suffering (apparently a nod to double-effect or collateral-damage theory), but to garner crucial information, waterboarding, along with the other techniques, was approved for use by the CIA on Abu Zubaydah. He was waterboarded eighty-three times in one month.

Therefore, torture under another name, "enhanced interrogation" or "harsh interrogation," was sanctioned for use by operatives of the United States. Two years later, the pictures from Abu Ghraib appeared and the chaplains at my Pearl Harbor PDTC admitted that although they were ashamed of what had occurred at Abu Ghraib, when they were deployed in Iraq they had witnessed or knew of similar "interrogation techniques" used by Marines. Some also noted that it was not as bad as the "long step" technique they had heard was used in Vietnam, which entailed taking Viet Cong prisoners up in helicopters and, if they would not talk, pushing one out to his death. The others, as they understood it, then would divulge just about anything.

There are at least two kinds of torture: terroristic and interrogational. Bybee and others in the Bush administration who wrote memoranda approving of torture techniques were not trying to justify torture for the sake of the terror it instills in its victims, that is, torture engaged in sadistically as a form of punishment or as a means of exacting revenge. For them, it was to be a primary method for gaining actionable information in a timely fashion when the United States was woefully ignorant of what was going on within the radical elements of the Arab and Islamic world. Anything else that it may have produced was of no significant consequence to them. Two months before the Bybee memorandum was written, Secretary of Defense Donald Rumsfeld said: "Our interest is not in trying and punishing him. Our interest is in finding out what he knows."[3]

In 2002, when he was White House counsel to George Bush, Alberto Gonzales engineered another ploy in the pseudo-legalistic campaign in the administration to justify enhanced interrogation techniques. Gonzales, in providing a decision as to whether the Geneva Convention on Prisoners of War applied to Taliban and al-Qaeda[4] members who were captured in Afghanistan, recommended that they be identified not as prisoners of war but as "enemy combatants." Insofar as the Geneva Conventions do not speak of enemy combatants, the captives were not covered by the protections in the Conventions, he opined. They were

[3] He was speaking about Jose Padilla on CNN, June 11, 2002.

[4] Al-Qaeda is also spelled al-Qaida. In this case, I am using the former spelling because that conforms to the spelling used in the memorandum and a number of other government documents. Al-Qaida is more commonly used.

neither incarcerated convicted felons nor prisoners of war. He wrote that the designation of enemy combatants would shield from domestic and international prosecution interrogators who committed "outrages against personal dignity" while interrogating detainees.

What the Bush administration was clandestinely doing, as characterized by Ken Kipnis,[5] was creating a wholly new category of "social institution," a social structure predicated on the way they defined those who would be housed within it. Abu Ghraib was a prison under Saddam Hussein in which prisoners were reportedly brutalized either as a form of punishment or for the sadistic enjoyment of the guards. Prisons are social structures within the judicial/penal institution for those who have been tried and convicted under law of crimes and sentenced by legitimate courts to penal servitude. Their purpose is to punish convicts and, possibly, to rehabilitate them. Some of those who were incarcerated in Abu Ghraib after the U.S. invasion of Iraq were common criminals, but many – and in particular those held in what was known as the "hard site," Cell Blocks 1-A and 1-B – were picked up primarily by Army and Marine units in the cities and towns of Iraq as suspected insurgents or "enemy combatants." They were not there as the result of criminal convictions. For them, Abu Ghraib was not a prison, but it also was not a prisoner-of-war camp. As Kipnis writes: "POW camps are intended to confine those who surrender or are captured on the battlefield. . . . They are there solely because they have been taken prisoner while serving in an opposing army."[6] The capturing forces are held to internationally endorsed standards of care for the POWs they have within their control, and at the end of the hostilities, POWs are repatriated to their own countries.

During the Bush administration, so-called enemy combatants were collected and warehoused in sites like Abu Ghraib; Camp Delta at Guantanamo Bay, Cuba; Bagram in Afghanistan; and in black-site facilities in countries throughout the world. All of those locations were primarily designed to function as interrogation centers, places where, purportedly limited to the permitted techniques, interrogators would extract actionable intelligence for the Bush administration's global war on terror. The only reason to hold enemy combatants at those centers was to

---

[5] Ken Kipnis, "Prisons, POW Camps, and Interrogation Centers: Reflections on the Juridic Status of Detainees," *Intervention, Terrorism, and Torture: Contemporary Challenges to Just War Theory*, edited by S. Lee (New York, 2007), 289–98.
[6] Ibid., 291.

get information from them, and it did not seem to matter how long doing so might take, which is odd granted that time was supposedly of the essence in order to prevent planned terrorist attacks. The captives were "detainees," another clever term to avoid the very thought that they were prisoners serving out duly authorized penal sentences or POWs. There were no sentences because there were no trials; there were no formal charges. They could be and were detained indefinitely, and even if they had no information to impart, releasing or properly trying them in normal courts presented serious risks the Bush administration was reluctant to run. For example, detainees with no prior connections to terrorists or insurgents had probably been radicalized by the treatment they underwent and so would likely join up with terrorist cells as soon as they were freed. Detainees also could not be tried under American law in an American courtroom for a number of reasons that were trotted out by the Bush administration, including that evidence of culpability obtained during "enhanced interrogation" would be inadmissible, and any publicly held trials would confirm to all the world that the United States, in violation of international law, the UN Convention, and treaties, tortured. Places like Abu Ghraib and Guantanamo were the "legal equivalent of outer space"[7] as far as the status of the detainees and the techniques of the interrogators working on them were concerned. The identities of the detainees typically were not made available to families and the Red Cross. In fact, as Kipnis notes, there was little difference between being detained and being disappeared. Neither prisons nor POW camps, whatever the interrogation centers run by the United States are, or whatever international law ultimately makes of them, morally disgusting things were done to human beings in them in the name of national security and the perceived need to get actionable intelligence. Little of which, apparently, was ever accomplished, although defenders will argue heatedly on something that sounds like utilitarian grounds: no follow-up attacks after 9/11/01 on American soil, thus the whole process was justified.

The pictures taken of the treatment of detainees in Abu Ghraib, as noted by Gregory Hooks and Clayton Mosher,[8] fall into two general categories: "(1) intentional violent or sexual abuse, and (2) actions taken

---

[7] Quoted by Kipnis from the website www.globalsecurity.org.

[8] Gregory Hooks and Clayton Mosher, "Outrages Against Personal Dignity: Rationalizing Abuse and Torture in the War on Terror," *Social Forces* (June 2005), 1627–46.

based on misinterpretation or confusion regarding law or policy." Most of the released pictures depict events that fall into the former category. They include, but were not limited to, the following:

> (a) a contest between two army dog handlers to see who could make the detainees urinate or defecate in the presence of dogs; (b) three detainees stripped of their clothing, handcuffed together while nude, placed on the ground, forced to lie on each other and simulate sex while photographs were taken; (c) the rape of a female detainee and the rape of a 15- to 18-year-old male detainee; (d) a detainee being forced to bark like a dog and crawl on his stomach while MPs spat and urinated on him; (e) several instances of detainees being forced to wear women's underwear, often on their heads; (f) a detainee who was beaten with a broom and had a chemical light broken and poured over his body. MPs then used the broom to sodomize the detainee while two female MPs hit him, threw a ball at his penis and took photographs.[9]

What was going on? The ostensible reason for such actions by American troops was that they were acting under orders, possibly given by contractors or CIA operatives, if not their own superiors, to "soften up the detainees," "to give them a bad night." The techniques they utilized, however, could not just be called "enhanced sleep deprivation." They were acts of extremely callous cruelty intended to dehumanize and humiliate the detainees through forced sexual perversion. The Abu Ghraib torturers seemed bent on trying everything their obscene minds could conceive of to torment the detainees by exploiting Arab modesty in sexual matters through reducing detainees to objects for demented sexual and vulgar scatological play. Unlike the trained interrogators for whom they were "softening up" the detainees, the Abu Ghraib Army guards' cruelty seemed to be fueled with passion, but was it a passion to do what they had been ordered to do, or a passion born of a deep-seated belief in their own superiority that they believed granted them a right to treat the detainees as subhumans and to get as much of a kick out of it as possible? To them, their victims were not soldiers, they were enemy combatants, which gave them no more moral status than had they been an invading swarm of space aliens.

The use of torture tactics to gain actionable intelligence was a natural progression from the military policy of the United States to limit casualties in any conflict in which it is engaged. The primary way that

[9] Ibid., 1629.

limitation is accomplished is by fighting engagements, as much as possible, at a distance and by the use of robotics and other technologies that limit the exposure of humans to deadly risks. That, however, puts the highest premium on getting truthful data on targets and also on knowing what sorts of collateral damage are likely to occur when attacking those targets. Gathering intelligence is, therefore, a first priority, and in a war against nonstate enemies, interrogation of captives is a primary source of that information. Insofar as those who are members of such groups are most likely to be highly committed to their causes and not likely to willingly divulge information that could jeopardize the success of their missions, coercive interrogation techniques were believed necessary to pry the information from resistant captives, even though they are prohibited by U.S. and international law.[10]

Larry May provides a number of important observations about the moral status of captives, although he couches them in terms of POWs and does not respond to the Bush administration view that they are not prisoners of war. Nonetheless, what May identifies as derivable from Hugo Grotius's seventeenth-century work *De Jure Belli Ac Pacis* regarding the humanitarian treatment of captives in war is instructive. POWs cannot be subjected to reprisals, summarily dealt with, and treated inhumanely. Most important, May claims that captives "are in a special moral situation since they are utterly dependent on their captors, and vulnerable in ways that soldiers on the battlefield are not."[11] That special moral situation that May identifies is a kind of fiduciary or stewardship relationship between the captor and the captive that has been confined, whether or not against his or her will. (Whether surrender is willful confinement is not an issue with respect to the relationship between the parties.) That relationship, a fiduciary responsibility for the welfare of the captive, according to May, is triggered by the utter vulnerability of the captive to the captor's care and protection. In effect, the captive becomes a ward of the captor (or the captor's military force); he or she can no longer be conceived of as a competitor or, in other words, as a combatant. The

---

[10] This role for coercive interrogation was established in the CIA's *KUBARK Counterintelligence Interrogation Report* in 1963, which maintained that physical abuse was not likely to result in useful information, but that sensory deprivation and the other techniques, such as those detailed in the Bybee memorandum in 2002, were more likely to produce valuable results. As Hooks and Mosher note: "These techniques had been laid out in manuals first prepared in the 1960s." See Hooks and Mosher, 1636.

[11] Larry May, "Humanity, Prisoners of War, and Torture," in *Intervention, Terrorism, and Torture*, 221–34, 225.

captive is in a dependence relationship with the captor. The two parties in the relationship do not share the same status. Unfortunately for May's argument for the humane treatment of captives, Gonzales and others in the Bush administration (with the complicity – probably unthinkingly – of the media) short-circuited the argument by maintaining that the captives held in interrogation centers are still combatants. They are, in their view, competitors, not POWs, and therefore if their captors have any sort of fiduciary relationship to them, it is minimal at best. Insofar as some detainees died during interrogation, affording them such protections as would insure their continued existence does not seem to have been in the package of what was believed to be a responsibility of the captor. I strongly suspect that few philosophers and legal theorists, when trying to evaluate what the United States was doing at its interrogation centers, grasped the significance of the Gonzales ploy in negating the traditional moral status relationship of captor to captive. Of course, it could be argued that it does not matter what Gonzales called them, they just are prisoners of war. The logic of continuing to consider them combatants may be supported by the theory that even when captured, as supposed deeply committed members of an international terrorist organization, they may conceive of their current incarcerated condition as but a different venue in their war and use it to mislead and misdirect their sworn enemy in whatever way they can. Movies about Allied prisoners of war during the Second World War typically depict the captives in such a manner. The use of enhanced interrogation techniques is supposed to counter that commitment by driving detainees over the brink of willful control and getting them to divulge actionable intelligence. It is puzzling, however, if that is the goal, why interrogators favored the techniques described in Bybee's memorandum rather than the administration of drugs such as scopolamine, temazepam, or sodium thiopental. Of course, the use of such drugs is internationally identified as torture and the Bush administration was arguing that the enhanced interrogation techniques did not constitute torture. Still, waterboarding, by virtually all authorities, is a form of torture even if the term used to describe what used to be called water torture is a euphemism for what actually occurs to make it more palatable to the general public. It may sound to some to be a relative of surfboarding or snowboarding, some form of recreation. Vice President Cheney was reported to have once referred to it as "a dunk in the water."

There are a number of very serious moral problems with the interrogation centers approach that utilizes torture or techniques that approach torture in order to try to gain actionable intelligence. Interrogational torture will become terroristic torture if the interrogator does not stop the use of the techniques once the detainee has divulged the information he or she has on the subject sought by the interrogator. Another round of waterboarding for good measure, for example, is terroristic. There is at least an implicit – although in most cases likely an explicit – bargain between the parties that the technique will cease when the detainee provides the information. The interrogator says repeatedly, "If you just tell us what we want to know, I can stop doing this to you." There is, however, clearly a dependency relationship between the torturer and the tortured regarding when the torture will cease. The person being tortured cannot really ensure that the torture will stop. Henry Shue characterizes it: "The supposed possibility of escape through compliance turns out to depend upon the keeping of a bargain which is entirely unenforceable within the torture situation and upon the making of discriminations among victims that would usually be difficult to make until after they no longer mattered."[12] What Shue has in mind is that escaping from the torture in the interrogational situation requires compliance, and because that means divulging information to the detriment of one's cause, it is more likely to come readily from the least committed members to "the cause." The most committed, those who have associated their very identities with "the cause," are likely to hold out and suffer severe episodes until they break, and when they break they will do so with a sense of loss of integrity, self-image, and identity. But what of those who have no information to provide? How does the interrogator distinguish between the deeply committed enemy combatant and the utterly innocent person who was rounded up by the military and deposited in Cell Block 1-A in Abu Ghraib? How can a person who knows nothing convincingly demonstrate that to a torturing interrogator? Surely not by undergoing more and more torture.

Epistemologically, the interrogator is in a terrible bind because he or she is likely to get identical answers to questions from two types of detainees, the committed and the innocent: "I know nothing." If there is no independent way to sort the detainees with respect to the likelihood that they possess actionable intelligence, then those who will be most severely tortured will be those who have nothing to say because they know nothing, and it is likely that they know nothing because they are innocent, they are not enemy combatants of any stripe. Of the thousands detained by the U.S. forces in Iraq, how many were innocent or had no knowledge

---

[12] Henry Shue, "Torture," *Philosophy and Public Affairs* (1978), 140.

that would constitute actionable intelligence? When has an interrogator exposed such people to the enhanced interrogation techniques long enough to know that the detainee is not withholding information because of a personal identification with the insurgent cause? How much pain and suffering is it morally permissible to administer in such a state of uncertainty? Suppose that a detainee has suffered through days and nights of sleep derivation and still insists that he has no knowledge of enemy combatant locations or whatever sort of information is being sought. Should the interrogator ratchet up to waterboarding at the next session? Although these are meant to be rhetorical questions, too many Americans, particularly those in government positions of authority and power, think they can be answered in a nuanced fashion, which is a telling commentary on the sad moral state of the U.S. interrogation center approach and its identification of those it warehouses in them as outside the moral boundaries of the established categories of prisoner of war or convict.

In the public debate on torture, few have unashamedly defended torture per se as a morally justifiable procedure, though many have used consequentialist arguments to try to justify torture techniques when, hypothetically, some desired end is the guaranteed result. They do that, of course, because no one seems really prepared to admit that inflicting grotesque suffering, physical and/or mental, on someone, even a demonstrably wicked person, is not evil in and of itself. When it is done for a higher purpose such as saving millions of lives or preventing the advent of nuclear warfare on a global scale, however, its moral status or character is supposed to change.

The most common retort to moral questions that challenge torture or enhanced interrogation techniques is what has become known far and wide as the ticking-time-bomb scenario. The scenario can be attributed to Jeremy Bentham, who used it to induce utilitarian intuitions. In the political debate in America surrounding the Iraq War and the War on Terrorism, the ticking time bomb usually has been set off by neoconservatives in an attempt to disarm their opponents of the notion that there should be an absolute prohibition against torture.[13] The strategy is to get the prohibitionist to concede that there is one type of case in which torture should be permissible: to prevent a catastrophe. If prohibitionists

---

[13] It also has been used by Michael Walzer and Alan Dershowitz. See Michael Walzer, "Dirty Hands and Ordinary Life," *Philosophy and Public Affairs* (1972), 160–180; and Alan Dershowitz, *Why Terrorism Works* (New Haven, 2002).

will admit torture in such a case, a slippery slope could be constructed on which to slide them down to the admission that most of the uses of torture in the interrogation centers are really ticking-time-bomb cases.

Allowing torture, even in what is an extreme case, explodes the prohibitionist's principled platform against torture. A concession on the ticking-time-bomb case amounts to the prohibitionist's surrender of the moral high ground to the utilitarian. The idea is that if terrorism is a constant threat of catastrophes affecting the lives of large numbers of innocent people, then torture used to try to gain actionable intelligence of the plans of terrorist groups and their locations should be permitted. When President Bush maintained that 9/11 changed everything, certainly one of the things he, or those in his administration such as his vice president, probably had in mind was that the prohibition against interrogational torture must be obsolete. But if eyes not clouded with fear examine it, the ticking-time-bomb scenario may not be as persuasive as it is reputed to be.

Here is the simplistic version of the ticking-time-bomb scenario that frequently is slipped into the debate on the moral status of torture with the intent of bringing the discussion to a screeching halt. A terrorist has planted a nuclear time bomb in the heart of an American city, but we do not know in which city or where in the city it is planted or when it is set to explode. We have in our custody the person who has planted the bomb, but although he brags about having planted the bomb, he refuses to answer any of our questions. Should we not be morally permitted to torture him until he reveals the location of the bomb so we can prevent the deaths of hundreds of our fellow citizens? The expectation, of course, is that the prohibitionist will relent in order to get the vital information and save the people.

What is wrong with the scenario? Other than the fact that it is an utter cheat? In order to gain from the prohibitionist what it wants, it has to posit far too much. We have to accept that there is a ticking time bomb and that the authorities know there is one and that they have the terrorist in their custody and that he is telling the truth when he claims to have planted a bomb. None of those factors ever actually occurs. David Luban offers what he calls "more honest hypotheticals."[14] My version of one of Luban's hypotheticals has the following elements: suppose that CIA operatives are convinced that one of a hundred detainees in Abu Ghraib

[14] David Luban, "Liberalism, Torture, and the Ticking Bomb," *Intervention, Terrorism, and Torture*, 249–62, 254.

Cell Block 1-A might know the plans of an insurgent unit in Baghdad that might include a concerted rocket attack on the Green Zone in conjunction with an assault on the Iraqi Parliament. However, they do not know which detainee. Should they start torturing the hundred detainees until they hit on the one who has the information? Suppose they do not come upon him until they have tortured seventy-five detainees for nothing, and suppose they learn nothing of value from any of them. They have, in effect, assaulted the defenseless. Is that to be allowed as collateral damage? Also, when they get to the one who might know something, it turns out that what he believes he knows is false because the insurgents had given him false information, never having trusted him to stand up under torture were he to be captured. Was there any point to the torture of seventy-five detainees? Was it not a fishing expedition launched on rumor, rather like "they are really biting down at the south end of the lake?" Luban puts the point well. He writes:

> We do not know in advance when al-Qaeda has launched an operation. Instead interrogation is a more general fishing expedition for any intelligence that might be used to help "unwind" the terrorist organization. Now one might reply that al-Qaeda is itself the ticking time bomb, so that unwinding the organization meets the formal conditions of the ticking bomb hypothetical. This is equivalent to asserting that any intelligence which promotes victory in the War on Terror justifies torture, precisely because we understand that the enemy in the War on Terror aims to kill American civilians.[15]

If the torture advocate allows torture on such grounds, then any perceived threat to the lives of American citizens would justify torture, making torture a morally legitimate tool of American defense policy. But why stop at defense? Why couldn't torture be utilized in the pursuit of any goal that is thought to be worthwhile for American interests? The slippery slope down the other side! More important, the decision to torture in the ticking-time-bomb scenario could be made responsibly only in an extremely desperate situation. Such situations are rare and whatever may need to be done in them, although it makes engrossing fiction and film, is no basis for policy.

There are still those who insist that torture works and should not be abandoned even if it has a deleterious impact on the moral fiber of the culture. When asked to cite examples of its success, they, like former Vice President Cheney, claim that supposed plots to cause havoc

---

[15] Ibid.

in certain American cities were foiled, but the evidence that the plots in question were real or had any hope of being actualized is dubious at best, and evidence that torture actually played a significant role in the apprehension of the plotters is left vague, purportedly and conveniently for "reasons of national security." In most of the reported cases, standard FBI infiltration operations seemed to be the telling factors. Then there is the oft-cited 1995 case of Abdul Hakim Murad in the Philippines. The Filipino police tortured Murad for sixty-seven days. Agents beat him, waterboarded him, crushed cigarettes into his genitals. But they already had his laptop on which the details of the plot to bomb eleven airliners and the CIA headquarters were found before the torture began. Testimony during his trial in the United States revealed that during torture in the Philippines, the details of other plots that Murad provided were "police fabrications that Murad mimed to end the pain."[16] Many in the intelligence business claim, based on their own experiences, that as a practical matter, torture is not a dependable way to get actionable intelligence.

In order to be persuaded by the ticking-time-bomb scenario that torture should be morally permissible, we must grant a ridiculously large number of dubious assumptions. Once all of those are slipped in, then torture is left as the only option, but that is a form of begging the question. If we are told that there is no other way to uncover the crucial information than to torture someone until they reveal it and that hundreds of lives are at stake, what choice is left to us? What we are not told is that in order to reduce the options down only to torture, an amazing amount of detailed information must already have been uncovered. How? Not by torture. If, for example, it is known that the bomb-planter is in custody and we know which of all of those folks held in custody is the person who planted the bomb, how did we come to know that? At least, we will not have to torture everyone we have detained! The scenario is so wrought with fantastic assumptions that it cannot serve as a useful moral thought experiment. Its simplicity is its flaw, and philosophers and legal theorists who take it seriously are far too ready to engage in the torture justification game. In doing so, they become pawns in the political tactics of the neoconservatives who trumped up the Iraq War on the basis of falsified intelligence. They inadvertently elevate something so

---

[16] Alfred McCoy, *A Question of Torture: CIA Interrogation from the Cold War to the War on Terror* (New York, 2006), 112.

morally unpalatable as torture, which has sometimes led to the death of detainees and is typically unproductive, to the level of a morally justifiable instrument in a never-ending global war on terrorism, and they encourage the metastasizing of torture into a cultural artifact. Baseball, apple pie, and torture! I agree with Shue: "Artificial cases make bad ethics. If the example is made sufficiently extraordinary, the conclusion that torture is permissible is secure. But one cannot easily draw conclusions for ordinary cases from extraordinary ones, and as the situations described become more likely, the conclusion that the torture is permissible becomes more debatable."[17]

We might, I suppose, decide that torture is not morally permissible, but that it is morally excusable in ticking-time-bomb – like situations. Claudia Card suggests such a ploy and explores potential excuses that might be proffered by defenders of torture in those situations.[18] She wants, however, to reach the conclusion that torture is inexcusable. Unfortunately, in order to avoid begging the question regarding the nature of torture as evil and so morally inexcusable, she opens the door to excusing it by ruling out some tempting candidates. Her problem, as she admits, is that she cannot ensure that she has ruled out all of the possible candidates for excusing interrogational torture, and so she either must accept the possibility that an excuse might be forthcoming that will work or declare that by definition torture is inexcusable.[19] After all, inexcusability just means that searching for an excuse is futile. There are no excuses to be found or invented. Stop looking. Once you allow searching for possible excuses, you defeat inexcusability. "Murder is inexcusable," for example, does not mean that up to now no one has offered a good excuse for murdering someone. There are, of course, some morally acceptable excuses for killing someone. "Killing in self-defense" is not a euphemism for "murder" and, by the same token, "enhanced interrogation techniques" should not be treated as a euphemism for "torture." The fact that it has been used that way as a substitute for "torture" is yet another clever move by the Bush administration, adopted by the media, to try to block the conclusion that torture of the interrogational variety is an appropriate descriptive for what was being done at Guantanamo, Abu Ghraib, and the black sites.

[17] Shue, 141–42.
[18] Claudia Card, "Ticking Bombs and Interrogations," *Criminal Law and Philosophy* (2008), 1–15.
[19] Clare Chambers convincingly makes this point in her response to Card, "Torture as an Evil," *Criminal Law and Philosophy* (2008), 17–20.

Is interrogational torture morally inexcusable?[20] The answer is yes, but not because we cannot think of a good excuse for doing it, even in ticking-time-bomb situations. It will be because there is something about torture used in that way in itself that makes it morally abhorrent, indeed evil.

I defined moral evil in previous chapters as human action that jeopardizes another person's (or group's) aspirations to live a worthwhile life (or lives) by the willful infliction of undeserved harm on that person(s). I believe that by "undeserved harm" I mean something comparable to what Card means by "intolerable harm" in her definition of evil.[21] That is, it is a normative rather than a subjective concept. I think that a convincing assessment that interrogational torture is evil can be based on a certain feature of such torture that has not been adequately exposed, perhaps because so much attention has been paid by philosophers to the moral status of the participants and utilitarian justifications or excuses in concocted "urgent" situations.

Interrogational torture, as far back in history as anyone wishes to go, has been successful only when the will of the tortured individual is broken. Breaking the will of the subject is the primary technique of all forms of torture. The idea in interrogational torture is to inflict pain severe enough to get the tortured person to do or say what the torturer wants, regardless of what the person wills him or herself to do, just to stop the suffering the body is undergoing. Suffering pain in itself is not torture, nor is suffering pain necessarily undeserved harm. Sometimes pain is inflicted willfully or requested by the individual enduring it. What happens in interrogational torture is that the will of the tortured person is commandeered by the torturer's intentional imposition of pain and suffering. The more intense the pain and the related fear that it will be worse yet, the more the tortured person realizes how fragile is his (or her) control of his (or her) will and so his (or her) personhood, until will and personhood are gone altogether. As Louis Michael Seidman maintains, torture reveals to all of us what we know but do not want to admit to

---

[20] In what follows, I am talking only about interrogational torture and not terroristic torture or torture purely as punishment. Although I think all versions of torture can be shown to have serious moral problems, the use of torture in punishment, and only for that purpose, may be more difficult to rule out other than on cruel and unusual grounds. In *The Virtues of Vengeance*, I argued for a fitness condition for justifiable punishment that might not exclude certain forms of torture depending on the crime being punished.

[21] She writes that "evils are reasonably foreseeable intolerable harms produced by culpable wrongdoing." Then she opts to alter her definition by changing "culpable" to "inexcusable." Card, 6.

ourselves: namely, that we are slaves to our bodies.[22] When someone else gains control of one's body by inflicting pain on it, one's will is soon surrendered. A chaplain who worked with Navy SEALS told me, "They learn that no one is unbreakable." All wills and with them senses of identity can be enslaved and destroyed. That is the predicate on which the use of torture in interrogation rests. Jean Améry, who was a victim of severe torture by the Nazis, writes: "Whoever is overcome by pain through torture experiences his body as never before. In self-negation, his flesh becomes a total reality.... Only in torture does the transformation of the person into flesh become complete ... the tortured person is only a body, and nothing else beside that."[23]

In developing a compelling account of the will and the concept of personhood, Harry Frankfurt[24] distinguishes different types of desires. First-order desires are the desires we have to do something or get something or have something and such. The first-order desires a person has at any time may be incompatible and range all over the place. We may have some first-order desires of which we are unaware and some we may not think we have. Our actions are caused by first-order desires becoming effective motivators. When a first-order desire moves one to action, when wanting something motivates a person to do something, that first-order desire is that person's will in that case. In effect, a person's will is not just what that person desires, but those desires that he (or she) has that actually are motivationally effective at a particular time in his (or her) life.

It seems reasonable to assume that in most interrogational torture cases, a first-order desire of the person being tortured is to terminate the pain. The interrogational torturer counts on inducing that desire and sustaining it. However, the torture subject, assuming that he (or she) is really committed to his (or her) cause, does not want that desire to be his (or her) effective desire. He (or she) does not want to end the pain because to do so, as he (or she) knows, requires divulging actionable information regarding the cause in which he (or she) is enlisted. The torture subject wants his (or her) first-order desire to be to endure the pain and not tell the interrogator whatever he (or she) knows or believes

---

[22] Louis Michael Seidman, "Torture's Truth," *University of Chicago Law Review* (Summer 2005), 881–918.

[23] Jean Amery, "Torture," in *Art from the Ashes: A Holocaust Anthology*, edited by Lawrence Langer (Oxford, 1995), 121.

[24] Harry Frankfurt, "Freedom of the Will and the Concept of a Person," in *The Importance of What We Care About* (Cambridge, 1988).

he (or she) knows. That is what Frankfurt calls his (or her) second-order desire. Second-order desires are wanting to want something one wants in the situation and not something else one wants, for example, wanting to want to endure the pain and not tell the interrogator anything and not wanting to want to terminate the pain because that requires telling the interrogator. Second-order desires are desires to have certain desires, and some second-order desires are wanting a certain first-order desire in the situation to be one's will, to motivate one's actions.

A second-order desire that identifies a first-order desire as the desire one wants to be effective, to motivate one, to be one's will, is what Frankfurt calls a "second-order volition," and having second-order volitions, on his account, is essential to being a person. In other words, what makes something (for example, a human being) a person for Frankfurt is that it wants its will to be a certain desire at a certain time. As far as we know, other animals do not have second-order volitions. A necessary condition of being a person is that one desires that one's will, which is the desire that effectively motivates one's action, be a certain first-order desire and not some other first-order desire one may have at the relevant time. John Kekes summarizes Frankfurt's position succinctly. "What is most important in the lives of persons is to shape their characters by willing themselves to have and act to satisfy some of their desires and not others."[25]

Consider how we might, using the conceptual picture that Frankfurt has drawn, describe a person under interrogational torture. We may assume that he is not a masochist, so he hates what he is undergoing. The pain is excruciating and so he has a first-order desire to make it stop. He also has a first-order desire not to reveal information that could put the mission of his unit at risk of failure. Because he is committed to his cause, he has a second-order volition to make his desire not to reveal the information his will. His will is to remain silent. It matters to him which of his first-order desires is effective. He has much in common with the person Frankfurt describes as an unwilling addict who wants to take the drug and also wants to refrain from taking it and who has a second-order volition to make the latter constitute his will, "to provide the purpose that he will seek to realize in what he actually does."[26] The detainee wills to endure the torture. The torture continues and intensifies.

The focus of torture is to destroy the subject's second-order volitions or to make it extremely difficult and then impossible for the subject to

---

[25] John Kekes, *The Art of Life* (Ithaca, NY, 2002), 228.
[26] Frankfurt, 17–18.

form second-order volitions. In effect, it is to put him in the position of not having a preference with respect to his first-order desires, to not care what his will is. It is to bring him to the position where he believes he no longer has a stake in preferring his desire to refrain from telling what he knows regardless of the pain. It is to replace his will to remain silent with the needs of his body to terminate the pain. Seidman puts this well when he writes: "Torture is about the body, not the mind – or, more precisely, it is about what happens to the mind when we realize that we are only body."[27] The detainee, now lacking second-order volitions and having no preference among his first-order desires, likely will make his desire to end the pain become the first-order desire on which he acts; ending the pain will thus be his will. In effect, however, he then can be swayed to do whatever the torturer wants him to do. He has been turned from a person into what Frankfurt calls a "wanton."

Frankfurt writes about the wanton that

> he does not prefer that one of his conflicting desires should be paramount over the other; he does not prefer that one first-order desire rather than the other should constitute his will. It would be misleading to say that he is neutral as to the conflict between his desires, since this would suggest that he regards them as equally acceptable. Since he has no identity apart from his first-order desires, it is true neither that he prefers one to the other nor that he prefers not to take sides.[28]

When the torturer has his victim in this state, he can extract whatever information he wants from him, for he is like the drug addict who must at whatever price have a fix to satisfy his bodily craving. The fix in the case of torture is relief from the pain. What issues from the detainee's mouth, however, may well be useless information or an ersatz confirmation of what the interrogator wants to hear because the tortured human's will is no longer independent of his body's craving to end the pain. The torture process, because it has destroyed his capacity for forming second-order volitions that evaluate his first-order desires and determine which to prefer as his will, has annihilated him as a person. He has become "a helpless bystander to the forces that move him."[29] And that is the desire to stop the pain. He does not want to want the pain to stop. He just wants it to stop.

Torture destroys personhood by paralyzing the will, leaving only a human animal in its wake. It does not thwart the will. Were that the case,

[27] Seidman, 909.
[28] Frankfurt, 18.
[29] Ibid., 21.

the person could still have the second-order volition to want a specific desire to be effective, to be his will, but something blocks that desire from resulting in an action, from being effective. All of us have had our wills thwarted from time to time when we are unable to perform the actions that we want ourselves to perform because of something outside of ourselves that stands in the way. Thwarting may occur in some early stages of interrogational torture but not as the process continues into such techniques as waterboarding. Then, the tortured human no longer has a free will because he cannot conform his will to his second-order desires, for he no longer has any second-order volitions. Even if he has some second-order desires, none of them are paramount; none is his preferred second-order desire. He has lost control. He ceases to be a person. His will has been hijacked. He is not free to have the will that he would want to have were he not under torture.

When we develop a neurotechnological devise that allows us to invade someone's brain without drilling a hole in his skull and extract the information we are seeking, we might not regard our using it as torture, but we certainly would concede that in gaining it, we bypassed the subject's will. It would not be true that he divulged the information. He did not do anything. In the interrogational torture cases, the detainees do something, at least some of them do: they talk. But, when subjected to the more advanced phases of torture, they do not do it because they want to want to talk. They are humans talking, but, no longer having second-order volitions, no longer persons, and I doubt anyone, even members of their terrorist or insurgent group, would be inclined to hold them morally responsible for saying what they say.

A ploy sometimes used by interrogational torturers is to tell the detainee something of this sort: "Look, tell me what I want to know and you can save yourself a whole lot of pain and suffering. You are going to tell me eventually. Make it easier on yourself." The weak of will, of course, will then talk, but the deeply committed and the totally innocent will say nothing the interrogator wants to hear. The interrogator is right about those deeply committed to the cause. They will eventually lose their second-order volitions and say something to terminate the pain. Sadly, the innocent will lose their personhood and have no way to stop the pain until the interrogator tires of torturing them. We will never know how many who died during enhanced interrogation in Iraq and the other interrogation centers had nothing to tell interrogators who could not be convinced of their ignorant innocence.

What is so morally wrong about interrogational torture is that it annihilates the fragile personhood of its subjects to accomplish its ends. It treats potentially obtaining information as more important than the moral status of persons. It turns members of the moral community into wantons by making it virtually impossible for them to form second-order volitions as the pain is ratcheted up. The interrogator who inflicts the torture on the subject to prevent him "from identifying himself in a sufficiently decisive way with any of his conflicting first-order desires, destroys him as a person. For it either tends to remove him from his will and to keep him from acting at all, or it tends to remove him from his will so that his will operates without his participation."[30] It is instructive that Frankfurt is not talking about the effects of interrogational torture in the previous passage but rather drug addiction. The interrogational torturer, on my account, has much in common with the drug pusher.

It might be argued that the demolition of personhood in torture is only temporary. When the interrogation is over, the detainee reclaims his or her personhood and is again able to form second-order volitions. What torture victims learn from the experience, however, is not temporary. They learn how fragile is their claim to personhood that sets them apart from the other animals and bestows moral rights and responsibilities on them, on which their moral status as agents depends. They learn how readily they are likely to relinquish control of their wills to appease their bodies, to stop the pain. "Whoever was tortured, stays tortured. Torture is ineradicably burned into him."[31]

---

[30] Ibid.
[31] Jean Amery, *At the Mind's Limits* (Bloomington, IN, 1998), 34.

8

Community and Worthwhile Living in *Second Life*

According to Linden Lab's reports, more than nine million people are residents of *Second Life*. Many residents spend (on average according to Linden Lab) up to four hours a day in *Second Life*, some considerably more. What are they doing in that three-dimensional virtual environment, or rather, what are their avatars doing there? They are visiting art galleries, going to concerts, having sex, gambling, consuming and manufacturing products, attending webinars, taking college courses, worshipping, buying and selling, trying to make a profit in Lindens (Linden dollars), which are convertible to real-world currency. In short, living, or, at least, living it up!

Although some commentators and critics have interpreted *Second Life* as a game on a par with *World of Warcraft*, it is not a game in the usual sense of the term, although Wittgenstein might disagree. In any event, there are no rule-constitutive actions peculiar to *Second Life*, no winning or losing, no definable success or failure other than what is understood by those terms in real life (or perhaps I should say in "First Life"). Whatever *Second Life* now is and whatever it will become is, in very large measure, a product of its residents, who are provided or purchase the programming tools in *Second Life* to manufacture the objects that give their experiences of *Second Life* whatever character and content they may have. Residents create or manufacture everything in *Second Life*, from cars to mansions, and they sell on E-Bay to other residents the programs to do likewise. The *Official Guide to Second Life* says the following: "*Second Life* is often held up as the perfect place to get your fantasy on – and yes, there's no other place like it for becoming something you aren't, or even for working out just what it is you want to be. In a sense, it's the epitome of the 'walled garden', a place where reality dare not intrude."[1]

---

[1] Michael Rymaszewski, et. al., *Second Life: The Official Guide* (Indianapolis, 2007), 301.

My interest in *Second Life,* or any other virtual world design platform comparable to it, was started by a question posed by Hubert Dreyfus. Dreyfus gave a paper at my institution in which he writes:

> thanks to virtual worlds like *Second Life,* we can forget our finitude and lose ourselves in a rich, safe metaverse. Thus we now face a clear choice between a captivating life of diversion, which existential philosophers like Pascal consider empty and inauthentic, and the authentic life they favor in which one is called to face up to one's finitude and the vulnerability of all one cares about and yet, at the same time, find something meaningful to which to dedicate one's life. At the limit the question becomes: how much misery should one confront? When would it be preferable and ethically permissible to be under the illusion that one was free of finitude?[2]

Consider a case the basics of which were offered to me by a chaplain concerned about a seriously wounded Marine whom he got to know in a rehab center. The Marine is a white male I will call Bob. He no longer has the use of one arm and both of his legs. A roadside bomb shattered his spinal cord and horribly disfigured half his face during a patrol in Western Iraq. Bob also suffers from PTSD and frequent and lengthy attacks of severe depression. He spent the better part of his waking life in a wheelchair, typically slumped and disinterested, before a computer that he is able to operate with his damaged but functional right hand until he was told by a nurse about *Second Life* and decided to visit its site. Mildly intrigued by what it offers, he registered and, for reasons he cannot articulate, created as his avatar, his persona in *Second Life,* an African American woman with long platinum blond hair and a body that would rival that of Halle Berry. He located the marketplace and bought revealing clothes with Linden dollars, then navigated to a singles bar in search of a partner.

He returns daily to *Second Life,* exploring many of its locations and entertainments, and meets and sustains friendly relations with a number of other residents. He decided to design bathing suits and purchased the programming tools necessary to do so; then, in partnership with another resident, also a female avatar, opened a shop where he sells his creations. After a few weeks, he purchased real estate and built a two-story house and invited his business partner to live with him in the house. Months passed during which Bob spent most of his waking hours in *Second Life*

---

[2] Hubert Dreyfus, "Virtual Embodiment: Myths and Meaning in *Second Life*" typescript. My understanding is that this paper is to play a role in a book on which Professor Dreyfus is working. (There is little point citing page numbers for the typescript I have as I received it as an attachment to an e-mail.)

absorbed in his avatar's experiences, including what blossomed into a lesbian relationship with his business partner.

Should we be willing to grant that Bob, who shows no signs of depression during his time as a resident of *Second Life*, is now living a meaningful, albeit an illusionary, life by manipulating his female avatar through a variety of three-dimension virtual experiences? Dreyfus argues that we should not consider Bob's life, so dramatically augmented by residency in *Second Life*, meaningful, although I am not certain that he would deny that Bob's *Second Life* existence is to be preferred to his first life existence and that it may be ethically permissible for him to immerse himself in the illusions afforded by *Second Life*, given the condition in which his wartime service has left his physical body. Dreyfus's primary argument against *Second Life* depends on what he regards as design or engineering flaws in *Second Life* that he believes prevent anyone from experiencing a meaningful life. Dreyfus also raises additional arguments against the possibility of living well in a metaverse – that is, a virtual world – arguments worth noting before examining his own position.

An existentialist might raise one such argument. Its core would be that living in a metaverse cannot be an authentic life because it promotes a denial of the basic facts of human life: pain and suffering, finitude, impotence when pitted against the other forces in the universe, Stephen Crane's moral indifference of the universe. *Second Life* is a diversion, an escape, from the reality of the human condition of fragility, vulnerability, and ultimate nothingness that must be confronted with a commitment to something, some project, that one undertakes without despair, or "on the far side of despair," if one's life is to be meaningful. The meaningful and worthwhile life is the one that grasps the depressing facts of the human condition and yet makes something of value in the face of them. It is not one that escapes into the illusion of full control and immunity. In *Second Life*, virtually (literally) all of one's real-world disabilities and weaknesses are, by one's own choices, banished, and one's avatar can be involved in all manner of experiences in which one could never engage in reality. When things do not go as desired, one can simply exit the program. In fact, if you are screwing up relationships in *Second Life* in much the manner you do in reality, you can just dump the whole thing and start over from scratch with a new avatar body and a new identity. There are no repercussions.[3] On the existentialist's criticism, avatar-existence in

---

[3] Maybe not! A Japanese woman has been arrested, according to AP reports, in first life for "murdering" the avatar of a person to whom her avatar in a virtual world was married

Second Life is escapism into mere illusion and can never substitute for a meaningful or worthwhile life.

The existentialist's critique, however, depends on a singular conception of a worthwhile life. Why should the criterion of such a life be bravely facing the truth of human finitude and the vulnerability to failure and the impermanence of all of our most treasured projects and still striving to find something to which one could dedicate one's life, even if the result is only gaining the peace of mind of knowing that one tried? Why should stoically enduring with a "stiff upper lip" the physical and psychological suffering brought on by the contingencies of the world and pushing on toward one's transitory, and possibly unrealizable, goal be a prerequisite for living a worthwhile life? This is not to deny that one could be properly described as having lived a worthwhile life were one to have lived a life, in John Kekes terms, "whose successfully completed project was to come to terms with the misfortunes that had derailed it."[4] But that is not the only way, and perhaps not even the most advisable way, of living a worthwhile life.

A second criticism of *Second Life* as a way of living a worthwhile life, as noted by Dreyfus, arises from a Nietzschean admonition that the truly worthwhile life is the one lived dangerously, the life of daring and willingness to risk everything. Dreyfus notes that in *Second Life*, one could build one's city "on the slopes of Vesuvius," although it would be a virtual volcano, but that *Second Life* throughout its literature touts itself as the place for "safe experimentation." There appears to be no real possibility of one having to confront the consequences of the monumental failure of one's projects. Nietzsche would argue that the definite possibility of such failure is what makes the undertaking of those projects worthwhile in themselves and especially worthwhile to the individual.[5] Dreyfus suggests that Nietzsche would appreciate the fact that *Second Life* offers a place where the most debilitating aspects of our finitude are easily shunted far off to a sidetrack where one never has to go. However, as I see it, *Second Life* can be most deceptive in this regard. It is not as benign as advertised. There apparently are a number of cases in which once residents have "found themselves" and created lifestyles played out by

because that avatar suddenly divorced her avatar. The woman, using the other player's password, entered the virtual world and "killed" his avatar by canceling out his account, thereby removing his avatar from the virtual world.

[4] John Kekes, *The Art of Life* (Ithaca, 2002), 201.

[5] Friedrich Nietzsche, *The Gay Science*, translated by Walter Kaufmann (New York, 1974), 283.

their avatar in *Second Life*, they become invested in their lifestyles, care about them (in Harry Frankfurt's sense) in a most profound way, and care about their caring about them far more than they do their real-world lifestyles and even their real-world bodies. An NBC report on *Second Life* told of someone who died of starvation because he found it impossible to move from his computer for a number of days while a resident in a virtual world. Residents that become so engrossed and invested in their metaverse existence then are prone to the same sort of vulnerabilities that plague human relationships and human endeavors in the real world and at least to the same degree.

Although *Second Life* advertises itself as a place of risk-free enjoyment and freedom from finitude, it actually invites deep commitment and profound caring by its residents for the world that they have and are creating. That is its selling point. The residents make the world, not the Linden Lab programmers. There is a god-like element in *Second Life* for all residents. They are worldmakers. We may imagine that it is very difficult for a god or any creator not to invest some significant part of itself or himself or herself in the creations. When those creations meet with disasters or failures or rejection, the psychological risks the creator has run typically become evident and the consequences can be not at all superficial. Sometimes, even in *Second Life*, one cannot just exit the program. There are messes that one must clean up in order to go on, albeit psychologically. Dreyfus is right that there is a "carnevalesque relation to reality" in *Second Life*, but residence is not as risk-free as the notion of masquerading may suggest. Acts of creation always come with psychological risks for the creators, and psychological injuries sometimes may be as or more devastating than physical ones. You may build your beautiful home on the slopes of Vesuvius and escape physically unscathed when the volcano erupts, yet experience personal devastation watching from a safe distance as it is engulfed in lava and ash. Creation always comes with a price, whether in a virtual world or the real one.

Dreyfus believes that his strongest criticism of *Second Life* as offering the possibility of a meaningful life derives from a view he attributes to Heidegger and Merleau-Ponty. He argues that Heidegger's concept of practices that create "local worlds" is a key to having a worthwhile life experience. Such interpersonal experiences or local gatherings are supported, Dreyfus argues, by learned practices regarding how our bodies obtain meaningful behavior directly from the behavior of the bodies of others. Maurice Merleau-Ponty calls the social skills and practices that are involved in the creation of local worlds "intercorporeality."[6] Dreyfus maintains that unless *Second Life* can actually introduce intercorporeality into the experiences of its residents, genuine local worlds, or what Albert Borgman calls "focal practices,"[7] cannot be generated or sustained in the virtual world and so residents in those worlds must fail to have worthwhile or meaningful lives in them. Examples of focal practices or events that Dreyfus mentions are family dinners, sporting events, weddings, reunions, memorials, funerals, religious rituals, graduations, and the like. "Much that gives life meaning is organized around such focal occasions.... All these focal events depend for their success on the gift of a shared mood and the appreciation that it is shared."[8]

What Dreyfus seems to have in mind is illustratable by an example he mentions of people attending a baseball game. The home team's centerfielder leaps up against the wall and catches a ball that otherwise would have flown over the fence for a home run. There is grace, there is artistry, there is skill in his success in making the catch and the crowd rises "as one" with cries of awe and shouts of approval. All of the members of the crowd are swept up in the same excitement and joy, and "each one senses that they are all swept away by it. Indeed, the sense that the shared mood is shared is constitutive of the excitement. It is what makes the occasion into a self-contained world and binds the participants together in a focal event."[9]

Dreyfus maintains that the ability to share moods is a primary element in what makes a life worth living, and his concern is that in a virtual world, such as *Second Life*, experiencing, communicating, and sharing moods is not possible to the extent necessary to set up and sustain genuine focal events or Heideggerian local worlds. He notes that typically in philosophical psychology, moods are thought of as inner mental states. On the Cartesian model, moods are in people, people are not in moods. The picture that model encourages is that, for example, when I am angry, I have a particular inner mental state, and to communicate that state I have to use a certain set of more or less conventional bodily movements, perhaps including saying certain things or emitting certain sounds, so another person may observe and interpret those bodily movements, sounds, and so forth as my being in that mental state and then respond in some fashion.

---

[6] Maurice Merleau-Ponty, *Phenomenology of Perception*, translated by C. Smith (London, 1981).

[7] Albert Borgman, *Technology and the Character of Contemporary Life* (Chicago, 1984).

[8] Hubert Dreyfus, "Virtual Embodiment: Myths and Meaning in Second Life."

[9] Ibid.

Dreyfus notes that this Cartesian conception is the way feelings are now communicated in *Second Life*. If a resident of *Second Life* wants another resident to know that he is unhappy with the way their relationship is working out, he has to order his avatar to use a preprogrammed gesture to express his unhappiness, and then the other resident has to interpret the gesture and may then transmit her feelings by commanding her avatar to use a gesture, and back and forth in this manner it may go. Moods can be communicated to other residents only by the use of generic gestures or emoticons. The essentially private Cartesian experience of one's feelings that is communicated indirectly to others is hardly, Dreyfus argues, sharing moods and is insufficient to allow for the creation of focal events or local worlds. Dreyfus maintains that in ordinary life (or First Life), communication of our feelings to others is direct, not Cartesian; in *Second Life* it must be indirect. On the Cartesian conception, if the communication of the range of feelings were to be possible in *Second Life*, the Linden Lab technicians would have to design programming for a repertoire of gestures that express feelings, and residents would have to select the one to use each time they want to convey their feelings to another resident.

By "direct communication of feelings," Dreyfus means that our bodies in some spontaneous and nongeneric way express our situation-specific moods and that others "directly pick them up." Our feelings are spontaneously embodied, and that is the typical way they are expressed. His point is that expressing feelings is not a matter of choosing to adopt certain bodily movements to signal to an audience that we are experiencing those feelings. Communication of feelings, crucial to sharing moods, is direct body-to-body interaction, Merleau-Ponty's intercorporeality. This, Dreyfus thinks, following Heidegger, explains both the contagion of moods among people and that the moods we have and share "determine what matters to us and so govern our social behavior."

Dreyfus's critique of *Second Life* as incapable of supporting and sustaining a worthwhile life depends on his argument that *Second Life*, because it relies on a Cartesian conception of the communication of feelings, cannot provide a venue in which genuine communication between residents is possible. Direct communication of feelings and the sharing of feelings with other residents is blocked by the need to choose gestures (or type in emoticons) to express the emotions one is privately experiencing.

This argument has the following elements: an attack on the Cartesian conception of having and expressing feelings; an appeal to the Heidegger/Merleau-Ponty account of the importance of intercorporeality (direct mood sharing) to focal events or local worlds; the notion that focal events are what make life worth living; an argument that the Linden Lab technicians working from the Cartesian paradigm inherent in programming communication of inner mental states cannot make possible for residents the contagion or sharing of moods, thereby rendering focal events in *Second Life* impossible; therefore, living a worthwhile and meaningful life in *Second Life* is not possible.

I am not convinced that focal events are all that crucial to living a worthwhile life, although I am not interested in disputing the matter here. I agree with Dreyfus that at its current stage of programming development, *Second Life* relies on a Cartesian conception of the expression of emotions that is woefully inadequate for a resident's avatar to express the range of moods or feelings of the resident. Also, direct communication of moods between residents is not possible, and so neither is the sharing of moods, unlike in real-life human encounters. That acknowledged, Linden Lab programmers, as Dreyfus is aware, are working on the programming of direct communication of feelings between the resident and his or her avatar by the use of webcams trained on the resident's face and upper body. The programming apparently under development will enable the resident's computer to access the resident's facial and upper bodily movements and translate them directly into comparable movements of the resident's avatar. The avatar would then express the feelings and moods of the resident just as the resident does, without Cartesian translation and bodily expression choice sequences intervening. The avatar then becomes an extension of the resident's body, another body part, although one in a metaverse. For this to satisfactorily occur, however, there are upgrading problems that must be solved with the design of the avatars. Currently, *Second Life* avatars lack the human facial characteristics necessary to reproduce the detail of the subtle movements of the resident that will be captured by the webcam on his or her computer. If, however, the software problems are overcome, and there is reason to think they can be conquered even with existing technology, the moods and feelings of residents, including ones of which they may not be aware, will be reproducible instantaneously in their avatars. But will that result in contagious mood sharing between residents that would not be under the control of any one resident, in other words, focal events? And would Dreyfus have to withdraw his claim that living a meaningful life in *Second Life* is not possible?

There may be a catch that still defeats genuine shared moods: the resident who is on the receiving end of an avatar's expression of a mood (via the webcam translation method) will need to express a mood that is caught by his or her webcam, translated by the programming onto that person's avatar, and, hopefully, picked up by the originating resident. There would seem to be an intermediate step in the communication of moods that would not be there were the two residents to meet on a real-life street corner. Of course, that may be overcome when a resident's avatar is just an extension of that resident, another bodily part motivated and moved by the resident's will. At that point, however, I have what I think may be other serious concerns, for example, concerns about personal identity.

If Bob's *Second Life* avatar is an African American woman, can she be Bob, who is a White male ex-Marine? I have no idea what we should say, but I do not want to say that Bob has multiple personalities or that he is many different persons, for certainly his avatar, call her Babs, is not really a person. Babs is Bob or a certain manifestation, extension, or instantiation of Bob. When Babs smiles, it is because Bob smiles, Bob approves, Bob is pleased. Babs smiles with perfectly formed, lipstick-reddened lips. Bob smiles with lips that only partially can form into the classic configuration of a smile because he has little control over half of his disfigured face. But, clearly, Babs's smiling is not independent of the mood Bob is in. Babs is never in a mood independent of the mood Bob is in. Avatars are not in moods, residents are. Babs cannot express pleasure while Bob is in pain. But, paradoxically, the pleasure Bob experiences in Babs's activities and relationships may be a cause of great sorrow in Bob, because Bob is not always in *Second Life*, and his first-life, his real-life, deprivations are highlighted by recollections of the "Babsian" joy he experiences in *Second Life*. Little wonder Bob has the first-order desire to spend his every waking moment in *Second Life*, and his second-order volition is to have such a desire. He wants that desire to be his will.

The currently proposed programming solution to the problem of communication of moods among avatars, in any event, relates to a resident's creation of his or her avatar. Bob's face is so seriously disfigured that it may be a nearly impossible task to design a program that translates a webcam recording of his expressions of feelings and moods into the appropriate expressions on his chosen avatar, a woman who is definitely not disfigured. In order for the direct mood or feelings expressions to function from resident to avatar, will the avatar created by the resident have to have many of the same facial features as the resident? Wouldn't that significantly weaken the fantasy attraction of *Second Life*? Escaping into one's avatar's body and lifestyle would be restricted, and someone like Bob is not likely to find his life in the metaverse so attractive as to want to devote most of his waking hours to residence there. The attraction of escapism will have been diminished.

Let us stipulate that Linden Lab programmers overcome these worries and Bob's avatar can directly express his feelings and moods. Dreyfus's primary concern then is not a defeating issue for a resident living a worthwhile life in *Second Life*, given Dreyfus's account of what is required to live such a life. But is a Dreyfusian meaningful and worthwhile life a worthwhile life? Sharing moods in focal events may well contribute to one's sense of one's life being worthwhile, but I think that to live a worthwhile life, a person must really give a damn about something, perhaps many things, in his or her life, and those things, no doubt, are things about which one has deep feelings. That is what really giving a damn involves. Can a resident really give a damn, care in a profound sense, about anything in *Second Life*?

My question may appear to be embedded in some of the criticisms about *Second Life* that Dreyfus attributes to philosophical positions other than the one he favors, in which the illusionary essential nature of *Second Life* and its safe haven for fantasy and play were argued to be sufficient to defeat its meaningfulness. The argument might go that there is far too much fantasy to take it seriously enough to give a damn about it. I want to suggest that is no drawback because a person can really give a damn about an illusionary experience, a fantasy, a fiction, make-believe. That it is a safe haven for a person's spirit may be a reason why a person really gives a damn about it.

To give a damn about something is to care about it. Not really giving a damn about it is not to care at all about it. If you care about something, as Frankfurt noted,[10] it is important to you. You only give a damn about what is important to you, and for something to be important to you, you must give a damn about it. If you "really give a damn" about something, what you care about is very important to you. It is an element in defining the sort of person you are. If it were not, you would not give such a damn about it. Really giving a damn about something is guiding your behavior in a particular manner, along a specific course, intentionally avoiding other courses.

Frankfurt writes, "A person who cares about something is, as it were, invested in it. He identifies himself with what he cares about in a sense that he makes himself vulnerable to losses and susceptible to benefits depending upon whether what he cares about is diminished or enhanced."[11]

---

[10] Harry Frankfurt, *The Importance of What We Care About* (Cambridge, 1988).
[11] Ibid., 83.

Really giving a damn involves structuring a life in a certain way. Greenpeace in the United Kingdom is well aware of this feature of giving a damn and puts out an Internet cartoon on "Giving a damn" intended to encourage behavior that, if practiced by a significant number of people, could stem the tide of global climate change. They want all of us to really give a damn about that.

To give a damn about something, one must conceive of oneself as a being that casts itself into a future and so as a more or less consistent identity over time. Really giving a damn about something is not merely being moved by a momentary impulse. One may make the decision to give a damn about something in an instance, for example, while watching the Greenpeace website cartoon, but actually giving a damn about something cannot be identified with the decision one makes to give a damn about it. The decision to give a damn about something may be momentary, spur of the moment; really giving a damn about it takes time and involves structuring one's life in a specific sort of way in order to realize what one gives a damn about. At various times in our lives, some of us decide to give a damn about things that we never get around to really giving a damn about. Giving a damn about something, however, is not always dependent on making a prior decision to give a damn about it. Like falling in love, we can sometimes fall into giving a damn about some things and some of those things we really give a damn about. Frankfurt writes: "It certainly cannot be assumed that what a person cares about is generally under his immediate voluntary control."[12]

Because what one really gives a damn about is intimately intertwined with one's identity, the things one gives a damn about are largely constitutive of the possibility of one's choice rather than the objects of one's choice. What a person really gives a damn about determines what is relevant and irrelevant within that person's life. It frames and filters which means and (subsidiary) ends are in the field of possible actions or potentially worthy of choice for that person. Mitchell Haney refers to what one gives a damn about (although he, like Frankfurt, frames it in terms of what one cares about) as the "horizon" of one's will.[13] If you can imagine someone who really gives a damn about nothing at all, you would imagine a person who really makes no choices, who just doesn't care, a wanton.

What a person really gives a damn about is located in what Frankfurt calls "the structure of a person's will." As discussed in Chapter 7, I take

[12] Ibid., 85.
[13] See P. French and M. Haney, "Changes in Latitudes, Changes in Attitudes," *Contemporary Philosophy*, XXIII (2002), 22.

Frankfurt's account of the will to be salient. He distinguishes between first-order desires and second-order desires in a way I alluded to earlier. One of Bob's first-order desires, we may stipulate, is through his avatar to have a lesbian sexual experience with the partner in Babs's bathing suit business. He also may have a first-order desire to avoid such an experience, believing it may not be good for their business relationship. First-order desires are the effective motivators, and when a first-order desire moves him to action, that desire is his will. Bob, we continue to stipulate, has the second-order desire to have the desire to have a lesbian sexual experience with the partner in Babs's bathing suit business. Furthermore, Bob has the second-order desire that that first-order desire be his will, that it motivate his actions. He wants it to be the case that he is moved to cause his avatar to try to achieve his first-order desire. If that is the case, his second-order desire is what Frankfurt calls his "second-order volition," and having second-order volitions is "essential to being a person," as noted in Chapter 7. Frankfurt contrasts real persons with wantons who simply follow any first-order desire that strikes them and have no second-order volitions to make any of those desires their will. We may have all sorts of desires and will all sorts of actions, but the ones that we desire, give a damn about, to be our wills shape our characters. Consequently, perhaps the most important thing for a person to do in order to live a worthwhile life is to really give a damn about what is worth giving a damn about.

It might be suggested that *Second Life* is designed for wantons to realize many of their first-order desires. To no small extent, I suppose, that is true. Perhaps a great deal of avatar behavior should be classified as the expression of the first-order desires of *Second Life* residents that are not aligned with their second-order volitions. They really don't give much of a damn about what their avatars are up to most of the time. It is just fun, only make-believe, reminiscent of the Jack Nance and Conway Twitty song of the 1950s: "People see us everywhere. They think you really care. But myself, I can't deceive, I know it's only make believe."[14] Bob wanted to have a lesbian experience, and he acted on that desire through his avatar Babs. But he may not have wanted it to be the case that his first-order desire was his will. In that case, Bob had no second-order volition that aligned with his first-order desire, and he might be described as acting wantonly. It then will not be the case that Bob really gives a damn about that experience he desires in *Second Life* and through his avatar causes

[14] Jack Nance and Conway Twitty, "It's Only Make Believe," Marielle Music (1958).

to happen. I am not suggesting that Bob has a second-order desire not, through Babs, to have the lesbian experience. He may or he may not. Probably he doesn't.

Frankfurt's notion of the centrality of the will in personhood leads him to an account of what can occur when persons realize that what they deeply care about (really give a damn about) matters to such a degree to them that they cannot "forbear from a certain course of action." Such persons are in the grip of what Frankfurt calls "volitional necessity." Volitional necessity, though it may bestow meaning on the lives of those in its grip, is the extreme case, really giving a damn "on steroids." (I say more about this notion in Chapter 12.) It is possible that Bob's life as Babs in *Second Life*, and all that entails in terms of lifestyle commitments, is volitionally necessary for him. If that is the case, I do not see how we could deny that his *Second Life* existence through the avatar Babs is meaningful for Bob, although it is still unclear whether it is worthwhile. Living in *Second Life* is what Bob really gives a damn about, and he may give so much of a damn about it that any other course of action for him is unthinkable. He has not the will to give up his metaverse life, not because his will is weak, but because his will is so strong as to constrain him from any other course of action. The temptation is to think that Bob (under such a description) has become addicted to living through his avatar and that such an addiction is a sign of a weakness of character. That, however, need not be the case. Frankfurt describes the situation as follows: "Unlike the addict, he does not accede to the constraining force because he lacks sufficient strength to defeat it. He accedes to it because he is unwilling to oppose it and because, furthermore, his unwillingness is itself something which he is unwilling to alter."[15]

Generally, I think we should say that the life a person leads is worthwhile if what he or she really gives a damn about satisfies some condition(s) of value. Hence, the question, "What to care about?" as Frankfurt says, is a "fundamental preoccupation of human existence." What conditions of value should be applied to determine if someone's second-order volitions are aligning with worthwhile first-order desires, desires that make a person's life worthwhile? What makes something worth giving a damn about it?

That is a large and complex question that I cannot hope to answer in this chapter. I think there are at least two types of answers that might be offered. The first takes the form "X is worthy of giving a damn about if X

---

[15] Frankfurt, 87.

is important to the person independent of whether the person actually gives a damn about it." The idea is that there is some list of things or commitments or beliefs (virtues, maybe) that have the capacity to affect a person's life in important positive ways even if the person is unaware of them and does not have second-order volitions that he or she desire those things. In terms used by Michael Slote[16] and discussed earlier, I think such an answer could be called agent-focused. In Aristotle's ethics, for example, as Alasdair MacIntyre writes, "The virtues are precisely those qualities the possession of which will enable an individual to achieve *eudaimonia* and the lack of which will frustrate his movement towards that *telos*."[17] Possessing the Aristotelian virtues is antecedently important for persons, even if persons really do not care about possessing them just because, on an Aristotelian account, they are requisites of living a good life, a contented and worthwhile life.

On the basis of other accounts of the life well led or the good life or something in that vein, other things will be deemed worthy of our caring about them, that is, important to us, independent of our recognition of them as we align our second-order volitions with some of our desires, as we form our wills. If what Bob cares about in his residency in *Second Life* coincides with what is on some such theory important to him antecedently, or independent of his willing it, then his *Second Life* existence is worthwhile, at least given that theory.

I am not arguing that reaching the bar set by theories of what is independently important for persons is achievable in *Second Life*. I am not suggesting that a resident in *Second Life* can achieve *eudaimonia*, for example, although I cannot think of a good argument why a resident in *Second Life* could not possess and cause his or her avatar to act on the Aristotelian virtues. My point, a modest one I think, is that if we were convinced that there is something or there are some things or (possibly) states of mind the possession of which, independent of the person desiring them, are essential to living a worthwhile life, then we could determine whether someone like Bob living through Babs in *Second Life* has attained them regardless of whether his reasons for occupying himself at his computer in *Second Life* have anything at all to do with the attainment of those things or states of mind.

---

[16] Michael Slote, "Agent-Based Virtue Ethics," *Midwest Studies in Philosophy*, XX (1995), 83–101.
[17] Alasdair MacIntyre, *After Virtue* (Notre Dame, 1981), 148.

The second type of answer takes the form, "X is important to a person just because that person gives a damn about it." The second answer, again adopting language from Slote, could be called agent-based. One type of agent-based motivation noted in Chapter 5 and that I have written about more extensively elsewhere,[18] and that can determine what is important to a person, is inner strength. A person of "inner strength" might be described as self-sufficient,[19] self-assured, independent, a person of personal courage, fortitude, or integrity. The actions of a person of inner strength that are morally praiseworthy in an agent-based moral theory either directly demonstrate or express the person's inner strength or they express or exhibit motivations that are derivative of his or her inner strength. Slote catalogues some of the identifying characteristics of a person of inner strength as not self-deceptive, motivationally independent of others, and not weak of will.[20] In Chapter 5 and elsewhere,[21] I have suggested that Emersonian self-reliance may be the basic virtue of those with inner strength. The self-reliant person is his or her own direct moral "task-master." The worth of the life of an inner-strength anchored person is self-certified. Emerson writes, "Insist on yourself; never imitate."[22] Bob may be doing just that, although he would not say that is what he is doing. I cannot see why living through one's avatar in *Second Life* could not be an expression of inner strength and render that life that one really gives a damn about worthwhile, worth living in just that way.

It is important, however, to stress that I am not suggesting that Babs's life is worthwhile if Bob's life is. Babs has no life. It is Bob's life in *Second Life* as Babs that can be worth living for Bob, and that invites us to think about a number of what may in the future for philosophers become significant metaphysical issues. It seems to me that we need to come to grips with the anthropogenic fact that human beings are design spaces. Further, those spaces are not stable nor, for that matter, may the concept of a person be stable; that may already be contingent on the outcomes of engineering/design projects. The minds and identities of persons can

---

[18] See Peter A. French, *The Virtues of Vengeance* (Lawrence, 2001).

[19] Although I used the term "self-sufficient," among others, to characterize the person of inner strength, I do not mean to suggest that inner strength is a version of the Stoic *autarkeia*. The Stoic defines self-sufficiency as freedom from all pleasures and desires outside of one's direct control.

[20] Slote, 91.

[21] See note 19.

[22] Emerson, "Self-Reliance," 60–1.

be distributed over alternative information systems and design platforms and spaces, and actively engaged in multiple realities. What it is to live a meaningful and worthwhile transworld life will have to be focused in the will of the translife person, but it may become increasingly difficult to isolate that person and so identify the operative will across design platforms. Assuredly, I am convinced, nothing like a Cartesian conception will emerge.

The question to which I don't know how to frame an answer is, "Who is Bob?" Bob really gives a damn about his life as Babs, and that is the case regardless of whether his *Second Life* existence satisfies external conditions of worth or even manifests his inner strength in a way that he cannot otherwise do. I am tempted to say that Bob's will motivates Babs's behavior in a way that is more than his willing his only usable first-world physical hand to move a mouse on a pad. Alhough, of course, that is all Bob moves or needs to move. The rest is redescription. His moving the mouse is Babs acting, is Bob acting, is Babs designing a new bikini for her shop and everything else she ever does in *Second Life*.

9

Of Merels and Morals

Musts and Oughts

Before I go on in the next chapter to discuss the relationship between moral judgments of institutions, organizations, and the individuals functioning within them, it is important to clarify the role of institutions in matters of morality and obligation. Much that has been written on the significance of institutions in understanding moral obligations I believe evidences a basic misunderstanding. The remedy for certain aspects of that misunderstanding is first to clarify the concept of "institutional obligation" and then show that "moral-ought" judgments, although in one sense parasitic, are yet importantly independent of institutional obligation-creating rules.

I

I use the term "institution" more or less in the same way John Rawls did when he wrote that "by institution I shall understand a public system of rules which defines offices and positions with their rights and duties, powers and immunities, and the like."[1] Their formal character and their imposition of order and structure on participant behavior by rule and regulation are typical characteristics of institutions. Institutional rules, regulations, and customs define certain kinds of behavior; that is, they make certain kinds of descriptions of experience possible. Indeed, they make possible certain experiences.

An institution's set of rules (broadly defined to include regulations and customs) is not merely a collection of devices that regulate antecedently existing behavior patterns. Rather, the rules define, or, in John Searle's

---

[1] John Rawls, *A Theory of Justice* (Cambridge, 1971), 55.

terms, are constitutive of,[2] new kinds of activity; that is, they identify the performance of certain actions as "counting as" the performance of an institutional act. We may say that a rule is constitutive if and only if it is a member of a system of rules such that behavior that accords with at least a large subset of the rules of that system can receive descriptions that could not be given if the system did not exist.[3]

My account of constitutive rules may seem unnecessarily imprecise. Searle maintains that a rule is constitutive if and only if behavior that accords with it can receive descriptions it could not receive if there were no such rule. But Searle also speaks of constitutive rules "on the fringe" of some system of constitutive rules. He talks of degrees of centrality in such a system. According to Searle's account, every constitutive rule, including all fringe rules, would have to make new descriptions possible. Given my version, a rule would still be constitutive even though in itself it does not make a new description of behavior possible, as long as it is a member of a system of rules that does make new descriptions possible.

The following are plausible ways of construing the relationship within an institution between its constitutive rules and the behavior they pro-hibit, permit, and require of participants:

(1) Within institution I, X (a person) has the right to do y in circum-stance C if and only if there is a rule in I that specifically gives permission to X to do y when circumstances of the sort C arise.[4]

(2) Within I, X has an obligation to do y in circumstance C if and only if there is a rule in I that specifically requires the doing of y when circumstances of the sort C arise.

(3) Within I, X has an obligation not to do y in circumstance C if and only if there is a rule in I that specifically prohibits the doing of y when circumstances of the sort C arise.

(4) Within I, if doing y is not specifically prohibited by any rules in I, then X is at liberty to do y in I.

All four of these are controversial. I want to extract from them a great deal, some of which will fly in the face of standard treatments of deontic logic and many moral theories. I hold that:

---

[2] John Searle, *Speech Acts* (New York, 1969).

[3] I am indebted to Howard Wettstein for this definition of a constitutive rule.

[4] This form is based on a discussion with Haskell Fain. He is not responsible for my employment of it in this way.

(a) The proper way of understanding a right is to treat it as a permission given to someone to do something within an institution.

This removes any temptation to treat "rights" as properties of persons. To have a right to do something is not to be in possession of some property or other, but to be in a position to do something without penalty and with justification when one chooses to do it.

(b) Rights are always intra-institutional (or, if you will, institution-specific).

There are no such things as natural rights because the mechanism of permission granting does not exist out of the context of institutions. I do not have, for example, the right to life by virtue of the fact of my birth, although I may have that right by virtue of the rules of, for example, a legal institution. The "state of nature" is not only a state without obligations, as Hobbes allowed; it is a state without rights as well.

That the granting of permissions is an institutional affair is made especially clear in that the sentences used to grant permissions contain act-descriptions that would not be possible if the institution that provided their context had not a specific subset of constitutive rules. That is, the descriptions of those acts are made possible by the introduction of terms created by or given their special sense by a subset of the constitutive rules of that institution. For example, chess players are given permission by the rules of the game to castle if neither king nor rook has previously moved, the king is not in check, and the intervening spaces on the back line are clear. All chess players whose circumstances in a game of chess are truthfully described in that way have the right to castle. The expression of that right is impossible (that is, it is totally senseless) outside of the game's context, which is just to say, and not surprisingly, that the act of castling and the right to do so are completely bound to chess.

(c) The sentence (S1) "X has the right to do something" is a description of X's institutional situation.

This should be understood as equivalent to the sentence (S2) "X has been granted permission by the rules of I to do something." (S2) is truth-apt. Settling whether or not X has a right to castle is in principle no different from determining that the object on which the chessboard is resting is a yellow table.

(d) What I have said of rights (that is, permissions) is also true of obligations (so-called positive and negative duties).

Hence, the sentence (S3) "X has an obligation to do something," is a description of X's institutional situation. It should be understood as equivalent to (S4) "X is required by the rules of some institution to do something." This point will be of greater concern momentarily.

II

The remark "X has the right to do z but ought not do z," made in an institutional setting, can be nothing other than a prudential or tactical remark. In an important sense the remark is extra-institutional.

Games have proved to be useful for examining intra-institutional relationships and behavior.[5] So, in order to set a basis for the development of my general thesis, I shall use as an example a relatively primitive game (with a minimum of rules). It was originally associated with the shepherds of the Salisbury Plain and was popular in Elizabethan England. It is the game variously called "Merels,"[6] "Morelia," or "Nine Men's Morris."[7] The game is played on a rectangular layout of concentric rectangles with lines connecting each of the rectangles halfway on each side of the pattern, creating a number of intersections. The entire set of rules for the two-person game of "Merels" is as follows: each player is provided with nine men of distinguishable colors, and each in turn places one man on the layout at any intersection, corner, or meeting of the lines, hereafter called *spaces*. (a) Turns alternate after each move throughout the game. The object is to get three men in a line. (b) A player who succeeds in getting a line of three men has the right to remove from the layout any one of his adversary's men, except that he cannot take one from a line of three unless there are no others remaining on the layout. After all nine men are entered, turns are taken by moving any man to any adjoining space, provided it is vacant. (c) When a new line of three is formed in this way, the player has the right to remove an adversary's man from the layout. (d) It is advantageous for a player to place his men in a position to form and reform two lines alternately several times. Play continues in this way until one player has only three men left. Any of the three men can then

---

[5] Examples: William Alston, "Linguistic Acts," *American Philosophical Quarterly*, I, 2 (April, 1964), 138–46; John Searle, "How to Derive 'Ought' from 'Is'," *Philosophical Review*, LXXIII, 1 (January, 1964), 43–58; Rawls, "Two Concepts of Rules," *Philosophical Review*, LXIV, 1 (January, 1955), 3–32.

[6] "Merel" was often corruptly used, or both "moral" and "miracle."

[7] In *A Midsummer Night's* Dream, Shakespeare refers to the game, Act II, Scene 1.

hop over to any vacant space on the layout. (e) When either player is reduced to two men, his game is lost.

Let us suppose that two shepherds, having etched the layout in the turf of the Salisbury Plain, reach the point where shepherd X forms the first line of three. Shepherd X has the right [see (1)–(4)] to remove one of Y's pieces; he is not obliged or obligated to do so. The game will not stop nor even be corrupted if X does not exercise his right.[8] Suppose X's friend tells him that he *ought* to remove the piece if he intends to disadvantage Y and hence ultimately win the game. "Ought" there would have either a prudential or a tactical use, and it is not derivative of the rules of Merels, although those rules make it ("X ought to remove the piece") an intelligible remark.

Imagine now that the game has progressed to endgame and that, if X exercises his right of removal (earned in the appropriate way), Y will lose the game. Furthermore, suppose that Y had struck a bet with X that the loser would forfeit five of his best sheep to the winner, that X is well aware that his victory will cause great personal and family hardship (Y's children will starve, for example), and that he (X) could absorb a similar loss without difficulty. It may seem appropriate in such circumstances to say that X has the right to do something (remove Y's piece from the layout), but he ought not do so, and that is clearly not a tactical remark. The force of that "ought not," like that of the prudential "ought," falls outside the game of Merels. It is a moral "ought not."

If X removes the piece, X might be blamed for ruining Y or for making such a bet with Y in the first place, but X will not be penalized within the game of Merels for exercising his right of removal. The rules of the game of Merels have nothing at all to say about sheep or the financial status of participants, or about wagers.

Let us take a closer look at the tactical and prudential uses of "ought" just exemplified. (I return to moral uses of "ought" in Section III.) When ought-statements are made in institutional contexts (and when their force is not moral), they do not state obligations. Institutional obligations, that is, those obligations that are created by an individual for himself or herself by his or her participation in a particular institution, cannot characteristically and best be expressed by using "ought"; rather, they can best be expressed by using "must." In the first example,

---

[8] This must be true of all rights. For example, the fact that I have the right to sell my house does not entail that I have an obligation to do so.

X *ought* to (as a matter of tactics) remove Y's piece, Y *must* (is *obliged* to) allow his piece to be removed; that is, Y has an institutional obligation (Y is required) to do so. Y must. Or, to use an example from chess, a player *must* (not "ought to") move his king out of check.

If the standard modal deontic logicians and moral philosophers remain insistent on using "ought" to render institutional obligations, then that "ought" will have to be understood as a very special "ought." We could call it an "institutional ought," but it will convey what the ordinary "must" conveys.[9] "Must" can do the institutional work for which it is suited: its ordinary use in institutional contexts as well as in non-institutional contexts straightforwardly signals the binding requirement or prohibition we want it to express. Moreover, the use of "ought" in statements of institutional obligation is apt to be misleading. If the constitutive rules of Merels define what it is to play Merels in the sense that they make it possible for behavior that accords with them to be described as Merels playing, they have to exclude the possibility that someone may be playing Merels and not acting in accord with a large subset of those rules. That possibility is not excluded if the accepted way of stating the institutional obligations derived from those rules does not itself convey the sense of a binding requirement on participant behavior; that is, if it conveys a concessive "requirement" or that it is optional, as "ought" does.

Statements of institutional obligation, then, *must* report binding requirements of action for participants qua participants within the institution and *ought* to be formulated, as "Y must do z." Whether or not someone must do something is simply a question of fact, of finding the correct description of his or her institutional situation, and that such a description is made possible by institutional rules of a certain sort. The upshot is that we should equate the institutional "must" with the predicate "ϕ is required to do (something)." We can, using that monadic predicate, render institutional obligations for logical purposes in the existential modality. No disguise of the purely descriptive nature of an obligation-stating sentence, no undefined deontic categories, such as characterize standard systems of deontic logic constructed analogously to that of the alethic modalities, need enter the picture.

"Ought," as in settings like those just mentioned, signals or at least allows for the presence of option or choice available to the addressee. "Must," however, forecloses the possibility of choice; it conveys the sense

---

[9] It alternatively can be stated as "_____ is obliged to _____."

that the course of action is inescapable insofar, at least, as the participation status in the institution is maintained. Of course, one can always escape the requirement to move the king out of check by ceasing to play chess at the point when one's opponent places one's king in check. This might suggest that the institutional obligation could best be expressed by "Y ought to move Y's king out of check if Y wants to continue playing chess." But such a conditional directs attention away from the moves in the game toward Y's state of mind or to what Y wants. Even if the intent to participate is assumed in the rules, it is not assumed in sentences that state the obligations that derive from those rules. If we were to ask a chess player, participant qua participant, why he or she moved his or her king out of check when certain game situations occurred, the answer would most likely not be that he or she recognized he or she ought to do so insofar as he or she wanted to continue playing, but indeed that the rules of chess dictate that he or she must do so, that the set of all his or her possible next institutional moves has been greatly limited, and that the effect of his or her next move will be a very particular kind of modification of his or her status [the placement of his or her pieces] in the game. Y's situation is best described by using the dyadic predicate Ryk (Y is required to move Y's king out of check), in conjunction with a set of sentences that describe the placement of the pieces on the chessboard at that time, and that that conjunction entails (stipulated for simplicity) that Y's next move is a if and only if it is not b (where a and b are move-descriptions such as "K to K3"). The question "Ought Y's next move be a or b?" can be completely and satisfactorily answered intra-institutionally by the application of game-theoretic methods (in the case of chess and Merels) for zero-sum nonnegotiable games. It will be solely a question of strategy, consequences, and preferences. Y would be in a classic game-theory choice situation in a perfect information game, and so a best-play strategy could easily be devised for Y. The tactical "ought" can always be given a game-theoretic analysis. Hence, it always can be reduced to sentences describing a "best-play" strategy. "Y ought (tactical remark) to move the king to K3" will be true if that move occurs in a "best-play" strategy devisable for Y at that juncture of game play.

III

Returning to the other uses of "ought," the shepherds on the Salisbury Plain, and their game of Merels: suppose that, as mentioned earlier, shepherd X has shepherd Y in a bad way in the game. Upon making one move, X will end Y's game. Further, Y and X have struck up a wager that will, in the circumstances of defeat, make it impossible for Y to meet his legal/parental obligation to provide for his children's welfare. In simplified fashion, let us say that at least three institutions are involved in the situation: (1) the game of Merels; (2) wagering; and (3) the legal institution insofar as it concerns parental obligations to insure their children's welfare. The rules of Merels grant the right of removal to X and also force on Y the obligation to (he must) cease his play (do s) in this circumstance; he has lost. The rules of wagering create an obligation for the loser of the wager to (he must) pay in full the amount of the wager (Y must do p).

The legal institution admittedly is much more complex than two-person games such as Merels or wagering, but that complexity does not appreciably alter the types of obligations (in this case, parental duties) that may arise therein. For the sake of simplicity, let us stipulate that one legal rule of the community of the shepherds is that parents are obliged to provide the necessities of survival for their young children. Shepherd Y, a father, must then provide for the sustenance of his children (he must do c). We may say then that Y has institutional obligations to do s, p, and c.

Y cannot, of course, do s, p, and c. Doing p precludes doing c, and vice versa. We are presented with the interesting question, the sort that typically perplexes ethicists: "Ought Y fulfill p or c, since he cannot do both?" Any definitive answer to that question is what I take to be paradigmatic of a "moral-ought" judgment. The logic of institutions can in no way settle the issue. Richard Brandt set up the situation nicely when he wrote: "If there are two conflicting obligations . . . and a decision must be made as to what should be done, we do not normally say, 'What then really is my obligation?' To ask this is somewhat odd, since it is already clear that there are two obligations, which conflict. . . . [T]he preferred phrasing in this situation is 'what *ought* I to do?'"[10]

As previously mentioned, "ought" has myriad uses (tactical, prudential, institutional). When "ought" is used either to identify one obligation as paramount in a conflict of institutional obligations or as a reminder that one obligation in such conflicts is paramount, its use is paradigmatically moral. (This is not meant to suggest that every "moral-ought" judgmental use is bound to occur in obligation conflict situations

---

[10] "The Concepts of Obligation and Duty," *Mind*, LXXIII, 291 (July 1964), 374–93, 378.

or that each such judgment makes some oblique reference to such conflicts.) Judgments as to what is paramount obviously rest on some structure of priorities, on some kind of hierarchy of institutions and activities.

In the best of all possible worlds, all people would be able to fulfill
all their institutional obligations without having to postpone, delay, or
fail to meet any. There would be no moral obligations in such a world.
In the next best possible world, most of the time persons are able to
fulfill all their obligations, although on occasion circumstances arise
such that people cannot fulfill two or more obligations that fall due at
approximately the same time. In those cases, "moral-ought" judgments,
moral principles, and the notion of moral obligation have a role to play.

The *Oxford English Dictionary*'s seventh definition of "principle" is "a
general law . . . adopted or professed as a guide to action; a settled ground
or basis of conduct or practice." Julius Kovesi distinguished moral principles from moral judgments, suggesting that principles contain what he
calls "complete notions" from the moral point of view, whereas judgments
do not.[11] For example, "Murder is wrong" is a moral principle because
"murder" from the moral point of view is a complete notion; hence,
there is a sense in which the word "wrong" in the sentence expressing
the principle is redundant. "Killing someone suffering from a terminal
disease is wrong" is a moral judgment because "Killing someone suffering
from a terminal disease" is not a complete notion from the moral point of
view. "Wrong" in that sentence functions as a discriminator, marking off
as morally forbidden killing someone because he or she is in a particular
medical state, and so forth.

Although I am in sympathy with Kovesi's approach in general, I prefer
to make the distinction between moral principles and moral judgments
along somewhat different lines. A moral principle for me is any former
"moral ought" judgment that has ceased to serve a judgmental role for
members of a community, but nonetheless would likely be cited as a guide
to their actions by the majority of the membership if they were pressed
to explain their ways of behaving in certain situations and, importantly,
provides analogical support for the "moral-ought" judgments they do
make.

It is one of the sociohistorical facts about a community that its members
at certain times simply cease making certain discriminatory judgments
regarding certain actions and the fulfillment of certain obligations rather
than others in genuine conflicts, although they continue to guide their

---

[11] See Julius Kovesi, *Moral Notions* (London, 1967).

lives by what once were the dictates of those judgments; that is, they start acting on principle in those cases. They use those principles as the bedrock of the reasons they give in support of the "moral-ought" judgments they do make. In language used by Wittgenstein for quite another purpose in *On Certainty*, I prefer to think of moral principles as "hardened"[12] "moral-ought" judgments. They are no longer judgments, insofar as no one in the community actually judges them to be the case; for example, no one judges that he ought not to commit murder. If one is convinced that the act one contemplates is an act of murder, the "ought" in "I ought not to do it (commit murder)" is redundant.

Community moral beliefs can and do alter over time. The fact that certain beliefs about the paramountcy of one institutional obligation vis-à-vis another are no longer thought to be subject to question, or are only extraordinarily so subject – that is, that they have privileged status – is not a logical matter. It is simply a function of community history that some things are done on principle and others need to be decided.

It might be convenient if all the "moral-ought" judgments supportable within a community could be logically derived from its moral principles as the obligations of an institution can be derived from its rules in conjunction with true sentences describing someone's institutional state of affairs. But, unfortunately, it does not work that way. Moral principles may form a part of the framework in which "moral-ought" judgments are made, but the maker of a "moral-ought" judgment does not infer his or her judgments from those principles. He or she will, however, justify his or her moral judgments either by citing a moral principle or by trying to identify them by analogy with a moral principle.

To justify "moral-ought" judgments is to indicate the relative status of moral beliefs. If a speaker is asked to justify his or her expression of the belief that (1) "X ought not to do a," he or she might respond by uttering a sentence of the form (2) "Because X ought not to do b." When asked for a reason why (2) should be the case, he or she might again offer an "ought" or "ought not" judgment, but if he or she does, he or she will still be vulnerable to another "Why?" question. The chain of reasons cannot end with a sentence containing an "ought" or "ought not" if these are used in a judgmental, a discriminatory, way. Discriminations are always subject to further justification. The justifier's chain can terminate either in a sentence of the form "c is paramount to a" or in a sentence of the

---

[12] Ludwig Wittgenstein, *On Certainty*, translated by C. Paul and E. Anscombe (Oxford, 1969), 95–8.

form "That would be (moral term)." It can also terminate in a sentence that contains "ought" if "ought" is not functioning as a discriminator in that sentence. For example, "One ought not to commit murder." If a "why" question were asked of any of those responses, the justifier could only assume either that the questioner is ignorant of the language or that he or she is questioning the scope of the application of the moral term, for example, "murder," or the first term of the paramountcy predicate. "Why would that be murder?" is quite a different question from "Why ought I refrain from pulling the plug of the support system of a comatose human being for whom there is realistically no hope of recovery?"

Moral principles, including those stated in "ought" sentences, do serve as final answers, bedrock responses, to questions of justification. "Moral-ought" judgments cannot play such a role. In fact, most "moral-ought" judgments cannot be nonanalogically related to moral principles in a justificatory process. That should come as no surprise; for, if a direct implicational relationship always could be drawn from moral principles to appropriate "moral-ought" judgments, the discriminatory feature of those judgments would be only a facade. If, as I maintain, "ought" sometimes does have a discriminatory (judgmental) moral use, then the only justificatory avenue open to the maker of such judgments is an analogical appeal to a principle; for example, "Euthanasia is murder." The success or failure of such an appeal when broadcast generally across the community is an indicator of whether or not the "moral-ought" judgment – that is, "Persons ought not to pull the plug of the support system of a comatose human being for whom there is realistically no hope of recovery" – will eventually harden into a moral principle itself. If it were to harden, a chain of justificatory reasons in the future might then be successfully terminated with "That would be euthanasia!" This process I take to be the moral corollary, or exemplification, of the process suggested by Wittgenstein's "river metaphor" in *On Certainty*.[13]

Insofar as the "ought" in the statement of a moral principle about obligations is at best redundant, the sense of such a principle can be rendered in logical notation by the dyadic predicate, "● is paramount to ♦," so long as an institutional obligation is introduced in the first free-variable place; for example, "The obligation to do c." Moral principles are not ad hoc, not addressee-specific, and not time-specific. Hence, there is

---

[13] See my "Why Did Wittgenstein Read Tagore to the Vienna Circle?" *Proto Soziologie* (1993). Republished in *Protosoziologie im Kontext: "Lebenswelt" und "System" in Philosophie und Soziologie*, edited by Preyer, Peter, & Ulfig (Wurzburg, 1996).

little virtue in complicating their logical representation. We may simply represent, for example, "the obligation to do c" with the singular term "c" (but only as a shorthand device, in no way implying that obligations are individuals). If there were a moral principle regarding the obligations to do c and a, it could be sufficiently rendered by "Pca" (read as "The obligation to do c is paramount to the obligation to do a").

It will, however, take a radical innovation to properly treat in logical notation the "ought" that appears in "moral-ought" judgments about obligations. I shall offer only a suggestion for doing so. Suppose we treat the "ought" that appears in such judgments as the copula of the triadic predicate, "X treat ♦ as paramount to ●" (or, what amounts to the same thing, "X fulfill ♦ before ●"). Using F as the predicate letter representing the triadic predicate in the case of shepherd Y, we would have Fycp. But that can best be understood only as the imperative "Y fulfill c before p" and does not capture the moral "ought."

Copulation in assertoric discourse is not represented at all. It is assumed in the juxtaposing of a predicate letter and a variable. Suppose we distinguish assertoric copulation from "ought" copulation by using a like device in the nonreducible "moral-ought" judgment cases, for example, Oy(Fycp) (read as "Y ought to fulfill c before p").

IV

I have distinguished four basic uses of "ought." The prudential or tactical "ought" is convertible to a description of a best play or plays and can be rendered fully in purely assertoric discourse. The institutional use of "ought" is collapsed in terms of its sense into "must" and can best be rendered by the predicate "X is required to do (something)," without leaving assertoric discourse. Two moral uses of "ought" were identified. "Ought" is, for all intents and purposes, redundant in the statement of a moral principle. The only noneliminable use of "ought" that cannot be rendered in the assertoric modality is that which occurs in the making of moral judgments, for example, that a particular institutional obligation in a conflict situation is paramount.

I prepared a session for the chaplains to discuss conflict situations in which I used the case of Agamemnon at Aulis. Agamemnon assembled the Greek naval army in a cause demanded by Zeus, avenging the kidnapping of his sister-in-law Helen. His ships carrying the Greeks to Troy were becalmed by the anger of the goddess Artemis because Agamemnon, boasting he was as good a hunter as Artemis, killed an animal she regarded as sacred. A plague struck the troops and the wind was prevented from blowing so the ships could not sail away from Aulis. Agamemnon's soothsayer Calchas divined that the only remedy for the situation was to placate the wrath of Artemis by sacrificing Agamemnon's daughter Iphigenia. The Greeks demanded the sacrifice. Were Agamemnon not to kill Iphigenia, he would be abandoning the expedition, causing the useless deaths of many if not all of his troops, and utterly failing in his duty as the commander of the Greeks. To perform the sacrifice, however, is to violate his parental obligation as a father. It is to commit a horrible deed. As a commander he must do x. As a father he must do y. The two things he must do are incompatible. What morally ought he to do? A utilitarian will probably say that he ought to sacrifice his daughter to avoid losing the Greek army on the beaches of Aulis. And that, of course, is what he does. He will also pay the ultimate price for doing so. It is to revenge the sacrifice of Iphigenia that ten years later, when Agamemnon returns victorious from Troy, Clytemnestra, his wife and Iphigenia's mother, will slaughter him. Doing what one morally ought to do may not always end happily. It doesn't for Agamemnon.

Another case that illustrates the point, and one the chaplains had no trouble in identifying the moral obligation among competing institutional obligations, is that of Robert Boisjoly, a rocket seal expert with Morton Thiokol, Inc., who, after the explosion of the *Challenger* space shuttle, revealed to the investigating commission that not only did his company know of defects in the O-ring seals, but that it and NASA decided to launch the shuttle against the strong recommendations of Boisjoly and other engineers on the project. On the day before the *Challenger* launch, he recommended against it to his superiors and managers at NASA because the temperature at launch was forecast to be 18 degrees Celsius and he had run tests that proved that the primary and secondary O-ring seals were prone to be compromised by hot gasses that eroded the seals if launches occurred at low temperature. He was reprimanded by his boss for revealing that he and the other engineers did not support the managers' decision to recommend launching and for "airing the company's dirty laundry." He was castigated as being disloyal and accused of seriously damaging the company's image. Six months after the *Challenger* explosion, he was granted extended sick leave and never returned to work for Morton Thiokol or any other company in that industry. He had an institutional obligation of loyalty to his company and an obligation from the legal institution to truthfully report what he knew of the case to the investigators. He decided that he ought to do the latter and made that choice on moral grounds. In his case, doing what he morally ought to do was imprudent and destroyed his engineering career.

The case of Captain Vere in Herman Melville's *Billy Budd* offers an additional example, one yielding what may be called a recipe for moral tragedy. The childlike Billy, an impressed sailor on a British warship, is falsely accused of plotting mutiny by the master-at-arms Claggart. Billy suffers from a speech impediment and cannot verbally respond to the charges. Like a child, he strikes Claggart, killing him. Captain Vere is in a serious predicament. He has a duty as captain of a naval vessel in a time of war to punish Billy to the full extent required by the Mutiny Act and the Articles of War – to hang him. It does not matter that Claggart was killed. Merely striking a superior is a capital crime. But Vere knows, because he was the only witness to the event, that Billy's actions lack what in law is called *mens rea* and as such he does not deserve to be executed. Perhaps Billy should not, under the usual administration of justice in law, be exonerated, but he does not deserve the death sentence. Vere cannot both punish Billy as martial law requires and be lenient as he also believes justice requires because he believes Billy to be "innocent before God." Vere must hang Billy and he must be lenient to him. He has two institutional obligations, one as captain and one as a judge with the duty of administering the law justly. Obviously, he cannot do both and Christopher Gowans seems to be right that Vere's case is "morally tragic in this sense: Whatever he did, in the wake of Billy's killing of the officer, he would have committed a serious moral wrong."[14] But Vere must do something, just as Agamemnon must choose between his obligations as a military commander and his obligations as a father. Vere hasn't the luxury of putting off a decision. What ought he to do? If that is a moral ought, the answer to that question will identify the obligation in the conflict that is primary, not which is prudent. "Struck dead by an angel of God! Yet the angel must hang!" Vere says over Claggart's corpse. There is considerable discussion in the literature about *Billy Budd* as to which way Vere ought to have gone, and I am not saying that the matter is at all settled. In *Billy Budd* and in Agamemnon's plight at Aulis, we have a recipe for unavoidable moral tragedy, and that is the makings of important and lasting literature.

Given my account, there can be no class of obligations that is the moral class; we do not have, on the one hand, institutional obligations

---

[14] Christopher Gowans, *Innocence Lost* (Oxford, 1994), 7.

and, on the other, moral obligations. Saying that someone has a moral obligation to do something is to characterize an institutional obligation as paramount in a conflict situation. We do not have obligations and moral obligations, as Farmer Jones has cows and pigs. We have institutional obligations, some of which are moral in certain circumstances. Furthermore, there can be no such thing as the Moral Institution because there are no moral rules of a constitutive type. In fact, if there were a moral institution, its rules would no doubt at times create obligations that would conflict with those incurred from participation in some other institution. The resulting conflict could be resolved only by appeal to a paramountcy principle that in all fairness could not be derived internally from the institutions party to the dispute, *ad infinitum, ad nauseam.*[15]

[15] I am indebted to Howard Wettstein, D. E. Cooper, and David Pears for their helpful criticisms and penetrating questions on earlier drafts of this chapter, and to Bernard Baumrin, who was kind enough to share an unpublished manuscript on a nonmodal deontic logic with me.

10

Inference Gaps in Moral Assessment

Individuals, Organizations, and Institutions

In *Notes on the State of Virginia*, Thomas Jefferson acknowledges that slavery is a moral wrong and at odds with the principles he so eloquently laid down in the *Declaration* and with respect to which the American Revolution was motivated. He proposed legislation to abolish the slave trade and the extension of slavery into the Western territories, legislation that failed by a single vote. Throughout his entire adult life, Jefferson owned hundreds of slaves on his two plantations, and he freed only a very few. There appears to be little doubt that Jefferson was a racist, as a sampling of comments he wrote in the *Notes on the State of Virginia* attests.[1] He nonetheless identified the enslavement of Blacks as immoral, although he regarded Blacks as unfit by nature to participate in the American social experiment.

It is tempting to think that Jefferson is the epitome of hypocrisy, and we would think that because we likely hold the view that from a slave owner's assenting to the judgment that "the institution of slavery is immoral and should be abolished," some course or courses of action follow on the part of that slave owner with respect to his/her slaves, namely, that he/she should free them.

The argument looks like this:

[A] (1) The institution of slavery is immoral and should be abolished.
(2) I own slaves.
(3) Therefore, I should free my slaves.

---

[1] "I advance it therefore as a suspicion only, that the blacks are inferior to the whites in the endowments both of body and mind, and that... their inferiority is not the effect merely of their condition of life.... It appears to me that in memory they are equal to the whites; in reason much inferior, as I think one could scarcely be found capable of tracing and comprehending the investigations of Euclid; and that in imagination they are dull, tasteless, and anomalous."

Such a conclusion, from a practical point of view, might be said to follow from the premises if attached to it is a *ceteris paribus* clause: I should free my slaves, other things being equal, or something of that sort. Or, it might be read that I have a *prima facie* moral obligation to free my slaves. That obligation, being *prima facie*, of course, may be overridden by more important moral concerns in the circumstances, and in Jefferson's case, he believed that such concerns existed. Ethically speaking, of course, such conclusions drawn from those premises are a cheat, for the very reason that things in such cases are seldom equal or morally insignificant.

I think that it is not at all clear what conclusion(s), morally speaking, regarding my behavior were I a slave-owner follows from the previously stated premises. That is, it is not at all clear that Jefferson morally ought to have freed his slaves, even though both premises are true and he would have agreed that they were so.

Marcus Singer argues, in a paper that has not received the attention it deserves,[2] "no moral judgment of an institution-constituted action follows from a moral judgment of the related institution."[3] By "an institution-constituted action," Singer means an action whose description as an action of that sort depends on the existence of an institution or social practice for its sense. Simply put, in the absence of the institution, no one could perform the action. Owning slaves and freeing them are examples of such actions with respect to the institution of slavery. Singer's point is that from the negative moral assessment of the institution, all that could follow deductively is that we have a moral problem with the institution. What morally ought to be done by an individual engaged in actions constituted by the institution is not inferable from the assessment. If Singer is right, then, although I concur wholeheartedly with [A] (1) and acknowledge that [A] (2) is true, it would not be illogical for me to decide, even having adopted the moral point of view, that I should not free my slaves. And that is what Jefferson concluded.

What I morally ought to do with my slaves may be dependent on crucial factors other than the moral assessment that the institution of slavery is immoral and should be abolished. This is not to say that the moral assessment regarding the institution is utterly irrelevant with respect to what I ought to do with my slaves. Jefferson could have reasoned that if he were to free his slaves, the law might allow someone else with a

---

[2] Marcus Singer, "Institutional Ethics" in *Ethics, Royal Institute of Philosophy Supplement: 35*, edited by A. Phillips Griffiths (Cambridge, 1993), 223–45.

[3] Ibid., 239.

reputation for extreme sadistic cruelty toward Blacks to capture and enslave them. Then he might be condemning them to a life much worse than he provided on his plantations because no provisions are made in his society for Blacks who are freed or ex-slaves to participate in the community in a meaningful and productive or even basic way other than as slaves. In 1820, Jefferson made a paternalistic argument along similar lines. The very fact that the possible outcomes of emancipation for his freed slaves are considerable from the moral point of view suggests that it would be, at best, morally callous to ignore them when deciding what to do. In effect, morally speaking, the individual action decision is not directly inferable from the premises in [A]. The point is that there is an inference gap of sizable proportions between the premises of [A] and any conclusion about what a slave-owner (like Jefferson) morally ought to do in any specific case.

Another inference gap problem relates to premise [A] (1). The premise maintains that from the negative moral assessment of the institution, it follows that slavery should be abolished. I suppose such an inference rests on the generalized claim that immoral practices or institutions ought to be abolished. In the case of slavery, it is indisputable that it should be abolished, or at least it is in the case of forced slavery (contractual slavery may be another matter, but not one I want to explore), but that is because slavery is a special case among institutions. It may not be the case that most other institutions in a society, such as capitalism or democracy, that may be assessed as immoral even in very serious ways in whole or in part ought to be abolished. In this I depart from Singer's account. If I were to convince you that capitalism is seriously flawed in very fundamental ways from the moral point of view (because it is unfair to those from lower economic classes or to those in developing countries), it does not follow that you must endorse abolishing capitalism. You must, on pain of inconsistency, be willing to endorse doing something to correct its moral deficiencies, reforming it, fixing it. But reform is not abolition. The reason we cannot reform slavery to satisfy moral principles of justice and fairness, particularly those that protect human dignity, respect, and worth, is that were we to do so, the resulting institution would not be slavery. I am arguing that we should not generalize from the slavery case to the position that all institutions that are rightly assessed to be immoral with respect to some of their fundamental elements or to some, perhaps significant, degree should be abolished. What does follow is that something corrective, perhaps even radical, must be done about the institution for it to pass moral muster. However, nothing specific about what individuals engaged in the institution, some of whose actions are institution-constituted, morally ought to do with respect to exactly those actions seems to follow from the negative assessment of the institution in and of itself.

My point so far is that it is a mistake to think that negative moral assessments of institutions entail that those who perform actions that are constituted by those institutions ought or ought not to be performing them. Also, the inference gap exists in both directions, from the moral assessment of the individual's institutionally constituted actions to the moral status of the institution or the system of rules that constitute it and vice versa. The inference gaps expose a very important structural aspect of the moral world. They reveal, I suggest, that the elements of the moral world, although related, are distinct and require separate moral attention when it comes to moral assessment.

Institutions are abstractions. They are, as Singer, leaning heavily on Rawls, describes them, "complex[es] of rules defining rights and duties, roles, functions, privileges, immunities, responsibilities, and services."[4] Most, though not all, institutions are concretely embodied in what I call organizations. And, of course, individuals perform institutionally constituted actions within organizations. For example, there was slavery, the Monticello Plantation, and Thomas Jefferson owning, emancipating, buying, and selling slaves. There is the military, the Marine Corps, and a sergeant in Iraq leading his unit in a house-to-house battle in Fallujah or al-Sadr City.

Not all institutions have concrete organizational embodiments. Promising does not. Promising, however, is a prerequisite institution for other institutions that do have organizational embodiments even if only rudimentary ones, for example, marriage. There may be multiple linkages between institutions on which an organizational embodiment of one or more than one is or are based. There are also institutionally constituted actions that persons can perform in the absence of any specific organization, for example, my promising to meet you for lunch.

Rawls maintains that the principles of justice for institutions must not be confused with moral principles that apply to individuals. "These two kinds of principles apply to different subjects and must be discussed separately."[5] He adds that institutions as systems of rules are abstract objects, but that they are also "realized." By that, I take him to mean that

[4] Ibid., 228.
[5] John Rawls, *A Theory of Justice* (Cambridge, MA, 1971), 54–5.

they are actually practiced in social life. Promising may be understood as an abstraction that will be just if certain principles govern it, but it is the institution as realized in the behavior of people in a society that is just if it is practiced in accord with certain principles. I want to distinguish, where Rawls is only suggestive, between the realized institution and an institution's concrete embodiment in an organization. On my account, the institution of promising can be seen as an abstract object and as realized in the occasions in which people promise each other different sorts of things, but it is not concretely embodied in an organization. I would extend Rawls's point that we should not confuse the moral principles and judgments made with respect to institutions with those relevant to individuals practicing within those institutions to organizations that embody institutions, or through which many institutions become effective in social life.

This may be somewhat harder to accept than the distinction that Rawls admits between the principles that govern institutions and those that ought to govern individual behavior within those institutions. After all, organizations, on my account, are to be understood as concretely embodying institutions. An institution is the coherent organizing of a certain set of norms, and an institution is realized when a group of people act in ways that they understand to accord with those norms. An organization is a social structure that concretizes, systematizes, arranges, administers, and typically polices the roles and activities of persons that are made possible by the rules and norms of the institution. So some institutions are realized through embodying organizations or even fleets of organizations. The military is such an institution, capitalism is another.

Imagine that the realized institution of capitalism (through a number of associated organizations) falls significantly short of achieving what morality requires, say with regard to providing for the welfare of the least well off of employees. (Call that judgment [S].) [I am not going to offer an argument to support this claim, although I suspect it is the case.] Then think of those tightly or loosely associated organizations that concretely embody the institution of capitalism, where it exists, such as banks, business corporations, government agencies, and the like. What judgment follows from the negative assessment of the morality of the institution with respect to the institution-constituted actions of a particular corporation? Does the judgment that corporation X ought to adopt a policy of sharing its profits through stock options or some other scheme with its least well-off employees follow from [S]? I do not think that it does. It might be persuasively argued that X ought to adopt some set of operating policies that respond to [S], that we should hold X morally deficient if it did not do so. But whether or not those would include providing stock options or profit-sharing to all of its employees is not clear. On the other hand, all that might follow from [S], morally speaking, with respect to X is that X ought to work, in conjunction with other concrete embodiments of the institution of capitalism, public and private, toward the reform of the realized institution while continuing to conduct business as usual in order to remain competitive in its markets and maintain its value to stockholders.

With respect to institutions, their concrete embodiments, and those who practice within them (perform institution-constituted actions specific to those institutions), it makes sense to worry about the appropriate moral evaluations and assessments made relative to each element in large measure independent of the others because there exist significantly wide inference gaps between moral assessments made about institutions, those made with respect to their concrete embodiments, and those made about the actions of individual practitioners. That point seems virtually incontestable regarding institutions and individual practitioners, as noted by Singer and Rawls, but neither has anything to say about organizations. In Rawls's case, that is no surprise because, at least in his most famous work, he adopted a methodological individualist's conception of organizations. On such an account, organizations are just collections of individuals, and moral and other judgments made about them are supposed to reduce without remainder to like judgments about the individuals who are organized within them. I have argued against that view for more than three decades. On my view, organizations, such as the Marine Corps and business corporations, should be understood as moral agents in their own right and therefore bearers of moral responsibility. Institutions can be morally assessed, but they cannot be held morally responsible, although their concrete embodiments that qualify as moral agents can and should be held accountable for their moral defects and failings.

My view has long been that corporately organized entities, organizations of a certain sort, are more capable of causing undeserved harm across significant portions of the population and the environment than are individual human beings. And that, in no small measure, is because they embody our institutions. If an ethical theory systematically cannot address the organization offender qua organization offender, then it will be impotent with respect to minimizing a great deal of undeserved harm, and, I believe, a failure in ethics.

In my work on corporate or organizational moral agency, I defended three positions: (1) corporations or corporately structured organizations exhibit intentionality that is not reducible to the intentions of the individual members of the organizations; (2) organizational intentions can be rational; and (3) organizations can alter their intentions and patterns of behavior for any number of reasons. The keystone element in my picture of such organizations, of course, is my claim that it makes sense to understand some organizational behavior in terms of organizational intentionality.

In my earlier work, I held the rather traditional view that having intentionally done something is essential to being held morally responsible for its occurrence. I no longer think that such a strict intentionality condition is defensible. People and organizations often do considerable undeserved harm when not intending their actions under the specific description of which the causing of that harm was an explicit element. In such cases, of course, the agent does not act without intention. But the agent does not intend the action under the description that would have been required for moral responsibility on the strict intentionality condition. Some of Aristotle's ignorance cases might fall into this category, but I suspect that the majority of cases are those in which, for whatever reasons, the agent(s) are factually but not logically incapable of seeing the circumstances in which they act or the outcomes of their actions under descriptions that describe them as undeserved harm-causing.[6] In the military, this is sometimes referred to as collateral damage. (As a side note, I was struck in sessions on the just conduct of war by how ready chaplains of virtually every denomination were willing to adopt a doctrine of double effect to handle cases of civilian casualties.) I am no longer persuaded that the intention to do the deed under the relevant description is as important to moral responsibility as the fact that undeserved harm was done and that morality must not allow such actions to pass without condemnation. Nonetheless, intentionality still sits at the core of the issue of moral agency and thus of organizational agency and organizational moral responsibility. Simply put, something must be a moral agent, which is an entity that is functionally capable of acting intentionally, in order to be held morally responsible for its chosen and unchosen harm-causing. I do not think that is a controversial position.

---

[6] See Peter A. French, "Unchosen Evil and Moral Responsibility," *War Crimes and Collective Wrongdoings*, edited by Aleksandar Jokic (Oxford, 2001), 29–47.

My intent when I first raised the issue of organizational moral agency was to provide a structure that would allow us to understand how describing an action as "organization-intentional" makes sense, and I worked out the Corporate Internal Decision (CID) Structure theory to serve that purpose.[7] At the core of my earlier view was the widely held position that intentionality should be understood in terms of a desire/belief complex.

If intention is understood on that model, it is natural to think that any talk of the intentions of organizations (and so organizations as moral agents) must be metaphorical or reducible to the intentions of a human (or humans) who has (or have) the requisite desires and beliefs. Organizations cannot, in any normal sense, desire and believe. Consequently, in my earlier accounts, I redescribed desires and beliefs into organizational policy in order to match the model. Many objected that I had overly formalized the notions of desire and belief to fit the CID Structure approach I had created. I now agree that if intention must be understood on the desire/belief model, then organizations will fail to make it as intentional agents.

More than a decade ago, I modified my work on intentionality, organizational or individual. To intend to do something, I now believe, following the work of Michael Bratman, is to plan to do it, and although there may be desires and beliefs provoking planning or related to planning, planning is not just or reducible to a desire/belief complex. If I intend to go to Naples in May to teach a PDTC, then I plan to go to Naples in May. Or, at least, I have made some plans to do so. It is not that I just desire to go there in May and have a belief that I can do so. In fact, I may intend to go even though I do not desire to go there. I would rather go to Ireland, but my agreement with the Navy Chaplains Corps requires that I be in Naples. I am committed, resolved, to doing it. That is what it is to intend to do it. To say that some entity acted intentionally is to say that his or hers or its actions were planned, or undertaken deliberately to accomplish a goal or goals; they were schemed, designed, even premeditated by that entity. I may do little to indicate what intentions I have or what my plans are. I may put off buying the tickets and packing my clothes. You might not be able to tell from any of my present behavior that I am intending to go to Naples in May. The reason for this is that I might now be doing any number of things that are compatible with my intention

---

[7] See French, "The Corporation as a Moral Person," *American Philosophical Quarterly* (1979), 207–15.

to go to Naples in May, although they have nothing to do with a Naples trip. On the other hand, I cannot be intending to go to Naples in May if I book up that month with trips to Asia. Some things are excluded from my possible present activities. That is what it means to be committed to, to plan on, doing something.

It might be worried that saying that I intend to go to Naples is distinct from saying that it is my will to go to Naples because I have, following Frankfurt, identified my will with my effective first-order desire in the circumstances. This is a rather confusing matter, but I think we should say that the first-order desire that is effective in moving me to action, although in some cases not aligned with my second-order desire or my will, may be but is not always what I intended to do. What I have in mind is what Austin referred to as the "machinery of action" having many departments. The will is the effective element in the executive stage, but there are also "departments of intelligence, and planning, of decision and resolve,"[8] and appreciation. I am associating intention with the planning stage of action, rather than the executive stage where something gets done. Despite possessing excellent intelligence and firm resolve, if one's intention, one's plan, is defective, the action will likely result in disaster and that not because the execution was faulty. Then everyone will be asking, "What the hell were you intending?" This seems to be a frequent occurrence in military operations.

Of course, "plan" might be used in at least two ways, one to refer to a set of plans, as for example a blueprint; and second, to talk of what one plans to do. "Here is the plan that I plan to bring to reality." It is the second sense that captures intentionality, the sense in which "plan" entails commitment. The rejection of the desire/belief complex model of intentionality also removes most of the subjectivism from my earlier accounts of organizational intentionality. I am not saying that intentions never involve desires and beliefs. They may enter into the various planning stages and, in a sense, they may be equated with second-order volitions, identifying one's will as the will one wants to have.

I hope that a cursory mention of work I have previously done on CID Structures will suffice to make the case for organizational intentionality on a planning theory. An essential feature of a corporately structured organization is that it has an established way by which it constructs plans, makes decisions, and converts them into actions, a CID

---

[8] J. L. Austin, "A Plea for Excuses," in *Philosophical Papers* (Oxford, 1961, 1970, 1979), 193–94.

Structure. CID Structures have two elements crucial to our understanding of how intentionally acting organizations emerge at certain levels of the description of events: (1) an organizational flow chart that delineates stations and levels within the organization; and (2) rules that reveal how to recognize plans and decisions that are organizational ones and not simply personal decisions or intentions of the humans who occupy the positions identified on the flow chart. These rules are typically embedded, whether explicitly or implicitly, in statements of organizational policy.

Its CID Structure is an arrangement of its personnel for the exercise of the organization's power with respect to its ventures and interests and, as such, a CID Structure's primary function is to draw various levels and positions within the organization into decision-making, ratification, and action processes. In effect, it is the machinery of action for the corporation drawn out in lines and boxes. An activated CID Structure subordinates and synthesizes the intentions, desires, and actions of various human persons (and sometimes even the behavior of machines) into an organizational action. What I mean by that is that the CID Structure not only organizes the various human beings in the organization into a decision-making and acting entity, it makes it possible for us and those within the organization to describe what is happening as an organization's actions, plans, positions, and so forth, and not just as the actions of a specific manager or officer of the organization. In the absence of the structure, many of the activities of the humans and machines would be unintelligible.

CID Structures generally are, and need to be, epistemically transparent, significantly differing from humans whose machinery of action is rather opaque, even to the very humans making the decisions. Anyone with access to CID Structures should be able to discover everything about how they work. Hence, CID Structures can be confidently used as licenses of redescription to transform descriptions of certain events as the actions or the mere behavior of humans and/or machines into descriptions of actions of the organization. A CID Structure provides the means by which we gain access to a certain kind of intentional agents, namely, organizations, at a different level of description than the one we typically use to describe the behavior of individual humans. And, as maintained earlier, this is an ethically distinct level, with respect to inferring morally required or appropriate actions, from the level on which we morally assess human behavior, and from the institutional level as well. In effect, the attribution of organizational intentionality is referentially opaque with respect to other possible descriptions of the event in question; for example, as the intentional actions of a specific member of the organization.

I have elsewhere identified two sorts of rules in CID Structures: organizational rules and policy/procedure rules.[9] The organizational rules distinguish players, clarify their rank, and map out the interwoven lines of responsibility within the organization. They provide the grammar of organizational decision making. Policy/procedure rules supply its logic. Every organization creates a general set of policies and procedures that, at least ideally, should be easily accessible to both its members and those with whom it interacts. When an action performed by a bona fide member of an organization is an implementation of its policy, and accords with its procedural rules, then it is proper to describe the act as done for organizational reasons or for organizational purposes, to advance organizational plans, and so as an intentional action of the organization.

The Arthur Andersen obstruction of justice case related to the Enron collapse may illustrate the point I am making. The American government in prosecuting Andersen argued that its employees followed the policies and procedures found in the Andersen CID Structure when they destroyed documents relative to Enron's accounting practices. Hence, the company and not just a few of its employees should be found guilty. Andersen defended itself by maintaining that the employees involved were acting on their own and not following corporate policy. That defense became harder to sustain as the prosecution piled up the evidence regarding the corporation's policies and decisions relative to the matter.

The plans of an organization might, perhaps often, differ from those that motivate the human persons who occupy positions in its CID Structure and whose bodily movements are necessary for the organization to act. Using its CID Structure, we can, however, describe the concerted behavior of those humans as organizational actions done with an organizational intention, to execute an organizational plan or as part of such a plan. Organizational intent, then, is dependent on relatively transparent policies and plans that have their origins in the social psychology of a group of human beings. Organizational intent might look like a tarnished, illegitimate offspring of human intent. If, however, we concentrate on the possible descriptions of events and acknowledge that there are distinctly organizational plans and policies that provide the

---

[9] I toyed with associating them to what MacIntyre calls "practices," but I found his account too broad for my purposes. See Alasdair MacIntyre, *After Virtue* (Notre Dame, IN, 1984), 187–93.

reasons why organizations do the things they do, then we should not feel compelled to reduce statements about organizational actions to ones about the actions, reasons, plans, desires, or interests of humans who happen to hold membership in the organization.

An organization's policies provide sufficient reasons and the other intentional elements needed to redescribe certain events as organizational actions, allowing, of course, that the member's actions are procedurally correct. The recognition of procedural rules in CID Structures is a bit easier than identifying policies, even though some procedures may be the result of common practice rather than official sanction. The policies of an organization seem to be inviolate. The basic ones generally are; indeed, they have to be for reasons of maintaining organizational identity. In that respect, they are unlike policies adopted by individual humans. You could adopt a policy of honesty, but you may occasionally violate that policy by lying. When you lie, it is still you lying. If members act in ways that violate organizational policy, their acts are no longer organizational. But whether or not a policy is actually in place in an organization is dependent not on just what is on the written record of the organization, but on how members respond to apparent violations of it. So, the sociology of the organization is often necessary in identifying its real policies.

To be a proper target of ethical evaluation, it seems to me indisputable that something must be capable of responding to what it learns about those with whom it interacts, as well as to ethical criticism. It must be able to responsively adjust its patterns of behavior and its policies and procedures to proactively head off predictable failures as well as prevent reoccurrences of disvalued outcomes. Such a responsive capacity, especially to moral criticism, seems to me to be crucial to anything being considered a moral agent. Organizational policies must be somewhat flexible so that organizations can respond to unexpected circumstances in ways that will further their interests, and fully realized CID Structures build in that capacity. In effect, organizations, if they are to survive for very long, must be capable of making rational nonprogrammed decisions directed to the achievement of their interests. Their CID Structures must encourage some reactive, responsive, discriminatory elements with respect to policies. Insofar as corporately organized entities demonstrate nonprogrammed responsive decision-making capacities, they would seem to qualify as moral agents in that regard as well. It therefore should not be too troubling to talk about organizations as members of the moral community, to treat them as proper subjects of moral assessment and judgments, and to hold them morally responsible, even if those judgments do not reduce to similar judgments about individual human beings or if similar judgments about individual human beings who work within or are members of organizations are not directly inferable from them.

To summarize to this point: I have maintained that there is a substantially wide inference gap between moral judgments or assessments of institutions, such as the military and capitalism, and like moral judgments or assessments of the organizations that are concrete embodiments of those institutions, such as the Marine Corps and corporations. I have also maintained that those organizations should be thought of as moral agents in their own right and not as mere collections of human individuals. The Jefferson situation again serves for illustrative purposes. We should grant that the institution of slavery is immoral and must be abolished whenever and wherever it exists. And we must admit that Monticello Plantation during the Jefferson years was a slave-based organization. From that we cannot directly infer that during the Jefferson years the Monticello Plantation should have been abolished. It is not unimaginable, morally speaking, that one might reach the conclusion Jefferson reached: that although the institution must be abolished, Monticello Plantation should not be abolished at that time. Of course, in the case of slavery, this becomes a very hard sell because slavery is inherently immoral and the organizations that embody it surely are also immoral. That, I think, is undeniable and fuels our concern that Jefferson was a hypocrite, as well as a racist. If the institution is not one that is inherently immoral, but riddled with unfair or unjust practices, such as capitalism may be, inferences to the operations of the specific organizations that embody it – namely, corporations – although tempting, are more problematic and illustrate the inference gap problem in moral assessment to which I am drawing attention.

The picture, albeit still quite primitive, of the moral world that I have been trying to sketch takes as its foundation that there are unbridgeable inference gaps with respect to moral judgments or assessments between institutions and the institution-constituted actions of their concrete embodiments (organizations), between institutions and the institution-constituted actions of individuals, and between the institution-constituted actions of organizations (e.g., the Marine Corps) and those of individuals who are members of those organizations. There are also, although I am not concerned with them here, moral assessments of individual actions that are not institution-constituted, and there probably are organization actions that can be the subject of moral assessment that are not institution-constituted either.

Because they are intentional agents, even if organizations are somewhat limited with respect to the scope of their actions, it makes sense to morally assess and hold morally responsible individuals and organizations in terms of both their actions and their characters. Institutions do not act, and if we were to talk about the "character" of an institution, we would not be using the term in the same sense that we do to talk about individuals and organizations. Actually, I am not at all sure that we can talk sensibly about the character of an institution in any meaningful way. I suppose there is a sense of "character" that is understood to mean something like "nature" and that we could well ask, "What is the nature of a particular institution?" "What is the nature of slavery?" for example, could be answered by saying that it is an institution constituted by a system of rules that yield a certain set of rights, duties, and so on. Or we might say that it is an inherently immoral institution because it is constituted by a certain system of rules that yield a set of rights, duties, and so forth that violate basic moral standards of human dignity, respect, and worth. In any case, that seems to be a somewhat different matter than assessing Mary's character or the quality of her will as defective or as exemplary based on our observations of her actions or her telling us of her intentions.

Institutions are basic to a social system, and the moral assessments of institutions, as in Rawls's theory, are generally given in terms of justness and fairness. Institutions are typically judged as just or unjust, fair or unfair, with respect to their fundamental, although abstract, conceptual structures. To say that the institution of slavery is inherently immoral is to say that it is fundamentally flawed because it is unjust and/or unfair and to found that judgment on defensible principles, typically those regarding the morally appropriate distribution of the goods based in the institution or the society as a whole, or with regard to basic moral principles regarding human dignity, worth, respect, and so on. Judging that the institution of the military is unjust or unfair requires citation to comparable principles. Whether or not the military or militarism is inherently unjust or unfair is not a matter I am prepared to discuss. However, I think a negative moral assessment of the institution of the military would likely take the form of a hypothetical of the sort [C]: "The institution of the military in the United States would be just, or more fully just, if its concrete embodiments, for example, the Army, Navy, Marine Corps, Air Force and such, through which it functions, were structured to deliver their services in a just and fair way and they actually did so." Perhaps that would include not abiding by a "Don't ask, don't tell" rule regarding the gays serving in the ranks. In effect, moral judgments about institutions that are not inherently immoral will generally include hypotheticals that relate to the organizations that deliver the goods or services of those institutions. That being the case, we may be tempted to think that no inference gap exists between [C] and a negative or positive judgment regarding a particular branch of the military and the way it does or does not do certain things in carrying out its services for the country. That would, however, be a mistake. From the fact that the military would be just or fair (or more so) if the organizations that concretely embody it acted in a certain way nothing directly follows about what policies and procedures a particular branch or unit of the military ought or ought not to adopt or that that branch or unit should or should not, in any particular case, enact a particular policy regarding its actions or personnel. If we should decide that the military per se as an institution is morally flawed, what we are deciding is that our conception of the institution fails to meet the standards of our principles of justice and fairness. We are saying that we need to "rethink it," to reconceive it, until our conception does satisfy those principles. We should expect, of course, that once we have reconceived an institution to satisfy our moral principles, we would make efforts to reform the organizations that embody that institution. But organizations operate in the practical sphere, in the real world, not in a world of abstractions, and the gulf, from a moral and a logical point of view, between those worlds is sizable.

Another related point: unlike organizations and individuals, institutions are not intentional agents. They are abstractions. They do not, they cannot, act and they cannot be held morally responsible. They are, to paraphrase Singer and Rawls, relatively permanent systems of social relations organized around a social need or value and regarded in a society as a way of meeting that need or realizing that value. They involve systems of rules that are built on shared beliefs, values, cares, and purposes within a society. They are not simply customary ways of doing things because customs and habits may not be rule-based.[10] Individuals, collectively, in effect, hold the institutions of their society in their shared worldview and have the capacity to modify most institutions and bring them closer to the principles of justice and fairness by which they are morally measured and to then restructure the organizations that concretely embody them.

[10] Rawls, 55.

The reason that I qualified the previous statement is that I do not think they can modify certain institutions, although they can abolish them. I have in mind slavery, of course, but also promising.

Organizations can act, and included in the panoply of their possible actions, as already noted, is planning for organizational change, even the termination of the organization's existence or its merger with another organization. Other organizations and individuals also can effect change in an organization, and the same holds true for individuals. The primary point I want to make, however, is that the moral assessment of organizations and of individuals is a conceptually different matter than the moral assessment of institutions. It makes sense to talk of the ethics of institutions, the ethics of organizations, and the ethics of individuals without assuming that they can be reduced to a single set of moral principles. Rawls seems to have understood this point. And even if one were convinced that there is a single moral principle that applies to all elements of the moral world that I have sketched, perhaps the principle of utility or the Categorical Imperative, the inference gap between the various elements still would exist. In accord with Rawls's view in *A Theory of Justice*, the principle(s) applies to different subjects and "must be discussed separately."[11]

What I have said about the inference gaps between moral assessments of institutions, organizations, and individuals performing institution-constituted actions comes into focus when we think about whether a Marine following lethal orders during a village house-to-house sweep in an unjust war should be adjudged as acting unjustly. Suppose that the matter of the justice of the war itself is settled negatively. Suppose also that the Marine Corps or the unit in which the Marine is serving is fighting the war in a manner consistent with the principles of *jus in bello*. The Marine is ordered to bust into a house and secure it. In doing so he encounters a woman he believes to be hiding a weapon under her clothing, he searches her, and discovers she has no weapon. He hates anyone and everyone in that village since a good friend was killed by an IED nearby. He opens fire on her. He is guilty of murder and the unjust nature of the war is irrelevant to our judgment of him, as is whether or not his Marine unit was following the principles of *jus in bello* in its rules of engagement. But if he follows the rules of engagement but kills the woman, wrongly believing she is concealing a weapon she will use on his unit, we would likely say that it is unfortunate that she was killed, but

---

[11] Ibid., 54.

that he did not act unjustly in an unjust war. It is also conceivable, in fact, there are a number of cases where this has occurred, that a soldier, carrying out immoral orders that he did not know were in violation of the principles of *jus in bello*, is not held morally responsible for his actions. That is the case despite the Nuremburg Tribunal's rejections of the "Jodl defense" of "following orders." If the Marine unit is operating unjustly, it does not follow that any member of the unit is acting unjustly even when following orders, and it does not follow that the organization, the Marines or the Marine unit, is acting unjustly, even if the war in which it is acting is unjust or the institution of which it is a concrete embodiment is unjust.

It should also be noted that there is a fourth level or element in the moral world: the social system, composed of institutions, taken as a whole. Rawls writes: "The primary subject of the principles of social justice is the basic structure of society, the arrangement of major social institutions into one scheme of cooperation."[12] Rawls notes that from the justice or injustice of the social system as a whole, one cannot infer anything about the justice or injustice of any of its institutions or all of its institutions. A social system is an arrangement of institutions according to some rules. Some or all of the rules of arrangement for any given social system may be unjust while the institutions within the system are just. An institution within a social system may be unjust, but the social system containing it may not be unjust, but I suspect that can be the case only when the institution is not a dominant one in the system. Where it is dominant, as was slavery in the antebellum American South, I do not see how the social system could be just. Rawls suggests that in some social systems, one institution that is unjust might be compensated by another that is just so that "the whole is less unjust than it would be if it contained but one of the unjust parts."[13] It is also conceivable that none of the institutions in a social system are unjust taken independently of each other, but that the system, the arrangement of them into a single system, is unjust taken as a combination. From a moral assessment of the social system and/or its rules of arrangement, therefore, we cannot infer a similar moral assessment about its institutions, nor about the organizations that are the concrete embodiments of those institutions.

[12] Ibid., 57.
[13] Ibid.

Blaming Whole Populations

The American People and the Iraq War

As noted in Chapter 1, among the disturbing revelations in a Pentagon report on the ethics of the troops in Iraq was the fact that only 38 percent of the Marines serving in country believe that noncombatants (Iraqi civilians) are to be treated with dignity and respect. Other reports indicate that U.S. Marines in Iraq participated in a significant number of gross violations of the Uniform Code of Military Justice with respect to civilians, and some were sentenced to lengthy prison terms for rape and murder. For example, Corporal Marshall Magincalda admitted to the Associated Press on August 9, 2007, that he and members of his unit planned to shoot an Iraqi they believed to be an insurgent and make it look like they killed him while he was planting a roadside bomb. They did not get to kill the man they had targeted, so they went next door in order to kill another Iraqi, a retired policeman and father of eleven children. They dragged that man to a roadside ditch, tied him up, and killed him. Corporal Magincalda's squad members were charged with murder, kidnapping, conspiracy to commit murder, larceny, and housebreaking. Magincalda was acquitted of murder but convicted of conspiracy to commit murder, larceny, and housebreaking. He was sentenced to the time he served in the brig while awaiting trial and reduced in rank to private. "I didn't want to have anything to do in the killing," he said. "But at the same time, I was willing to support my guys because I wasn't going to let them go off into the night on their own." A psychiatrist testified that Magincalda suffers from post-traumatic stress disorder, depression, and nightmares. The leader of the group, Sgt. Lawrence G. Hutchins III, was sentenced to fifteen years in prison for unpremeditated murder.[1]

---

[1] The Associated Press story on this case was reported by Thomas Watkins on August 10, 2007.

Predictably, when atrocities committed by American troops during hostile occupations or combat operations are exposed in the media, commentators raise a certain set of legal and moral-responsibility issues. The legal questions, despite the typical facileness of the usual commentators, are often complex and may involve determinations of whether or not the perpetrators were acting under superior orders and what rules of engagement governed the action in which they were participating. By and large, the answers to those questions may or may not expand the net of legal culpability, although they seldom direct matters of legal responsibility altogether away from the actual perpetrator(s).

On the moral side arise questions that not infrequently also are posed by "talking head" commentators of one political stripe or another. These have to do with the applicability of "broad brush" ascriptions of moral responsibility to whole populations for wartime atrocities that are committed "in their name." Of course, that is not to be taken literally in many of the most egregious cases because it is virtually unimaginable that a young American Marine, pulling down his pants to rape an Iraqi girl, says either to himself or out loud that he is raping her in the name of the American people. He, however, may in fact likely believe that the American people would approve of what he is doing and that any other "red-blooded American male" would gladly do the same in the circumstances.

Some commentators have endorsed absolving the perpetrators of wartime atrocities of moral responsibility for their heinous deeds by blaming the provoking circumstances on the people of the nation that employs them. Some pundits in the 1970s, for example, maintained that the American people were to blame for the atrocities committed by American troops in Vietnam.[2] In recent years, similar things were said on cable television news and commentary shows or written on op-ed pages after the graphic revelations of the torturing of prisoners in Abu Ghraib prison and other atrocities in Iraq made the media. One difference in public reaction from the Vietnam-era analyses that was reflected in the opinion polls is that the bulk of the blame as the war continued was dumped on former President Bush and the members of his administration and not on the American people per se. A not insubstantial number

---

[2] Even Lt. William Calley made such a claim. "The guilt: as Medina said, we all as American citizens share it.... I say if there is guilt, we must all suffer it." "The Concluding Confessions of Lieutenant Calley," by William Calley, Jr., interviewed by John Sack, *Esquire*, September 1971.

of Americans, apparently, no longer regard the Iraq War as "theirs." It is "Bush's War." Even if they had been gung ho about the invasion, by 2006 the zeal of the people for the war had seriously waned. Realization sunk in that the country was lied or misled into this war by the Bush administration following the September 11, 2001 attacks that destroyed the World Trade Center in New York City. Their patriotic fervor and fear had been manipulated, and many resented the way their support had been purchased. So, if the polls and the 2008 election are good indicators, for some, and perhaps many, the American people are not to be morally blamed for the way Marines and soldiers behave in Iraq. The Bush administration put them there. They, not the American people, are to be blamed for what the troops do while outside the wire.

Whether the disconnecting of the American people from the war can be morally or politically justified is doubtful. In any event, some antiwar protesters, as was also the case during the Vietnam War in the 1960s and 1970s, maintain that the American people are morally responsible for the atrocities committed by their troops. It is pointed out that Bush was reelected in 2004 by a majority of the American voters even after most of them were aware of the way the war had been "ginned up" by his administration. As a people, a collective, they can, many will argue, be held to blame for how the war transpired, how it was fought, and the atrocities committed by their troops in Iraqi villages and in prisons and detention centers. Such an ascription, in many cases of its utterance, is intended not only to capture in its net the killing and torturing of Iraqi civilians but also the physical and mental injuries and deaths of the American soldiers and Marines who served in Iraq and Afghanistan and were often compelled to extend tours of duty, redeployed more frequently than standard policy recommends, and returned to inadequate medical and psychiatric treatment. In fact, some recent op-ed pieces have focused more on the moral responsibility of the whole population of America for the lack of care provided to its physically and mentally damaged troops during the pointless war than on the atrocities American Marines and soldiers committed against Iraqi noncombatants.

The perplexing philosophical question is, "Can ascriptions of moral blame to whole populations be justified?"

I

The etymological roots of "to blame" lie in "to blaspheme" ("to speak evil of"). Although there are numerous everyday occasions where blaming is identifying the cause of unhappy or untoward events (for example, "Blame the weather for ruining the vacation"), there is more to blaming than the determination of causes or faults. There are at least two major senses of "blame." In the first, to blame is to identify the cause or causes of an untoward or disvalued event: the weather is to blame for a ruined vacation, the dead battery is to blame for the flashlight's failure, and so on. In the second sense, to blame is to hold responsible or accountable. We cannot hold the weather responsible or the dead battery responsible for the unhappy events for which they are to blame. Also, both legally and morally, some things and some people[3] may be *to blame* for certain unhappy events, although they are not *to be blamed* for them, for example, very young children and the severely mentally handicapped.

Expressions of disapprobation are central to all blaming episodes. Where blaming is an expression of displeasure directed at animate and inanimate objects, persons, and things alleged to be the causes of unhappy or untoward events, it is nonmoral. Nonmoral blaming is not inappropriate in cases of accident, mistake, and where the blamed party is not believed to have wanted to cause the event that occasioned the disapprobation or even to be capable of controlling what it does. A child, for example, is to blame for breaking his toy train, even though he is only four years old and it was surely an accident. To resurrect one of J. L. Austin's famous illustrations,[4] I am to blame for killing your donkey even though I shot it in the mistaken belief that it was my donkey. Nonmoral blame does not necessarily occasion evaluations of intelligence, states of mind, intentions, desires, or responsibilities. We only need to know (or have sufficiently good reasons to believe) that someone or something did bring about the unpleasant or unwanted circumstances in order to blame him, her, or it.

A further characteristic of nonmoral blaming (although I think this can be shown to be the case with blaming in general) is that occasions of its use are not necessarily directed at altering future behavior, either of the object of blame or of others. Deterrence has no essential relationship to blaming. This is most obvious in the example of blaming the weather. It is entirely consistent with this type of blaming to blame sociopaths and psychopaths for their antisocial behavior and to blame children for

---

[3] See my "On Blaming Psychopaths" in D. E. Cooper, ed., *The Manson Murders: A Philosophical Inquiry* (Cambridge, MA, 1973).

[4] J. L. Austin, "A Plea for Excuses," The Presidential Address to the Aristotelian Society, 1956, *Proceedings of the Aristotelian Society*, 1956–57, Vol. VII, 1957, reprinted in *Philosophical Papers* (Oxford, 1961, 1970, 1979).

breaking toys insofar as a causal relationship can be shown between the occurrence of the disapproved event and the thing or human being blamed.

To nonmorally blame is to answer the question, "Who (or what) has caused or brought about this (disvalued event)?" To blame the December weather in Minnesota for my automobile accident is not necessarily to grade (downgrade) the December weather. After all, it is standard, normal, for the weather in December in Minnesota to be snowy and icy, and many of the residents like it that way. My blaming expression just identifies the weather conditions as a major contributory factor in a disvalued occurrence. The brakes are to blame for an auto accident if the brakes did not work; had they worked, the accident would not have occurred. But this is not to suggest that standards or norms never play a role in nonmoral blaming.

Nonmoral blaming differs from just citing the causes of disapproved events insofar as it is not dispassionate. It is to use animadvertives in an objurgatory way toward the thing, event, or human blamed.[5] And more is also involved.

Consider the following contrasting examples:

(A) While driving at a legal speed down a residential street, Mr. X is shocked to see a young child dart in front of his car. The shock of what is about to occur is too much for Mr. X's heart. He suffers a massive attack. The car swerves directly at the child. She is dead on impact, but later Mr. X recovers.

(B) While driving at a legal speed down a residential street, Mr. Y suddenly is shocked to see a young child dart in front of his vehicle. Mr. Y panics and instead of braking, slams his foot on the accelerator. The child is killed instantly.

X and Y both caused the deaths of children. But we are, I think, inclined to blame Y for the child's death and reluctant to do the same in X's case, although we might blame X's heart for the accident. For that matter, automobiles also caused those deaths. But in neither case are we likely to

---

[5] There is a whole class of expressions and idioms that might be called animadvertives (utterances of criticism, censure, or reproof), including "despicable," "detestable," "diabolical," "evil," "insufferable," "reprehensible," and so forth. Animadvertives might best be described as the verbal expression of what might be called disapprobatives (e.g., disapproval, disvaluation, dislike, disfavor, dispraise). The boundaries of and relationships between disapprobatives, animadvertives, abusives, and possibly objurgatives need to be clarified in the map of blame.

blame the car or its manufacturer. After all, the cars operated as advertised, as cars are expected to operate. Had there been some mechanical fault in the construction of the car that made emergency stopping
impossible, we would blame not only the car but also its manufacturer or
perhaps the most recent mechanic to have serviced it. Cars are expected
to perform according to a certain automotive standard, and when accidents occur because of failures to meet that standard, we are entirely
justified in blaming the car for the accident and often exonerating the
driver. Where standards are harder to determine, as in the case of the
weather being to blame for an accident, there is a reluctance to exoner-
ate the driver completely. Unless the weather unexpectedly changed, we
are likely to say that the driver is to blame for having ventured out at all.

In regard to (A), we might be tempted to blame the child for her own
death, but that likely would be contingent on the age of the child. If she
were only one or two years old, it would seem unlikely we would say she
was to blame for her death, unless we were consoling Mr. X. If the child
were somewhat older, say four or five, and of normal health, we might
be more inclined to include her in the blame. Our reluctance to ascribe
even nonmoral blame to the very young child is due to our expectations
with respect to standards of performance for such children.

I think that we would not blame X for the child's death. It makes little
sense to talk of standards in regard to heart attacks. X's heart was to blame
for the child's death because it malfunctioned, tragically falling below the
standards normally expected of hearts. But, assuming X does not have
a history of heart ailments, that he should not have been expecting an
attack, X would seem to be blameless in the nonmoral sense of blame for
the child's death.

Y, on the other hand, is to be blamed, nonmorally, for the child's death.
Y's performance behind the wheel was substandard. Panic is not sufficient
exculpation for driving directly at the child. Most drivers do not do that;
they are expected not to do so. Keeping the car under control is the first
rule of the road. Y should have known which pedal was the brake, and he
should have swerved to avoid the fatal accident. Y is more than just the
cause of the child's death; he merits blame (in the nonmoral sense) even
if it is claimed that he was so gripped with panic that he could not have
acted other than he did, that his will never entered into the situation.
Panic overwhelmed his will. Primary in nonmoral blaming is the notion
of *should have*, not *could have*.

A word is in order distinguishing "should have" from "could have."
Consider the following:

(C)Teacher to pupil: "You should have written more on Wittgenstein's private language argument. I'm afraid I can't give you a very good grade."

Two elements are worth noting: (1) "should have" in cases such as this refers to a standard (explicit or implicit), and (2) "should have" does not depend for its sense on the capacities, dispositions, or abilities of its subjects. It does not depend on what Frankfurt famously called the "Principle of Alternate Possibilities,"[6] specifically that one could have done something other than what one in fact did. Suppose the pupil in (C) has no capacity or ability to understand or write more on Wittgenstein's discussion of a private language. He could not have written more on it in his essay without producing gibberish. Would the teacher be speaking nonsense were she to say that he should have written more? I think not. When the teacher says to the pupil in (C) that he should have written more, she need not believe that "if (such and such), he would have." What she has told the student is that he failed to reach a certain expected standard, one that is involved when judgments are made within the type of activity in which he was engaged.[7] There is much more on that subject that must be said if a good grade is to be earned on the essay.

Our practices of nonmoral blaming rest on the existence of standards and expectations that are relevant to our various activities and the events of our lives. Someone or something is to blame (nonmorally) when the major criterion of our adverse judgment of him, her, or it is of the "should have" variety.

Some types of blaming are like scolding or rebuking or chiding, whereas others are merely expressions of attitude (what J. L. Austin may have had in mind when he referred to the behabitive sense of blaming). To say the weather should have been better, that is, to blame the weather for our ruined vacation, is to express the attitude that we disvalue the weather. We had counted on sunny days and it rained for a week. "The weather should have been better" amounts to something like "We had in mind a standard of acceptable weather that was not met when it rained for a week." There is no scolding, rebuking, or chiding about it.

---

[6] See Harry Frankfurt, "Alternate Possibilities and Moral Responsibility," in *The Importance of What We Care About* (Cambridge, 1988), chapter 1.

[7] There is, I suppose, a hypothetical suppressed in the notion of a standard of the sort that if he had satisfied the criterion he would have been successful, but I do not think that is an important element in the logic of "should have."

An ascription of nonmoral blame to the American people for atrocities committed by U.S. Marines in Iraq might be justified if there is (1)
good reason to treat the American people as a specific collectivity, for
example, there is a solidarity (to use Feinberg's term) that binds them
together as a group; (2) evidence that the Marines in Iraq who committed the atrocities would not have had opportunities to perform them
had not that collectivity acted in such a way as to have allowed themselves, for example, to be led or misled by political leaders, to have paid
taxes without protest, to have failed to question governmental decisions,
and so forth; (3) some standard(s) or behavioral norm(s) by which the
conduct of a people in relation to their government is judicable (the
American people in relation to the American state); and (4) a demon-
stration that those acts [as in (2)] of the collectivity did fall short of the
standards [as in (3)] regardless of whether or not anyone or all of the
members of the population could have altered the whole population's
pattern of behavior or their government's policies, even if they had had
a mechanism for such alteration and knew how to operate it. By claiming
that the American people are to blame (nonmorally) for the atrocities
committed by Marines in Iraq, events that aroused in the blamer feelings
of disapprobation, the blamer is saying that he or she believes that the
American people should have done x, y, and z, and, of course, that they
did not do x, y, and z.[8]

II

The types of judgments that signal the practice of moral blaming are
"should haves" of a particular kind, that is, judgments based on our
moral standards.

It would not be profitable here to compare and contrast the various
positions taken in the discussion of whether responsibility may be rec-
onciled with some form of determinism. I take it to be a fact of our
ordinary language and everyday behavior that we do hold certain individuals morally blameworthy for some, although not all, of their actions.[9]
That is, we hold ourselves and others morally responsible for some of our
behavior and some of its consequences. It is also a fact that we refrain

---

[8] Clearly, this is far more complex than a series of things not done: a time element would
be necessary, among other things.

[9] Austin, I believe, would call this type of blaming verdictive. See *How to Do Things with
Words* (Oxford, 1965), 152.

from holding morally responsible some human beings no matter what they do: certain mental defectives and infants. And we never literally hold animals or mechanical devices morally responsible. What distinguishes those cases where we are inclined to hold people morally responsible (blameworthy) from those where we are reluctant to do so?

I have maintained that an essential element of all blaming is the existence of standards of performance, either implicit or explicit. When moral blaming is the issue, "He should have done something other than he did when he fell below standard" is a moral judgment. That is, the standard of behavior is derived from or reflects a moral principle or moral assessment.

"Should haves" are the primary grounds for judgments of blame for untoward or disvalued events. "Should haves" express our moral or nonmoral standards usually by citing specific courses of action that have not been met.[10] If there is persuasive evidence that the blamed person could not have achieved the expected moral standard of behavior when achieving that standard in what he or she had wanted to do, moral blame is typically thought to be inappropriate. Notice, however, that this has nothing to do with whether or not, for some reason external to the person, he or she could not have done anything other than what he or she did. As Frankfurt famously argued, what matters is the reason why persons do what they do, not that in the circumstances they could not have done otherwise. If a person could not have done otherwise than what he or she did, although doing what he or she did is not what he or she wanted to do in the circumstances, moral blame is withheld. In the manner of the Frankfurt-style counterexamples to the Principle of Alternate Possibilities, we are justified in morally blaming someone only for doing those things they did because they wanted or intended to do them (they were the product of their wills), regardless of the fact that had they not wanted or intended to do them, some external force would have seen to it that they did them.

Frankfurt-type cases have met with an avalanche of objections in the philosophical literature since Frankfurt first unleashed them in his landmark paper in 1969. It may be recalled that the counterexamples are cases of overdetermination such that if the person decides not to do

---

[10] Daniel Ellsberg said in blaming Robert McNamara for the Vietnam War, "It must occur to him that the things he did not know were things he should and could have discovered." J. Robert Moskin, "Ellsberg Talks," *Look* (Oct. 5, 1971), 31–34, 39–42. Similar things have been said about Donald Rumsfeld with respect to his leadership in the Department of Defense during the first three and a half years of the Iraq War.

something that an intervener wants the person to do, the intervener will cause the person to do it anyway. The usual way that is accomplished in the counterexample scenarios is for the intervener to have embedded some sort of control device in the brain of the person that the intervener activates only if the intervener discerns that the person will not do what the intervener wants done. As long as the person decides to do what the intervener desires, the device is not activated. Consequently, even though the person has no alternate possibilities of action in the case, as long as what he or she does was the result of his or her wanting or intending to do it, there is no reason not to blame (hold responsible) the person for doing it. Ishtiyaque Haji persuasively attacks one of the popular anti-Frankfurt responses, the so-called Dilemma Objection, by offering what I believe is an original way of resisting the first horn of the dilemma identified in the objection.[11] That horn maintains that if there is an infallible sign that can be identified by the intervener to the effect that the intervener does not have to intervene, "it can only be so because states of the agent prior to the occurrence of the supposedly free choice (or action) are causally sufficient for this choice (and the sign indicates this)." But that would mean that a deterministic relation obtains between the sign and the choice a person Z makes, and that will beg the question against the incompatibilist's position. To respond to this objection, Haji develops an elaborate Frankfurt-type case that involves two causal routes to the agent's action, one of which is causally deterministic. To get his point, imagine that Z indeterministically decides to do x (something untoward) and also that there is a deterministic mechanism functioning in Z that will cause Z to arrive at the same decision at the same time. If the two causal routes to Z's decision were to diverge, the deterministic one will override the indeterministic one, so Z will decide to do x and Z will do x no matter what. Our intuitions, Haji points out, should tell us that if they do not diverge and Z does x, Z should be morally blamed for doing so. Z is morally responsible for Z's choice even though Z could not have chosen otherwise. The reason we would morally blame Z is because we would blame Z were the deterministic, causal sequence to be totally absent; its presence plays no role in Z's deciding to do x.

What appears to be necessary for moral blameworthiness in the Frankfurt-style cases is that the person must have ultimate control over the

---

[11] Ishtiyaque Haji, "On Frankfurt-type Examples," *APA Newsletter on Philosophy and Law*, edited by Steven Scalet and Christopher Griffin (Spring 2008), Volume 07, Number 2, 1–5.

decision to act, and ultimate control may be understood, depending on whether one is a compatibilist or an incompatibilist in one way rather than another. I am persuaded that Z has such control because the cause of Z's doing x is internal to Z and issues from Z. That Z has no alternatives in the circumstances does not diminish Z's responsibility-grounding control and thus Z's being morally blameworthy for doing x.

But, it may be worried, is the cause of Z's doing x agent-causal? As Haji points out, that is not a relevant condition for moral responsibility or blameworthiness. One does not have to be partly responsible for everything that is a sufficient cause of one's choices for those choices to be responsibility grounding. But we still need a plausible account of a decision being someone's (in the sense relevant to moral responsibility grounding), even if all of its causally sufficient antecedents (including those internal to the person and issuing from the person) could not have been otherwise. I think that what is needed for ownership of actions in the responsibility-grounding sense, agreeing with Frankfurt, is that the person's first-order desires align with the person's second-order desires or second-order volitions or intentions.[12] In other words, that the choice or action is appropriately identified as the person's will regardless of whether or not the person could have done otherwise.

When these criteria are applied to the driver in (A), we see why no moral blame is due him. Also, regarding (B), we may not want to morally blame the panic-stricken driver if only because we may think of his state of panic as not a product of his will and so his driving as something not within his control sufficient for responsibility grounding. If the pupil in (C) lacks the ability or the capacity to succeed at his task (writing more on Wittgenstein's private language argument) owing to some condition that is external to his will and that prevents him from doing what he wants to do in the circumstances, then the pupil is not to be morally blamed for his failure to succeed at the task.

III

What should we say when the "should have" judgment is a moral one (the standard is a moral standard) and its subject is a collectivity such as the American people? Three issues are prominent: (a) Can anyone be morally to blame for the acts of another?; (b) Can a collectivity such as

---

[12] See Harry Frankfurt, "Freedom of the Will and the Concept of a Person," in *The Importance of What We Care About*, chapter 2.

"the American people" be the bearer of moral blame?; and (c) Is "vicarious collective moral blame" reducible to individual vicarious liabilities?

Many philosophers have rejected the whole idea of collective responsibility because they feel compelled to answer (a) in the negative.[13] Common usage, however, suggests that there do exist cases in which we hold persons morally responsible (blameworthy) for the acts of others. Possibly underlying the negative answer to (a) is a confusion of the concept of guilt with that of blame. "Guilt" is typically applied in cases of willful breach of legal codes. No one, to be sure, can be guilty of the illegal acts of another, although as history has painfully shown, one can be found guilty of the acts of another. If my daughter steals a car, she is guilty of stealing. I cannot be guilty of her stealing, but I may well be to blame for her stealing. I may, of course, be guilty of raising my daughter a thief, but that is not to be guilty of her thievery (assuming she was not acting under my orders to steal the car). For me to be guilty of stealing the car, I have to have been an abettor, accomplice, inciter, and so forth of her crime. Even then, however, I am not guilty of her stealing. I am guilty myself of stealing. The point: "Guilt" and "blame" are not synonymous. Furthermore, blame can be vicarious (I am to blame for my daughter's thievery, even though I am not the thief). Because there are a number of things I might have tried to do that would normally be expected in order to raise a daughter with a greater respect for private property and as I do not qualify for any acceptable exemptions, others are justified in morally blaming me for my daughter's thievery. I might even blame myself. It is not simply that I should have raised her better than I did; there were no significant impediments to my having done so, no Frankfurt-type interveners ensuring that I fail to do so.

It might be objected that I am really morally to blame only for being a poor parent and not vicariously to blame for my daughter's thefts. I think, however, such an objection misses the point of expressions such as "The girl stole the car, but the parents are to blame."

I am inclined to the view that to be guilty is to have done the deed or something that in law amounts to doing the deed, that the paradigmatic use of the word is its legalistic use. I assume, then, that to be "morally guilty" is to have transgressed a moral norm, principle, code, or some such, but that is only the first step in moral blameworthiness. After

---

[13] See, for example, H. D. Lewis, "Collective Responsibility," *Philosophy* (January, 1948), XXIII, 84, 3, and R. S. Downie, "Collective Responsibility," *Philosophy* (January, 1969), XLIV, 167, 66.

all, psychopaths, mental defectives, young children, and idiots regularly transgress moral norms. The notion that such persons cannot transgress moral norms because they cannot appreciate the moral nature of such norms begs the question. To argue that "moral guilt" is the willful transgression of such norms will not do either. Surely some of those just mentioned transgress those norms not only willingly but with finesse. What the illustration of my thieving daughter shows is that moral blame is transferable.

Another example may be made to bear more specifically on the issue of justifying the blaming of collectivities. Recall those science-fiction movies in which a scientist attempting to probe the limits of knowledge in search of the "secret of life" (and often for some humane reason) creates a human-looking monster that soon goes berserk and ravages the countryside. The scientist is beset with overwhelming pangs of self-blame, and the good people of the town also blame him for the monstrous evil deeds of his monster. They march on his castle with torches and pitchforks! Despite the fact that the scientist has no control over the monster, despite the fact that he had only good intentions at its creation, I think the townsfolk are justified in holding him morally blameworthy for the monster's deeds. He should have expected dire consequences to occur when he created a monster. But not only should he have refrained from creating the monster; creating it was what he wanted to do. The scientist I have in mind also is not of the "mad" variety, although he may be obsessed with his theories.[14]

Now suppose the scientist was not working in isolation, that he was one of a team of scientists. I think that we would not be reluctant to morally blame the team of scientists for the monster's deeds. Assume that the team of scientists was organized in such a way that they could make group decisions on the value and advisability of various avenues of research in their project. (They had something like a CID Structure.) As a team they were capable of making team judgments and acting on those judgments.[15] Also, assume that no one was forced to join the team and that they all knew they were "searching for the secret of life." They are

[14] See my "Monsters and Their Makers," in Peter A. French, editor, *Individual and Collective Responsibility* (Cambridge, MA, 1972).

[15] Virginia Held convincingly argues that a collectivity is distinguishable from a random collection of individuals by its possession of a decision method for action. See Held "Can a Random Collection of Individuals Be Morally Responsible?" *Journal of Philosophy* (July 23, 1970), 461ff.; and "Moral Responsibility and Collective Action" in my *Individual and Collective Responsibility: Massacre at My Lai*, 101–18.

an identifiable collectivity, a team, and not just a gathering of scientists for, say, a convention in Las Vegas. We may legitimately say that not only should they have chosen a different avenue of research, they also could have done so had they wanted to do so. Monster-making was within their control. Importantly, however, once we have blamed the team, we have not necessarily blamed each scientist individually for the monstrous deeds of their collective creation.

If X, Y, and Z form collectivity A, and if A can and does act as a collectivity – for example, it has and makes use of its decision methods for action – then we may be justified in finding A morally blameworthy for its acts, although the sum of X, Y, and Z's moral blameworthiness is not necessarily, if each is blameworthy of anything at all, equivalent to that ascribed to A. "Collectivity A is blameworthy for event e and A is composed of individuals X, Y, and Z" does not entail "X is blameworthy for e, Y is blameworthy for e, and Z is blameworthy for e."

Herein, of course, lies one of the stickiest problems with the notion of blaming collectivities: how can a collectivity be held morally to blame for event e when not all of its members are held morally blameworthy for e? The approach I am suggesting appears to make the collectivity an entity capable of bearing blame over and above the sum of the blame due each individual member for e. I think that there are good reasons for holding such a view. Collectivities are, in fact, often organized in such a way that they may shoulder blame for the failure of their projects qua collectivity without depositing that blame on individuals who are associated in the collectivity. For example, the Honeywell Corporation was said by many during the 1960s to be to blame for the damage done in North Vietnam by the antipersonnel bombs it designed and manufactured.[16] It would be unjust to blame every Honeywell worker from that time period individually for the destruction those bombs wrought.

It should be noted, however, that from "Collectivity A is blameworthy for event e and A is composed of X, Y, and Z" it would be presumptuous to conclude that X, Y, or Z do not warrant any blame for e, or that either X, Y, or Z is not himself or herself blameworthy in the case of e. Such judgments assessed on members of the collectivity, however, do not follow necessarily from judgments of collective blame. There is an inference gap here comparable to those discussed in Chapter 10. We

---

[16] Honeywell disputed being blamed for the damage done in North Vietnam. The company insisted that it made the bombs for the United States government only as a patriotic service. That government ordered them dropped on Vietnamese citizens.

may expect that at least one of the scientists in the team merits individual blame for the creation of the monster, but the grounds for justifying such blaming are not solely those by which the collective blame is justified, and the individual case is not inferable from the collective one.

Some years ago, Virginia Held argued[17] that the assessment of responsibility on a collectivity is not distributive but that it can be concluded from such an assessment that at least some members of the collectivity are responsible for the event in question. I maintain that although that is often, perhaps typically, the case, it is not a defining characteristic of blaming collectivities that one is able to conclude from the ascription of collective blameworthiness that some members of the collectivity are liable for the event in question.

Two questions bear most significantly on the issue of justifying morally blaming collectivities: (1) Can collectivities act in ways not simply reducible to the acts of their members?; and (2) Does it make sense to say that a collectivity should have done something other than it did do? (Or, do moral norms of collective action exist?)

There are a number of things one can say about the actions of a collectivity that cannot be said of or cannot be reduced to statements about the acts of individuals, or at least such reductions destroy the sense of the original statement about the collectivity. In the case of the team of scientists, under certain conditions it might be said that the team created a monster, although no individual scientist on the team could have done or did so alone. "The X, Y, Z team of scientists made a monster" does not entail "X made a monster," "Y made a monster," and "Z made a monster." If the point is not yet clear, compare this to the statement, "The football team lost the big game," which does not entail "The quarterback lost the big game" or "The middle linebacker lost the big game," and so forth. It does not even entail that any of the players played poorly as individuals. The team effort was just not up to the occasion. Perchance a general spirit was lacking or perhaps the team, through circumstances for which no individual could be cited, is so constituted that even when all members play as well as they possibly can, the total performance is dismal. The team simply lacks a certain complementarity and talent.

Some have argued[18] that although fault may be collective, group liability is always distributive. I think a confusion is embedded in such a view. Take the example with which we were first concerned:

---

[17] Held, "Moral Responsibility and Collective Action."
[18] Joel Feinberg, *Doing and Deserving* (Princeton, 1970), 249.

(D) The American people are to blame for the atrocities committed by U.S. Marines (such as those in Corporal Magincalda's unit) in Iraq.

How is (D) to be justified? Anyone sincerely uttering (D) must be able to show (1) that there exists a recognizable or referable collectivity designated by the term "the American people"; (2) that events describable as "atrocities" took place in Iraq and were committed by U.S. Marines; (3) that a causal relationship can be drawn from acts of the collectivity to those "atrocities"; (4) that the American people should have acted (collectively) in a manner different from the manner in which they did act; (5) that the American people were not unaware of the nature of their behavior (that is, the American people did not believe they were authorizing a cultural exchange of ballet troupes with the Iraqis); and (6) that the collectivity had the ability to act in those alternative ways citable in (4) had they wanted or decided to do so.

It might be argued that my position seems to ignore the fact that collectivities are collections of individuals, that "the American people" is a composition of all Americans (comparable to humankind being a composition of all humans), and that it seems intuitively unjust to blame the American people (all Americans) when a goodly number evidenced a lack of support for the Iraq war. Such a view, however, rests on a serious misunderstanding.

The terms "the American people" and "all Americans" are not equivalent, intersubstitutable without loss of meaning. In "all Americans," "Americans" is a general term. What is true of all Americans is true of each and every American. If we were saying "All Americans are to blame for the atrocities in Iraq," then we would have to justify blaming each American, a task that would be most difficult in the case of many Americans, and by 2008 maybe most. On the other hand, "the American people" is not a general term. It is a singular term that names or purports to name a collectivity. What is true of "the American people" need not be and often is not true of each and every American. For example, "the American people have one of the highest standards of living on Earth" certainly does not mean that each and every American has one of the highest standards of living on Earth. Notice also that the statement "the American people have grown tired of hearing about the Iraq war" may be true when the statement "American John Doe has grown tired of hearing about the Iraq war" is false. (D) does not ascribe blame for the atrocities committed by U.S. Marines in Iraq to each and every American citizen.

Those who might seek to preserve the notion that responsibility is primarily an individual matter might propose we treat (D) as a shorthand version of

(E) All American citizens who did not manifest in some fashion their nonmembership in the collectivity "American Iraq War supporters" are individually to blame (degrees of blame would probably be appropriate) for the atrocities committed by U.S. Marines in Iraq.

However, (E) is not an acceptable substitute for (D); they mean entirely different things. The membership of a blamed collectivity (like the American people) cannot be defined ad hoc in terms of individual participation (overt or covert) in the untoward events that were the occasion of the blaming. When someone blames "the American people" or "the Honeywell Corporation" or the team of scientists or the football team, he is not usually adding (softly under his breath so that he and a few methodological individualists can hear) some qualification to the effect "except those who did X." The collectivity likely would soon die the death of "a thousand qualifications."[19]

Furthermore, if it were the case that the meaning of a statement about "the American people" were identical to the conjunction of a number of statements about the members of the collectivity "the American people," then had one of the individuals belonging to the American people (collectivity) not in fact been a member, the meaning of the original statement would have been different. It is a mistake to seek grounds for exculpation for individual collectivity members when (D) is not individually blaming anyone (which is not to say that individuals are not to blame). The only issue of exculpation in regard to (D) is that of whether or not in the relevant sense we are justified in saying that the collectivity picked out by "the American people" could not have tried to do anything other than it did in the circumstances even if it should have and even if it had wanted to do something different than it did.

Membership in "the American people" or "the Honeywell Corporation" or "the football team" (the collectivities picked out by those terms) is not determined by whether one materially contributed to the particular untoward event for which the collectivity is being blamed, but instead whether one has the "credentials" of membership in that collectivity that acted in such a way as to be productive of such an untoward event. The credentials of membership in "the American people" would

---

[19] This term is borrowed from Antony Flew.

seem to include at least citizenship, perhaps maturity, common descent, language, history, or heritage. But the expression "the American people" surely does not refer to "only those people of American citizenship who support program x or y or z of their government." That is another collective on whom blame might also be heaped in certain cases. In fact, "the American people" is used in ordinary discourse to name not only a collectivity of individuals but also the nation for which the president of the United States speaks and in whose name the armies of the United States march.

Another possible objection: it might be argued that we are not justified in blaming whole populations without blaming individuals because there is really no point in it. That is, there is no reason to expect our blaming to alter the future behavior of the collectivity. Probably few national populations alter their actions because of a fear of blame or censure. Perhaps, however, such a statement as "The German people are to blame for Dachau" has had some impact at least as a kind of warning (the plaque at Dachau reads, "For the past, honor, for the future a warning."). The confusion here, however, is in treating the efficacy of blaming as the grounds for blaming. Whether or not blaming X for e is or should be expected to be productive of any morally desirable results is not the same problem as whether or not X merits blame for e. It must be remembered that blaming in its important moral sense is "to hold responsible" or "to deem blameworthy." It is not "to punish." The only justifiable reason for morally blaming a whole population is that that population merits such blame.

To the question "Why should we blame the American people?" the answer "because it will make the American people act differently in the future" rests only on the weakest of hopes and goes counter to most of what we know of history. But then history gives us little precedent for morally dealing with the powerful technological conglomerates and political machines that proliferate the globe.

Standards for individual behavior and standards of collective behavior should not be thought a priori to be ineffably linked. If we are going to blame whole populations for the untoward behavior of those who act in their name, standards of morally appropriate collective behavior are being, at least implicitly, referenced. How, morally, should collectives act? The task of defining moral standards of collective action or uncovering them from our more-and-more-typical practices of morally blaming collectives of all sorts needs to be carefully undertaken. We should not assume that reverting to traditional theories of individual moral responsibility necessarily will prove adequate in justifying our moral blaming of collectives. As maintained in the previous chapter, we should expect the moral assessment of collectives to be a conceptually different matter than the moral assessment of individuals, and we should expect that different standards or different interpretations of standards that respond to our higher ethical norm of correctness are relevant.

12

The Moral Challenge of Collective Memories

In *The Virtues of Vengeance*, I maintained that there are two types of morally impaired people and that the differences between them are crucial for whether or not they ought to be held morally responsible for what they do.[1] I want to offer some reasons that I believe suggest that a potential source of one of the types of moral impairment for individual members of groups is the "collective memories" of those groups.

I. The Morally Challenged

Throughout the history of moral philosophy and in ordinary discourse, we find various versions of the "could-not-have-done-otherwise" argument to justify not holding a person morally responsible for what he or she did. As previously noted, Harry Frankfurt famously attacked such arguments,[2] maintaining that unavoidability is not what John Martin Fischer calls "a responsibility-undermining factor."[3] What then does undermine moral responsibility? I think that it is the absence in a person of what I will call (with a major debt to Fischer and Mark Ravizza) the moderately moral-reasons responsiveness of the person's own "springs of action." What that means is that a person may be held morally responsible when his or her actions issue from a process in the person that is

---

[1] Peter A. French, *The Virtues of Vengeance* (Lawrence, 2001), 194–206.

[2] Harry Frankfurt, "Alternate Possibilities and Moral Responsibility," *The Importance of What We Care About* (Cambridge, 1988), chapter 1. The crux of Frankfurt's argument is that "if someone had no alternative to performing a certain action but did not perform it because he was unable to do otherwise, then he would have performed exactly the same action even if he could have done otherwise." So that person should be held morally responsible for doing it and for its consequences.

[3] John Martin Fischer, *The Metaphysics of Free Will* (Oxford, 1994), 162.

at least moderately moral-reasons responsive, regardless of whether or not the person could have done otherwise in the circumstances. In cases where a person's actions issue from a process that is not at least moderately moral-reasons responsive, the person is morally incompetent with respect to that case and should not be held morally responsible for his or her behavior in that case. If a person's actions never issue from his or her own moderately moral-reasons-responsive springs of action, the person is profoundly morally incompetent and ought never to be held morally responsible for what he or she does.

What then is moderate moral-reasons responsiveness? Consider the following example (derived from Fischer and Ravizza[4]). Imagine that there is a moral, sufficient reason for me not to spend tomorrow driving around the state of Arizona in search of a woodworker to build me a certain type of end table. That reason is that I need the time to do the proofreading I have promised my editor to finish by the day after tomorrow. Despite the fact that there is a sufficient moral reason anchored in my promise, which my editor and her staff are relying on, and that I recognize this reason as such, I decide to spend tomorrow driving around the state because that is what I feel like doing. When tomorrow rolls around, that is what I do. My editor and other moralists are likely to blame me for putting finding a woodworker ahead of fulfilling my promise to finish the proofreading on time. In effect, she would be holding me morally responsible for doing something other than what I promised to do. I need to stress, however, that the actual process in me that issues in my driving around Arizona recognized but did not react positively to the sufficient moral reason I have to do the proofreading because I made a promise to do it. This is a case of moderate moral-reasons responsiveness. It is a case of moral-reasons recognition or receptivity, but not one in which those reasons motivate actions. It might sometimes be a case of weakness of will. Contrast it to cases in which the agent cannot recognize or is not receptive to moral reasons to do one thing rather than another and so those reasons do not motivate him or her. That may be what I called in Chapter 4 an amoralist. Also, contrast it to cases in which the agent recognizes or is receptive to moral reasons as sufficient reasons to act in a certain way and always acts in that way because of those reasons. We could call the latter type a person of strong moral-reasons responsiveness.

There are two crucial elements in moral-reasons responsiveness: (1) recognizing moral reasons as sufficient reasons to act a certain way in

[4] John Martin Fischer and Mark Ravizza, *Responsibility and Control* (Cambridge, 1999), 42–44.

the circumstances, and (2) translating those reasons into choices and acting on those choices. Call the first moral-reasons receptivity and the second moral-reasons reactivity. Persons are moderately moral-reasons responsive in a particular case if they recognize that there is a sufficient moral reason for them not to do what they are about to do, and if they conceivably would react to that reason by choosing to do otherwise in the circumstances and thereby acting differently, even if that is a rather remote possibility.

To hold a person morally responsible for doing something, we need to be aware of at least one sufficient moral reason to act differently that the person is receptive to and will recognize as such. We also need to be able to imagine that the person could react to that moral reason such as to choose to act differently in the case in question. (This might be given in terms of possible worlds. The world in which the reactivity occurs may be rather remote from the actual world, although not so remote that it strains imagination to the breaking point.) For example, it is conceivable that a career burglar might react to a moral reason to which she is receptive not to steal the jewels by not stealing them; still, she nonetheless steals the jewels. She is morally responsible for the jewel theft even if it is only a remotely conceivable possibility that she would react appropriately to the moral reason she recognizes, or is receptive to, as sufficient for not stealing the jewels by not stealing them. She is morally challenged as regards to stealing jewels. For some reason that may or may not be of her choosing, there is a disconnect between receptivity and reactivity to sufficient moral reasons in her springs of action with respect to jewel thievery. It is more difficult, but not unimaginable, for morally challenged persons to do the morally appropriate thing in certain circumstances than it is for the person who is not morally challenged, that is, the person for whom receptivity and reactivity to moral reasons are aligned in their springs of action in those same circumstances.[5]

To the concept of moderately moral-reasons responsiveness I need to add another concept to provide the foundation for what I want to say about the potential moral-impairment capacity for members of a group because of their collective memories. I am going to help myself to a concept I have already used in Chapter 8. It is Frankfurt's account

[5] I wonder if Kant may have thought that it is those I am calling morally challenged who deserve moral credit when they act against inclination and do the right thing for the morally sufficient reason to do it. Those who are strongly moral-reasons responsive, particularly if that is their habit of acting, seem to earn less, if any, moral credit from Kant when they do the right thing.

of "volitional necessity." Frankfurt writes, "There are occasions when a person realizes that what he cares about matters to him not merely so much, but in such a way, that it is impossible for him to forbear from a certain course of action... [such that] every apparent alternative to that course is unthinkable."[6] As an example, Frankfurt provides Martin Luther's famous declaration before the Diet of Worms, "Here I stand; I can do no other." The impossibility alluded to by Frankfurt when he describes volitional necessity is not logical or causal. It is a felt necessity arising out of aligning one's sense of identity with a certain collection of cares. Although calling this "necessity" risks misleading or confusing, insofar as the term has found currency owing to the reception in the literature of Frankfurt's work, I use it to refer to the force of constraint in the will that Frankfurt describes in explicating the term. It is crucial to my account that Frankfurtian volitional necessity does not exclude the possibility, albeit remote, that a person could choose to act otherwise. Volitional necessity may block reasons reactivity, even if it does not necessarily block reasons receptivity.

When Luther uttered his response to the Diet, he was not saying that he had no choice in the matter, nor that he was incapacitated and thus could not form the sentence in which he would have recanted, nor that it was logically impossible for him to do so, nor that he was weak of will. We confidently may assume that he recognized sufficient reasons (prudential ones) for doing otherwise in the circumstances. He had the capacity and the power to recant but not the will to do so. He felt constrained by his own will, and that constraint rendered it impossible for him in the circumstances to utilize his capacities to recant.

However, there is surely a conceivable set of circumstances – that is, a possible world, even if a remote one – in which Luther does recant, where he overcomes the constraint of his own deeply held cares and convictions and reacts to prudential reasons to do otherwise. After all, he is not a passive victim of his own will. He accedes to his own constraining force "because he is unwilling to oppose it and because, furthermore, his unwillingness is itself something he is unwilling to alter."[7] He acts in the way he does because his sense of identity and will have been formed, whether or not voluntarily by him or through other influences over which he may or may not have had control, in a way that in this circumstance renders it extremely difficult for him to do something other than refuse

---

[6] Frankfurt, "The Importance of What We Care About," 86.
[7] Ibid., 87.

to recant the positions he has publicly taken against the Catholic Church. I think we would agree with the Diet that Luther is morally responsible for his refusal to recant. Among his followers, then and now, he is praised for his stand.

The force of volitional necessity can arise in a person's will by any number of involuntary processes as well as by free choices of the agent. Acting on such deeply engrained cares, what one really gives a damn about (to use the expression for the attitude I adopted in Chapter 8) may become volitionally necessary for some people who do things that are morally objectionable, whereas any other course of action is unthinkable for them in the circumstances. Nonetheless, it is conceivable that the processes they actually employ that issue in their actions in those cases satisfy the conditions of moderate moral-reasons responsiveness. That will be the case if they recognize that there are moral reasons that are sufficient to motivate alternative actions by them, although they are, for all intents and purposes, constrained by a force in their own wills that they are unwilling to oppose and so behave immorally. I am uncertain as to whether such people should be described as perverse or preferential wrongdoers. (See Chapter 4 and the Appendix to Chapter 2.)

When it results in untoward behavior, volitional necessity as I understand it could render remote the possibility that the agent is moral-reasons reactive, although he or she is still moral-reasons receptive with regard to the behavior in question. Put another way, the agent may recognize that there is a sufficient moral reason for him or her not to do x but cannot align his or her will with that reason and act accordingly because it is volitionally necessary for him or her, given his or her deeply-held cares, to do x under the circumstances. If that is the case, the person is profoundly morally challenged in those circumstances but should be held morally responsible for what he or she does in them. Doing the right thing in cases of that sort will be difficult for the agent in the extreme, but that fact about his or her will is not morally exculpating when the agent acts immorally in those circumstances.

I turn now to try to lay the basis for believing that the collective memories of groups may have the capacity to render individual members of those groups morally challenged. They can engrain cares in the wills of some group members, what they really give a damn about, that are productive of the force of volitional necessity and that constrains their actions and causes them to regard as unthinkable acting in a way differently from the way they act, although they would or do recognize or are receptive to sufficient moral reasons to act differently. For some group members in some circumstances, inculcated collective memories are the root cause of a volitional necessity that blocks both moral-reasons receptivity and moral-reasons reactivity. Typically, group members so affected believe they are doing what is right and sheath themselves in the armor of self-righteousness. They are then perverse wrongdoers. If, however, they recognize that what they are doing is morally wrong, they often report feeling that, being the people they are, acting otherwise is not a live option. I am not certain as to whether we should regard them as preferential wrongdoers.

II. Memories and Collective Memories (Heritage)

Taken at face value, it sounds as if a collective memory is any memory that is held by more than one person. That, however, is likely to confuse collective memories with other kinds of memories that are held by more than one person.

What follows is a rough-and-ready taxonomy of memories, a taxonomy that I admit is rather superficial but I hope sufficient for my purposes. The perceptual, factual (that distinction is Norman Malcolm's[8]), and habitual memories persons have can be called their "Personal Memories." You have a personal perceptual memory (or at least I am assuming that you do) of what your lunch yesterday tasted like and a personal factual memory of where you were the hour before reading this. Similarly, I do not have a perceptual memory of my mother, but I factually remember that she died when I was five years old. (Oddly enough, I have both a perceptual and a factual memory of her funeral.) Maybe we both have habitual memories of how to ride a bicycle. (Perceptual memories involve mental images, or what Malcolm called "definite perceptible physiognomy"[9]; factual memories need have no accompanying mental imagery.)

A number of us could have personal memories of the same event that we each experienced, perhaps in different ways. Following Margalit's lead,[10] I call personal memories of the same event had by a number of persons "Common Memories." When we have a common memory of an event, there has been no communication among us to arrive at or polish that memory, no negotiation, no agreement on the contents

---

[8] Norman Malcolm, "Three Forms of Memory," *Knowledge and Certainty* (Englewood Cliffs, 1963), 204.

[9] Ibid., 207.

[10] Avishai Margalit, *The Ethics of Memory* (Cambridge, 2002), 50–1.

of the memory; its commonality is simply aggregative and, in a not-unreasonable use of the term, accidental.

"Shared Memories" are the result of communication and often negotiation. Imagine that you were my companion for dinner last night and that now you and I report personal memories of the experience to each other, but that our accounts are radically different with regard to certain particulars. We share the memory that we went to an Italian restaurant last night only if you have in your memory that we did and I have in my memory that we did, and we have those memories because each of us knows that the other has agreed that we went to an Italian restaurant last night and it is common knowledge between us that each of us has in his or her memory that we did, at least in part, because the other one agrees that we did. Sharing a memory is the cumulative outcome of the parties each having in his or her memory an account of an event that has the features it does because the parties have brought or negotiated their memories into agreement.[11]

I use the term "Collective Memory" to refer to a narrative representation of events that forms a part of the story that an encompassing and enduring group (Avishai Margalit and Joseph Raz's term[12]) tells itself about itself; such a memory contributes to its sense of itself or its identity. It is a part of, if you will, its heritage. Jan Assmann defines it as "the outer dimension of human memory."[13] It typically is given or repeated by members in the first-person plural, even when none of the current members of the group could have had a personal perceptual or a shared memory of the events involved. The transformation of factual personal memories into collective memories is described rather well, if not in those terms, in David Silver's account of the change in the speaker's report of historical information from the use of the third-person plural to the third-person singular, from "they did x" to "we did x."[14]

Collective memory is a way a group ensures "continuity by preserving, with the help of cultural mnemonics, its collective knowledge from one generation to the next, rendering it possible for later generations

---

[11] My account of shared memory, more or less, mirrors Bratman's account of shared intention.

[12] Margalit and Raz, "National Self-Determination," *Journal of Philosophy* 87 (1990), 439–61.

[13] Jan Assmann, *Das kulurelle Gedächtnis. Schrift, Erinnerung und politische Identität in frühen Hochkulturen* (Munich, 1992), 19.

[14] David Silver, "Collective Responsibility and the Ownership of Actions," *Public Affairs Quarterly*, 16, 3, July 2002, 297.

to reconstruct their cultural identity."[15] It is elemental in the strategy by which most groups instill and reinforce their peculiar collection of cares in the minds of members. The kind of groups I have in mind may be ethnic, tribal, national, regional, and possibly gender, sexual, and racial. The narrative form that collective memories take can bind together material objects, places, events, documents, and so on to provide a coherent and typically quasi-historical "fabric" that forms and preserves the group members' "perceptions and values . . . to create a sense of continuity and to act as a motor for development,"[16] to use Eric Kluitenberg's description.

The members of encompassing and enduring groups, through acculturation, commodification, and other institutional embedding processes, but typically not negotiation, become jointly committed[17] to collectively holding in their memories a certain narrative about their group and a distinctive collection of cares. Having a particular version of the group's story in one's memory is a crucial element of belonging to or identifying with that group. Collective memory is to peoples as personal memory is to persons.

Its collective memories incorporate what the group qua group cares most about, and so its members, or a significant subset of them, are jointly committed to defending, protecting, and nurturing those memories. Such joint commitments typically reveal themselves in group or individual actions when issues regarding the veracity of the content of their collective memories arise. For example, when historians or archeologists challenge some of their collective memories, group members have been known to reject the historical or the archeological evidence, sometimes violently.

Its collective memories not only define the identity of the group, they serve as an external horizon for the current events that involve the group. Edward Casey noted that collective memories provide a spatial/temporal framework for what it is to become a member of the group.[18] Important elements of the collective memories of, for example, Americans are

---

[15] Cornelius Holtorf, "Towards a Chronology of Megaliths: Understanding Monumental Time and Cultural Memory," *Journal of European Archaeology* 4 (1996), 119–52. Also available on the website https://tspace.library.utoronto.ca/citd/holtorf/2.0.html.

[16] Eric Kluitenberg, "The Politics of Cultural Memory," *Media*Revolution*, Campus Verlag, Reihe "edition bauhaus," Band 6, Herbst 1999. Reprinted at http://amsterdam.nettime.org/Lists-Archives/nettime-l-9907/msg00083.html.

[17] I borrow the term "joint commitment" from Margaret Gilbert.

[18] In a paper given at a conference on *Ethics in Place* at Arizona State University, February 2004.

stabilized, memorialized, in space. Think of the Gettysburg Battlefield, Wounded Knee, where the World Trade Center Towers once stood; and Americans tell the story about themselves with those elements of their collective memories as crucial signposts: "After Gettysburg...."; "Since Wounded Knee...."; "In the wake of 9/11...."

A distinction found in Malcolm's account of memory[19] (but not one on which he dwells, although it certainly produced its fair share of respondents) between something being remembered and something being in one's memory is useful in understanding a typical characteristic of collective memory. Memory reports have the appearance of being factive in that if I remember something having happened in a certain way, then it must have happened in that way or I am not really remembering it. As Alan White put it, "If this is what I remember, this is what must have been. 'Incorrect memory' is a logical solecism."[20]

Still, we often get things wrong when sincerely believing we remember them to be one way rather than another. The locutions we use to express our memories are instructive. "I remember our going to an Italian restaurant last night," on most accounts, entails that we did so, or that the proposition "We went to an Italian restaurant last night" is true. On the other hand, "As I remember" or "According to my memory" or "I have it in my memory that we went to an Italian restaurant last night" allows that we may not have gone to an Italian restaurant last night. Those locutions are hedges with regard to truth-value implications.

Without going further into this tangle at this time, I adopt what I think is a commonsensical position that there is no guarantee that what is in my memory is or was the case. False propositions may litter our memory banks. I can remember something that did not happen by remembering or recalling what is in my memory. Insofar as collective memories are among the memories in my memory bank, there is no guarantee that they are veridical.

Collective memories, because of the role they play in shaping a generally positive identity of a group, often include fabrications, myths, stories, plausible accounts of the group's past, and noble lies. An historical example, one Umberto Eco incorporated into his novel *Baudolino*, is illustrative. The collective memories of the people of Cologne, Germany, for eight centuries contained the story that the twelfth-century archbishop

---

[19] Malcolm, 204.
[20] Alan White, "As I Remember...," *The Philosophical Quarterly* Vol. 39, No. 154 January 1989), 95.

of Cologne, Rainald, stole the mummified corpses of the three Magi from Milan and transported them for display in the Cologne cathedral. The corpses exhibited in the Cologne cathedral until the early twentieth century, however, were not those of the biblical three wise men. Also, they were never in Milan. Rainald manufactured them from bodies dug up in a Cologne cemetery. He concocted the narrative of their having once been in the possession of Constantine, and in 314 taken to Milan in an ox cart by Saint Eustorgio, from whence they were pillaged in the aftermath of Frederick Barbarosa's siege of Milan and carried off to Cologne to become venerated patrons of that city. Through the centuries, the people of Cologne were alternately proud and ashamed of having stolen the "Magi" from Milan, and they expressed something of the latter when they allowed some bodily parts from the corpses to "return" to Milan in 1909. The Milanese, during the same period, collectively mourned, expressed regret and shame, and became incensed because their mummified Magi were stolen from them. Of course, no one in either city ever could remember the theft, although both groups could remember, and did for eight centuries, that according to their collective memories it occurred in the twelfth century.

The story of the people of Cologne's collective memory of their Magi suggests that, as Jon Elster writes, "what matters is not that a certain account of the past be correct, but that it be convincing to the particular group ... [and] that it be meaningful to the collective subjectivities and self-identities of the specific group which it addresses."[21]

David Lowenthal goes further along this path by maintaining that the collective memories of a group are typically fabricated.[22] He claims that the stories in a group's collective memories will survive over time only if they place the group both in a positive light and exalt its uniqueness, and that typically requires reengineering of the facts, a job usually taken on by the dominant institutions within the group's social/political structure. The collective memories of a group become largely immune to criticism by group members. They rest firmly on a prejudiced pride that affirms the group's worth for each member.

Let me offer an indelicate example. Each of us may have a personal memory of the September 11, 2001 attack on the World Trade Center

---

[21] Jon Elster, "From the Pyramids to Pausanias and Piglet: Monuments, Travel, and Writing," in S. Goldhill and R. Osborne, eds. *Art and Text in Ancient Greek Culture* (Cambridge, 1994), 226.

[22] David Lowenthal, "Fabricating Heritage," *History & Memory* 10, 1 (Spring 1998).

and the Pentagon. Many of us probably have common memories of those events, having been there or having seen the attacks on television, and I suspect that a number of people now have shared memories of 9/11/01; that is, memories that are the result of communication and negotiation with others. However, there is also the "candidate" collective memory of 9/11/01 and subsequent days artfully produced, test-marketed, and promulgated by the purveyors of our American storyline, and it seems to have won the allegiance of a significant majority of the American population. That narrative exaggerates, omits, and erases facts that future historians may determine are crucial to understanding the events. It has a great deal to do with the original justification for America invading Iraq, and it excludes a number of historical facts that would likely have weakened its attraction to the American people. Michael Moore, in his film *Fahrenheit 9/11*, and others attempted to correct that collective memory, for example, with respect to its depiction of the role of President Bush on 9/11/01, by displaying historical fact. However, that was bound to fail with the majority of the American people because of the unflattering image, even if historically correct, it revealed of the leader of the collectivity. That seven or ten minutes of film footage has been given a revisionist reading by the promulgators or propagators of the "approved" version, and that may well be what will be woven into the tapestry of our heritage narrative.

Lowenthal notes that group members characteristically lack concern for historical data and reflection on content with respect to their group's collective memories. He writes:

> From some legendary seed each group grows delusory faiths – faiths nutritive not despite but due to their flaws. A "mountain of false information" sustains all societies. The bad effects of wrong beliefs are more than compensated by the bonding a legacy confers and by the barriers it erects. Shared misinformation excludes those whose own legacy encodes other catechisms. "Correct" knowledge could not so serve, because it is open to all. Only "false" knowledge can become a gauge of exclusion. Heritage mandates misreadings of the past.[23]

III. Collective Memories Provoking Moral Challenge

The collective-memory mill is usually supervised by an established institutional structure within the group that may manufacture the narrative and

---

[23] Ibid.

that certainly adopts, promulgates, and preserves it for the membership of future generations. Those institutions (e.g., governments, libraries, museums, media, heritage foundations and organizations), themselves loci of authority and power in the group, typically focus their political and social agendas through the lenses of collective memories and fabricate new versions of the "approved" story to suit their purposes. Because they are constructed for general consumption and to serve as a unifying identity tool as well as a provocateur of group actions, collective memories will either portray the group's past behavior as better than it was, and so a matter of collective pride, or its struggles as worse than they were as a way of building the solidarity of oppression among the members.

In whatever guise they take, collective memories seem to be capable of generating extraordinarily influential collections of cares to which group members are jointly committed. Those cares frequently give rise to the force of volitional necessity in some group members, especially when collective memories are wielded by authority figures that understand and have mastered their motivational power over group members. This, of course, is an empirical claim and not one, as a philosopher, that I am qualified to test. I suspect that any attempt to construct a social-psychological experiment to test it would be ruled improper by institutional review boards concerned about the use of human subjects in experiments. A number of historical examples could be cited that I believe go some ways toward convincing us that the claim is on the mark, although disputes are prone to arise about interpretation of the facts in most if not all cited cases. In any event, the following could serve as possible examples where collective memories played a not-insignificant role in the behavior of group members toward those in other groups: Protestants and Catholics in Northern Ireland, the Irish Republicans in the first half of the twentieth century, Hindus and Muslims in India at the end of the British Raj, Shiites and Sunnis and Kurds in Iraq today, various American Indian tribes with respect to other tribes and to white Americans at various times past and present, members of the KKK since the American Civil War, and the list could go on and on.

Consider an example from the Balkans in the 1990s. Some Serbs reportedly committed atrocities against Muslims in Bosnia and Kosovo as a form of ethnic cleansing. It was reported that the Serbs carrying out massacres in Kosovo villages shouted "Remember the Field of Blackbirds" and that the number "1389" was often scrawled on the walls of buildings in which atrocities were committed. The Battle of Kosovo was

fought between the Serbs and the Turks on what was called the Field
of Blackbirds in the year 1389. The Turks won that battle and subju-
gated the Serbs to their rule for about five centuries. The Turks are
Muslims, the Serbs Christians. Historians tell us that the social, religious,
and political institutions of the Serbs sustained the memories of 1389 in
the Serbian population through all those years. When Slobodan Milosevic wanted to raise the Serbs to his cause, he enlisted those collective
memories that were a part of Serbian heritage. Those collective memories retained motivational power because they summoned deeply held
cares in individual members of the group, and those members, acting
out of volitional necessity, behaved in the manner they did notwith-
standing any moral compunctions they may have held proscribing such
behavior.

The historical record suggests that members of groups whose collective
memories are laced with hatred and intolerance for those not in the
group or toward a specific other group find resisting the urge to act
on those memories, particularly when those memories are invoked by
those in positions of authority, at minimum an extremely difficult task.
The consideration of questions about the veracity and the morality of
those collective memories, in fact, may be virtually unthinkable for most
group members. It would take a special person, what Margalit calls a
"moral witness,"[24] with uncommon insight from within the group to
raise the appropriate moral concerns. Such a person is highly unlikely to
be heeded by the general membership, mainly because those memories
are, as I have stressed, perceived by group members to be among the
essential features of their group identity.

The members of what Margalit calls a "community of memory" typically
are unconsciously habituated to having their collective memories and a
certain collection of cares and second-order cares about those cares. Put
simply, they care deeply about what they care about. For a group member to question the veracity and the moral value of the heritage story the
group tells itself about itself requires an extraordinary intellectual and
volitional effort. Group members, at some cognitive level, may be aware
of the strong disincentive to their making such an effort because of the
likelihood that it would threaten their personal and social identities, provoking a crisis of identity for them individually and for the group from
whose identity they glean no small measure of their own sense of who
they are. Nonetheless, their losing, erasing, or overcoming the attraction

[24] Margalit, chapter 5.

of collective memories, of caring about things different from those they were acculturated to care about, is at least conceivable for most group members. Volitional necessity engendered by the cares promulgated by collective memories is therefore not a block to their moderate moral-reasons responsiveness with respect to their behavior that was motivated by recollection of those memories. The block is in their will, not in their ability to recognize reasons, including moral reasons. There is nothing inconsistent in someone saying something like, "I know there are sufficient moral reasons for me not to do x, but I will do x, I can do no other." I suppose that in some cases where an agent would say something of that sort, we could rightly identify the statement as an admission of weakness of will. I think we would be wrong, however, to do so in many of the collective memory cases I have mentioned in which the inculcation of collective memories, in large part, is the cause of the agent's deeply held cares and the agent is acting in the grip of volitional necessity. Volitional necessity is not weakness of will. Some would say that it is strength of will, as in the Luther example favored by Frankfurt. In any event, I am suggesting that in certain circumstances, it can be best described as provoking a profound disconnect in the agent between moral-reasons recognition and moral-reasons reactivity. Importantly, although collective memories certainly provide group members with sufficient reasons to act in certain ways by instilling in group members a collection of group-identity-conferring cares, collective memories, like any other memories, are not irresistible instigators of action, triggering physical processes in the central nervous system that are not moral-reasons responsive.

Remember that moderate moral-reasons responsiveness requires only that there is a conceivable set of circumstances in which there is a sufficient moral reason for the agent to do otherwise, that the agent's own machinery of action operates, and that he or she does otherwise. The remoteness of that possibility is not an exculpating factor, but I suppose we often regard it as mitigating in certain sorts of cases. Moderate moral-reasons responsiveness does not require that realistically the agent could have done otherwise in the actual world.

IV. Concluding Note

Collective memories can be overridden by moral reasons that are sufficient to cause group members not to act as they do toward outsiders, if only in some remote possible world. Hence, collective memories are not responsibility-undermining factors, but they are morally problematic and probably noneliminatable features of our moral lives. We derive much of our sense of who we are from our memberships in groups, and we gain the sense of what it is to belong to such groups from the inculcation and acculturation processes, rituals and celebrations, and even, as Paul Connerton maintains,[25] the clothing we wear, all of which habituate the group's collective memories in our memory banks. I am not claiming either that collective memories are necessarily morally bad things or that they are a dispensable element of group life. I am claiming that we are often morally challenged when we interact with those who are outside of our groups and who are excluded and demonized by our collective memories or heritage narratives. In most cases, when that occurs, we cannot avoid moral responsibility for our untoward actions, qua group members, practiced on outsiders, albeit we were incited by the persuasive rhetoric of authority figures invoking those memories, and even though our acts were for us volitionally necessary.

Addendum: Thoughts about Team Mascots, Nicknames, Apologies, and Restitution

The Memphis Chicks were a professional baseball team from 1902 until 1960. After a number of years out of professional baseball, the Chicks returned in 1978. I was curious as to why a men's professional baseball team would choose the nickname "Chicks." I looked up their logo, and lo and behold, it was not a baby chicken or a bevy of young women or even the Memphis Belle. It was originally a forlorn looking Indian, and then in 1993 a stylized Indian, in both cases in the war bonnet of a Northern Plains tribe. It turns out that "Chicks" is a shortened version or a nickname of "Chickasaws," albeit the Chickasaws are not a Northern Plains tribe. Still, the puzzle remained: why was a Memphis baseball team using that name, that logo, and an Indian mascot?

I suspect that the Chickasaws could not have been especially pleased given their history with the Memphis area. The Chickasaw Nation was systematically swindled out of its lands in western Tennessee by treaties negotiated by Andrew Jackson in 1805, 1816, and 1818. When Jackson became president of the United States, he initiated the removal of all the Chickasaws to what is now Oklahoma. That removal began in the

---

[25] Paul Connerton, *How Societies Remember* (Cambridge, 1989).

summer of 1837. Today, the tribe is primarily located in south-central Oklahoma. Its only ties to the Memphis area are that prior to 1818, the bluffs along the Mississippi where Memphis is located had been part of the tribe's western Tennessee hunting grounds.

I could not find any references regarding whether or not the Chickasaws had ever expressed an opinion, one way or another, regarding the use of the tribal name or rather a diminutive version of it as the nickname of the Memphis baseball team. Did they regard it as an honor to have the shortened tribal name on the team jerseys, to have tee shirts with the logo on the front worn by Memphis fans, and souvenirs with generic Indian chiefs emblazoned on them sold at the games? Or were they offended, even outraged? As most of the existence of the Chicks was during the time of segregation in Memphis, I wonder if members of the Chickasaw Nation would have been able to attend the team's games or sit in the box seats rather than the distant bleachers.

Some supporters of the use of Indian mascots and logos for sports teams claim that they honor the tribes. Some further argue that the tribes should feel flattered, not offended, by the representation of their culture in the sports events that are one of the dominant features of American life during the last 100 or more years. The NCAA Executive Committee has come to see the matter differently. They announced a postseason ban from its sponsored tournaments of college teams that have "hostile and abusive" American Indian nicknames and imagery, including those with spears in their logos and mascots that pose as American Indian warriors. Eighteen schools are subject to this policy. They are the Alcorn State University Braves, the Central Michigan University Chippewas, the Catawba College Indians, the Florida State University Seminoles, the Midwestern State University Indians, the University of Utah Utes, the Carthage College Redmen, the Bradley University Braves, the Arkansas State University Indians, the Chowan College Braves, the University of Illinois Fighting Illini, the University of Louisiana-Monroe Indians, the McMurray University Indians, the Mississippi College Choctaws, the Newberry College Indians, the University of North Dakota Fighting Sioux, the Indiana University of Pennsylvania Indians, and the Southeastern Oklahoma State University Savages.

Being Irish, I wonder why the Fighting Irish of the University of Notre Dame are not on the list. The NCAA executives anticipated my query with the preemptive response: "the Fighting Irish refers to a nationality, not a race of people, and no ethnic group." But aren't the Chippewas, the Seminoles, the Choctaws, and the Chickasaws nationalities as well? A university with the nickname "Warriors" was not included on the NCAA's list because the NCAA learned the university's mascot and logo were of a Homeric Greek soldier. The Irish and the Greeks, I guess, cannot be offended.

Of course, there are not only caricature mascots and logos that are demeaning and stereotyping, there are outright historical and cultural falsehoods portrayed in the logos and the mascots. Take the case of the mascot of the University of Illinois: Chief Illiniwek. "To represent the Illini with a Plains Indian war bonnet, to name them the 'fighting Illini,' and to dress the mascot in the military regalia of a Sioux warrior, is totally inaccurate. It is like representing Italians or Germans with someone dressed in a Scottish kilt and playing the bagpipes."[26]

San Diego State University is not on the list. Its nickname is the Aztecs. The reason it escaped is that the NCAA could not find any currently existing organized tribe or group related to the Aztecs or now bearing that name. What does that imply? I guess the idea is that there is no one living to be offended by the use of the name.[27]

I am concerned only with the nicknames and mascots that relate to specific American Indian Nations, rather than the more generic ones like Indians, Redskins, Chiefs, Braves, and the like. My philosophical concern turns on the question: What is it to offend a collective or a group?

One plausible answer is that offending a group is to offend a certain percentage of the group's membership. How many? At least 51 percent? All of them? Is it plausible to claim that a group is offended by something even if none of its current members claim they are offended by it? Might something offend a group even if its representatives maintain that they are honored by the use of its name, for example, by a university? Some leaders of the Seminole tribe claim they are honored by the use of their tribal name as the nickname of the Florida State University sports teams. They do not seem to be put off either by the nickname typically being shortened to Noles. The FSU football teams have had a long run of victorious seasons, including a national championship. Had they a dismal

---

[26] Letter to the Board of Trustees of the University of Illinois, 2004.

[27] It is intriguing that the military has chosen to nickname its helicopter gunships after American Indian Nations. There is the Apache, the Kiowa, the Comanche, the Chinook, and the Blackhawk.

record year in and year out, perhaps those tribal leaders would be less pleased with the use of their name as the brand of the teams representing that institution.

In any event, I think the ethical issues regarding the use of tribal names as nicknames of sports teams should, in large measure, turn on the concept of heritage, and that it is the group's heritage and not necessarily its current membership that is being offended. Heritage, as noted herein, is the narrative representation of events that forms a part of the story that a group tells itself about itself, its sense of itself, of its identity. In that regard, heritage functions like our personal memories that are, in large measure, the keeper of our personal identities (the central element in Locke's theory of personal identity). Alexander McCall Smith writes in *The No. 1 Ladies Detective Agency*:

> Our heads are small, but they are as full of memories as the sky may some-
> times be full of swarming bees, thousands and thousands of memories, of
> smells, of places, of things that happened to us and which come back, unex-
> pectedly, to remind us who we are. And who am I? I am Precious Ramotswe,
> citizen of Botswana, daughter of Obed Ramotswe who died because he had
> been a miner and could no longer breathe.[28]

For a group such as an American Indian nation, the narrative form that heritage takes can bind together material objects, places, events, documents, and so forth to provide a coherent, typically quasi-historical, "fabric" that forms and preserves the group members' sense of continuity with past generations. The members of a tribal group, for example, through acculturation and other institutional processes, become jointly committed to collectively holding in their memories a certain narrative about their group. Having a particular version of the group's story is a crucial element of belonging to that group. Heritage is to peoples as personal memory is to persons. Being a member of a tribe is to share in a collective ownership of its heritage. It is to use the third-person singular rather than the third-person plural to recount its story, to handle its artifacts, and so on.

So what has all of this to do with the question of whether or not a tribe can be offended by such things as the use of its name as a nickname of a sports team even if none of the current tribal members regards that use as personally offensive? I am suggesting that appropriating the

---

[28] Alexander McCall Smith, *The No. 1 Ladies Detective Agency* (New York, 1998), 15.

heritage of a group, whether by a group member or a non-group member, in a way that is not consistent with the group's traditions, history, sacred and other beliefs is an offense against the identity of the group and hence offends all of its past, present, and future members, whether they appreciate it or not! It is a version of identity theft. Confusion may arise, even in the minds of group members, of the imagery of the appropriation and its quasi history with the crucial elements of the group's heritage.

Furthermore, it does not matter that a group's heritage is laced with fabrications and highly implausible tales on which the group's sacred ceremonies and beliefs about itself are based. The vetting of heritage in the face of historical fact is an entirely different matter from the confusion of heritage with commodified imagery that is utterly external to the group.

Which brings us back to the Aztecs of San Diego State. Apparently, there no longer exist pure Aztecs in an organized tribe to be offended by the use of the tribal name for a university's sports teams. So what? The use of the name and mascot is offensive because it reflects on all American Indian tribes. If the only thing that would make it permissible to use the name of a tribe or Indian nation is that the tribe no longer exists, then is genocide what makes it permissible? If we were to kill off all the currently existing Hopis, would it be morally permissible for Northern Arizona University to change its nickname from the Lumberjacks to the Fightin' Hopis? Or if the Navahos were wiped out, then would the Demon Navahos be okay?[29]

Much has been written in ethics about obligations to future generations. We can, of course, ensure that there will be no future generations by destroying the environment in which humans can exist. But do we also have moral obligations to past generations? Western European/majority American thought says very little about obligations to ancestors, although in our legal system the recently dead, at least, do command some power over the living if they do not die in testate. Honoring heritage may be a primary way in which we can meet moral obligations to our ancestors. But our ancestors also may have burdened us with obligations because of what they did to other groups.

A group's history, as well as its heritage, belongs to it collectively. It is ours, not yours or mine. The idea of collective ownership is crucial

---

[29] I understand that Wake Forest University's sports teams have the nickname the Demon Deacons.

to understanding a group's collective moral responsibilities for its past wrongs, its historical obligations to other groups. Consider the following from a debate in the Canadian Parliament. The motion under debate was "That a humble Address be presented to Her Excellency praying that she will intercede with Her Majesty to cause the British Crown to present an official apology to the Acadian people for the wrongs done to them in its name between 1755 and 1763." For those unacquainted with Canadian history or Longfellow's *Evangeline*, those were the years of the Acadian Diaspora, the Grand Derangement, in which the francophone Acadians were rounded up and shipped by the British to Louisiana (where they became the Cajuns) or to France and other places.

The motion sent the Canadian Parliament into a spin. Some of the members argued in favor of the motion because it "gives the Acadian people the opportunity to have the wrongs done to their ancestors, as well as concrete impacts that are still felt today, officially recognized." But others argued that guilt cannot be collective and cannot be passed from one generation on to another. A remark by former Canadian Prime Minister Pierre Trudeau was oft quoted. Trudeau said, "I do not see how I can apologize for some historic event to which we were not a party. We can only regret that it happened."

Regret, as used by Trudeau, seems to be something like indignation, perhaps only mild indignation, felt about what someone else did to someone other than the person who is at least mildly indignant. But can one have such regret, at least in the fullest sense of the term? "I regret what John did to Mary" seems odd, if not a misuse of the term. More normally we would say "I am sorry that John did that to Mary." However, we do sometimes say, "The incident was regrettable" when we had nothing to do with it. "Regrettable," in such cases, however, lacks in power as an expression of a strong negative reactive attitude. It gives off an antiseptic odor. Think of the politician telling us, "My use of that phrase was regrettable" when we would have preferred him to say, "I am ashamed of myself for having said that."

For an apology to have any sense, of course, the actions for which the apology is being made must be ones for which the apologist is at least morally responsible. Learning of the Grand Derangement may well arouse resentment in currently existing Acadians whose ancestors were dispersed, but who today can they legitimately resent? British and English-speaking Canadians living today might be their target. Suppose they are. Can British and English-speaking Canadians sincerely apologize to the Acadians alive today for what was done by their ancestors to ancestors of the Acadians in order, at least, to try to lessen the resentment that creates a barrier today between the peoples? Would not an apology uttered by someone, even someone in political authority, in the name of some group that had no control over what happened centuries ago be nonsensical, as Trudeau maintained?

I do not think that an individual can be personally responsible for an event if the person could not have had any control over the event, but the same person might be a member of a group that is collectively responsible for the same event. The ownership of actions is the justifying condition for holding someone or some group responsible for the events brought about by those actions. However, there are at least two different kinds of ownership, two distinct ways by which a person comes to have ownership of actions and events. One is by actually having done them, and the other is by membership in the collective that did them. The latter category breaks into two subcategories: collective membership in which my utterance "We did X" entails "I did X," and collective membership in which my utterance "We did X" does not entail "I did X." In individual cases ownership of actions, for moral purposes, requires that the person was at least moderately moral-reasons responsive with respect to the event in question. That is what Fischer refers to as guidance control. In collective cases, shared ownership in the absence of control is sufficient for collective moral responsibility.

Think again of the debate in the Canadian Parliament. Some of those speaking in favor of the motion claimed they were doing so because they recognized that the British people and the non-Acadian Canadians of today collectively own the events of the Grand Derangement and that it is therefore entirely proper for the Queen and the Canadian government to apologize to the Acadians for what "we did," although recognizing that the collective responsibility cannot be distributively assigned to the membership of the collective alive today. The Grand Derangement was officially sanctioned and promoted by the then-British government, that is an historical fact and something both those supporting the motion and those opposed acknowledged. The difference between the two positions is that the supporters reasoned from the premise "We engaged in the Grand Derangement," whereas the opponents reasoned from the premise "The British government of 1755 to 1763 engaged in a policy of deporting the Acadians." The difference between the two premises is profound. The supporters' position manifests a sharing of collective ownership with those who more than two hundred years ago engaged in the practice. It sees the past event as present in the present of the

Canadians, as an injustice that they committed and have yet to rectify. Doing what the supporters of the motion did – that is, adopting the third-person singular to talk of that historical event – is, to use Silver's term, "owning up" to their sharing of the collective responsibility for it. Of course, sharing in such a collective responsibility does not entail that any living Canadian or British subject is individually responsible for the Grand Derangement. That would be nonsense.

13

Corporate Responsibility and Punishment Redux

Colonel Ted Westhusing's suicide note in Iraq included the sentence, "I didn't volunteer to support corrupt, money-grubbing contractors." The Army psychologist who reviewed Westhusing's case concluded that the colonel was unable to cope with the concept of corporate profit making. Those who knew Westhusing do not agree with her report. He was not anti-corporations or anti-capitalism. He understood and appreciated the profit motive that drives the business world. His complaint was widespread corruption, outright theft and fraud in the dealings between corporations and the military in Iraq, the way that American corporate contractors with multimillion dollar no-bid contracts were dominating the conduct of the war, and the role that the regular military forces were playing in country and especially behind the wire. He hinted that Army officers at the highest ranks were complicit in the shady activities of the contractors. In Colonel Westhusing's opinion, the way the war was being conducted with the collusion of the Pentagon corrupted the mission and transformed the U.S. military into an ancillary operation for the enrichment of American corporations and their executives. In his suicide note, he did not name the contractors he regarded as the most egregious offenders, but there is good reason from his experiences in and around Camp Dublin to include Blackwater and KBR among his targets.

KBR (formerly Kellogg, Brown, and Root), a subsidiary of Halliburton from 1962 until 2007, had more than 20,000 employees in Iraq providing all sorts of services and support for the American troops. During the Bush administration's tenure, KBR was frequently under Congressional and General Accounting Office investigation because its very close relationship with highly placed members of the administration, including Vice President Dick Cheney, the former CEO of Halliburton, cast doubt on the propriety of the size of its contracts with the Department of

Defense (said to be in the $30 billion range) and the fact that many were no-bid arrangements. KBR was accused of inflating the prices it charged to the military for all manner of products and services, human trafficking, and shoddy workmanship. KBR set up at least two shell companies in the Cayman Islands that it admits were created only to avoid paying hundreds of millions of dollars annually in U.S. taxes for Medicare and Social Security. Most KBR employees in Iraq are listed as employees of those shell companies that list their home offices in Ugland House, a five-storey nondescript building on South Church Street in Grand Cayman that miraculously houses 12,748 corporations. Among the many charges against KBR related to work for which it was contracted by the Department of Defense is the shoddy electrical work in buildings housing soldiers and Marines, where eighteen or more electrocutions have occurred.

The *New York Times* ran the following account:

> Since the United States invaded Iraq in 2003, tens of thousands of American troops have been housed in pre-existing Iraqi government buildings, some of them dangerously dilapidated. As part of its $30 billion contract with the Pentagon in Iraq, KBR was required to repair and upgrade many of the buildings, including their electrical systems. The company handles maintenance for 4,000 structures and 35,000 containerized housing units in the war zone, the Pentagon said. Lawmakers and government investigators say it is now clear that the Bush administration outsourced so much work to KBR and other contractors in Iraq that the agencies charged with oversight have been overwhelmed. The Defense Contracting Management Agency has more than 9,000 employees, but it has only 60 contract officers in Iraq.[1]

KBR has typically responded to the charges of shoddy workmanship causing the deaths of military personnel with statements that amount to saying, "What do you expect in a war zone?" Colonel Westhusing expected that contractors would function for the benefit of the mission and the troops, not solely for their own greedy pecuniary aggrandizement. His suicide note holds the senior military command and contractors like KBR morally responsible for the perversion of the mission. A number of relatives of those electrocuted on the bases in Iraq in civil actions are trying to hold KBR legally responsible as well.

For decades, as discussed in Chapter 10, I have argued for the position that some corporations should be treated as proper subjects of moral

---

[1] *New York Times*, "Despite Alert, Flawed Wiring Still Kills G.I.'s," by James Risen (May 4, 2008).

responsibility ascriptions, that corporate actions are morally appraisable as corporate without the need to reduce them to the actions of individual humans who hold managerial positions in corporations. When "The Corporation as a Moral Person"[2] first appeared, there was a hue and cry from some quarters that corporations did not have souls so they could not be moral persons. This was, of course, a regurgitating of the old saw, "No soul to damn, no body to kick!" I responded to that concern in *Corporate Ethics*[3] by replacing the term "person" with "actor" and expanding my conception of corporate intentionality in such a way that it would clearly capture companies like KBR in its net. Nonetheless, the debate over corporate moral appraisability is far from being settled in my favor as my theory has regularly come under attack from outside its own battlements by those who prefer what John Danley[4] calls "moral individualism." Recently, however, I have been confronted by an assault from within the base, from what the Marines in Iraq would call my "fobbits," that uses my own work on the conditions for moral responsibility to undermine my theory of corporate moral responsibility. That seems to me a more serious matter than worrying about how to construct a corporate soul fit to be damned.

Deborah Tollefsen[5] has pointed out that my account of loss of innocence[6] requires affectivity in the members of the moral community. She cites a paper by Mitch Haney[7] that uses my account of loss of innocence to anchor his argument that I must exclude corporations from the moral community because corporations do not have the ability qua corporations to recognize their capacity to do evil, to care about the moral quality of their actions. The capacity for caring about the moral quality of one's actions is linked to the capacity for affectivity; hence,

---

[2] Peter A. French, "The Corporation as a Moral Person," *American Philosophical Quarterly* (July 1979).

[3] Peter A. French, *Corporate Ethics* (Fort Worth, TX, 1995).

[4] John Danley, "Moral Individualism and Ascribing Responsibility: Kantianism for Persons and Utilitarianism for Corporations," paper given in Washington, DC, at the Society for Business Ethics Conference (August 2001) at a session honoring Peter French's work on Corporate Moral Agency and Responsibility. (I do not know whether Professor Danley has published this paper or parts of it in another work.)

[5] Deborah Tollefsen, "Affectivity, Moral Agency, and Corporate-Human Relations," *American Philosophical Association, Newsletter on Philosophy and Law*, edited by Steven Scalet and Christopher Griffin, 7, 2 (Spring 2008), 9–14.

[6] See Chapter 3. Also see my *Responsibility Matters*, "Losing Innocence for the Sake of Responsibility," chapter 3.

[7] Mitchell Haney, "Corporate Loss of Innocence for the Sake of Accountability," *The Journal of Social Philosophy*, 35, 3 (2004), 391–412.

on my own account of the requirements for holding someone morally responsible, Tollefsen and Haney allege, corporations cannot be held morally responsible for what they do. Corporations, on their readings of different aspects of my work, may be intentional actors, but they must exist in an innocent state from which they can never escape. When we talk of holding a corporation (KBR) responsible for performing shoddy electrical work in the showers in Iraq and causing the electrocution of a number of American soldiers and Marines, or for bilking the American people by charging exorbitant prices for services and products in war zones and not actually doing the work or providing the services, or for concentrating its financial offices in tax havens like the Cayman Islands to avoid paying American taxes, we are either talking only about causal responsibility or, if we mean moral responsibility, some sort of code or shorthand ascribing moral responsibility to some genuine member of the moral community, presumably a human being in some authoritative position in KBR. Lacking affectivity, KBR itself cannot be held morally responsible.

I agree with Tollefsen, given what I have written about loss of innocence, that acquiring mature moral self-reflectivity (as well as trust, one of her concerns) requires affectivity, and that corporations cannot be moral actors if they lack the capacity for the requisite reactive attitudes. Tollefsen offers me three possible corrective strategies for responding to her attack. The first is to differentiate human moral agency from corporate moral agency, each having its own conditions for a subject being held morally responsible, where the corporation's conditions for responsibility would exclude affectivity. She rightly points out that I cannot use the first strategy because to do so I would have to jettison a central element of my general account of moral responsibility: that the ability to appropriately respond to moral criticism is constitutive of moral agency.

I might, she suggests, give up the general affective component and maintain that to be a moral agent, one does not need to have the capacity for reactive attitudes with respect to the behavior of others and oneself. Such an entity would have no sense of indignation (or sympathy) upon learning or witnessing an injustice visited on another member of the moral community, nor resentment when it is the target of undeserved harm or shame, nor regret and remorse when it reflects on its immoral behavior, nor gratitude when it is the recipient of benefits from others. I agree with Tollefsen, that the second strategy is unacceptable and for reasons that mirror my rejection of the first strategy. Tollefsen maintains that my best strategy is to deny that corporations necessarily lack affectivity.

The expression of moral emotions certainly seems to be a part of the moral responsibility picture and, indeed, we communicate them in and about our dealings with corporations, whether or not it is easy to identify that corporations have them, in any reasonable sense, or can reciprocate. Americans expressed indignation and anger when they were made aware of the Halliburton, KBR, Blackwater, and other contractor abuses, fraud, overcharging, and corruption in Iraq. Certainly, Colonel Westhusing expressed similar attitudes toward such corporations in his suicide letter. To salvage my position on corporate moral agency from the argument from affectivity to which I opened myself, I need to produce a convincing account of how corporations can have reactive attitudes, granted that they are indisputably and often the target of such attitudes held and articulated by humans.

Tollefsen rightly rejects any account of our reactive attitudes toward the behavior of corporations that associates them with our reactions to fictions. She makes a laudable double-barreled point addressing the problem at hand and dismissing the old fiction theory of the corporation that has been one of the dominant conceptions of corporations in legal history and a favorite refuge from corporate moral agency for many philosophers. She writes:

> Our reactive attitudes are often directed at corporations. We resent them, feel pride for their achievements, embarrassed by their actions; we feel guilt and shame when they harm others. Because corporations are not ideas but real entities in the world, these reactive attitudes cannot be understood in the way that some philosophers have understood our emotional reactions to fiction – as "make-believe." Further, the emotional responses we have toward corporations exhibit behavioral responses indicative of "real" emotion in a way that our responses to fiction do not.... [T]he fact that corporations are often the target of our reactive attitudes suggests, at the very least, that our interactions with them are more complex than those we have with mere objects. I don't resent my laptop computer when it fails to start properly. I do resent corporate American for attempting to turn my children into consumers. The fittingness of such attitudes suggests that they have the capacity for moral address – to consider and respond to moral criticism.[8]

Although she categorizes the general response of philosophers to the obvious fact that we are often moved by fiction, following Kendall Walton,[9] as just make-believe, there are other philosophical responses to the so-called Radford Paradox, some more convincing than Walton's,

---

[8] Tollefsen, "Affectivity, Moral Agency, and Corporate-Human Relations," 12.
[9] Kendall Walton, "Fearing Fictions," *Journal of Philosophy* (1978), 5–27.

that cover the spectrum from the position that our reactions to fictions are simply irrational and an indicator of an inherent irrational element in our nature to elaborate accounts of the biochemistry of our brains responding to certain stimuli or memes. In any event, I agree with Tollefsen that our moral reactions to corporate behavior are not ersatz or irrational. They are genuine and appropriate expressions of resentment when we are their victims, and indignation when we learn of what they have done to others, even other corporations and organizations.

Insofar as our reactive attitudes toward corporations are forms of what Gary Watson calls "incipient communication,"[10] we should ask what is required of the object of such addresses in order for it to participate in that type of communication. We can morally assess corporate behavior and express moral outrage about what corporations like KBR do, and that suggests that we presume they have the ability to consider our criticism and respond in a morally appropriate fashion. Tollefsen writes: "If the capacity to direct one's actions in light of reasons was absent, moral address would be futile. The reasons one provided would never result in the alteration of action and attitude. The capacity to guide one's behavior and actions in light of moral demands, in turn requires the capacity for deliberation. Agents must be able to attain some conformity between their values and their actions."[11] What she has in mind is what John Doris calls "normative competence."[12]

But some will say that when we express indignation about KBR's practices in Iraq, we are not really addressing KBR, we are addressing some human or group of humans as individuals: the executives that run KBR. That is what Danley means by "moral individualism." Tollefsen and Watson believe that we determine whether we are engaging in a dialogue with KBR or only with some unnamed, but nameable, human who presumably holds a position of significant authority in KBR (its CEO, for example), by opening a conversation with KBR and seeing if KBR responds or if we hear only from its CEO in his or her capacity as an individual.

What is it like to open such a conversation? Sue the corporation. File a complaint. Hold a Congressional hearing into the misappropriation of funds or the shell companies in the Caymans or the no-bid contracts

---

[10] Gary Watson, "Responsibility and the Limits of Evil," in Ferdinand Schoeman, ed., *Responsibility, Character, and the Emotions* (Cambridge, 1988), 256–86.

[11] Deborah Tollefsen, "Participant Reactive Attitudes and Collective Responsibility," *Philosophical Explorations* (September 2003), 226.

[12] John Doris, *Lack of Character* (Cambridge, 2002), 136.

garnered by KBR in Iraq. And also see whether the responding person answers as the CEO speaking for KBR or as Mr. Smith. What is it to do such things? It is to "communicate that it [the corporation] has failed to meet the [a] moral demand."[13] Tollefsen maintains that when a corporation enters into a dialogue about the moral appropriateness of what it has done – undoubtedly through its spokesperson, sometimes the CEO, who is not speaking as an individual – it is exposing the fact that it has the capacity for moral address.

Many will be skeptical that this shows as much as Tollefsen wants to claim. They will argue that all it exposes is that individuals, not the corporations, have the capacity for moral address because it is humans who answer the moral charges, albeit in their corporate roles. But by availing herself of an account of distributed cognition and tasks within corporate entities, Tollefsen suggests that collective normative competency can be shown to be an emergent property of corporate structures.

The Strawsonian strategy adopted by Tollefsen that is anchored in practices involving reactive attitudes attempts to circumvent the metaphysical issues of agency and personhood that I have tackled while reaching my conclusion that corporations in themselves can be held morally responsible. I am not unsympathetic to her approach; however, no matter how burdensome working through the metaphysical issues may be, skeptics will undoubtedly raise them when arguing that only humans can be full-fledged members of the moral community. Tollefsen admits that her objections to my position rest on a phenomenological reading of self-reflection and offers me an escape from her criticism: "If one subscribed to a purely cognitive theory of emotion corporations might meet the functional requirements for affectivity."[14] I am not inclined to adopt a purely cognitive theory of emotion as I joined with Haney in defending a hybrid account of care,[15] so I must return to the metaphysical issues I originally regarded as sufficient for corporate moral agency.

Carlos Gomez-Jara Diez defends the view I have maintained since the publication of "The Corporation as a Moral Person"[16]: that there are defensible metaphysical reasons to treat corporate entities that exhibit

---

[13] Tollefson, "Participant Reactive Attitudes," 227.
[14] See B. Huebner, "A Defense of Collective Emotion" (2008, unpublished), for a defense of collective emotion on the grounds that emotions need not be conscious and so collectives could have emotions even though they lack consciousness.
[15] See Peter French and Mitchell Haney, "Changes in Latitudes, Changes in Attitudes," *Contemporary Philosophy*, XXIII (2002).
[16] Peter French, "The Corporation as a Moral Person."

certain functional capabilities as moral agents.[17] Gomez-Jara champions Gunther Teubner's[18] autopoietic systems account that describes a corporation as "a system of actions/communications that reproduces itself by constantly producing from the network of its elements new communications/actions as elements."[19] He maintains that corporations "are not made up of human beings or human actions, but of corporate decisions. Individuals here are not part of the corporate system, but of the environment of the corporate system. They basically provide the energy for the on-going existence of the corporate system, but are not part of it."[20] As I have argued in a number of places and as Gomez-Jara agrees, corporations are not contractual relationships between human individuals. They are decision structures composed of their self-constituted elements and roles or stations, some of which are occupied (typically temporarily) by humans. Gomez-Jara notes, "It is through internal communication that they construct social realities of their own, quite apart from the reality constructions of their individual members."[21] Corporate entities make decisions that are sensitive to reasons to do them or reject doing them, and they do things, usually, through the faculties of the humans who work for them in various structurally defined positions. As Philip Pettit describes the process, "These entities [corporations] operate via their members in such a way that they simulate the performance of individual agents. They endorse certain goals and methods of reviewing goals and certain judgments and methods of updating judgments, and they follow procedures that enable them to pursue those goals in a manner that makes sense according to those judgments."[22] That describes corporations straightforwardly as reason sensitive. My structural/functionalist account explicates how that occurs.

On my view, corporations, at least many of them, are moral actors that play an ever-increasingly significant role in the social/global community. To be a moral actor, a proper subject of moral appraisability, is to exhibit functional capacities to act intentionally, to make rational decisions, and to respond to events and criticisms or reasons by altering intentions and

---

[17] Carlos Gomez-Jara Diez, "Corporations as Victims of Mismanagement: Beyond the Shareholders vs. Managers Debate," *Pace University Law Review* (2008), 101–20.

[18] Gunther Teubner, "Enterprise Corporatism: New Industrial Policy and the 'Essence' of the Legal Person," *American Journal of Comparative Law* (1988).

[19] Gomez-Jara Diez, 104.

[20] Ibid.

[21] Ibid., 110.

[22] Philip Pettit, "Responsibility Incorporated," *Ethics* (January 2007), 172.

behavior that are harmful to others or detrimental to one's interests. As noted in Chapter 10, the Corporate Internal Decision (CID) Structure[23] of a corporation synthesizes the actions, judgments, and attitudes of individuals into the intentions and actions of the corporation. It also provides mechanisms for self-reflection that are required for its responsive function and rational decision-making processes.

Those who interpret intentionality on the traditional desire-belief model will find my account of corporate intentional actions in decision making, communicating, endorsing, and so forth intelligible only if it is understood as metaphorical or reducible to the intentions of humans who have the requisite desires and beliefs, but that sort of reductionism would defeat an autopoietic account of corporations. Certainly corporations, we should probably all agree, cannot, in any normal sense, desire and believe.

I have, however, rejected the desire-belief model of intention and adopted a view of intention persuasively defended by Michael Bratman. He writes: "Our understanding of intention is in large part a matter of our understanding of future directed intention. . . . Plans are not merely executed. They are formed, retained, combined, constrained by other plans, filled in, modified, reconsidered, and so on. Such processes . . . are central to our understanding of . . . intention."[24] Bratman maintains that because we are rational agents with complex goals, the majority of our intentional actions will have been thought out, deliberated, or reflected on before we act. That is what it is to plan. Such an account helps to explain why it is usually senseless to ask someone whether he intentionally sat in a chair[25] if, when he entered the room, he just sat down in the chair. To raise the question of intention suggests that he was up to something besides sitting down. Was it an act of protest? J. L. Austin is correct when he notes: "I intend to" is, as it were, a sort of "future tense" of the verb, "to X." It has a vector, committal effect like "I promise to X," and again like "I promise to X," it is one of the possible formulas for making explicit, on occasion, the force of "I shall X" (namely, that it was a declaration and not, for example, a forecast or an undertaking).[26] Actions are "guided," willed. Mere movements are not. Intentional actions are planned. They are undertaken sometimes deliberately, sometimes on

---

[23] A term I coined in "The Corporation as A Moral Person." J. L. Mackie urged my using the initials. At the time he was writing about causation and coined the term INUS conditions!

[24] Ibid., 7.

[25] A point made by J. L. Austin, *Philosophical Papers* (Oxford, 1970).

[26] Ibid., 279.

purpose. The operative element in intentional action is planning, and to plan in the relevant way is to make commitments to perform certain future actions.[27]

Denis Arnold exposes two elements in the Bratman approach to intentionality as planning.

> First, plans are typically partial or incomplete. They need to be filled in over time. Second, plans typically have a hierarchical structure... one will fix certain portions of one's plan in advance, while leaving other aspects of one's plan open. The strategy of determining in advance partial elements of a hierarchically structured plan allows us to adapt to unanticipated events in a manner compatible with our inherently limited capacities for deliberation and information processing.[28]

Planning, in basically the way Arnold describes it, is indisputably a major corporate activity that is reasons sensitive.

Pettit provides an account similar to my revised theory of the corporation as a moral person to explain how a corporation and one or more of its individual members (employees) could be held responsible for the same event.[29] The corporation "may control in a reason-sensitive way for the performance of a certain action by some members.... It will do this, by maintaining a constitution for the formation and enactment of its attitudes, arranging things so that some individual or individuals are identified as the agents to perform a required task."[30] Of course, the individual(s) may fail to perform the task or perform it poorly. When that happens it may be appropriate to hold the corporation and the individual(s) responsible for the inadequate performance. "The individuals who act for the group [corporation] on any occasion will have to answer, of course, for what they do. But the corporate entity will also have to answer for what it ensures will be done, drawing on the resources provided by such members. It has all the capacities of reason-sensitive agency necessary to make this demand entirely plausible."[31] For example, although KBR should be held responsible for the electrocutions of U.S. military personnel in the showers on bases in Iraq because it was the

---

[27] Those commitments, of course, do not cause the actions.

[28] Denis Arnold, "Agents, Intentions, and Corporations," paper given in Washington, DC at the Society for Business Ethics Conference (August 2001) at a session honoring Peter French's work on Corporate Moral Agency and Responsibility. I do not know whether Professor Arnold has published this paper or parts of it in another work. The quotation is from his typescript.

[29] Pettit, 191–2.

[30] Ibid., 192.

[31] Ibid.

contractor, its electricians should also be held responsible for the same untoward events.

Corporate plans, as noted in Chapter 10, might radically diverge from those that motivate the human persons in corporate positions and whose bodily movements and judgments are necessary for the corporation to act. The CID Structure, however, licenses redescribing their actions as the execution of a corporate plan. That is my version of what Teubner called an autopoietic system. But that alone does not answer whether a corporation functioning through its CID Structure can have self-reactive attitudes or emotions, the issue raised by Tollefsen.

I was tempted after reading Tollefsen's challenge to my account of corporations as moral actors to take back the argument from knowledge by acquaintance of evil I made regarding loss of innocence to become a mature member of the moral community and adopt a purely cognitive account that identifies having an emotion with the making of a judgment or having a belief. Corporations, my critics such as Haney will allow, can be said to make identifiably corporate judgments about a number of things, that is, redescriptions as corporate judgments or decisions of a variety of decision processes performed by humans are licensed by the operations of their CID Structures. But Tollefsen did not take that handy escape route. I join her in trying to defend what may be thought by some to be a counterintuitive position: corporations can and do have reactive attitudes.

Tollefsen constructs a vicarious emotion theory in which corporate employees are "conduits for corporate emotions," a position that mirrors Gomez-Jara's conception of the role of humans in corporations as providing "the energy for the on-going existence of the corporate system" while not being part of it. An example that provokes what she has in mind would be that when a corporate employee in her role qua corporate employee tells me on the phone that she is sorry that I was double billed for a purchase on my credit card account, she is not expressing her personal regret for the double billing, she is conveying corporate regret. The voice on the phone is the vicarious moral-emotion expresser for the corporation. Tollefsen associates this idea with the fact that humans can have vicarious reactive attitudes for others even if those others do not (cannot?) have the same attitudes about themselves. We can be ashamed for others, particularly those with whom we stand in a relationship, and such shame is not being ashamed for ourselves because we have done nothing of which to be ashamed. I recall a scene in *Pride and Prejudice* in which Elizabeth Bennet witnesses the inappropriate and oafish behavior of members of her family at a ball and feels ashamed for them and expresses it, although they were not ashamed of themselves or they would have ceased acting like country bumpkins. Tollefsen goes on to propose that collective emotion (and presumably that includes corporate emotion) is a form of this sort of vicarious emotion. What we have is not corporations feeling emotions per se, but emotions being corporatized. (Elizabeth's shame in *Pride and Prejudice* might be thought of as an emotion that is "family-ized.") Tollefsen worries that this may not satisfy critics of allowing corporations into the moral community, and she turns the matter back to me.

I think the problem is manageable. It may be recalled that on my account of corporate intentionality, I maintained that all intentionality and, consequently, corporate intentionality, is a matter of redescription. My point is that an action is corporate if at some level of true description it is the action(s) of a person(s) (sometimes also machines or in conjunction with machines, and that is becoming more common) in a corporate role(s) and it is redescribable, as licensed by the rules of the CID Structure, as an action of the corporation. It is then appropriate to refer to the action as intended by the corporation. In effect, corporate intentional acts are typically human bodily movements (or the operations of programmed machines) under a corporate description. Human physical movements and actions usually are necessary for corporations to act on corporate reasons and interests. This is the same point made by Gomez-Jara when he referred to humans as "the energy for the on-going existence of the corporate system, but not part of it – just as the blood provides energy for the consciousness system, but is not actually a part of the system of consciousness."[32] CID Structures subordinate and synthesize the intentions and actions of various human persons (and often the running of machines) into corporate actions. They run on them. The corporate actor makes its appearance on the moral and legal responsibility stage at the level of redescription that those CID Structures, including their organizational and policy/procedural rules, make possible. The same sort of redescriptive account can be applied to reveal something that will pass as corporate affectivity.

CID Structures may contain conversion rules for descriptions of certain types of utterances by appropriate employees into descriptions of corporate reactive attitudes. When a corporate employee says, "We are sorry that we double billed your credit card account," I do not think the employee with whom I am speaking personally regrets the corporate act. I

---

[32] Gomez-Jara Diez, 104.

understand that I am receiving an apology from the corporation and that it is as sincere as apologies go. It makes no difference that it is conveyed to me in a digitally engineered robotic voice. By the same token, when the president of the United States apologizes to native Hawaiians for past actions taken by the United States military on the Hawaiian Islands, the regret being expressed is that of the collective, the United States of America, and it is so identifiable because of the redescription licenses that are a part of the decision structure of the nation the president represents or for whom the president speaks. The expressions of reactive attitudes are, generally, performative, ritualistic, conventional. They may be regarded as insincerely made if they are not "backed" by a certain sort of feeling, for example, an apology without the feeling of sorrow, but they are not void.

The idea of collective emotions, including regret, prima facie does not lack sense and is a topic of much current discussion in the literature. Although I am somewhat uncomfortable with Margaret Gilbert's plural subject account of group emotions,[33] what I like about her account is the idea that a group can become jointly committed to feeling an emotion as a group. She says that joint commitment is "a function of the understandings, expressive actions, and common knowledge of the parties."[34] I am inclined to the idea that something like her idea of a joint commitment in a corporate setting can be functionally engineered by the inclusion of certain rules and policies in a CID Structure. Such an account, of course, would not claim that the corporation feels or has "pangs" of regret or remorse or sorrow when it expresses affectivity, although members or employees may suffer such feelings (what Gilbert calls "membership remorse") because of their association with the corporate wrongdoer. I do not, however, think that employee feelings are essential to the truth of the claim that the corporation regrets what it did qua corporation, just as I do not think that we can say that a human does not regret doing something even if she does not experience the typical or expected "pangs" or emotions. I would not say, however, that a corporate employee expressing corporate regret for double billing my credit card account is necessarily vicariously feeling regret for the corporation. She is performing her corporate duty of expressing the corporation's regret, although she may have, incidentally, membership regret when

---

[33] Margaret Gilbert, *Sociality and Responsibility* (Lanham, MD, 2000), chapter 7.
[34] Ibid., 135.

learning how her corporation so badly treated me. In effect, I think that with appropriately constructed and largely transparent CID Structures, corporations are normatively competent.

I do not think this is a mere cognitive account of reactive attitudes. There is a cognitive element, of course. I do not see how anyone can have regret without believing one has, in a specific instance, done something wrong or is perceived to have done something wrong. However, regret is not just the belief that one has done something wrong or undeservedly harmed someone or something; it involves an intention, in most cases, to not repeat the wrongdoing and to make amends. Corporations can have such intentions in the form of plans for future actions. However, when we hear the mechanical voice on the phone offering regret for having double billed a credit card account, it is natural to conclude that the regret is insincere because it is difficult to believe that any plan to curtail the practice is in the offing in the offending corporation. Of course, that is cynical on our part, but many of us will take the expression of regret for anyone who has benefited from a wrongdoing, be it a human or a corporation, with a grain of salt. If a KBR spokesperson announces that the company regrets the shoddy workmanship that caused the electro-cution deaths of U.S. military personnel in Iraq, many of us are likely to have our doubts about the sincerity of the utterance. That, however, does not really touch on whether KBR does regret; it tells us something about the healthy skeptical bent of human psychology in such cases. In any event, I think there are sufficient reasons to support the view that corpo-rations, or at least some of them, are not illegitimate aliens in the moral community. They are normatively competent, can express affectivity, and should be treated as such and not as fictions or innocent children who are rather too big for the sandbox. This however, raises another problem that is discussed by Gomez-Jara: can corporations be victims as well as victimizers?

It will be crucial to answering that question to determine what, in general, are the interests of a corporation that can be harmed. I have in mind interests that are peculiar to corporations qua corporations and not the interests that their shareholders or stakeholders may have in protecting their investments or ensuring the continuation of the flow of products, services, or support they receive from their associations with a particular corporation. As Gomez-Jara points out, corporations have an interest in their own survival, that is, "in remaining within the 'society of organizations' i.e., modern society... permanence in such society may be regarded as a legitimate interest of the corporate actor."[35] That corporations have an interest, independent of the interests of their shareholders in surviving, which is clear from the fact that shareholders shift their investments sometimes daily, even many times in one trading day, does not, of course, entail that they have a right to survive. Humans also generally have an interest in surviving, but they can by their actions forfeit whatever rights they may have had bestowed on them.

A second interest that corporations have, following Gomez-Jara' account, is in financial security, probably the simplest way to explicate what might otherwise be called "corporate well-being." What is intended by that notion is that corporations have an interest in the protection of their assets. With respect to the fragility of that interest, we have a stagger-ing number of recent cases in which corporate assets have been sacrificed, harmed, and unreasonably, even criminally, risked by excessive executive compensation; bonuses; purchase of toxic mortgages, derivatives, and other near-worthless "paper"; waste; ill-conceived mergers; poor product design; misrepresentation of products; production and sale of danger-ous products; and so forth. Some of these harms to the well-being of a corporation reveal that the interests of stockholders or managers can be clearly differentiated from the interests of their corporations. Most of the scandals that beset the corporate world, toppling some of the once most powerful and financially successful corporations in the United States (e.g., Enron, Worldcom, Healthsouth, Lehman Brothers) and taking the global economic system to the brink of depression, are attributable to mismanagement with intent to increase personal financial gain. The vic-timized corporations in many of those cases, however, are also offenders, perpetrating undeserved harm on investors, ordinary people, customers, other corporations, government agencies, nations, and sometimes their own employees. As such serious offenders they should be morally and legally liable to punishment.

Corporate crime in combat zones in Iraq, according to many reports and the sad suicide note of Colonel Westhusing, was rampant in the first six years following the American invasion. But, how is corporate crime to be punished? Before suggesting answers to that question, it is helpful to draw a distinction between corporate and white-collar crime. "Corpo-rate crime" is crime attributable to a corporate entity or any responsi-ble person acting on its behalf. "White-collar crime" refers to offenses

[35] Gomez-Jara Diez, 114.

committed by persons from within their professional or corporate stations for personal reasons and includes criminal actions damaging the interests of the corporations that employ them.[36]

Brent Fisse and I, both jointly and separately, challenged the orthodox view that corporate liability for crime depends on proof of corporate intentionality for the causally relevant acts at or before the time of the untoward event.[37] To illustrate: it may be extremely difficult to identify corporate intentionality in the case of the electrocutions in Iraq attributed to KBR prior to the occurrence of the electrocutions. Fisse and I argued that corporate responsibility in many such cases could best be assessed on the basis of the corporate defendant's response to the harm it caused. Fisse called this the concept of reactive fault, and I developed the corresponding Principle of Responsive Adjustment (PRA).

Reactive corporate fault, according to Fisse, is an unreasonable corporate failure to undertake appropriate preventative or corrective measures in response to the corporate commission of an act that constitutes a violation of law.[38] PRA entails that the corporate intention that motivates a lack of responsive corrective action (or the continuation of the offending behavior) looks back to retrieve the actions that caused the offense, even though they may not have been corporately intentional at the time of the offense.[39]

Commonly, at the human level, when an untoward event occurs and the facts do not apparently support an ascription of moral responsibility to the causally responsible party because of the difficulty of defending a description of that party's behavior as intentional, that person's subsequent behavior is observed to see if measures are taken to avoid similar events. If appropriate behavioral changes are not made, not infrequently the perpetrator is held morally responsible for the untoward event. It is now regarded as a part of the perpetrator's moral record, something,

---

[36] I developed this definition and defended it in Brent Fisse and Peter A. French, *Corrigible Corporations and Unruly Laws* (San Antonio, 1985), chapter 1. To commit a white-collar crime, one has to occupy a certain kind of position in the professional/business world (including government service). See Peter A. French, *Collective and Corporate Responsibility* (New York, 1984), chapters 13 and 14.

[37] Fisse and French, *Corrigible Corporations*, especially chapter 10; Brent Fisse, "Reconstructing Corporate Criminal Law: Deterrence, Retribution, Fault, and Sanctions," *Southern California Law Review* 56 (1983), 1183–213; French, *Collective and Corporate Responsibility*, chapter 11.

[38] Fisse and French, *Corrigible Corporations and Unruly Laws*, 187.

[39] French, *Collective and Corporate Responsibility*, chapter 11.

for example, for which restitution may be appropriately assessed, regardless of the fact that at the time of its occurrence, the perpetrator may not have had a morally relevant intention to cause harm or to bring about the untoward event. Certain excuses, primarily those that claim continuing incapacity or diminished responsibility, defeat such a moral reappraisal.[40]

Intentionality has a significant role to play in PRA but, in corporate cases, as well as those involving individual humans, PRA and reactive corporate fault extend the time frame of moral responsibility appraisability for untoward events. In corporate cases, this is especially relevant because corporate policy at the time of harm causing ordinarily is boilerplate compliance. Reactive corporate fault extends the time frame on which moral appraisability focuses to include what the offender does subsequent and in response to its commission of the harmful act. When evaluating possible corporate wrongdoing, whether or not the corporate offender implements internal reforms to prevent repetitions is a relevant consideration in deciding the appropriateness of moral blame for the prior event. Refusal to reform clearly would be an intentional corporate act and may take many forms, from practiced indifference to blatant

---

[40] Suppose, suggested by the landmark strict liability case of *Regina v. Prince*, that a man, named Paul, contrary to law, had sex with a girl who is under sixteen years of age, and suppose at the time that he believed she was older than sixteen and that she gave him every reason to believe so. And suppose further that a reasonable person would have guessed that she was over sixteen. Let us stipulate that it was not Paul's intention to commit the act for which the law holds him strictly liable: statutory rape. On the basis of the traditional rule (I have elsewhere called it the "straight rule") of accountability, Paul should not be held morally responsible for his illegal assignation. An intuitively appealing, behaviorally oriented, principle of accountability, PRA, will, however, under certain conditions, license a radical alteration of the finding. Suppose that Paul, after serving his punishment, intentionally pursues another teenage girl to whom he takes a fancy and makes no attempt to discern her age (he has a penchant for young teenage girls). Paul's intention with regard to his behavior with such girls is formed within a personal history that includes his conviction for statutory rape. If, after committing the crime, Paul had taken precautions to ensure that he learned the ages of the girls he courted, we would allow his ignorance of the age of the girl in the legal case as an excuse, if not an exculpating one, for moral purposes (although he must bear the punishment for the strict liability offense). But, Paul makes no responsive adjustments in his behavior to assure that he not repeat the offense. He embarks on a course that has a strong likelihood of leading to a similar violation. By the adjustment principle, Paul's subsequently manifested intention to continue his romantic pursuits of underage girls constitutes an affirmation of the strict liability violation behavior. We no longer have reason to excuse him in the first instance because he has proven he is that sort of person, and in that sense he no longer escapes moral responsibility for the earlier strict liability offense. It is now a part of his moral biography, but had he not renewed his offending behavior, we could have dismissed it from his moral record as an aberration.

repetition. The intuition to which reactive corporate fault (and PRA) appeals is that an actor's past actions, even if unintentional, generally are captured in the scope of the intentions that motivate that actor's present and future actions. Intentions, whether individual or corporate, are not made in a vacuum; neither are moral evaluations. PRA/corporate reactive fault embodies the idea that after an untoward event has happened, those who causally contributed to its occurrence are expected to adopt courses of future action that will have the effect of preventing repetitions. Morality and social norms are embedded with expectations of behavioral adjustment that correct character weaknesses, habits, and so forth that produced untoward events. PRA/reactive corporate fault allows, when the expected adjustments in behavior are not made and in the absence of strong reasons for not adjusting, that perpetrators can be held responsible for the earlier untoward event that provoked moral disapprobation. PRA encompasses the idea that a refusal to adjust practices that led to an untoward occurrence is to associate oneself, for moral purposes, with the earlier behavior.[41] Adjustments in behavior that rectify flaws or habits that have caused past evils (or routinizes behavior that has led to worthy results) are morally required. Put another way, the intention that motivates a lack of responsive corrective action or the continuation of offending behavior may be taken as affirming the behavior that caused the harm. By the same token, failure to routinize behavior that has been productive of good results divorces that behavior from a person's or a corporation's "moral biography." Intentions certainly reach forward in planning, but they also have a much neglected retrieval function by which they illuminate past behavior. Humans and corporations are not purely prospective, ahistorical, or abstract centers of action. They have lives or pasts out of which intentions and planning emerge. Aristotle, it may be recalled, noted that we do not hold people morally responsible for unintentionally "slightly deviating from the course of goodness"[42] as long as they do not subsequently practice behavior that makes such deviations a matter of character.

Act descriptions have a well-known feature that Joel Feinberg called the "accordion effect."[43] Like the accordion, the description of a simple bodily movement can be expanded in different directions by causal linkages and other associations. For example, the act of pulling the trigger

[41] French, *Collective and Corporate Responsibility*. Especially chapters 3, 4, and 12.
[42] Aristotle, *Nicomachean Ethics*, translated by M. Ostwald (Indianapolis, 1962), 51.
[43] Joel Feinberg, *Doing and Deserving* (Princeton, 1970), 134.

of a gun, through a series of redescriptions, may be expanded to capture the description "the killing of Steven." The description of a present act also may be associated with past behavior by the ordinary relations "like yesterday," "as before," or "again." Descriptions such as "to pull the trigger again" clearly retrieve previous behavior, although they do not make that previous behavior intentional at the time it occurred if it was not.

Humans and corporations may plead that they never intend to do things under retrograde "accordioned" descriptions. They intend to do only what they are currently planning to do and nothing else. Such a plea must be rejected. The descriptions of events under which a human or a corporation intends actions are formed within a history. To ignore that fact is to reduce the actor to an unidentifiable entity trapped in the time slice of a single action. Blink and they disappear and a new, ahistorical actor magically appears.

PRA insists that moral actors learn from their mistakes and that the pleas of mistake and of accident cannot be repeatedly used to excuse frequent performances of improper behavior. "It was an accident" or "What do you expect in a war zone?" will only work if it was not the result of behavior that is repeated after the offending event. They will exculpate only if corrective measures are taken to ensure no recurrence. The KBR "war zone" excuse seems to claim that repetitions should be anticipated and so is not likely to exculpate, although in some cases it may be begging mitigation. Excuses can be, and often are, reevaluated after the individual's or the corporation's actions have been observed subsequent to the event for which the excuses were offered and accepted. It would, however, usually be wrong to say that, in such cases, we decide that the actor must have had the relevant intention in the first instance of the offending behavior.

Although a number of criticisms of PRA have been made, most seem to be based on a persistent misreading that claims PRA rewrites history. Time's arrow continues its inevitable course from past to future, but the shotgun of moral evaluation scatters its pellets in many directions. There is a major difference between thinking that the past can be changed by actions in the present (backward causation) and thinking that we can, and ought to, change our moral (and, I argue, legal) evaluations of those who were the cause of harmful things. And, most important, it is in the present and into the future that PRA allows holding moral actors responsible for a past deed where a specific intention cannot be ascribed in isolation of subsequent behavior. PRA does not say that if we had access at the crucial time, we would have discovered the specific intention. It says that now we have the intentional reactive fault that includes within its scope the past action that required responsive adjustment.

PRA offers a promising way of avoiding contentious attribution of criminal intentionality to a corporation. It is rare that a company displays any criminal intention at or before the time of the commission of the offense. Enron may be an exception, and some have suggested that KBR may be in that category as well. The typical legal solution, at present, is to either impose strict liability or impose liability vicariously on the basis of the intent of an identified corporate representative. The former approach avoids the issue by making intention irrelevant at the level of the attribution of liability (although intentionality may be relevant in relation to sentence). The latter approach (which is essentially a form of strict liability) is based on a representationalism that utterly ignores the fundamental criminal element of *mens rea*. To generate the relevant corporate intentionality that will displace strict or vicarious liability, focus should be on a corporate defendant's policies and how they are carried out in practice. That focus is achieved by an extension of the time frame of judicial inquiry to encompass what a defendant corporation has done *in response to* the commission of the *actus reus* of an offense. What matters, then, is not a corporation's stated general policies of compliance – most of them have that and trot it out on contentious occasions – but its specific implementation of a program of internal discipline, structural reform, and compensatory or restitutional relief subsequent to its untoward behavior or its causing of undeserved harm. This temporal reorientation flushes out blameworthy corporate intentionality more easily than is possible when the inquiry is confined to corporate policy at or before the time of the *actus reus*.

The expansion into a responsive time frame produces several new ways to handle corporate criminal liability. Three are worthy of consideration: interventionism, the due-diligence plea, and the design of penal sanctions. There has been a plethora of proposals for controlling corporate behavior through government intervention in the CID Structures of corporate offenders. Christopher Stone's book, *Where the Law Ends: The Social Control of Corporate Behavior*,[44] is a justly famous example from some years back. Stone championed the view that judicial means should be used to mandate new boxes in the flow charts of corporate offenders to be

---

[44] Christopher Stone, *Where the Law Ends: The Social Control of Corporate Behavior* (New York, 1975).

occupied by watchdog directors and the like.[45] Stone limited the use of interventionism to recidivist cases and to generically hazardous industries, suggesting that his interventionist strategy would be too draconian in the majority of cases. But what is to be done in such cases?

The American Bar Association proposed a continuing judicial oversight sanction.[46] But the ABA recommends that such a sentence should be imposed only when the criminal behavior is serious, repetitive, and the result of "inadequate internal accounting or monitoring controls,"[47] or when a danger to public safety exists. The ABA proposal takes no account of the corporate offender's responsive compliance activities unless the case is extremely severe. The only sanction recommended in cases that are not serious or repetitive is a fine.

Fines, even rather hefty ones, do not have a track record of producing the significant changes in corporate decision structures and standard operating procedures that bring them into compliance.[48]

If interventionism is too limited but also intrudes the courts too deeply into CID Structures, as does the ABA's continuing oversight sanction, whereas fines are ineffective, is there a better way to guarantee an appropriate corporate response to its offending behavior? I think there is. The assumption of the Stone and ABA approaches is that the courts can examine corporate responses to the commission of criminal offenses only by inserting themselves rather deeply in the corporate decision process. An alternative might be to require convicted corporations to file compliance reports that detail their own internal responses to the offense. Judicial intervention could, and should, be held in abeyance and used only if the corporation's own reaction is judged unsatisfactory. I have called this approach Enforced Corporate Responsive Adjustment (ECRA).[49]

ECRA requires a two-stage judicial hearing procedure. In the initial stage, the issue before the court will be whether the action resulting in the offense was committed on behalf of (or by) the corporate defendant. That established, the defendant corporation will be required to prepare a compliance report that spells out what steps it will take by way

---

[45] His views changed somewhat. See Christopher Stone, "Corporate Regulation: The Place of Social Responsibility," in Fisse and French, *Corrigible Corporations and Unruly Laws*, chapter 2.

[46] American Bar Association, *Standards for Criminal Justice* (Boston, 1980), 3, section 18.

[47] American Bar Association, *Standards for Criminal Justice*, section 18–28 (a)(V)(A).

[48] Andrew Hopkins, *The Impact of Prosecutions under the Trade Practices Act* (Canberra, 1978).

[49] See Peter A. French, "Enforced Corporate Responsive Adjustment," *Legal Studies Forum* (Fall, 1989).

of internal discipline, modification of existing compliance procedures, and, as appropriate, compensation to victims. The second stage of the judicial procedure will determine whether the corporate offender has satisfactorily responded to its harm-causing or risk-imposing actions. If adequate measures have been taken to adjust, the corporation will be acquitted of the offense. If not, the corporation will be convicted of the offense and be liable to a variety of further penal sanctions that could include even extreme forms of interventionism and judicial supervision. It is important that the use of such drastic violations of the integrity of the CID Structure should be contingent on the corporate defendant's own intentional failure to make a responsive adjustment to try to ensure that there are no repetitions of its harm-causing behavior.

ECRA preserves managerial freedom as long as the court is satisfied that effective responsive adjustment has been undertaken. ECRA is a cousin of John Braithwaite's model of enforced self-regulation, in which corporations are required to formulate their own regulatory standards,[50] and intervention is restricted to the development and enforcement of overarching principles and social goals. ECRA is not so sweeping. It requires corporate offenders to formulate their own reactive programs in response to specific violations. ECRA has the virtue of minimizing court-ordered intervention while not, as in the case of fines, excluding it altogether. Braithwaite, Fisse, and I have noted that although there probably are some fundamental, minimal requirements for effective corporate compliance systems, the variables differ widely from corporation to corporation without necessarily affecting the compliance outcome. Also, ECRA will not be restricted to only the more serious and repeated offenses. Lesser offenses will be more effectively dealt with by ECRA than by purely monetary sanctions.

ECRA does not respond to retributive intuitions. It does, however, preserve proof of *mens rea*, blocks a move to more and more strict liability offenses, and maintains a "commitment to the moral force of the criminal law."[51] The adoption of the responsive adjustment time frame approach also corrects some problems with the due-diligence defense.

Suppose that KBR offers a due-diligence defense in the electrocution cases. The charges that have been voiced against KBR usually focus on

---

[50] John Braithwaite, "Enforced Self-Regulation: A New Strategy for Corporate Crime Control," *Michigan Law Review* 80 (1982), 1466–507.

[51] John Braithwaite, "Taking Responsibility Seriously: Corporate Compliance Systems," in Fisse and French, *Corrigible Corporations and Unruly Laws*, 57.

the claim that KBR did not take due care to prevent the shoddy work-manship that resulted in the electrocutions. Its response is, "It's a war zone!" Presumably, that is meant to convey the idea that in a war zone, whatever KBR employees did by way of supervision constitutes as much due diligence as is reasonable to expect. Normally, the standard of care in due diligence generally is set by the prevailing industry standard. That standard may be adjusted to meet the needs of particular circumstances such as war zone situations, but there are clear limits on the amount of alteration allowed because the standard must still be applicable across the industry. In many industries, however, no generally accepted stan-dard for a compliance system exists. Perhaps that is what the war zone defense claims. Still, if there does exist a customary compliance system in the relevant industry, even one operating in a war zone, and if the corporate defendant has adopted it, should that exculpate?

If KBR could show that it had met the standards normally upheld by construction firms in war zones or in Iraq war zones, it would likely be judged to have exercised due diligence and, on the traditional theory, been acquitted of the criminal charges in the electrocutions. If it did nothing to change its operations after the first death, industry standards have not appreciably changed, and another electrocution occurs, it could again plea due diligence and should again look forward to acquittal. That makes no sense.

There have been at least sixteen electrocutions of military personnel. Due diligence, proactively understood, flies in the face of basic intu-itions about justice. However, if the industry standard does not set the benchmark, then a corporate offender is not provided with clear prior notice of conduct subject to criminal liability. Furthermore, if a court should determine that the industry standard was set too low, then good faith compliance with the standard will not shield a corporation from criminal liability. What then happens to fundamental fairness? It is surely unjust to disallow a due-diligence plea on the grounds that the corpo-ration should have anticipated a failure in its procedures that came to light in the industry only after the harm causing occurred. Also, the advance specification of acceptable standards only invites the search for loopholes.[52]

The proactive due-diligence defense cannot help but pull down the standard to a common denominator level that would put the force of the

---

[52] Discussions with Brent Fisse helped clarify for me the problems with due diligence.

law behind older, traditional compliance technologies. No legal incentives then are provided for corporations to find innovative solutions or to apply state-of-the-art techniques to prevent harm, even in war zones. Law tied to a proactive time frame for offenses is stuck in a dangerous rut that deprives potential victims of adequate protection. It can extricate itself only by imposing higher standards that the defendant can rightly claim are ad hoc.

Using the ECRA model, a corporate offender would be required to produce a compliance report in which it specifies the standards it will seek to meet in response to its harm causing. The standard setting is then reactive, not a matter of routine prevention. The standards are tailored not only both to the particular corporation and its activities, but also to the particular case that exposed its weaknesses. The due-diligence defense would not succeed even if the company could not have foreseen the harm produced by its following the existing standards of the industry. In fact, due diligence and due care would have little or no role to play.

ECRA provides fair notice of criminal prohibitions, but loophole-prone rules are eliminated. The focus is shifted from industry-wide standards, in this case for corporate contractors in Iraq, that may, in fact, be too low (the harmful result is evidence that they, indeed, may be too low) to the adequacy of the corporate offender's response to the need to develop a higher standard of care. Proactive due diligence imposes static and often undemanding requirements of care. ECRA, unconfined to ex-ante due diligence, looks to the care that *should be* taken regardless of any existing industry standard, and so it is more dynamic and demanding, often perhaps requiring state-of-the-art technology to satisfy its demands. ECRA then works to reduce the tension between stability-inducing rules of law and the rapidly changing corporate, technological, and social world to which they are to be applied.

Once we have established that a corporation is guilty of a criminal offense, appropriate sanctions also need to be determined. The proactive time frame commitment that has governed most thinking about corporate criminality produces a bias toward the adoption of the notion of vicarious liability that largely locks the judicial system into a restricted number of applicable sanctions, dominated by fines. Fines have been used because, viewed from the proactive perspective, it is nearly always impossible to prove that a corporation committed an offense with the appropriate corporate *mens rea*. Boilerplate compliance policies are intended to prove the absence of the corporate criminal state of mind. With access to the corporate *mens rea* effectively blocked, many U.S. jurisdictions have adopted the vicarious liability approach for corporate cases. All that is required is demonstrable fault on the part of an employee acting on behalf of the corporation. The *mens rea* of a manager or employee, of course, is typically easier to expose than corporate intentionality. No published policy of compliance can serve as a shield.

Vicarious liability, as Fisse has argued, "projects a noninterventionist attitude toward corporate decision making."[53] Little wonder it is championed by the staunchest corporate lobbyists. Avoidance of interventionism, conjoined with the historical relationship between vicarious liability and vicarious tort liability, generates the bias in favor of monetary remedies of damages and the offending corporation's identification of fines with enterprise costs. Fines, however, have serious limitations and can be passed on to undeserving populations in the form of higher prices, layoffs, and so on. In the KBR case, any fine would be more than adequately offset by the enormous sums paid to the company through its no-bid contracts. In any event, fines against most corporations have proven to have minimal deterrent effects. Oliver Wendell Holmes, Jr., noted that although there is a difference, or there should be, between a fine and a tax, in many cases the line is blurred until it disappears.[54] In most corporate criminal cases, drawing that line may be, in practice, extremely difficult. Taxes are often imposed to discourage activities that have not been made criminal. "Conversely fines payable for some criminal offenses... become so small [e.g., in relation to the offender's income] that they are cheerfully paid and offenses are frequent. They are then felt to be mere taxes because the sense is lost that the rule is meant to be taken seriously as a standard of behavior."[55]

Interventionist sanctions, such as punitive injunctions, are not so easily assimilated. But some noninterventionist sanctions should prove almost equally successful in producing the desired alteration in corporate procedures and policies, for example, court ordered and directed adverse publicity, or what I have elsewhere called the Hester Prynne Sanction.[56] If the proactive time frame approach is utilized, and the courts are blocked from adequate information about the "corporateness" of the

---

[53] Fisse and French, *Corrigible Corporations and Unruly Laws*, 204.

[54] See Oliver Wendell Holmes, *The Common Law* (Boston, 1881), 300. *The Pollock-Holmes Correspondence* (Cambridge, MA, 1953), 1:21, 119, 177, and 2:55, 200–234. See also H. L. A. Hart, *Punishment and Responsibility* (New York, 1968), 6–7.

[55] Hart, *Punishment and Responsibility*, 7, n.8.

[56] Peter A. French, "The Hester Prynne Sanction," *Business and Professional Ethics Journal* 4, 2 (Winter 1985), 19–32.

corporation's intention to commit the offense, fines would seem to be the only justifiable, if less than satisfactory, option. However, by shifting to an ECRA approach rather than proactive perspectives, corporate policies and procedures would be no longer shielded from the courts. Willful, deliberate noncompliance by the corporate offender can be exposed, and the offending corporation appropriately targeted for sanctions, and the innovative noninterventionist sanctions that have been championed by a number of writers as alternatives to fines, because they promise to be more effective in producing compliance, will be supported by far more reliable sentencing data.

The great danger in the fines approach is that corporate offenders may totally escape the gravity of their victimizing. Monetary sanctions are, at best, only oblique ways of changing defective corporate practices that have left victims in their wake, although with some corporations and some crimes, a monetary penalty may be sufficient. There is, however, no need to settle on only one type of sanction. An incremental escalation strategy or a mix of sanctions could prove both efficient and effective. Stone's interventionism is, of course, among the more severe options. Perhaps it comes in just short of revocation of business permits and corporate charters. Insofar as protection of the integrity of the corporate enterprise our economy depends on ought to be a major commitment of our society, Stone-style intervention should be used only in extremely serious cases where the sentencing data unequivocally demonstrate corporate intent owing to a seriously defective CID Structure. Still, even in such cases, Fisse seems to favor punitive injunctions rather than intervention in the CID Structure.[57]

My inclination in the case of KBR is to commend interventionist strategies. KBR has a record of accusations ranging from homicide and human trafficking to fraud and tax evasion. More important than its record of other offenses, however, the harm in the electrocution cases, even when death did not result, is especially egregious: the killing or injuring of American soldiers in a war zone by shoddy construction for which the company was paid exorbitant fees. It is bad enough that soldiers and Marines die or are maimed from enemy actions such as gunfire, IEDs, and suicide bombings. When a company is paid to provide services to military personnel such as safe shower facilities in FOBs, it has no excuse

---

[57] Fisse and French, *Corrigible Corporations and Unruly Laws*, 207. See also Richard Stewart, "Regulation, Innovation, and Administrative Law: A Conceptual Framework," *California Law Review* 69 (1981), 1256–377.

for constructing them or remodeling them in such a negligent way that they are lethal. It is also worth noting that the base military civil engineers who report to the base commanders may be complicit because they probably signed off on the electrical work that KBR did on the bases. That, of course, in no way exculpates KBR.

One of the families of an electrocution victim is suing KBR, whose motion to dismiss the wrongful death action was rejected by a U.S. district judge in Pennsylvania. KBR, through its spokesperson, responded with a statement that it was "disappointed with the ruling," that it was not responsible for the death of the soldier, and it will decide its next legal move after reviewing the ruling. In 2008, an Army investigation of the electrocution of the soldier in the wrongful death suit concluded that he had died as a result of negligent homicide by KBR. No criminal charges have been filed against KBR, Congressional hearings have been held, and an investigation into the electrocution cases is still open.

14

Mission Creep

The admiral told me not to raise the question. But in the second-year PDTCs, I asked the chaplains during the discussion of humanitarian intervention missions to identify the mission in Iraq. The answer that came back at San Diego, Kitsap, and Naples was "There is no mission" or "It keeps changing. Who knows?" At NSA Capodichino, a voice piped up, "Mission creep," and many of those in the room nodded or repeated "Mission creep" followed by a disgusted grunt.

Mission creep is mission expansion or alteration when the original goals change or when, as the chaplains liked to say under their breaths, "somebody in Washington moved the goal post." Mission creeps have a history of failure, not infrequently leading to disastrous outcomes. The relatively recent example that stuck in the minds of the chaplains in Iraq was the one portrayed, if somewhat inaccurately, in the movie *Blackhawk Down*: the debacle in the so-called Battle of Mogadishu in 1993 that cost the lives of eighteen American soldiers and left another seventy-three wounded. The Somali mission was originally humanitarian, called Operation Provide Relief. It then became Operation Restore Hope when the Marines, with support from the Army's 10th Mountain Division, were sent in to provide protection for the humanitarian efforts. The mission morphed into trying to disarm and arrest Somali clan leaders, particularly those of the Habr Gidr clan, and create a stable democratic state. The U.S. attack on a compound where the clan elders were meeting killed sixty-three elders and is generally regarded as having provoked the deadly battle in the streets of Mogadishu in October 1993. After the Somali missions, the Clinton administration was reluctant to enter into internal conflicts in Africa. Consequently, the United States did not become involved in the United Nations' missions during the civil war and genocide in Rwanda that we used in the PDTC to provide vivid focal incidents for the discussion of humanitarian intervention issues.

How did the mission creep in Iraq? Disregarding the UN missions to verify whether or not Iraq was developing a WMD program or already possessed WMD, the war was ostensibly launched to bring about regime change in Baghdad, which the Bush administration claimed was a just cause for a variety of, as it turned out, spurious reasons. The mission shifted to an occupation with the goal of finding and destroying nonexistent weapons of mass destruction and establishing a democratic political system. It changed again into an occupation primarily engaged in forays to search out and destroy insurgents and terrorists in order to bolster the fledgling democratic government. Then it became entangled in a bloody civil war fought mostly in urban settings between religious and political factions. It drifted into what some would call a humanitarian mission in conjunction with the protection of the Iraqi government and American contractors operating in the country. Then it surged into a secure-and-protect mission purported to give the Iraqi government time and space to function and build its own military and police force.

At every stage of the war, its supporters maintained or proclaimed with little or no argument that U.S. operations in Iraq were morally justified in their cause and their execution. Their citations were often explicitly to traditional just war theory and some recently suggested modifications, put forth by philosophers and theologians, dealing with preemption. In the PDTCs, the chaplains tended to regard discussion of just war theory to be irrelevant to their experiences, although some grasped that its two primary elements were being used as the moral justificatory grounds that put them where they were, ministering to Marines in Iraq and being asked to provide moral counsel regarding the conduct of the units with which they were deployed.

I

The Iraq War differs in some crucial respects, especially in its preemptive or preventive instigation, from most of the other foreign conflicts into which the United States has entered, whereas the kinds of justifications put forth to promote it by the Bush administration by and large utilized the rules, although somewhat strained, that characterize traditional just war theory. Traditional just war theory breaks into two, supposedly distinct categories: the justice of resorting to war (*jus ad bellum*) and the justice of the way the war is conducted (*jus in bello*). The usual way to think of the relationship between those categories is that a country could be fighting a just war using just means or a just war using unjust means or an unjust war using just means or an unjust war using unjust means. The morally best state of war, obviously, would be the one in which the war and the means used to fight it are both morally justifiable.

There are those who argue that it is nonsense to shape war rationales to reflect a well-worn moral theory and the way one conducts a war to a set of moral rules. They maintain that war needs no moral justification and employing such justifications demeans morality because war is conducted not in a civil state but in the state of nature where moral rules do not apply, echoing Hobbes. Nation-states go to war when they believe doing so will further their interests, and the way they fight wars is a matter of tactical prudence at best. Those who hold such a view are usually referred to as realists, sometimes as militarists, and might be identified with the old saw that "All's fair in love and war."

Tagging those that exclude moral appraisal from war as realists may give them a leg up in the discussion because the moral-justification folks then must be painted as antirealists, as unrealistic or out of touch with reality, and thus as idealists at best or just plain nuts. Nonetheless, few American elected officials have ever been willing in public to endorse realism and reiterate General Sherman's famous pronouncement, "War is cruelty, and you cannot refine it," or his "War is hell," and so they take refuge in just war theory to validate military adventures.

Although it is often identified with the realist position, strictly speaking, militarism is built on the doctrine that nation-states always have a right to go to war and that there are no limits on how they may conduct wars. Someone, I suppose, might be a realist with respect to *jus ad bellum* issues but hold out for some moral limits in the conduct of war. Militarists remove moral considerations from both entry and conduct questions. Historically, militarism about means in conjunction with religious fervor, despite proclamations or revelations of divine sanction, seemed to have underpinned a number of self-righteous barbaric holy wars such as the Crusades and most of the wars commanded by the Old Testament God against various non-Hebrew tribes in the land of Canaan.

On the extreme other end of the spectrum from the realists (and militarists) are pacifists who maintain that no war is morally justifiable and that acts of violence against other nation-states should never be undertaken.

Just war theory was developed – primarily in the Judeo-Christian theological tradition and reaching back at least to the writings on the subject by Saint Augustine, who regarded some wars as necessary evils as long as Christianity was being defended against heretics and unbelievers – to carve out a middle ground between the realists/militarists on the one side and the pacifists on the other. This middle ground was to allow that sometimes going to war is morally justified and that some tactics in fighting a war are morally legitimate, whereas others are not. Of course, realism/militarism and pacifism are not really comparable positions except that one claims that all wars are morally unjustifiable and the other says that moral justifiability is irrelevant in the case of war. The realist and the militarist do not say that all tactics adopted in war are morally permissible or that all causes for entering a war are morally acceptable. They claim that morality has nothing whatever to say about matters of war or conflicts between nation-states. Prudential logic, at most, governs entry and conduct decisions for them. Pacifists hold that morality, understood as dominated by a principle of nonviolence, is relevant to all elements of war, and presumably all aspects of human life, and they find a priori that all causes for war and all tactics in fighting a war must be immoral. Their nonviolence principle not only trumps prudential judgments, it is the only consideration that matters for them.

Just war theory falls between those two extremes in the sense that it recognizes some wars and some tactics as morally justifiable, but because the realist/militarist rules moral assessment out of order with respect to war, the spectrum on which these justifications of war are typically situated is not a moral continuum running from everything being morally permissible to nothing being morally permissible. Pacifism claims that war is immoral, just war theory that it is sometimes moral, and realism/militarism that any talk about the morality of war is nonsense, out of order, a category mistake.

(It is sociologically and psychologically intriguing that there are chaplains who represent religions that are doctrinally committed to pacifism, although the majority of the serving chaplains are ordained in faith groups that have adopted just war theory either formally or indirectly. *Jus ad bellum* concerns, however, seem to play no significant role in whether or not pacifist chaplains request nonbattlefield deployments; most do not.)

Jus ad bellum in traditional just war theory sets the boundary on just *casus belli* by excluding wars of aggression and revenge. Only wars of self-defense are morally legitimate, and such wars can be fought only to try to restore peace. Importantly, *jus ad bellum* rules out wars "waged to defeat a potential adversary before its military power can grow to rival your own."[1] *Jus ad bellum* includes additional troublesome restrictions for governments: declaring war must be a "last resort," war may be undertaken only if success is a probable outcome, the violence utilized must be proportionate to the aim of, or the intention in engaging in, the war, which must be, as noted, the promotion of peace and not the pursuit of national gains. The legitimate authorities of the combatant nations must also have undertaken the war.

The Bush administration, under the claim that it was a war of self-defense, although it clearly was preemptive, launched the Iraq War in March 2003. In reference to conducting a counterterrorism war, which under one of the depictions favored by the American government is what the Iraq War was supposed to be, Secretary of Defense Donald Rumsfeld said on CNN, "There is no question but that the United States of America has every right, as every country does, of self-defense. . . . That is in fact what we're doing. That is, in effect, self-defense of a preemptive nature."[2] President Bush defended a similar position in his speech at West Point in June 2002 in which he stated what became known as the Bush Doctrine and was incorporated in the *National Security Strategy of the United States* (September 2002):

> The security environment confronting the United States today is radically different from what we have faced before. Yet the first duty of the United States Government remains what it always has been: to protect the American people and American interests. It is an enduring American principle that this duty obligates the government to anticipate and counter threats, using all elements of national power, before the threats can do grave damage. The greater the threat, the greater is the risk of inaction – and the more compelling the case for taking anticipatory action to defend ourselves, even if uncertainty remains as to the time and place of the enemy's attack. There are few greater threats than a terrorist attack with WMD. To forestall or prevent such hostile acts by our adversaries, the United States will, if necessary, act preemptively in exercising our inherent right of self-defense.[3]

The challenge raised by the application of the Bush Doctrine to justify the American invasion of Iraq that was preceded by the "Shock and Awe" rocket and bombing stage is to determine the limits on a country's self-defensive interests. In the *National Security Strategy Statement*, what

---

[1] Neta C. Crawford, "Just War Theory and the U.S. Counterterror War," *Perspectives on Politics* (March 2003), 5–25, 7.

[2] Quoted by Crawford, 12.

[3] National Security Council (March 2006), "Summary of National Security Strategy 2002," *The National Security Strategy of the United States*. The White House. http://georgewbush-whitehouse.archives.gov/nsc/nss/2006.

are called "the enduring global political and economic interests" of the United States are included in the ambit of the national self that can be defended by preemptive war. Perhaps a convincing argument can be made that global economic forces operating in a certain way are vital to American interests. Surely the protected use of cyberspace is also a crucial domain for the furtherance of those interests. In fact, it is difficult to imagine where to draw the line on what might be regarded within the vital interests of a country, the United States, that is both the world's only superpower and yet is economically, and in many other ways, dependent on the operation of systems, environments, and platforms that exist outside of its borders or in an international cyberdomain.

President Barack Obama created an Office of Cybersecurity in recognition of the expansion of the vital interests of the United States in that area and the threats to which it is prone. There seems to be ample reason to regard cyberattack as a genuine threat to the self-interests of a country. Information warfare and cyberwarfare striking at communication nodes and infrastructures with weaponry deployed in cyberspace have already made appearances on the international scene. For example, in April 2007, the websites of the Estonian parliament, its banks, ministries, and media were brought to a standstill by hackers. In 2009, the Nashi, a Russian-government–backed youth group, claimed responsibility for shutting down Estonia's Internet access, and the head of the Russian Military Forecasting Center confirmed that Russia had the ability to launch widespread cyberattacks and pointed out that doing so does not violate current international treaties. The Estonian government maintained that the cyberattack paralyzed the country commercially, economically, and socially and so constituted a threat to its national security.

The Estonian case is not isolated. Cyberattacks occurred during the 2008 war in South Ossetia. They disabled a number of crucial websites in Georgia, Russia, South Ossetia, and Azerbaijan. The United States has not been exempt from such attacks. *Titan Rain* fell on American targets in 2003. It purportedly was launched by Chinese military hackers and gained access to the networks of the U.S. Army Information Systems Engineering Command at Fort Huachuca, Arizona, the Defense Information System Agency in Arlington, Virginia, the Naval Ocean Systems Center in San Diego, California, the Army Space and Strategic Defense Center in Huntsville, Alabama, Lockheed Martin, the Sandia National Laboratories, the Redstone Arsenal, and NASA. In 2009, a Chinese-based attack, given the code named *Ghostnet*, infiltrated at least 1,250 computers in

103 countries as well as the Dalai Lama's exile centers in India, Belgium, England, and the United States. It compromised cybernetworks in embassies, foreign ministries, and government departments of India, South Korea, Indonesia, Romania, Cyprus, Malta, Thailand, Taiwan, Portugal, Germany, Pakistan, Laos, Iran, Bangladesh, Latvia, Indonesia, Philippines, Brunei, Barbados, and Bhutan.

Given the dependence of many of the nations of the world on cybertechnology to run their power grids and their economic, political, social, and military operations, it is impossible to deny that the protection of their virtual networks is a vital matter of a nation's security, an interest a nation has in its self-defense. Cyberattack with weapons of mass disruption undoubtedly will be a primary tactic of future wars and may have the effect of weakening the dominant position in military might currently enjoyed by the United States, leveling a playing field that militarily has been lopsidedly tilted in favor of the United States since the end of the Cold War. In information warfare and cyberwarfare, almost any country or noncountry force successfully can fight using unconventional cyberweaponry.[4]

In the globally interlocked and entangled commercial and technological environment, it is unrealistic not to define the self-defendable interests of a country broadly, but there is clearly a problem in just war theory with doing so: there seems to be no way to limit the application of the self-defense justification for war. What would it exclude? What *casus belli* is not morally justifiable? (At least it should rule out the United States testing some new weaponry by declaring war on and attacking a peaceful tribe living in premodern conditions in the deepest regions of the Amazon jungle because it happens to be encamped on a massive oil field. Or would it?) In effect, when the concept of self-defense covers protection of everything related to the social, commercial, technological, and cultural aspects of life in a country, it ceases to perform a useful purpose in morally justifying *casus belli* against a country that is believed likely to weaken or destroy any of those self-interests were it to act in such and such a manner (which it just might do, or so it is believed). Whether a perceived attack on the culture of a country, believed to be imminent or actual, could ever suffice as a convincing moral justification for making war seems dubious, but it certainly was used successfully to recruit

---

[4] See John Arquilla, "Can Information Warfare Ever Be Just?" *Ethics and Information Technology* (1999), 203–12.

Christian nations during the Crusades and by non-state Muslim groups in recent years in urging a war of terror against the United States. Of course, the crusaders could have found their justification in Augustine's just war theory, which authorized war against heretics and idolaters.

If self-defense is the only legitimate grounds for war and if a country's "self" is, in large measure, bound up in the culture it has adopted, nourished, created, indulged in, and so forth, then a threat to destroy that culture or significant parts of it by another country that does not participate in that culture may well be regarded as a legitimate *casus belli*. The problem, however, is to define which elements of a culture are essential or significant within it. Is rap music such an element in American culture? What about baseball? What about the Christian religion? Or religious and ethnic diversity? President Bush regularly said, "They hate us for our freedom." Was the September 11, 2001 attack on the World Trade Center, among other things, an attack on what the terrorists perceived to be American culture? What, after all, is American culture?

Putting aside trying to define what is included in the "self" a nation has an interest in defending, the problem with national self-defense as the morally justifiable *casus belli* in the contemporary world is that in political discourse, it becomes a persuasive argument for preemptive and preventive attack and not just a response to actual aggression, as was seen in the rhetoric in the "run up" to the Iraq War in the United States. Article 51 of the United Nations Charter allows that the right of self-defense extends beyond an actual attack to an imminently threatened one, "provided there is credible evidence of such an imminent threat and the threatened state has no obvious recourse available, there is no problem – and never has been – with that state . . . using military force 'preemptively.'"[5] The threat of aggression may be claimed to be imminent based, however, on intelligence that may be less than accurate and so not credible, even if couched in terms that make it appear to be unimpeachable. The notion of imminence is also a rather slippery one. Any nation-state may regard, sometimes legitimately, that another nation-state means it ill and is engaging in what may be reasonably interpreted as insults and provocations that test the limits of the other state's commitment to avoid armed conflict. Those provocations, however, never cross the line into actual injury of the interests of the state. It is extremely vague where that line

---

[5] Gareth Evans, "When Is It Right to Fight? Legality, Legitimacy, and the Use of Military Force," 2004 Cyril Foster Lecture, Oxford University (May 2004). Reprinted on the website of the International Crisis Group at www.crisisgroup.org.

is transgressed such that one state is imminently going to harm the self-interests of another. Do blockades and no-fly zones have to be initiated? Do border incursions have to have occurred? Does a cyberattack have to be launched? Or do one state's military forces have to be gathered near the border? What if a massive military training program for hackers or computer programmers is detected in a rival state's territory?

Michael Walzer, in his well-known work on just war theory, writes:

> The line between legitimate and illegitimate first strikes is not going to be drawn at the point of imminent attack but at the point of sufficient threat. That phrase is necessarily vague. I mean it to cover three things: a manifest intent to injure, a degree of active preparation that makes the intent a positive danger, and a general situation in which waiting, or doing anything other than fighting, greatly magnifies the risk.[6]

Walzer interpreted his conditions justifying preemptive war as requiring incontrovertible evidence of current particular signs of actual preparation for war in the other state that intensifies the present danger to the interests of the state contemplating preemptive attack. It is little wonder that the Bush administration talked of mushroom clouds, purchase of yellow cake uranium, missile building, warehouses of chemical and biological weaponry, and so forth to support its call for an attack on Iraq in the aftermath of the September 11, 2001 terrorist attack using American commercial airplanes on the World Trade Center and the Pentagon, in which no Iraqis were involved. To bolster their argument, they decided to claim that Iraq's government was somehow in cahoots with the terrorist group al-Qaeda. Still, Walzer's criteria justify preemptive strikes and not preventive invasions. What the Bush administration did was, as Shaun Casey claims, "to collapse the distinction between preemptive war and preventative war."[7]

The distinction is not as academic as it may first appear. A preventive war would be any conflict entered into in order to eliminate the very possibility of a future threat to one's interests by attacking the as-yet-unrealized capabilities of a perceived enemy. Preemptive war requires that the threat is imminent. Of course, if the intelligence is "cooked" to give every impression that the threat is not just potential but about to erupt, then Walzer's criteria will appear to be satisfied and the war morally justified, at least on Walzer's version of the theory. Little wonder

---

[6] Michael Walzer, *Just and Unjust Wars* (New York, 1977), 81.

[7] Shaun Casey, "Iraq, the Just War Ethics, and Preemptive War," in Peter A. French and Jason Short, eds., *War and Border Crossings* (Lanham, MD, 2005), 31.

that as each of the claims of imminent threat proved to be nonexistent after the invasion of Iraq, the Bush administration crept the mission.

Threats, of course, may be real but not imminent. That means that they can be addressed in some fashion, typically diplomatically, to deter or weaken them. In fact, that was the situation during the Cold War in which no one would have denied that the threat of all-out nuclear war between two superpowers was real, but by both sides adopting a mutual assured destruction policy in their ostensive game of "Chicken," both were deterred from direct combat and sufficient security for both sides was preserved until the Soviet Union collapsed internally, in part owing to the cost of maintaining an arsenal sufficient to sustain the international status quo. The Bush administration shifted the policy that won the Cold War for the United States by substituting "a policy that aimed at peace through the prevention of war by a policy aimed at peace through preventive war."[8]

The Iraq War as a preventive war has much in common with a war that Saint Augustine decried as having planted the seeds of the eventual internal decay and fall of Rome: the Third Punic War. The Third Punic War occurred from 149 to 146 BC. Actually, there was only one battle of note: the Battle of Carthage. In 151 BC, Carthage had repaid the debt it owed Rome for the Second Punic War, the one that featured Hannibal and the elephants. The Romans, however, regarded the treaty that had included the debt as requiring Carthage to be subordinate to Rome in perpetuity. Also that year, Numidia attacked Carthage in a land grab, and Carthage countered with an attack on the Numidian army that had invaded its territory. The Carthagians, however, suffered defeat. Rather than attacking Numidia in defense of what it regarded as its subordinate state, Rome declared war in 149 BC on Carthage for having launched an attack on Numidia without its permission. Attempts by the Carthagians to placate Rome failed, and the Roman army invaded Carthagian territory. The Romans besieged the city of Carthage for nearly three years before it finally fell. The collapse of the city revealed that many inside the walls had died of starvation, and those Carthagians who survived were sold into slavery. The city was utterly destroyed and its territories were annexed to Rome. The story that the Romans sowed the soil of Carthage with salt so that nothing would grow there is most likely false, because a primary reason that Carthage was attractive to Rome was because Carthagian

---

[8] Arthur Schlesinger, Jr., "Eyeless in Gaza," *New York Review of Books* (October 23, 2003).

territory was good farming country and Rome was in need of agricultural products to feed its growing population.

Many historians believe that the primary reason for the Third Punic War was not to punish Carthage for its use of military force against its neighbor Numidia without Roman consent, but to get Roman hands on food, particularly grain. Saint Augustine maintains in *The City of God* that by so thoroughly destroying Carthage in a trumped-up war, Rome paved the way to its own decay because it removed a potential enemy that at the time could not have been an imminent threat and thereafter made Rome too secure. Security is, Saint Augustine quotes Scipio, "a danger to weak characters.... The abolition of Carthage certainly removed a fearful threat to the state of Rome, and the extinction of that threat was immediately followed by disasters arising from prosperity."[9]

Saint Augustine's long-range historical conclusions are suspect, especially considering that he was actually trying to defend Christianity against the charge that it was responsible for the decline and fall of Rome. What is striking, however, is that Rome, the superpower of its time, undertook war with Carthage, based either on poor intelligence (it was argued that Carthage was reconstructing its war fleet, which it was not) or on the strategy of destroying Carthage so that Numidia could not annex it and deprive the Romans of its grain while establishing for themselves a strategic port in the Western Mediterranean from which they might eventually attack Rome or its allies. The similarities to the Iraq War are striking, especially if "grain" is read for "oil" and one thinks of Iran for Numidia.

Even if preventive war is countenanced in just war theory, there must be some constraints reining in a superpower's realizing its global hegemonic desires by militarily annihilating any country it comes to believe in its wildest nightmares of insecurity could be a threat. Henry Kissinger cautioned the Bush administration against the invasion of Iraq, maintaining that it cannot be in its interest "to develop principles that grant every nation an unfettered right of preemption against its own definition of threats to its security."[10] The problem is the very one that Saint Augustine pointed out: if the nation-state's goal is total security, then virtually any perceived threat is going to pass the evidence test. Even a smidgeon of evidence that country X is in the early planning stages of a cyberattack would satisfy the sufficient evidence test and a preventive war could be justified. But that is nonsense and surely a reason why

---

[9] St. Augustine, *The City of God*, translated by H. Bettensen (London, 1972), 30.
[10] Quoted by Gareth Evans from a *Washington Post* op-ed column by Henry Kissinger.

preventive war is considered a very slippery slope into a Hobbesian state of nature of unending war of all against all. The Bush administration, in fact, declared that its War on Terror would be a permanent state of global conflict, implying that at any time it could use force to eliminate whatever it perceived to be a potential threat on whatever evidence it regarded as sufficient.

The traditional just war theorist's insistence on self-defense in response to actual aggression is a more morally viable position, although an objective conception of imminence will probably still be necessary to deal with some cases. In such cases, Evans argues, authorization of the use of force by the United Nations pursuant to Chapter 51 will be adequate as long as the Security Council addresses such moral concerns as to the seriousness of the threat; the real purpose of the use of force; what the consequences are likely to be; whether the scale, duration, and intensity of the military action is the minimum required to handle the threat; and whether all other avenues of resolving the matters have been tried and proved unsuccessful.[11]

The last-resort condition in traditional just war theory embodies a presumption against the use of violence, but it is also epistemically problematic. Because the onus of proving that the last resort has been reached rests on the state that believes itself to be endangered by the potentially hostile capabilities of another state, how does it know that all of its options to alleviate the situation short of violence have been exhausted? Walzer objects to the last-resort condition if it is understood literally because he believes it would make war morally impossible. "For we can never reach lastness, or we can never know that we have reached it."[12]

Defenders of the last-resort condition, however, maintain that it does not require a country to attempt every possible nonmilitary measure if there is no reasonable expectation of success from trying some of them. They read the condition as requiring only that every reasonable nonviolent measure must be attempted before the military option is used.

John Lango adds to the understanding of the last-resort condition that the stronger state is morally obligated to always use nonviolent means whenever it is reasonable to do so.[13] Montesquieu maintained that a weaker state, because it is more vulnerable than a strong state, has a

[11] Ibid.

[12] Michael Walzer, *Arguing About War* (New Haven, 2004), 88.

[13] John Lango, "Before Military Force, Nonviolent Action: An Application of a Generalized Just War Principle of Last Resort," *Public Affairs Quarterly* (April 2009), 117.

presumptive right to wage offensive wars ("Small societies more frequently have the right to wage wars than large ones, because they are
more frequently in a position to fear being destroyed"[14]), although they
are less likely to do so because they will realize that the stronger states
will possess considerable capacities of retaliation after they make a preemptive strike. The Bush Doctrine, however, reserves the offensive right
for the strongest of all states, the hegemonic power on the globe, as a
first resort. Neta Crawford writes, "When the Bush administration says in
the National Security Strategy that 'our best defense is a good offense,'
it suggests – despite its other statements about nonmilitary elements of
the strategy – that preemptive action is preferred and nonmilitary action
is only supplementary."[15]

Just war theorists who are not adverse to and embrace war in certain
cases include a last-resort principle in the package of restrictions they
impose on *casus belli*. That suggests that they believe that morality in
general includes a presumption against carnage and that the burden of
proof falls on those who would use violent means even in a good cause.
The obvious reason for morality's stance on these matters is that, at least
historically, war results in the killing of many human beings and the
destruction of property. Walzer recognizes this when he writes, "We say
of war that it is the 'last resort' because of the unpredictable, unexpected,
unintended, and unavoidable horrors that it regularly brings."[16]

Insofar as the last-resort condition places on the would-be aggressor
the burden of proof to demonstrate that there are convincing and transparent reasons not to pursue nonmilitary options, standards for doing
so should be available to the global community to ascertain whether the
condition has been met. As Lango notes, "just war theory should include
specific standards of reasonableness for the last resort principle."[17] Two
standards seem appropriate. The first is recommended by Lango and
also by C. A. J. Coady, who writes, "Clearly, some principle of feasibility is
required to screen the realistic availability of alternatives to violence."[18]
As noted earlier, traditional just war theory includes what might be called
a "reasonable success condition." What that means is that a country is
not morally justified in initiating a war if it has little or no reasonable

[14] Charles-Louis de Secondat, Baron de Montesquieu, *The Spirit of the Laws* (Cambridge,
1989), book 10, 138.
[15] Crawford, 15.
[16] Walzer, *Arguing About War*, 155.
[17] Lango, 121.
[18] C. A. J. Coady, *The Ethics of Armed Humanitarian Intervention* (Washington, 2002), 28.

likelihood of success in doing so, and "success" is typically defined in terms of restoring peace, bringing about the appropriate punishment of international wrongdoing, and so forth. If it is unreasonable to believe you will win, morally you should not launch a war that will bring only death and misery on your and the enemy's people, as well as defeat and all that may be expected to follow in its train (subjugation, humiliation, and much worse) on your country.

No one seems to take serious issue with the standard of reasonable chance of success, but the same sort of standard of feasibility should also be applied in the case of the last-resort condition. That is, to pass the last-resort test, there should be no reasonable chance that the morally justifiable end to which war is aimed can be achieved by nonmilitary means. The difference between the standards is, of course, obvious in that the feasibility test for the last-resort standard requires proving that it is unreasonable to believe that something will happen, whereas the feasibility test for the success standard requires proving that it is reasonable to believe that something will happen. In the case of the United States in its current global position as the only superpower with the greatest military might on the planet, demonstrating that it is reasonable to believe that war will achieve its goal does not strain credulity. On the other hand, providing a convincing argument that it is unreasonable to believe that nonmilitary means such as diplomacy will succeed is a far more difficult task because it requires convincing judgments about the mental states of the enemy and other factors that are much less objective than counting the number of tanks, planes, warships, uniformed warriors, materiel, and so forth on both sides. Of course, sometimes even such straightforward calculations are poor bases for predictions of success, especially when enemies are fighting on their own soil and are prepared to carry on the war by nonconventional means for an indefinite period of time. That was a lesson the British learned during the American Revolutionary War and one that the United States may be learning in Iraq and should have learned in Vietnam.

The second standard for the last-resort condition, suggested by Lango and Simon Caney, might be called a "comparative-awfulness standard." The last-resort condition embodies "the assumption that war is the most awful option."[19] Generally, nonmilitary options, if they pass the feasibility test, will be less awful than the military option when it comes to death and destruction and so will be favored by morality. However, in some cases,

---

[19] Simon Caney, *Justice Beyond Borders* (Oxford, 2005), 202.

that may not be the case. Economic and other types of sanctions may work enormous hardships on a targeted country's population and lead to more deaths than a strategic attack to eliminate a military threat. For example, the United States in 2001 blocked the import of pipes and bulldozers to Iraq, causing massive problems in dealing with sewerage, water delivery, and health issues. The United States allowed the import of chlorine but blocked the import of the equipment needed to safely handle it. Medical supplies worth $280,000,000, including incubators for babies, cardiac equipment, and vaccines for infant hepatitis, tetanus, and diphtheria, were prevented from reaching Iraq on the specious grounds that the vaccines might have minute particles of biocultures in them that could be converted into biological WMD. Clearly, the suffering and death that such nonmilitary measures predictably produce could make the choice of war less awful. Unfortunately for the historical moral assessment of the United States with regard to Iraq in the late 1990s and 2000s, both brutal, or what Sukumar Muralidharan calls "malevolent,"[20] nonmilitary and military options were used against the people of Iraq.

With the advent of what Michael Ignatieff called "virtual war," another way to calculate the awfulness of war versus the awfulness of nonmilitary measures such as sanctions presents itself. During the Kosovo War in the 1990s, it was reported that NATO forces killed about 5,000 Yugoslavian soldiers and 500 civilians, without suffering a single combat fatality. The reason for the disparity in casualties was that NATO fought the war from afar. The weaponry used by NATO forces was high-tech and insulated the soldier or flyer from the battlefield. It was something like a video game situation, comparable to the "Shock and Awe" stage of the American invasion of Iraq. War for the NATO forces was a simulacrum lacking risk for the more technologically advanced participant. Had NATO engaged Yugoslavian troops on the battlefield in Kosovo, surely the fatality numbers on both sides would have been greater. Following out the logic, if a war can be fought virtually, at least on one side if not on both, then it may well be less awful with respect to casualties than the impositions of sanctions that deprive a citizenry of the means to sustain life and economic well-being. Of course, even if war, not nonmilitary measures, scores better on the awfulness meter, it may still be the case that those nonmilitary measures will prove feasible and so using them will still be the morally justifiable means of dealing with a threat.

---

[20] Sukumar Muralidharan, "Brutal Wars and a Malevolent Peace: Anatomy of US Policy in Iraq," *Economic and Political Weekly* (May 17, 2003), 1938–1943.

What might still be worried about in the wired world of warfare that is fast upon us and in which casualties on the higher tech side of the combatants will be minimal is that the individual simulacral warriors will lose psychological and moral touch with what they are doing, a situation that worried Navy chaplains during the early stages of the Iraq War. They may become morally numb to the violence they are perpetrating but, on the plus side, they are less likely then to suffer PTSD.

Just war theory also has a proportionality condition that is intended to control revenge motives by insisting that the havoc, destruction, and death that a country causes in its enemy's territory must be proportional to the threat or actual losses that it suffered at the hands of the enemy. I cannot think of any formulaic way that proportionality in war should be measured except by asking a question suggested by Evans – namely, "Is the scale, duration, and intensity of the proposed military action the minimum necessary to meet the threat in question?"[21] The obvious extremes of overreaction are clear and easily ruled out. Dropping a nuclear bomb on the largest city of one's enemy when the enemy perpetrated a cyberattack on the e-mail network of the Department of Health and Human Services surely is excessive in the extreme. In a case of provocation in which one's enemy has assembled troops at one's border and announced the intention to invade, attacking and annihilating the enemy's force seems within the rule of proportionality, but continuing to launch rockets of napalm into the enemy's cities after the threat has been effectively removed is disproportional.

The United States entered the Vietnam War in force after the so-called Gulf of Tonkin incidents in August 1964. In retaliation for what turned out to be a falsified report of an attack on the *U.S.S. Mattox*, the United States sent a massive bombing raid into Hanoi. Even had a North Vietnamese gunboat fired on the *Mattox* – something that according to an NSA report declassified in 2005 most likely never happened – the reaction of the United States strains the notion of proportionality to the breaking. In any event, the best we seem able to do in judging the proportionality rule of *jus ad bellum* would be along lines comparable to the way we think of fit in criminal punishment cases. Some uses of military force appear to reasonable people to be more or less proportional to the threat or the actual aggressive harm suffered, and others are strikingly disproportionate. I draw a blank in trying to identify examples of inadequate responses, although I am certain there are some, perhaps many.

[21] Evans.

Examples of overdoing are relatively easy to cite, and those provide the rationale for the proportionality rule in traditional just war theory.

There also are cases where military response to an actual invasion must appear fruitless to any rational person because of a staggering imbalance in the military forces that would be involved. For example, should Belgium have committed its troops to defend the country from German invasion in either World War I or II? Belgium certainly had a right to do so, but having a right and acting on it are two distinctly different things. If there were no conceivable ways for a country to proportionately respond to an aggressor and no realistic hope of success were a response of any kind to be mounted, would not just war theory require capitulation? Engaging one's country in a war that cannot be won because one is exceedingly overmatched and there are no predictably successful ways of winning by the use of unconventional measures would seem to be morally unjustifiable. The Winter War between the Soviet Union and Finland in 1939 could be thought of as an exception. After the Soviet Union and Germany completed the Molotov-Ribbentrop Pact in 1939, the Soviets threatened to invade the Baltic States and Finland. Lithuania, Latvia, and Estonia capitulated and Finland did not. On November 30, 1939, the Soviet Union attacked Finland. The Finns were greatly outnumbered (4–1) and had only 30 tanks to face more than 6,500 Soviet tanks. The disparity in the air was equally one-sided. But the Finns had a number of factors working in their favor. They wore white uniforms that camouflaged them in the snowy terrain, whereas the Soviet Army was wearing its dark uniforms and so were easy marks for sharpshooters. The morale of the Finns defending their homeland was high, whereas the Soviet troops were poorly led and demoralized by recent purges that killed more than half of their officers. The Finns resisted the Soviet invasion for a number of months and were able to bring an end to the war in 1940 through a treaty in which they agreed to cede the Finnish part of Karelia to the Soviets, including the city of Viipuri and a part of the Salla area, and four islands in the Gulf of Finland. A few years into the Second World War, Finland associated itself with Germany in Operation Barbarossa and launched an aggressive war, usually referred to as the Continuation War, against the Soviet Union to reclaim the territory it had lost in the Winter War. By siding with Nazi Germany, Finland then had war declared against it by many of the Allied Powers, including the United Kingdom. To those who claim that democracies never declare war against each other, the Finnish World War II situation is a clear counterexample. In fact, it could be persuasively argued that one of the primary reasons for Finland's entry into the war on the side of Nazi Germany was to protect its sovereignty and democratic government.

Another troubling issue with just war theory is the extent of the right of self-defense once a country has violated the territorial integrity and the political sovereignty of another state. The violated state has the right to war, assuming that it has satisfied the other rules of just war theory and thus has a just *casus belli*. Does the invader state lose its right of self-defense against the retaliator? Morally ought it to just lay down its arms? In the case of the punishment of justly convicted criminals, we do not believe that they continue to have a right to self-defense on which they may act by attacking their jailors or, if they are sentenced to death, by trying to kill the state's executioner. They have forfeited their rights, or at least the right to self-defense. On many accounts of just war theory, a state never forfeits its right to self-defense no matter what it has done or how it has behaved in the community of nations. But should that also entail that no matter how bad a state is from a moral point of view – for example, because of the way it treats its citizens or those living within its borders – it may take whatever measures necessary to defend itself against the threat of invasion by another state? Suppose that to raise a military force adequate for its defense, it must conscript its citizens and impress others into its service. Did the Confederate States of America have the right to draft able-bodied men and slaves from within its borders into its army to defend itself against attacks from the Union armies? Can a state bind its citizens in its preservation when it is fighting a war to preserve a corrupt culture?

II

Just war theory seems to entail that although there may be wars in which neither side is fighting for a just cause and wars in which one side or the other has a just cause, there cannot be a war in which the *casus belli* on both sides are morally justifiable. If national self-defense (even broadly interpreted) is recognized as the only morally justifiable *casus belli*, then two countries engaged in war cannot both be justifiably defending themselves against the invasion of the other by prosecuting the war. A possible complication that might skew that conclusion arises if the theory is interpreted sometimes to allow justifying self-defensive preemptive military measures against a presumed threat based on a false belief supported by inadequate evidence or bad intelligence that an attack on the nation's self-interests is imminent. In any event, the theory cannot allow just any claims of intelligence that a threat is imminent to justify preemptively or preventively launching a war. And even if it did, then the country believing itself to be under such a threat would be morally justified in the war and the presumed threatening country would not. When the evidence proves to have been invented and the intelligence the result of fabrications and outright lies, the moral high ground shifts to the party once believed to be threatening, which is then morally justified in resisting invasion. Of course, if the fabricating country (that is, the country that launches the war because of intelligence "cooked" by its leaders to support an imminent threat scenario) is a superpower, say the United States, and the invasion is well underway or has passed into an occupation stage, little practical good will be gained by the invaded country from having taken the moral high ground.

There is, however, a much more important issue that falls out from the *jus ad bellum* analysis of the justifiability of a *casus belli*. If the identified *casus belli* fails the *jus ad bellum* tests, the war is nonetheless being prosecuted by the military of the offending country. It seems reasonable to say that fighting in an unjust war could not be just and that for those engaged in such a war, whether or not they have personally determined the war to have such a moral status, there is a *prima facie* moral reason to cease to participate. Failing to do so morally dirties their hands, indeed, leaves them morally stained, perhaps irreparably, regardless of the salve of patriotism that undoubtedly will be applied to try to cleanse them. Without their participation, the unjust war cannot be fought.

Traditional just war theory has a second part, *jus in bello*, and the idea that motivates that part of the theory is that it should be possible to draw a thick bright line between the justice of a nation engaging in a war and the moral appraisability of the way that war is fought on either side, regardless of the moral status of the nations that are engaged in the conflict. One way to think of this is that there are big war crimes – those having to do with starting an unjust war – and there are somewhat smaller war crimes, although war crimes nonetheless and not to be taken lightly – those involving ways in which the war or specific battles in it or other aspects of the war were conducted. The puzzling question the thick bright line is supposed to answer in the affirmative is, "Can an unjust war be fought justly?"

Members of the military, according to Walzer, exist in a realm of moral equality regardless of whether they are fighting on the just or the unjust side. They are presumed not to be responsible for the war itself, although they are responsible for their actions in fighting it. The moral rules to which they are held accountable are those of *jus in bello,* not *jus ad bellum.* The *jus in bello* rules are usually grouped in three categories. There are the discrimination rules that focus on the legitimacy of targets. Soldiers on either side until they surrender are legitimate targets, as are certain civilians, those currently engaged in what Walzer calls "the business of war."[22] Noncombatants are excluded. There are the proportionality rules that mirror similar rules in *jus ad bellum* regarding tempering methods to the legitimate ends. There is also a rule banning *mala in se* that could be treated as just an extension of the proportionality rule. What are banned are the employment of methods and the use of weaponry that shock "the moral conscience of mankind." The use of rape as a method to terrorize a civilian population and demoralize the opposing forces falls within *mala in se,* as does genocide and ethnic cleansing. Weapons that are intrinsically awful or horrendous and assault our moral sense are forbidden.

The combatants on both sides have what Walzer calls "a license to kill" as long as they act within those *jus in bello* rules. Walzer writes, "Though there is no license for war-makers, there is a license for soldiers, and they hold it without regard to which side they are on; it is the first and most important of their rights. They are entitled to kill."[23] The idea that combatants on both sides possess equally a license to kill, however, is morally preposterous. Suppose that country A, without justification and with the intent of seizing territory or valuable natural resources, attacks country B in force. By *jus ad bellum,* B is morally justified in responding in a proportionate and discriminatory manner to A's aggressive actions. Surely that gives those in B's military a license to kill members of A's forces, but why should that grant an equal right to members of A's military to kill B's forces? They are on foreign soil uninvited and by violent means. How can those in an aggressor's forces gain a moral right by participating in, indeed, making possible, an immoral act? They marched across the border weapons blazing, although the decision to do so was not their decision. They have been put in a position, presumably by their government, to receive morally justifiable deadly fire, but it seems equally preposterous to say that they should stand there, perhaps lay down their arms, and take whatever is incoming. By a personal right of self-defense, they should be able to protect themselves now that they have been put in

[22] Walzer, *Just and Unjust Wars,* 43.
[23] Ibid., 36.

harm's way. Their job is not just then to die for their country's immorality, "theirs not to reason why; theirs but to do and die."[24]

It seems more appropriate, in such circumstances, to grant those in the aggressor's military forces an excuse to kill, but not a license to kill. That is, they have an excuse to kill the soldiers that are firing on them, trying to thwart their invasion. But there are further complications. Whom will they be excused for killing and which methods will be excusable? *Jus in bello* proponents, as noted, set limits on what means soldiers may use when killing or carrying out acts of war and, importantly, against whom they may use them. Ordinary citizens, noncombatants, may not be intentionally targeted. Discrimination must be practiced. (I have no patience to descend into the shadowy depths of the double-effect arguments popular with higher ranking officers and government officials to try to excuse collateral damage involving the slaughter of innocent civilians when bombs drop on their homes, schools, hospitals, and so on.) They also may not kill prisoners and the soldiers of the enemy who are in the process of surrendering. If they do such things, they have no excuse. But what good moral argument supports excusing them for killing the soldiers that are fighting in a just cause? Suppose they are very good at killing because they possess the most technologically advanced weaponry, whereas the soldiers on the other side have only out-of-date equipment and devices they can rig up from whatever they can find lying around, such as Molotov cocktails, IEDs, and so on. By loosing their "dogs of war," the aggressor force can annihilate the troops of the morally just nation. Could the combatants fighting for an unjust cause have an acceptable excuse for killing soldiers of the self-defending nation and ensuring that the just cause in the conflict does not prevail?

Proponents of every soldier's right to kill regardless of what side he or she is on likely will invoke the proportionality rule in *jus in bello* to try to adjust what seems to be a profoundly unacceptable conclusion. But how is the proportionality rule supposed to work in a case like the one described? Normally, the rule would tell the military that it should not use more firepower than is necessary to achieve its objective. Morality cannot side with the aggressor whose objective is to dominate another country and appropriate its natural resources. If its objectives are not morally justifiable, the calculation of what minimal means are necessary to accomplish them is utterly beside the moral point. Bank robbers who use only just enough TNT to blow off the door to the vault rather than

---

[24] Alfred Lord Tennyson, *The Charge of the Light Brigade*, 1854.

so much that they collapse the whole building are still bank robbers. Thanks a lot for leaving the building standing! Jeff McMahan writes,

> If the requirement of just cause specifies the types of good that may legitimately be pursued by means of war, it is hard to see how in the absence of a just cause, there can be any goods to weigh against the harms that the acts of unjust combatants cause. For goods that may not legitimately be pursued by means of war cannot contribute to the justification for an act of war and thus cannot figure in the proportionality calculation for that act of war.[25]

If a war is unjust according to *jus ad bellum*, those tasked by the aggressor country to fight it should refuse to participate on moral grounds. If they were to do so, aggressor nations would be incapable of achieving their unjust ends and that could not be a bad thing, morally speaking. If they do fight it, their violent behavior cannot be morally legitimized even if they refrain from employing the most destructive weaponry, the *mala in se* weapons they have in their arsenal. Of course, one reason why just war theorists do not want *jus in bello* to collapse into *just ad bellum* is to try to block aggressors from adopting the position that insofar as they cannot avoid moral condemnation for the way they fight an unjust war, they might as well go all out and use the full extent of their arsenal and engage in scorched earth tactics in the manner of Sherman's March from Atlanta to Savannah. Laudable as that may be, it will not avert the collapse of *jus in bello* into *just ad bellum*. The best that *jus in bello* rules can do on the unjust side of a war is serve as a violence-limiting device. That is a good thing, of course, but it does not much touch on the moral culpability of the unjust combatants.

It would appear that there are no circumstances in which a soldier fighting on the unjust side can, in his or her military capacity, fight justly. But recall the discrimination rule in *jus in bello*, and imagine that some of those fighting for the just side conduct the war in an unjust manner. Suppose that a platoon on the just side has rounded up the women and children of a border village. The platoon wrongly believes the village to have aided the invading army, and they line the villagers against a wall to shoot them, both as a lesson to other border villages and because members of the platoon are in a high state of agitation and seek revenge for their fellow soldiers killed in a skirmish with the invaders. If soldiers from the invading army were to witness what was transpiring in the village and mounted an attack before the executions could be carried out in order to prevent the killings of the innocent, they would be acting

[25] Jeff McMahan, "The Ethics of Killing in War," *Philosophia* (2006), 28.

justly despite fighting for an unjust cause. The good they would achieve by preventing the murders of the innocent women and children would outweigh the harm they will cause by killing or wounding just combatants in the platoon. In other words, were such a situation to arise, it would be morally permissible for combatants on the unjust side to commit an act of war against just combatants. A whole war, of course, would never be anything but a series of such incidents. The injustice of the cause of the unjust combatants will usually morally trump their use of proportional force and their properly discriminating by not attacking noncombatants.

Just combatants, however, can fail to satisfy the *jus in bello* rules by employing excessive measures to defeat the aggressor army and by attacking civilian targets and indiscriminately killing and wounding noncombatants. In effect, there is an asymmetry in the application of the *jus in bello* rules. They apply as moral requirements to control the military actions of the just combatants and, if they are not satisfied, those combatants lose their moral shields, although not the justice of their cause. Aggressor combatants are morally condemned by the *jus ad bellum* rules, and nothing they can do in the conduct of the hostilities can erase that fact. We may, however, regard their nonetheless fighting within the proportionality and discrimination parameters of *jus in bello* as, to some extent, mitigating, but not exculpating, the moral condemnation they are due as unjust combatants. The point is that "an unjust war *cannot* be fought 'in strict accordance with the rules.' For except in the limited range of cases in which unjust combatants act to prevent wrongful acts by just combatants, their acts of war cannot satisfy the proportionality requirement, and satisfaction of this requirement is a necessary condition of permissible conduct in war."[26] Put another way, those fighting an unjust war on the side of the aggressor cannot avoid doing wrong. Perhaps some awareness of that provoked mission creep in Iraq. If the cause of the war is not just, "mission accomplished" cannot be a good thing.

Another point is worth mention: it is not morally permissible for unjust combatants to attack just combatants, other than in a case like the one noted where the just combatants are acting wrongly by attacking noncombatants. That follows from the *jus ad bellum* rules. However, what that means with respect to the discrimination rule of *jus in bello* is that unjust combatants have no one to morally attack. They have no legitimate targets. Both noncombatants and just combatants are illegitimate targets. But unjust combatants who pose unjust threats to just combatants are

[26] Ibid.

legitimate targets of attack by those in the just forces. A caveat may be in order: if there are unjust combatants who are not morally responsible for being members of the unjust military force, then they may not be legitimate targets for the just forces. But what would make a combatant not responsible for being in the military force that is engaged in an unjust war? Perhaps conscription, impressments, or slavery would get such a combatant off the moral responsibility hook, but in the case of conscription, draftees can refuse to serve or flee the conscripting country. In any event, the military force of the United States now is filled entirely by volunteers.

McMahan offers some possibilities that might ground excuses for unjust combatants. "They may have been deceived, manipulated, indoctrinated, or coerced or compelled by threats or perhaps they just believed, reasonably but mistakenly, in the moral authority of their government."[27] Some of the conditions cited by McMahan might be regarded as legitimate excuses for participation in an unjust war on the side of the aggressor, but they cannot serve as exculpating excuses absolving unjust combatants of all moral responsibility for the unjust threats they pose as long as they can avoid military service or have enough native intelligence and access to a public discussion of the war issues to reach a reasonable personal decision that the war is unjust. However, the plea that one was systematically lied to by one's government in a most convincing manner and access to sufficient information for a citizen to reach a decision on the moral status of the war was intentionally blocked by the government in collusion with media might have a diminishing impact on an unjust combatant's moral responsibility. Again, however, that can go only so far in the case of the Iraq War because not every American was taken in by the charade that Iraq was prepared to launch an imminent attack on the United States or its allies and had something significant to do with the terrorist attacks of September 11, 2001; neither was every American driven to a state of frenzy for revenge by the rhetoric. I agree with McMahon that usually only if an unjust combatant were demonstrably lacking in the capacity for moral agency qua combatant would it make sense to absolve him or her of the moral responsibility for his or her actions on the side of the aggressor, harsh as that may appear. Walzer's position that combatants are sanitized from moral responsibility as long as they abide by the *jus in bello* rules is far too lenient.

[27] Ibid., 34.

However, another type of defense that has been used to try to absolve unjust combatants of the moral responsibility for their actions deserves some attention to see whether it is persuasive enough to soften my hard stance. It is sometimes identified as the Jodl Defense or the Nuremburg Defense. Simply, it is the defense of "just following orders." Importantly, although the defense is regularly trotted out to excuse unjust combatants, it was specifically ruled unacceptable by the London Charter of the International Military Tribunal when it issued the rules, principles, and procedures by which the Nuremberg trials were to be conducted in August 1945. Principle IV of the Charter states that the "fact that a person acted pursuant to orders of his Government or of a superior does not relieve him from responsibility under international law, provided a moral choice was in fact possible to him." Alfred Jodl, Oberkommando der Wehrmacht, tried unsuccessfully to offer the defense at his Nuremburg trial. It was rejected, and he was found guilty of war crimes and hanged. William Calley's attorneys offered it at his trial for the My Lai Massacre during the Vietnam War; it was also rejected, and he was found guilty. Some of the defendants at the trials of those accused of torturing prisoners at Abu Ghraib also trotted it out without success.

A soldier fighting on the just side who is ordered by a superior to perform an action that satisfies the rules of *jus in bello* and that is intended to result in the killing of enemy soldiers, all but the pacifist will agree, has an obligation to obey the order. If a legitimate superior gives a soldier fighting on the unjust side the very same command, does that soldier have an obligation to obey? A Walzer-type account will say that both soldiers have a moral duty to obey the command as long as it satisfies *jus in bello* rules. But combatants on the just side who are killed or wounded by the actions of the unjust combatant have been grievously wronged, so should that not entail that the person who wronged them acted wrongly and could not have been morally obligated to perform the action that caused the wrong? In other words, there is no moral obligation to obey orders in an unjust cause.

David Estlund does not agree. He writes, "Under the right conditions, even though the victim is wronged by the unjustly warring side, the soldier on that side is nevertheless morally obligated (and so morally permitted) to follow all normally binding orders – those that would be binding at least if the war were just."[28] The right conditions for Estlund

[28] David Estlund, "On Following Orders in an Unjust War," *Journal of Political Philosophy*, 15, 2 (2007), 213–34, 217.

are going to involve an epistemic authoritative procedure in the soldier's country that is sufficient to sanitize the soldier's actions and make it the soldier's duty to fight an unjust war. He writes, "If the war is declared by way of the appropriate deliberative procedure, most citizens ought to regard it as authoritative because this is now the citizen's best evidence about whether the war is just."[29] His point is that nations with certain democratic political arrangements that embody epistemic authoritative procedures that are engaged in the decision to go to war sanitize their soldiers' knowingly killing innocent people, including the members of the armed forces of a justly warring country. This is a procedural principle as Estlund develops it. He admits that democratic political processes are prone to a range of error in such matters, but, on his account, within that range of error the authority nonetheless is "entitled to obedience even when it is mistaken." The analogy that seems to be in place is that the judicial system is also prone to a range of error when deciding the criminal cases before it, and sometimes an innocent person is punished when the system has procedurally worked properly, but that does not give a license to those who function in various parts of the judicial and penal system to adjust punishments according to their senses of justice. They have a moral obligation to carry out the punishments that are decreed by the system, and they are held morally blameless for miscarriages that occur.

Applying the range-of-error approach to the military situation, Estlund is comfortable holding that a soldier is not obligated to carry out deadly orders if "an order to go to war or an order to fight in a certain way is not even close to what would be just if the facts were as the authority states them to be, or if the stated view of the justifying facts is not even close to a reasonable conclusion based on the appropriate materials."[30] The idea is that a country can obligate its warriors to fight for it and to do so in specific ways and sanitize them from moral responsibility even if it is mistaken as to the justice of the *casus belli* as long as its mistake is not "too unreasonable a conclusion based on the appropriate materials, and the procedures leading to this decision meet the . . . honest mistake standard."[31] What Estlund intends is that warriors for a country in an unjust cause have an obligation to obey commands that are not too far from a just response in the circumstances "in light of a reasonable view of the facts, by a legitimate authority that has, in a publicly recognizable way,

[29] Ibid.
[30] Ibid.
[31] Ibid.

a general capacity to respect the justice of waging and fighting wars."[32] Presumably, the United States passes the legitimate authority test.

Recall the case, recounted in Chapter 1, of the platoon in their amtracs outside Ash Shatra on the road to Baghdad commanded by a sergeant who became suspicious of an Iraqi woman in a black burqa who was walking on the other side of the road. The sergeant decided that either they had to kill the woman or she was going to blow them up by detonating a bomb she must be carrying under her burqa. He fired two shots at her. His platoon, following suit, fired on her and nearly cut her in half. Although the sergeant may not have explicitly ordered them to fire, his opening fire probably constituted an implicit order in the circumstances, and the other Marines certainly understood that to be the case. The sergeant inspected the corpse and discovered that she was not a threat and that she carried only a small white flag. By the rules of *jus in bello*, killing a noncombatant is forbidden. But the sergeant believed that any native met on the roads is a potential enemy combatant bent on defending his or her country by killing as many invaders as possible. Given the sergeant's circumstances of being in an invading army and on the basis of other reported and rumored roadside incidents, perhaps his belief was not too unreasonable. On Estlund's theory, the Marines were obligated to fire on the Iraqi woman. It was an honest mistake, and in the U.S. political system, honest mistakes are occasionally made that send its military forces into unjust wars and put them on roads in places like Iraq where orders are given to kill what turn out to be noncombatants. The country, of course, commits a serious injustice by acting on the mistaken belief that it has a legitimate *casus belli*, but that belief might be reasonable enough that it does not also lose its authority to command its troops to kill and destroy supposed enemy combatants in the invaded and occupied country.

The United States is an open democratic country in which public debate on political and foreign affairs is encouraged, and it certainly attempts through its political process to send its military to war only in just causes. If that were not the case, the Bush administration would not have spent so much effort in tilting the discussion about invading Iraq in favor of the view that it posed an imminent threat, had connections to al-Qaeda, and possessed stockpiles of WMD. But, for Estlund,

> so long as the mistaken view about Iraq's threat is nevertheless not too unreasonable, the authority's judgment is within an acceptable range of error, and the soldier's duty is to carry out the orders. The justice of the

---

[32] Ibid.

war is being duly looked after elsewhere by his nation, and that nation is entitled to have its will done...even when it is making a mistake.[33]

The range-of-error view championed by Estlund has the effect of morally sanitizing unjust combatants as long as they act within the *jus in bello* rules. But that view seems to me to be far too generous. As with all range theories, somewhere a line gets crossed and the moral obligation to obey orders no longer applies; but, in Estlund's case, although he admits there is a line, it is defined by reasonableness, which is itself a rather shady business. Why is it reasonable to think that an attack on Israel was imminent in the case of the Six Day War but not that Iraq was about to attack somebody in 2003? In the former case, it was patently obvious that Egypt had moved a thousand tanks and about a hundred thousand troops to the Israeli border and closed the Straits of Tiran to Israeli shipping. In the latter case, the best effort to provide the sort of proof that would bring the case down on the reasonableness side was Secretary of State Colin Powell's pathetic attempt to show and tell the United Nations Security Council that Iraq had a terrorist network headed by a member of al-Qaeda, operated a poison- and WMD-development program in full swing, sent envoys and trainees to Osama bin Laden, and was preparing to attack, presumably, U.S. targets or its allies such as Israel. None of Powell's charges against Iraq, even if they could have been substantiated, which they could not, reasonably would support an imminent threat. Still, a rather large portion of the American public, although not the major players at the Security Council table, were convinced that it was reasonable to believe that Iraq was an imminent threat and that the U.S. Congress was justified in authorizing military force against Iraq. So the U.S. invasion of Iraq would have passed Estlund's range-of-error test even though objectively it was unreasonable to believe that Iraq did constitute the threat claimed.

The hardliner's refusal to be so generous by adopting a range-of-error approach to sanitizing combatants has the benefit of acknowledging the most basic fact of war: people die and when those people are innocents, killing them is never morally justifiable. Francisco de Vitoria rightfully maintained that no one morally may kill an innocent on any authority.[34] Robert Nozick argued that soldiers who know they are waging an aggressive war may not morally in self-defense fire on the planes of the

---

[33] Ibid.

[34] Francisco de Vitoria, "On the Law of War" (1539), *Political Writings*, edited by Anthony Pagden and Jeremy Lawrence (Cambridge, 1991).

opposing force even if those planes are dropping bombs on them. Could any rational member of the U.S. forces invading Iraq not have thought that invading another sovereign country that was not attacking or had not attacked your country was not an aggressive action? Nozick also, and rather eloquently, makes the point that it is the individual soldier's duty to determine if his side is just. "Thus we return to the point that some bucks stop with each of us; and we reject the morally elitist view that some soldiers cannot be expected to think for themselves."[35]

The Bush administration may well have been aware of the shaky grounds of reasonableness on which it trod, and it reframed the Iraq War not as preemptive but as preventive. In doing so, however, it not only proposed a new type of war – one against not a current threat but against a possible future threat – but it, in fact, negated the last-resort criteria of *jus ad bellum*. Reframing the war as preventive had the effect of rendering its war unjust according to just war theory, thus defeating the very thing it was trying to do, namely, morally justify the war it wanted to fight.

III

The mission crept on. The goal posts were moved farther back. Giving up on most of the traditional *casus belli* to try to justify what shamelessly was referred to as a preventive war, the Bush administration focused its justification on that criteria of *jus ad bellum* that insists that the intentions of the war-making country must be morally good. Of course, the intention of taking control of the Iraqi oil fields or of funneling billions of dollars to contractors who are political supporters and friends will never pass that test. So the intention became regime change to turn Iraq from a dictatorship into a democracy and a beacon of democracy for the entire region. What could be more morally admirable than democracy at the point of a gun?

It should be recalled, as pointed out by Mohammed Abu-Nimer, that under the administration of another Bush in the early 1990s:

> the U.S. Army, with its allies, liberated Kuwait and restored a dictator-ship that has not improved its human rights record (treatment of women, refugees, or foreign workers) or created democratic institutions. If the United States was genuinely interested in democratization of the Middle East, Kuwait would have been an excellent place to invest in democratic

---

35 Robert Nozick, *Anarchy, State and Utopia* (New York, 1974), 100.

institutions, instead of reinstalling a corrupt monarchy that only allows male and royal voters.[36]

History and sarcasm aside, the type of democracy that was to be bestowed on the Iraqis seems never to have been discussed, even though the debate over that very subject had been raging for decades back in the United States between two camps: the liberal democrats and the communitarians. We may never know which of the two camps the *casus belli* of the Iraq War had mission-crept into when the democracy gambit was played by the Bush administration, but anyone who believes that the two camps are committed to conceptually the same understanding of what democracy involves is dead wrong. Consequently, in order to determine whether the intention was not only a good one but a practical or reasonable one for Iraq, it matters what conception of democracy the Bush administration thought it was gifting to Iraq and the Arab world. We all know what road is paved with good intentions. It is the road to Baghdad.

"Democracy" has quite different meanings to and is realized in radically different political structures for the liberal democrats and the communitarian democrats. The fact that "democracy" seems to fit both of their conceptions is an indication of how vague that term is in sociopolitical and global discourse. It is also indicative of its enormous cash value, especially when all other justifications for preemptive or preventive aggression have shriveled up under the harsh light of reality and are gone with the desert wind.

Both democracy camps swaddle themselves in thick blankets of political nostalgia, although subscribing to very different narratives of the "good old days." Their distinct stories are mistakenly often interwoven into a single tale that identifies seventeenth- and eighteenth-century liberals as the progeny of the classical Athenian democrats. The Athenian model of democracy to which the communitarians trace their lineage is not even a distant cousin of the Enlightenment conception. Benjamin Barber[37] calls it a "strong democracy," whereas the liberal democratic conception requires a rather "thin" democratic political structure that Barber calls "weak." Athenian-style democracy is conceptually thick, building political order and structure out of its participatory demands. "Active citizens govern themselves directly..., not necessarily at every level and in every instance, but frequently enough and in particular when

---

[36] Mohammed Abu-Nimer, "Pax Americana and the Bush Doctrine in the Middle East," in *War and Border Crossings*, 83.

[37] Benjamin Barber, *Strong Democracy* (Berkeley, 1984).

basic policies are being decided and when significant power is being deployed. Self-government is carried on through institutions designed to facilitate ongoing civic participation in agenda-setting, deliberation, legislation, and policy implementation."[38] It is proximate self-legislation. Its success depends on the conversion of a not-insignificant amount of individual interests into public goods.

The Athenian model adopted by the communitarians is characterized by the transformation of multiple individual conceptions of the good into a commonly held, and rather singular, communal conception of the good toward whose achievement and/or maintenance political process is directed. The Athenian model derives its strength from the fact that the individual interests of citizens are seen to orbit around their shared conception of the good, tending, by exclusion, to produce a homogeneous population. Citizens in the participatory process of governing, in the Athenian-style democracy, formulate the public ends toward which their community will strive and thereby define itself. Barber writes, "In such communities, public ends are neither extrapolated from absolutes nor 'discovered' in a preexisting 'hidden consensus.' They are literally forged through the act of public participation, created through common deliberation and common action and the effect that deliberation and action have on interests, which change shape and direction when subjected to these participatory processes."[39]

Communitarian democracy, at least in its pure form, amateurizes politics and government, creating a community out of a collective. That community transforms the individual while it sustains itself. It educates its citizens to become effective public participants and to appreciate and adopt its values, its shared vision, and purpose. The sustenance of the "strong" democracy requires nurturing in the members an abiding sense of civic responsibility that is developed through training in the arts of citizenship.

Although this "strong" or communitarian conception of democracy can be identified with classical Athens, for that was its purported "golden age," there is a healthy dose of Rousseau's political theory in it as well. The communitarian democracy, it is typically maintained, is necessary for individuals to achieve true moral freedom and to live worthwhile lives. Rousseau, frequently quoted by communitarians, wrote that the primary task in the formation of a democracy is "to change human nature, to

[38] Ibid., 150.
[39] Ibid., 151.

transform each individual . . . into a part of a larger whole from which
this individual receives, in a sense, his life, his being."[40] The great accomplishment, the goal, of the communitarian conception of democracy was
framed by Rousseau when he wrote, "If each citizen is nothing except in
concert with all the others . . . one can say that the legislation has achieved
the highest possible point of perfection."[41]

As Michael Sandel notes, this conception of democracy is, at heart,
coercive.[42] It links the moral improvement of its citizens and, perhaps
more to the point of difference with the liberal conception, the freedom
of its citizens, to the formative project of democracy. The political community attends to the moral character of its citizens as a condition of their
freedom. Statecraft is a part and parcel of, to use Sandel's term, "soul-
craft." Or, within Aristotle's framework, the epitome of virtue requires
active citizenship in the *polis.*

It is virtually impossible to imagine that anyone with even a modicum
of knowledge of the history of Iraq could hope, let alone intend, to bring
about a communitarian democracy in that country. About the only element of its conception that the Iraqi people might fully appreciate is its
coercive nature, but for them that would not exactly mean what it means
for the communitarian. A country of feuding religious sects and no real
history of cohesion other than that forced on those in its arbitrarily drawn
borders by a colonial power and then internal dictatorships is hardly a
breeding ground for common deliberation in a participatory governing process. The fact that the Iraqi Parliament, when finally convened,
found it almost impossible to get any legislation accomplished is evidence
that communitarian democracy would have been an unreasonable "good
intention" to justify the invasion.

Other than sharing some of the basic terminology of democracy, there
is very little in common between the Athenian/communitarian democratic ideal and the conception of the liberal democrat that has dominated the political scene in the Euro-American developed countries for
the past three or four centuries and that has the only reasonable chance
of being what the Bush administration had in mind when it shifted its
jus ad bellum argument from preventing imminent attack with WMD
to regime change to instill democracy. Consider the way in which the

[40] Jean-Jacques Rousseau, *On the Social Contract* (1762), trans. by D. A. Cress (Indianapolis, 1983), 39.
[41] Ibid.
[42] Michael Sandel, *Democracy's Discontent* (Cambridge, 1996), 318.

liberal democrat formulates the relationship between the "people" and their government.

Lincoln, famously, talked of "government by the people and for the people," and the Constitution of the United States begins, "We the people." For the communitarian democrat, government is the province of the participating citizen, not the people, definitely not the untutored and uninitiated masses. For the communitarian, to be a citizen is to be capable of participation and to be actually involved in government. Barber writes, "To be a citizen is to participate in a certain conscious fashion that presumes awareness of and engagement in activity with others. This consciousness alters attitudes and lends to participation that sense of the 'we' associated with community. To participate is to create a community that governs itself, and to create a self-governing community is to participate."[43] For the communitarian democrat, participation and community are the defining characteristics of the citizen. They are not the most evident properties of the people who happen to make their home in Iraq – Sunnis, Shiites, and Kurds, with a few Christians here and there, and each group more or less isolated and insulated from the other.

The liberal democrat's roots, on the other hand, are firmly planted in the individualism that marks the political philosophy and history of Europe and America since at least the seventeenth century. Enlightenment political thought and rhetoric stirs the hearts of those who see human society as an aggregate of free individual humans contracting together for individual personal benefit. The great political theorists of atomistic individualist liberalism, Hobbes and Locke, understood individual natural persons to be the elemental parts of society. The civil state, for them, is built on and composed of consenting individual contractors each committed to the protection and preservation of his or her natural rights to life, liberty, and property. Freedom is a precondition of civic association. It is not a goal of the formative project of the state. Collective enterprises, including democratic government, are to be thought of as goal-directed activities in which individual humans freely engage and disengage, usually for prudential (self-interested) reasons.

Among the primary aims of the atomistic individualist liberal democrats of the Enlightenment were the sociopolitical transformations of (1) the medieval feudal subject into the independent, prudentially

---

43 Barber, 155.

motivated, enlightened person; and (2) social relations from matters of status to matters of contract. The latter conversion reflects the conceptual chasm between Athenian-style communitarian democracy and liberal democracy because membership in the citizenry of the communitarian state is an exclusionary matter of status, albeit moral status.

The Enlightenment conception on which liberal democracy is based culminates an individualist movement in Western philosophical and religious thought that appears to have budded in the twelfth century, even within the Catholic Church, and flowered in the sixteenth century with the Protestant Reformation and its rallying cry of the "priesthood of all believers." It embraces individual autonomy, and its politics is the politics of individual interests and interest groups comprised of individuals. Charles Taylor writes: "We inherit atomism from the seventeenth century.... [E]ven though we no longer understand the origins of society as reposing in agreement, we nevertheless both understand and evaluate its workings as an instrument to attain ends we impute to individuals or constituent groups."[44]

The democratic process for the liberal democrat is an adversarial encounter of factions, individuals associated into loosely confederated groups that are generally united only with respect to a single issue, likely with quite distinct conceptions of the good, collectively and individually, each seeking majority support. Its basic conception of government is that of decision making between competing points of view. Although the liberal democrat may seek consensus, he or she is not interested in the formative project of citizenship. Liberal democracy rejects the notion that moral freedom and character development are crucial elements of the civic enterprise, radically disassociating the public from the private sphere.

The liberal democrat conceives of the decision, whether it be made by the single voter in the booth choosing over a list of candidates or cast in the vote of the representative in the halls of the legislature, as the heart and soul of the political process. The priority of the decision in the liberal democratic scheme of things can be observed during congressional sessions in the United States as a near empty hall fills only when a vote is taken. Representatives and Senators rush into their respective chambers to have their votes recorded on a bill, then depart with equal haste. It's the vote that matters, not the debate of the issue. The majority rules (sometimes a supermajority in the Senate), and its rule is not constrained

[44] Charles Taylor, *Sources of the Self* (Cambridge, 1989), 195.

with respect to the outcomes to be reached, except that it cannot infringe on the political freedoms of its citizens who are protected in its founding documents, such as the United States Constitution and its Bill of Rights. Brian Barry[45] adds two other conditions to the list of constraints: the rule of law will govern and there will be formal voting equality. Robert Dahl adds a third: voting rights and other formal aspects of citizenship are extended to all adult members, excepting transients and the mentally defective.[46]

This formalistic view of liberal democracy, however, generates a paradox, as Amy Gutmann notes, "in the tension between popular will and the conditions of maintaining the popular will over time."[47] (This is not Wollheim's paradox.[48]) A liberal democrat should oppose any decision of the majority that restricts any of the basic protected liberties because it would not be democratic to restrict them, but the same liberal democrat should support the majority's decision because not doing so would be undemocratic. What then should the liberal democratic Iraqi do if the majority, being Shiite, votes to restrict the freedom of Kurds or Sunnis to practice their religion?

There is a Rousseauian way of overcoming the paradox that involves drawing a sharp contrast between the general will and the will of all. Liberal democrats, however, should reject Rousseauian-type solutions; he is not really in their camp. But liberal democrats may discover themselves trapped in their own rhetoric once they start using theoretical stratagems to salvage majority rule from its illiberal and undemocratic tendencies. The referendum process in California has frequently produced such embarrassments. Gutmann writes, "A practically inevitable tension exists between any actual procedure of popular rule and the corresponding ideal of popular democracy. The ideal requires outcomes – unmanipulated political preferences, the rule of law, formal voting equality, and inclusive citizenship – that can, and do, conflict with the actual popular will as revealed by any procedure designed for the sake of popular rule."[49] In other words, Iraqis displaying purple ink on their thumbs

---

45 Brian Barry, "Is Democracy Special?" in P. Laslett and J. Fishkin, eds., *Philosophy, Politics & Society*, 5th Series (New Haven, 1979).

46 Robert A. Dahl, *Democracy and Its Critics* (New Haven, 1989).

47 Amy Gutmann, "The Disharmony of Democracy" in J. W. Chapman and I. Shapiro, eds., *Democratic Community* (New York, 1995), 126–60.

48 Richard Wollheim, "A Paradox in the Theory of Democracy," in P. Laslett and W. G. Runciman, eds., *Philosophy, Politics, & Society*, 2nd Series (Oxford, 1974).

49 Gutmann, 130.

indicating that they voted are hardly a sign that even liberal democracy has found a home in Iraq. Although the primary emphasis in liberal democracy is on the decision, there is rather more to it than tallying votes, and media while seeking photographs supposedly emblematic of the accomplishment of a *casus belli* often forgets that. A picture of purple ink-stained thumbs and fingers may not be just a picture of purple ink-stained thumbs and fingers, but neither is it a picture of a mission accomplished if the mission has crept into instilling a liberal democracy in Iraq.

In a communitarian-type democracy, the highest premium is placed on what Barber calls "talk."[50] "Talk" is understood to be not merely speech. It includes listening. A better term might be "conversation." The liberal democrats have also appropriated "talk," but for them it does come to mean something like speechmaking or "sound-biting." Looking again at those Halls of Congress, when a vote is not being taken, a C-Span viewer is likely to see a single member of Congress at a microphone rambling on and on about something or other while the rest of the chamber is empty. To whom is he or she talking? To no one, the speech is for the record, a record that is seldom read. "Talk" in the liberal democrat's lexicon is, at best, the expression of an opinion, regardless of whether or not anyone is listening. It is the noise that precedes the vote. Media, especially electronic media, have reduced talk to the ten- to thirty-second sound bite in which, at most, a slogan is beamed forth to the less-than-attentive audience. Listening is not required. In fact, listening to talk is something of a lost art. Politicians do not listen to their constituents and citizens do not listen to their representatives. Then again, the electronic media does not encourage listening. As Barber notes, "One measure of healthy political talk is the amount of silence it permits and encourages, for silence is the precious medium in which reflection is nurtured and empathy can grow."[51] Silence may be golden according to the adage, but it has only a negative value on television and radio.

Communitarian democracy is deliberation oriented, and it is deliberation over how the social world, the community, is to be formed and sustained. So it is talk to a practical purpose. It is not merely the statement of preferences. It is, crucially, involved in persuasion and the critical examination of options. It is what Barry calls "decision by discussion of

[50] Barber, 173.
[51] Ibid., 174.

merits."[52] It leads, of course, to the vote, but the vote is not the be-all and end-all of the democratic process, although it embodies the sense of urgency that marks the process as political.

The choice-oriented liberal democrat who sees the political process as a combat between various individual and group preferences can only stave off what could easily become an "anarchy of adversary politics" with the principle of majority rule, despite its potential paradoxes. "Majoritarianism," Barber bemoans, "is a tribute to the failure of democracy."[53] It is the failure of communitarian democracy to sustain itself in the post-Enlightenment world, but less so the failure of liberal democracy, which seems prepared to live with the paradoxes in the name of getting to closure on an issue.

It might be fair to characterize communitarian democracy as will dominated and liberal democracy as choice dominated. Barber writes, "Strong [read "communitarian"] democracy decision-making is predicated on will rather than choice and on judgment rather than preference. Strong democracy understands decision-making to be a facet of man as maker and as creator and consequently focuses on public willing."[54] Communitarian democracy is to collectively will a world that fits a certain description, one that permits certain types of human actions and organizations.

Independent rational preference based on one's conception of one's own best interests lies at the foundations of liberal democracy and drives its political and economic theory. Political arrangements and choices are the result of aggregated individual choices. Compromise, sometimes called the art of politics, is typically understood as the Pareto optimal choice when one cannot maximize one's preferences, where preferences and their orderings are prepolitical and independent of communal relationships and commitments, even unchosen commitments such as those embedded in culture and heritage. The need for compromise arises, of course, when conflicts of interests occur. Such conflicts, although intractable, are bargainable. The conflicts do not disappear in the compromise; they are put aside as the competing individuals or groups settle for something less than the realization of their interests in total.

[52] Brian Barry, *Political Argument* (London, 1965).
[53] Barber, 198.
[54] Ibid., 214.

The communitarian democrat requires that citizens develop and practice conversational techniques that allow the forging of a common vision and plan of action for the community. Such techniques are not conducive to a pluralistic or diverse citizenry like Iraq or the United States. Media has certainly discovered this and has, for example, proliferated special-interest channels and programming to appeal only to those who are proficient in the conversational techniques of narrower and narrower topic ranges. The catering to such individual interests and the encouraging of narrow bands of conversational proficiency, in large measure, works against anything like the communitarian's common-vision ideal.

Underlying this encouragement of narrow-banding interest development and the virtual obsession with the glorification of diversity that characterizes liberal democracy is the rejection of the communitarian idea that the identity of a person and the identity of a citizen are not distinct or separable. The liberal democrat draws a bright line between the public sphere and the private sphere of a person's life. One's public or political life is bounded by the obligations of a procedural democracy and the choices one makes as a rational and independent chooser. Those choices are conceived of as not being encumbered by ties antecedent to choice. Sandel, however, comments, "This vision cannot account for a wide range of moral and political obligations that we commonly recognize, such as obligations of loyalty or solidarity. By insisting that we are bound only by ends we choose for themselves, it denies that we can ever be claimed by ends we have not chosen . . . , for example, by our identities as members of families, peoples, cultures, or traditions."[55] The liberal democrat, however, can respond that his or her vision does not exclude such obligations. It reserves them for the private sphere.

In the liberal's conception of democracy, governmental neutrality with respect to conceptions of the good is preserved by a procedural emphasis that restricts the political sphere to operations within boundaries set by the protection of individual rights. Those rights are, of course, neutral with respect to the ends citizens might pursue, provided gaining those ends does not trespass the boundaries. The ends at which citizens aim, their conceptions of the good, are, at least theoretically, of no real political or governmental interest, provided that in getting to those ends citizens do not overstep the constraints that give teeth to their basic rights

[55] Sandel, 322.

or liberties. Liberal democratic proceduralism is merely a constraint theory, and a rather minimal constraint theory at that. It is not a formative theory like the communitarian version.

The rejection of formative democracy, in which the civic virtues the communitarian believes essential to effective self-government are positively fostered in the citizenry, in favor of pluralistic proceduralism has given rise, the critics stress, to a general discontent with (or disaffection for) democracy. So why not export it to an occupied country like Iraq! Sandel writes of procedural democracy that "its vision of political discourse is too spare to contain the moral energies of democratic life."[56] What he means is that procedural democracy requires citizens to bracket their moral and their religious commitments and their cultural heritages outside of political debate. Perhaps that is the only way for something resembling democracy to survive in complex and diverse countries.

The communitarian's conception of democracy, rooted in the Athenian model, is place dominated. For Aristotle, that place was the *polis*, the city-state, a rather small place at that! Loyalty to place, to a way of life peculiar to that place and to a common language and heritage, and a commitment to the maintenance of that place and that way of life are the impetus for the development of the art of self-government and for the fostering of the civic virtues in the residents (citizens). The communitarian ideal of democracy is, first and foremost, a story of place, a narrative of a people in a place. Commitment to that narrative drives the communal conscience to sustain the institutions of self-government.

No such narrative would seem to be possible in Iraq because it has not been possible in the pluralistic United States. That is not to say that Americans and Iraqis have no stories or no sense of place. In fact, since the American invasion of Iraq, they probably share a number of stories, although often from radically different perspectives and with much different plots. In the United States, with the help and urging of the liberal democrat, there may be the dawning of a realization, although probably regretfully, that it is impossible to compose a single coherent narrative that would make interpretive sense for most Americans of their current conditions, explain their commonality, and bring order and a sense of place to their lives. There are far too many strands in the story of America for the communitarian storyteller to weave a coherent communal identity to provide the exemplar for the formative project of communitarian democracy. The same, I suspect, is true of Iraq.

[56] Ibid., 323.

Our shared stories are not those that sustain Athenian-style democracy. They are what Sandel calls the "vacant, vicarious fare of confessional talk shows, celebrity scandals, and sensational trials."[57] To which should be added the story of the debacle of an unjust war in which maybe as many as 100,000 Iraqis have died, approximately 5,000 American have lost their lives, tens of thousands of other Americans have been severely physically or psychologically harmed, and a select few have become fabulously wealthy.

Postscript

I taught the sessions in the PDTCs on just war theory only at the Little Creek Amphibious Base in Norfolk, Virginia, in late March to early April of 2004. At the PDTCs in which I participated during the first year, the discussion of just war theory almost exclusively was restricted to the classical statement and a legalistic paradigm version of the theory that restates it in terms of the rights of countries vis-à-vis each other. I did not raise the unjust-war allegations with the chaplains in my presentation, although in the discussion period at Little Creek I was asked why chaplains should be at all concerned or aware of the various elements of the theory. One of the chaplains urged that the theory should not be taught at the Naval Academy for fear that knowledge of it could provoke a young officer to give too much thought to the moral status of the war he or she was fighting. Raising such concerns, he feared, could lead at minimum to a difficult session with his unit's chaplain or the loss of a career as a Marine officer. Patriotism should trump morality. Some agreed with him, others seemed perplexed and looked to me to answer. Although tempted to divert the session into a deeper discussion of unjust war, I stuck to the validated power point slides and said only that we should all hope that patriotism and morality are not at odds. Some grunted ambiguously. I felt I had been a pedagogical coward.

In the second year of the PDTCs, there was much more concern with the unjust status of the war, and trying to identify the mission had become something of a joke. "See what it says today in *Stars and Stripes*." Most of the chaplains were ready to declare that the mission had crept into something humanitarian, but they couldn't exactly say what. When patrols left the bases, they still were heavily armored and too many Marines and soldiers were returning to CONUS in coffins. If the mission had become

---

[57] Ibid., 351.

humanitarian, did that alter its moral status at the time of the invasion? It is difficult to see how adopting the Doctrine of Rapid Dominance "to affect the will, perception, and understanding of the adversary to fit or respond to our strategic policy ends through imposing a regime of Shock and Awe"[58] and killing about 6,000 Iraqis could be seen as the first stage of humanitarian intervention. Or was it terrorism by another name, as reported in the British newspaper *The Guardian*? Calling the mission humanitarian hardly seems consistent with killing somewhere between 85,000 and a million Iraqis and causing the disruption of the lives of the nearly five million Iraqis who fled their homes and communities, approximately half of which sought refuge in other countries, creating their own humanitarian crises in those countries.

[58] Harlan K. Ullman and James P. Wade, *Shock and Awe: Achieving Rapid Dominance* (National Defense University, 1996), XXIV.

Bibliography

Albo, Joseph, *Sefer ha-'Ikkarim [Book of Principles]*, translated and edited by I. Husik, (Philadelphia, 1929).

Amery, Jean, *At the Mind's Limits* (Bloomington, IN, 1998).

Aristotle, *Nicomachean Ethics*, translated by M. Ostwald (Indianapolis, 1962).

Ashley, Robert, *Of Honour*, edited by Virgil, Heltzel (Huntington Library, San Marino, CA, 1947).

Augustine, *The City of God*, translated by H. Bettensen (London, 1972).

Austin, J. L., *How To Do Things With Words* (Oxford, 1965).
    Philosophical Papers (Oxford, 1970).

Barber, Benjamin, *Strong Democracy* (Berkeley, 1984).

Barry, Brian, *Political Argument* (London, 1965).

Bittel, Lester R., *Management by Exception* (New York, 1964).

Borgman, Albert, *Technology and the Character of Contemporary Life* (Chicago, 1984).

Bradley, F. H., *Ethical Studies* (Oxford, 1876, reprinted 1989).

Cairns, Douglas, *Aidos* (Oxford, 1993).

Caney, Simon, *Justice Beyond Borders* (Oxford, 2005).

Coady, C. A. J., *The Ethics of Armed Humanitarian Intervention* (Washington, 2002).

Connerton, Paul, *How Societies Remember* (Cambridge, 1989).

Cooper, David, *The Manson Murders: A Philosophical Inquiry* (Cambridge, MA, 1973).

Dahl, Robert, *Democracy and Its Critics* (New Haven, 1989).

Danielson, Peter, *Artificial Morality* (London, 1992).

Darwall, Stephen, *The British Moralists and the Internal "Ought" 1640–1740* (Cambridge, 1995).

Darwin, Charles, *The Descent of Man* (London, 1888).

Dawkins, Richard, *The Selfish Gene* (Oxford, 1976).

Dershowitz, Alan, *Why Terrorism Works* (New Haven, 2002).

Doris, John, *Lack of Character* (Cambridge, 2002).

Emerson, Ralph Waldo, *Essays* (New York, 1926).

Feinberg, Joel, *Doing and Deserving* (Princeton, 1970).

Fischer, John Martin, *The Metaphysics of Free Will* (Oxford, 1994).

Fischer, John Martin and Ravizza, Mark, *Responsibility and Control* (Cambridge, 1999).

Fisse, Brent and French, Peter A., *Corrigible Corporations and Unruly Laws* (San Antonio, 1985).

Foot, Philippa, *Virtues and Vices* (Oxford, 1978).

Frankfurt, Harry, *The Importance of What We Care About* (Cambridge, 1988).

French, Peter A., *Collective and Corporate Responsibility* (New York, 1984).

    Corporate Ethics (Fort Worth, TX, 1995).

    Responsibility Matters (Lawrence, KS, 1991).

    The Scope of Morality (Minneapolis, 1979).

    The Virtues of Vengeance (Lawrence, KS, 2001).

French, Peter A., editor, *Individual and Collective Responsibility* (Cambridge, MA, 1972).

French, Peter A. and Short, Jason, *War and Border Crossings* (Lanham, MD, 2005).

Gilbert, Margaret, *Sociality and Responsibility* (Lanham, MD, 2000).

Gowans, Christopher, *Innocence Lost* (Oxford, 1994).

Hanson, N. R., *Patterns of Discovery* (Cambridge, 1958).

Hart, H. L. A., *The Concept of Law* (Oxford, 1961).

    Punishment and Responsibility (New York, 1968).

Hobbes, Thomas, *Leviathan* (1651).

Holmes, Oliver Wendell, *The Common Law* (Boston, 1881).

Hopkins, Andrew, *The Impact of Prosecutions Under the Trade Practices Act* (Canberra, 1978).

Hutcheson, Francis, *An Inquiry Concerning the Origin of Our Ideas of Virtue or Moral Good* (1725, 1738).

Iraneaus, *Adversus Haereses*, translated by W. W. Harvey (1857).

Kant, Immanuel, *Religion Within the Limits of Reason Alone*, translated by Greene and Hudson (New York, 1960).

    Critique of Judgement (1790), translated by J. C. Meredith (Oxford, 1978).

    Kant's Critique of Practical Reason and Other Works on the Theory of Ethics, translated by T. K. Abbott (London, 1873, 1909).

    The Metaphysics of Morals, translated by Mary Gregor (Cambridge, 1996).

Kekes, John, *Facing Evil* (Princeton, 1990).

    The Art of Life (Ithaca, 2002).

Kierkegaard, Soren, *Either/Or*, translated by Walter Lowrie (Garden City, 1959 edition).

Kovesi, Julius, *Moral Notions* (London, 1967).

Laslett, P. and Fishkin, J., editors, *Philosophy, Politics & Society*, 5th Series (New Haven, 1979).

Laslett, P. and Runciman, W. G., editors, *Philosophy, Politics, & Society*, 2nd Series, (Oxford, 1974).

MacIntyre, Alasdair, *After Virtue* (Notre Dame, 1984).

Mackie, J. L., *Ethics: Inventing Right and Wrong* (London, 1977).

Margalit, Avishai, *The Ethics of Memory* (Cambridge, 2002).

McCall Smith, Alexander, *The No. 1 Ladies' Detective Agency* (New York, 1998).

McCoy, Alfred, *A Question of Torture: CIA Interrogation from the Cold War to the War on Terror* (New York, 2006).

Mencius, *The Book of Mencius*, translated by D. C. Lau (London, 1970).

Merleau-Ponty, Maurice, *Phenomenology of Perception*, translated by C. Smith (London, 1981).

Midgley, Mary, *Wickedness* (London, 1984).

Montaigne, Michel de, *Essays*, translated by J. M. Cohen (London, 1958).

Montesquieu, Charles-Louis de Secondat, Baron de, *The Spirit of the Laws*, translated by A. M. Cohler, B. C. Miller, and H. Stone (Cambridge, 1989).

Morris, Herbert, *On Guilt and Innocence* (Berkeley, 1976).

Murphy, Jeffrie, *Getting Even* (Oxford, 2003).

Murphy, Jeffrie and Hampton, Jean, *Forgiveness and Mercy* (Cambridge, 1988).

Nietzsche, Friedrich, *Beyond Good and Evil*, translated by Walter Kaufmann (New York, 1966).

The Gay Science, translated by Walter Kaufmann (New York, 1974).

Noddings, Nel, *Women and Evil* (Berkeley, 1989).

Nowell-Smith, P. H., *Ethics* (London, 1954, 1964).

Nozick, Robert, *Anarchy, State and Utopia* (New York, 1974).

Philosophical Explanations (Cambridge, 1981).

Nussbaum, Martha, *The Fragility of Goodness* (Cambridge, 1986).

Peristiany, J. G., *Honour and Shame* (Chicago, 1966).

Posner, Richard A., *A Failure of Capitalism* (Cambridge, MA, 2009).

Pringle-Pattison, A. S., *The Idea of God in Modern Philosophy* (Oxford, 1920).

Rawls, John, *A Theory of Justice* (Cambridge, MA, 1971).

Ross, David, *The Nicomachean Ethics of Aristotle* (Oxford, 1925).

Rousseau, Jean-Jacques, *On the Social Contract* (1762), translated by D. A. Cress (Indianapolis, 1983).

Russell, Bertrand, *Problems of Philosophy* (Oxford, 1912).

Rymaszewski, Michael, et. al, *Second Life: The Official Guide* (Indianapolis, 2007).

Sandel, Michael, *Democracy's Discontent* (Cambridge, 1996).

Schoeman, Ferdinand, editor, *Responsibility, Character, and the Emotions* (Cambridge, 1988).

Searle, John, *Speech Acts* (New York, 1969).

Shapiro, Ian, *Democratic Community*, editor J. W. Chapman (New York, 1995).

Spierenburg, Pieter, *Men and Violence* (Columbus, 1998).

Stone, Christopher, *Where the Law Ends: The Social Control of Corporate Behavior* (New York, 1975).

Strawson, Peter, *Freedom and Resentment and Other Essays* (London, 1974).

Taylor, Charles, *Sources of the Self* (Cambridge, 1989).

Taylor, Gabrielle, *Pride, Shame, and Guilt* (Oxford, 1985).

Thomas, Laurence, *Vessels of Evil* (Philadelphia, 1993).

Ullman, Harlan K. and Wade, James, P., *Shock and Awe: Achieving Rapid Dominance* (National Defense University, 1996).

Vitoria, Francisco de, *Political Writings*, edited by Anthony Pagden and Jeremy Lawrence (Cambridge, 1991).

Walzer, Michael, *Arguing About War* (New Haven, 2004).

Just and Unjust Wars (New York, 1977).

Wiesenthal, Simon, *The Sunflower: On the Possibilities and Limits of Forgiveness* (New York, 1976).

Wittgenstein, Ludwig, *On Certainty*, translated by C. Paul and E. Anscombe (Oxford, 1969).

Tractatus Logico-Philosophicus, translated by D. F. Pears and B. F. McGuinness (London, 1961).

Wyatt-Brown, Bertram, *Southern Honor* (New York, 1982).

Yan, Jiaqi, *Wode sixiang zichuan (My intellectual autobiography)*, translated by D. S. K. Hong and Denis Mair (Honolulu, 1992).

Index